Panpsychism in the W

Panpsychism in the West

revised edition

David Skrbina

The MIT Press
Cambridge, Massachusetts
London, England

Set in ITC Stone Sans Std and ITC Stone Serif Std by Toppan Best-set Premedia Limited. Printed and bound in the United States of America.

Library of Congress Cataloging-in-Publication Data

Names: Skrbina, David, author.
Title: Panpsychism in the West / David Skrbina.
Description: Revised edition. | Cambridge, MA : The MIT Press, 2017. |
    Includes bibliographical references and index.
Identifiers: LCCN 2016059702 | ISBN 9780262534062 (pbk. : alk. paper)
Subjects: LCSH: Panpsychism--History.
Classification: LCC BD560 .P35 2017 | DDC 141--dc23 LC record available at
https://lccn.loc.gov/2016059702

10 9 8 7 6 5 4 3 2 1

dedicated to all those who seek alternatives to the mechanistic worldview

Contents

Acknowledgments

There are of course many individuals, past and present, to whom I owe inspiration and gratitude. Among them are Peter Reason, Brian Goodwin, Alan Rayner, and Chris Clarke, all of whom provided encouragement and feedback when this material was still a work in progress. In more recent years, many people contributed to my thinking on this subject, and dialogue with them has been most helpful; I particularly want to acknowledge Ludwig Jaskolla, Phil Goff, Gordon Globus, Bill Seager, Riccardo Manzotti, Giulio Tononi, Pierfrancesco Basile, Michael Blamauer, and Galen Strawson.

A special acknowledgment goes to my great friend, mentor, and peerless source of inspiration, Henryk Skolimowski.

1 Panpsychism and the Ontology of Mind

1.1 The Importance of Panpsychism

Few topics in the history of philosophy have proved as persistently inscrutable as the mind. In many ways, we scarcely know more than the ancient Greeks did. The brain, of course, is much better understood today, as are most aspects of human physiology. Physically speaking, our knowledge has expanded greatly. Mentally speaking, though, our progress has been much less impressive. We have many new, intricate philosophical concepts and tools at our disposal, and yet philosophers of mind seem unable to reach any substantial consensus about what the mind is, or how it is related to the body. The enigmatic nature of mind is so pervasive and so compelling that some current philosophers have given up on the problem, calling it intractable or unsolvable in principle. Even granting this, philosophy of mind will not cease. We will continue to inquire into its nature—*our* nature—and thus will continue to examine one of the fundamental riddles of existence.

The many difficulties surrounding the concept of mind seem to call for a deep reexamination of the entire situation. I begin with two basic assumptions that are held by nearly all present-day theorists: (1) that mind is limited to humans and perhaps "the higher animals," and (2) that mind is somehow dependent on or reducible to the physical substrate of the brain.[1] Point 1 is usually taken for granted and rarely argued for, even though there are intrinsic difficulties with establishing, for example, what exactly constitutes a "higher animal" and how we can know that only they have minds.

1. Others go to the opposite extreme and hold that mind is really a soul, something distinct from the body and fundamentally nonphysical. I examine this issue below.

Point 2 implies a belief that there is something fundamentally, ontologically unique about the brains of higher animals, and that they alone among all the physical structures of the universe can support mental processes. This second point seems reasonable at first glance, but upon reflection is almost inconceivable; we have not a trace of a theory that would account for such a situation, and there is no physiological data that would support it. Certainly there are unique physical characteristics of the human brain, among them the number and density of neural cells, the modes of input for sensory information, and the language-processing centers. These factors most likely account for our uniquely human mental capabilities, including our powers of abstract reasoning, our ability to experience rich emotions and feelings, to hold complex beliefs, and the like. But we have found nothing so unique as to account for the presence of a mind in humans alone. In any case, what is at issue here is not the nature of the uniquely human mental capabilities, but rather a general understanding of the phenomenon of mind in its broadest sense.

Many thinkers, past and present, have seen fit to challenge these two assumptions. On the basis of their philosophical reasoning, intuitive insights, and investigations into the natural world, they came to reject such assumptions as largely groundless and unjustifiable. They saw no compelling reason to limit mind or mental capacities to humans and higher animals. On the contrary, they found justification for seeing mind in the lower animals, plants, microbes, and even the inorganic realm. On such a view, mind becomes a general and perhaps fundamental property of nature. Mind would then exist, in some form, in all things. Broadly speaking, this is the view known as panpsychism.

To put a bit more structure to our definition, we may say that panpsychism holds that all things have a mind or a mind-like quality. It is an ancient concept, dating back to the earliest days of both Eastern and Western civilizations. In fact, until the past hundred years or so, panpsychism was a respected and widely held viewpoint. In many cases it was regarded as obvious and in no need of defense. But with the rise of analytic, linguistic, and anti-metaphysical philosophy in the early twentieth century, panpsychism was pushed to the sidelines of intellectual discourse. Even today, it is spoken of in dismissive tones by many orthodox philosophers. In the past few decades, though, it has witnessed something of a renaissance, both in and outside conventional analytic circles. The time is right, then, to conduct a detailed investigation of the phenomenon of panpsychism within Western philosophy.

If we take panpsychism to be the view that all things possess mind, this raises at least two immediate questions, one concerning the nature of "things" and the other concerning the nature of "mind." Generally speaking, panpsychist philosophers attempt to make some progress on both central issues; that is, they attempt to elaborate on precisely which entities in the universe qualify as mind-possessing, and they attempt to describe in some detail the mental qualities of such objects. I should note here that panpsychism doesn't entail that every conceivable entity possesses mind. For example, valid panpsychist theories may exclude composite or collective entities, such as piles of sand, or tables and chairs. They may exclude physical ultimates such as atoms—or they may include *only* physical ultimates. They may include matter but exclude various forms of energy. They may exclude conceptual or logical entities, such as numbers. I will therefore interpret panpsychism in a soft sense: that mind is very widespread, is nearly universal in extent, and crosses deeply into the inorganic realm. The precise extent of mind depends on the particular theory at hand.

The nature of things and the nature of mind are, of course, central to many aspects of philosophy. Panpsychism, however, lies at a unique intersection of the two concepts, in that mind is seen as fundamental, in some sense, to the nature of existence and being. If all things (appropriately defined) have mind, then any theory of mind is necessarily a theory about ontology, about the nature of extant things. This is unlike most other notions of mind, virtually all of which either make no statement on which objects possess it, or make implicit or explicit assumptions about its confinement to humans or, occasionally, the higher animals. Panpsychism alone is at once a conception of mind and a conception of reality.

And there are further distinctions. First, panpsychism is a unique kind of theory of mind. Its central feature is not that it examines or describes mind *per se*—although many panpsychists do this—but rather that it argues for a widespread or universal extent. In this sense it is a higher-order theory, a meta-theory, of mind. It is a theory about theories. It simply holds that, however one conceives of mind, such mind applies to all things. Because of this, there are panpsychist extensions of most conventional theories. For example, one could be a *panpsychist dualist*, holding that some Supreme Being has granted a soul or a mind to all things. Or one could be a *panpsychist functionalist*, interpreting the functional role of every object as mind, even if such a role is only to gravitate or to resist pressure. Or one could argue for a *panpsychist identism* in which mind is identical to matter, or a *panpsychist reductive materialism* in which the mind of each thing is reducible to its physical states. In fact panpsychism could apply, in principle, to almost any current theory of mind by explicitly extending its range of applicability. The only theories not applicable would be those that expressly target a specific physiology, such as biological organisms, neural structures, Homo sapiens, etc., or those that deny mind altogether, such as eliminativism. Such theories, though, are rare and, for many, unconvincing.

In fact, as we will see, it is arguably more logical and more natural to assume broad or even universal applicability of mind, unless one is able to convincingly argue to the contrary. In other words, it is plausible that panpsychism should be the default stance of any theory of mind, and only abandoned if it can be shown to be false. A related sentiment was put forth by Galen Strawson, who argues for "the theoretical primacy of panpsy-chism" (2015a: 203). This thesis, he says, "obliges us to favour some ver-sion of panpsychism ... over all other positive substantive theories." The strongest version of this thesis is not merely that "it would take extraordi-narily hard work to justify preferring any substantive metaphysical position that isn't panpsychist"; rather, "that it can't be done." I will elaborate on Strawson's views later on. For the moment, suffice to say that panpsychism has widespread theoretical applicability, and arguments to the contrary are surprisingly difficult to articulate.

In order to qualify as a complete theory, a panpsychist outlook must be complemented by a positive theory of mind that explicitly describes how mind is to be conceived and how it is connected or related to physical objects. Some philosophers have stopped short of this by simply expressing an intuition or belief that mind is universal in extent, and leaving it at that. This approach clearly and justifiably opens one up to philosophical criti-cism. Not that intuitions are unimportant; they do matter, and can often point to fruitful lines of inquiry. But to rely primarily on them is to open the way for a broad attack on panpsychism generally as not sufficiently grounded or analytic.

Another distinction for panpsychism is the unique role that it has played in the history of philosophy. As I mentioned, it is almost certainly the most ancient conception of the psyche. In the forms of animism and polytheism, it was probably the dominant view for most or all of the pre-historical era. Eastern cultures have a nearly continuous record of panpsychist metaphysics, right through the modern era.[2] It was also widely accepted, though not often explicitly argued for, in the early years of Western thought. With the emergence of Christian theology, panpsychism fell into decline for a number of centuries, but it made a comeback with the naturalist philosophers of the sixteenth century. Support grew steadily in the seventeenth and eighteenth centuries, reaching a zenith in the late 1800s and the early 1900s. With the advent of logical positivism and conventional materialism or physicalism,[3] panpsychism was once again driven down, along with most metaphysical theories, to a relatively low standing. In the past few years there has been a resurgence of sorts, and it has once more become a topic of serious philosophical inquiry. Panpsychism poses a unique challenge to the dominant physicalist view of today, and thus assumes a role of special importance.

Hence, both an investigation of panpsychism's historical background and a comparative study of the field are highly significant for present-day philosophical discussion. The main reasons, in sum, are the following.

Panpsychism occupies a unique and valuable position in philosophy. As has been mentioned, it is at once an ontology and a meta-theory of mind. It intimately links being and mind in a way no other system does. It tells us something important about mind, and something important about reality itself.

Panpsychism offers resolutions to mind-body problems that dualism and materialism find intractable. Present-day philosophy of mind is dominated by materialist theories that cannot adequately address issues of consciousness, qualia, or the emergence of mind in the universe. Dualism is the traditional alternative, but it too suffers from long-standing weaknesses

2. I will say little here about Eastern or other non-Western approaches to panpsychism. I have addressed this topic briefly elsewhere (2009a: 4–6). See Parkes 2009 and Manjaly 2009 for more detailed discussions.

3. I will use 'materialism' and 'physicalism' interchangeably. In their standard formulations, matter is intrinsically mindless.

and unanswered questions. Panpsychism offers a third way that avoids or resolves certain difficulties while providing inherent advantages.

Panpsychism has important ethical consequences.   It argues that the human mind is not an anomaly in the universe, but that the human and the non-human alike share the quality of enmindedness. By virtue of this common and universal characteristic, we may come to know the universe more intimately and perhaps find ourselves at home in it. This in turn can serve as a basis for more compassionate and ecological values, and therefore of new ways of acting in the world.[4]

Panpsychism brings into sharp relief the nature of conventional "mechanistic" physicalism.   Present-day philosophical thinking, and even present-day social and political systems, are largely rooted in a mechanistic view of the cosmos that was inherited from Hobbes, Descartes, and Newton: the view of the universe as a place of dead, insensate matter driven by mechanical forces. In such a universe, mind is an unexplained and perhaps unexplainable mystery, a "great exception" in the cosmic scheme. Throughout history, panpsychism has served, at almost every point, as an antipode to this mechanistic theory of mind and reality. Panpsychism stands in stark contrast to the long-dominant worldview.

Panpsychism is perhaps the most underanalyzed philosophical position in Western philosophy, and is long overdue for a detailed treatment.   The present volume is the first formal, systematic survey of the field. A few other works have made partial attempts, but they have either been too restrictive in scope or have addressed the topic from a narrow philosophical perspective.[5] This is a grievous oversight insofar as there have been nearly three dozen major philosophers in the past five centuries, and far more lesser figures, who have articulated versions of panpsychism. It is scarcely an exaggeration to say that panpsychism is utterly unknown to a large majority of present-day philosophers.

The remainder of this chapter will explore some general issues surrounding philosophy of mind and how they relate to the relevant ontological and psychological concepts. Subsequent chapters will address the specific

4. See Skrbina 2013 for a further discussion and a defense.

5. Such works would include Paulsen 1892/1895, McDougall 1920, and Griffin 1998.

writings of various thinkers in detail, documenting their panpsychist views and indicating something of their rationale. The final chapter will summarize the arguments for panpsychism, compare these with recent opposing arguments, and then attempt to place the panpsychist movement in a larger perspective.

1.2 Panpsychism Defined

Philosophical arguments often turn on interpretations of definitions. This is particularly so with issues of mind and consciousness—and perhaps even more so with panpsychism. Though the concept is ancient, the term itself was coined by Italian philosopher Francesco Patrizi in the late sixteenth century. It derives from the Greek *pan* ("all") and *psyche* ("soul" or "mind"). The association of *psyche* with "soul" is problematic for many contemporary secular and naturalist philosophers, and thus I will, for the most part, leave that issue aside. Here I will take *psyche* to mean "mind," as commonly—if vaguely—understood.

If we can agree that 'panpsychism' broadly means "all has mind," further articulation becomes difficult. Once we begin to categorize "all," and to break down the concept of mind, numerous issues arise and opinions diverge. Analysis of mind inevitably addresses such matters as consciousness, sentience, cognition, belief, qualia, and so on—all of which are ambiguous and contentious. The issues are serious enough when we are (implicitly) restricting our discussion to human minds, but these terms become very problematic as we move down the phylogenic chain. When we attempt to universalize them, the problems can become enormous.

In the attempt to minimize these concerns, it will be constructive to examine some of the associated terms. First, though, I will review various definitions of panpsychism in the literature. Timothy Sprigge, in the entry on panpsychism in the *Routledge Encyclopedia of Philosophy*, offers this definition:

Physical nature is composed of individuals, each of which is to some degree sentient. … [They may be said to have] sentience, experience, or, in a broad sense, consciousness. (Sprigge 1998a: 195)

However, one rarely finds the same definition twice. Here are some others:

All objects in the universe … have an "inner" or "psychological" being. (Edwards 1967: 22)

Everything has a soul, or ... a rudiment of a soul. (Popper and Eccles 1977: 15)

Mind is a fundamental feature of the world which exists throughout the universe. (Seager 2001)

Panpsychism is the view that mentality is present in all natural bodies with unified and persisting organization. (Clarke 2003: 1)

We even find variability within the same source. Chalmers (1996), for example, defines it once as "everything is conscious" (216) and elsewhere as "everything has a mind" (298), apparently regarding the two as equivalent. More recently, he has refined and restricted his definition: "I will understand panpsychism as the thesis that some fundamental physical entities are conscious." (2015: 246) The divergence here from the other views is striking. Despite this considerable variability, we may agree that the general meaning is understood, and may be captured—at the highest level—as the notion that all things have a mind, or a mind-like quality.

As soon as we allow the possibility that all things may possess mind, we are anxious to elaborate. What, precisely, do we mean by such a claim? Which specific mental qualities apply to non-human animals, or plants, or rocks, or atoms? There are many terms in the philosophical literature that relate to noetic qualities and abilities, and a brief survey will unearth the following (among many others): consciousness, self-consciousness, thought, cognition, intelligence, feelings, experience, inner life, what-it-is-like (to be something), qualitative feel, qualia, will, phenomenal feel, awareness, belief, perception, sense, sentience, and subjectivity. All these terms obviously evolved in a human context, and the meanings of all are rooted in our collective human experiences. This makes any textual definition or philosophical usage problematic, when it comes to subject at hand.

With respect to a definition of panpsychism, certain terms seem particularly troublesome. Let me highlight three of them: 'consciousness', 'soul', and 'thought'. 'Consciousness' is highly anthropocentric, and its meaning is very closely associated with specifically human mental states. The term derives from the Latin *com* (with) + *scire* (know), meaning "to know something with oneself"—in other words, self-knowledge or self-awareness. For most of us, 'consciousness' refers to the aware and alert mental states that human beings normally experience in their waking hours. This meaning is firmly entrenched, even for philosophers. Thus, to attempt to expand its applicability to all things is, arguably, to fight an unnecessary uphill battle.

This is not to suggest we should abandon it, even in a panpsychist context. The term is certainly useful for primates and so-called higher animals, and probably the "lower" ones as well. It gets more difficult when speaking of plants, or collective entities such as forests, coral reefs, or the Earth as a whole. Very few would allow the term for inanimate objects, and any attempt to do so likely poses insurmountable conceptual barriers.[6]

In general, panpsychists are highly sensitive to the use of the word 'consciousness', and for good reason. Upon laying out a panpsychist position, one is immediately faced with the charge that he believes that "rocks are conscious"—a statement taken as so obviously ludicrous that panpsychism can be safely dismissed out of hand. Such a tactic is clearly a logical fallacy, but it has some rhetorical force. To maintain consciousness as a universal quality demands an intricate and detailed defense, one that is arguably doomed to failure. Comparisons to human consciousness are inevitable and yet potentially irrelevant. And this is apart from the fact that human consciousness is very problematic in itself—notably, its definition, its qualitative nature, and its physical correlates. This makes it a poor candidate for universal ascription.

Different issues arise with the notion of the soul. As has been mentioned, my focus here is on naturalistic panpsychism, and thus I will generally set aside any supernatural or theological variations. The exceptions will be with those philosophers who themselves utilize the term, either explicitly or via common translation. The Greek word *psyche* is, of course, typically translated as 'soul', and thus we find extensive reference in the pre-Socratics, in Plato, and in Aristotle. Soul is also a point of discussion for the Italian naturalists, for Leibniz, and even for the French vitalistic materialists. The last major panpsychist philosopher to discuss the soul was Gustav Fechner, in the mid 1800s; since that time, there has been almost no such talk in serious philosophical discourse. We find occasional reference to the somewhat preferable term 'spirit', but even this carries an air of superstition and mystery, and thus is best avoided. Talk of the soul is best left to the theologians, or to those philosophers who prefer to speak poetically or metaphorically.

The larger message here is that present-day philosophers should not avoid use of, or reference to, panpsychism for fear of invoking unacceptable

6. Though, as stated above, Chalmers does precisely this.

religious or theological concepts. With perhaps one or two minor exceptions, panpsychism has not involved the soul for more than 200 years. No present-day panpsychist interprets *psyche* as "soul." Panpsychism is not a spiritual or theological theory. It is as naturalistic, rationalistic, and hard-nosed as any current theory of mind.

The third term, 'thought', typically involves purposeful planning, considering of alternatives, basic logical calculation, and perhaps even holding of beliefs. Most would attribute these qualities only to animals, in various degrees. A related concept, cognition, refers to an especially deep and insightful thinking, a reasoning power through the use of inference or deduction—primarily the rational thought process of humans. Thinking thus seems to be an authentic feature of the so-called higher animals, is therefore best restricted to them. There is perhaps a very loose sense in which "to think" could mean to process information, and this would naturally involve a much wider scope, arguably universal. But there seems to be little benefit in doing so. Information processing is a generally distinct property from thinking, on most accounts, and is best treated as such. Therefore thinking, along with consciousness and soul, are probably best avoided when speaking of properties of universal mind.

The central point here is that discussions of the meaning of panpsychism should avoid the most heavily anthropocentric terms, which cloud the discussion more often than they provide clarity. And the use of such loaded terms is in any event unnecessary, as is demonstrated in the working definition above. Certain terms seem to be the most general and least restrictive; these might include *mind, mentality, experience,* and even *qualia.* There are good arguments for certain intentional qualities, such as *will* and *belief,* to serve as universal properties. Even *psyche,* left untranslated and suitably defined, may serve as a universal noetic quality. Hence, these concepts are perhaps more appropriately used in connection with panpsychist descriptions of reality.

Some philosophers have recognized these definitional problems and made efforts to alleviate the situation. One tactic is to use a qualifier, such as 'proto' with 'mentality', 'low grade' with 'awareness', or 'occasions of' with 'experience'. But this approach has at least two weaknesses. First, if the base term is anthropocentric, then it is hard to see the advantage of softening it through some qualifier. Proto-consciousness, for example, is still inevitably seen as something comparable to human consciousness, and thus doesn't avoid the underlying anthropocentrism. Second, philosophers who use such qualifiers seem to want to have their metaphysical cake and eat it too. Proto-mind, they claim, is something more than pure insentience, but something less than true mind. But this is arguably incoherent. Does proto-mind have a foot in each camp? Or is it some new, third category? Does it share qualities of each side? If so, how does this work? Ultimately, either proto-mind is mental, or it is not. Whichever way it falls, it seems to exclude the other possibility. Therefore it doesn't serve its claimed purpose as a kind of bridging concept or middle ground.

It may be useful at this point to propose a sort of panpsychist hierarchy of terminology, ranging from the most human-like to the most universal. This is by no means the commonly accepted order, and certainly every philosopher would construct a different arrangement,[7] but it may serve as a framework for furthering the general discussion of panpsychism.

Humans clearly admit to all standard mental attributes, and I will assume for present purposes that the same apply to all primates; efforts to find uniquely human mental qualities, vis-à-vis our primate cousins, have yet to succeed. They seem to possess counterparts of all our mental aspects. If we consider the animal kingdom as a whole, we find a vast range of creatures, from the more complex mammals to such simple organisms as sponges, hydras, and flatworms. I reject an ontological distinction between higher and lower animals as meaningless and arbitrary, but I do acknowledge a presumed wide range of mental qualities, commensurate with physiological complexity. Looking at the other kingdoms of living organisms, we see gray areas between them, and we find difficulty comparing the more complex organisms of one kingdom with the less complex organisms of another. It isn't clear, for example, that a complex plant such as an orchid is less sentient or aware than a sponge or a flatworm, or that a mushroom—a multicellular member of the fungi kingdom—is less mental than a one-celled diatom. Even the border between living and non-living is vague, in view of the status of things like viruses and prions.

Nonetheless, it may be useful to attempt to assign various terms to different high-level phylogenic categories. I make one such proposal in table 1.1. The terms in the first grouping—'mind', 'mentality', 'experience', 'belief',

7. For an example, see Plumwood 1993: 135.

Table 1.1
A proposed terminological hierarchy for panpsychism.

	All objects	Living organisms	Non-primate animals	Humans and other primates
Mind	X	X	X	X
Mentality	X	X	X	X
Experience	X	X	X	X
Belief	X	X	X	X
What-it's-like	X	X	X	X
Qualia	X	X	X	X
Nous	X	X	X	X
Psyche	X	X	X	X
Will	X	X	X	X
Awareness		X	X	X
Sensation		X	X	X
Sentience		X	X	X
Feeling		X	X	X
Thought			X	X
Consciousness			X	X
Self-conscious				X
Cognition				X

'what-it's-like', 'qualia', 'nous', 'psyche', 'will'—are, I suggest, most suitable for a panpsychist application. All these terms recur in the various historical positions, as we will see.

Definitions of panpsychism are one source of confusion; synonyms are another. The philosophical literature contains a number of terms that are related to panpsychism, and are often inappropriately identified with it. Such terms bear a brief discussion. In no particular order, they are animism, hylozoism, pansensism, panbiotism, vitalism, pantheism, panentheism, and panexperientialism.

'Animism' derives from the Latin *anima* ("soul"), and is the belief that everything in the world has a soul or a spirit. Typically connected to pre-Christian or tribal religions and indigenous cultures, animism has a strong air of superstition and mystery. It is most commonly used in a primitive, pre-scientific sense in which objects have identifiable and characteristic spirits—e.g., "the spirit of the tree" inhabiting an oak or "the water-spirit" inhabiting a lake. These spirits typically have a human-like personality or other qualities that exhibit the properties of a rational person, perhaps including intelligence, belief, memory, emotion, and agency. Furthermore, such spirits are typically not bound to the physical realm; they are, in some vague sense, immaterial and supernatural beings. This dualistic, spiritual, and highly anthropocentric nature characterizes animism and distinguishes it from philosophical panpsychism, which generally doesn't attribute high-level capabilities to non-human entities. Animism is thus taken as having little if any philosophical standing.

'Hylozoism' derives from the Greek *hyle* ("matter") and *zoe* ("life"); it is the doctrine that all matter is intrinsically alive. The term was coined in 1678 by the Platonist Ralph Cudworth in his influential work *True Intellectual System of the Universe*. It has traditionally been used in reference to the early Greek philosophers, given that they spoke the most explicitly about life in all things. Their language thus provides the term something of a philosophical pedigree. But the concept is not restricted to the ancient Greeks. Even into the late 1800s, the philosophers Ernst Haeckel and Friedrich Paulsen openly described themselves as hylozoists; Paulsen called hylozoism "a conception which almost irresistibly forces itself upon modern biology" (1892/1895: 100). This view continued into the early twentieth century, as certain prominent scientist-philosophers—including Wilfred Agar and John Haldane—argued for a hylozoist worldview. Things began to change by the middle of the twentieth century, though, as scientists developed more precise notions of life. In 1944, Kasten Tallmadge asserted that "to call a contemporary scientist hylozoist would be simply to utter an anachronism" (187). And yet there continue to be exceptions. As late as 1982, the physicist David Bohm posited that "in a way, nature is alive ... all the way to the depths" (39).[8]

Of all the synonyms for panpsychism, hylozoism is perhaps most commonly and closely associated with it. But panpsychism is now the preferred term, largely because we have a better understanding of what constitutes life. Except for such borderline cases as viruses, we generally understand

---

8. The views of all these individuals are discussed in later chapters.

what it means to be alive, and it is clear that tables, rocks, stars, and atoms are not formally living things.[9] As with the various concepts of mentality, the notion of life can become an unnecessary point of disagreement and confusion. It is perhaps best to take it in the ordinary scientific sense and apply it only to living organisms as conventionally understood. As such, there is little place for hylozoism in the present-day philosophical discourse.

Panbiotism is essentially identical to hylozoism. It was apparently introduced by the philosopher Paul Carus, editor of the journal *The Monist*, in 1892. He defined panbiotism as the view that "everything is fraught with life; it contains life; it has the ability to live." Following the ancient Greek usage, he defined life as exhibiting "spontaneity or self-motion." Why he did not use 'hylozoism' is unclear. Regardless, panbiotism is now rarely used, as is the case with the related term 'panzoism'.

Vitalism gained prominence in the eighteenth and nineteenth centuries as an attempt to explain the mysterious nature of living organisms. Emerging sciences of chemistry and physics seemed to account for much of the universe, but the phenomenon of life resisted easy explanation—as, in many ways, it does today. Scientists and philosophers thus speculated that an extra substance or principle of some sort, something non-physical, was present in living organisms. This vital force or *élan vital* was widely sought, but never found. Notably, nothing about vitalism ever suggested panpsychism; it was a nominal account of the nature of living things, not all things. Be that as it may, we do find a link to panpsychism in the work of Henri Bergson, who was an explicit vitalist and borderline panpsychist. But this aspect of his thinking failed to win adherents. By the 1930s, vitalism had largely been discredited, and it is now considered mere pseudoscience. Critics of panpsychism occasionally deride the view as vitalistic, but this is a meaningless logical fallacy. In any case, vitalism is no longer a part of serious philosophical discourse, and has no bearing on the question of panpsychism.

9. Though certain dissipative structures, such as stars and atoms, do exhibit a form of metabolism and homeostasis that closely parallel those of living systems. So too do certain systems of living things, such as specific ecosystems or the Earth as a whole. Eric Chaisson (2001) applies the concept of life to galaxies, stars, and planets: "Life likely differs from the rest of clumped matter only in degree, not in kind." (122)

Pansensism—"everything senses"—is typically associated with the pan-psychist views of Bernardino Telesio, Tommaso Campanella, and Ernst Mach. It is synonymous with the rarely used 'hylopathism'. Pansensism, like panpsychism, deserves to be more widely discussed. The word 'sense' derives from the Latin *sentire*, "to feel"; this suggests that sensation is not merely a mechanism of perception, but involves a qualitative aspect as well. In common usage, sensation frequently takes on an anthropocentric mean-ing, in that it is associated with our five sense organs and the corresponding mental perceptions. In its broader meaning, however—that of a mecha-nism of perception—it becomes an awareness of, and reaction to, external stimuli. This meaning is much more amenable to a panpsychist interpre-tation. It is clear that all things react to, and thus in a way perceive, their environment; the questions then are "Is there a corresponding mental state of any kind?" and "Is there an actual feeling, a qualitative state, a quale?" These questions must be answered in the affirmative if true pansensism is to be defended.

Pantheism is the view that all (*pan*) is God (*theos*)—that God is identical with everything that exists, i.e., the universe. What precisely this means is not entirely clear, but it seems to suggest, at a minimum, that all material objects—including humans—are part of that divinity, and that the divine is a unity. It also typically implies that God is a non-personal being, that there is no creator or intentional providence in the world, and that there is no transcendent or supernatural realm.

The Greeks were the first pantheists. Plato writes: "this world, which [the Creator] begat for himself, is a blessed god" (*Timaeus* 34b9). Later, reject-ing the possibility of multiple universes, he remarks that "there [is] but one world, a god" (55d6). The Stoics then followed his lead. According to Diogenes Laertius, "Zeno says that the entire cosmos and the heaven are the substance of god, and so does Chrysippus" (*Lives of the Philosophers*, 7.147). Centuries later, Spinoza resurrected the idea when he equated God with Nature. A point of interest: Even though there is no logical connection between pantheism and panpsychism, it remains true that many major pantheists in history were also panpsychists—including those mentioned above.

Panentheism is related to pantheism and is often confused with it. The etymological meaning is *pan-en-theos*: "all in God," or, more simply, "God is in all things." The term seems to have originated in the writings of Karl Christian Friedrich Krause around 1828. An analogy can be made to a sponge: Just as water can saturate a sponge without being the sponge, so too God is said to saturate all things while remaining transcendent and unchanging. On an alternate reading of the term, God is the soul of the cosmos, a world-soul, and the physical universe is his body. This view isn't far from the standard Christian interpretation of the omnipresence of the Holy Spirit.

Thus understood, we can see the possibility for confusion with panpsychism. On the traditional view, God is omnipresent. If God represents spirit or mind, then all things can be said to contain mind—the mind of God. The central issue here is whether there is ultimately only one mind in the universe (God, the Absolute, the World Soul, etc.), or if the cosmic mind differentiates itself into individual enminded entities. The former is a highly monist conception of panentheism, and would seem to disallow the existence of even individual human minds. The latter view is difficult to articulate clearly, but might conceivably point to a kind of pluralistic panpsychism.

Finally, we have panexperientialism, the doctrine that "everything experiences." The term was coined by the process philosopher David Ray Griffin (1977: 98) to define a particular version of panpsychism deriving from Alfred North Whitehead and Charles Hartshorne. Whitehead took events, or "occasions," to be the fundamental metaphysical reality, and this was linked to the concept of experience—a move undoubtedly influenced by William James' theory of "pure experience" as the basis of all reality. Thanks to the persistence and diligence of the process philosophers, panexperientialism is at present a well-developed form of panpsychism. Hartshorne, Griffin, Christian de Quincey, David Clarke, and other process philosophers may be credited with keeping alive the debate over panpsychism in general, and they have marshaled a large amount of evidence, both to support their position and to criticize the dominant materialist and dualist ontologies. For an early account, see Hartshorne 1937; for more recent articulations, see Hartshorne 1977, Griffin 1998, de Quincey 2002, and Clarke 2003.

On the question of definitions, synonyms, and possible confusions, a final brief word should be said about the connection to idealism. Metaphysical idealism is the view that mind, or something mind-like, is the fundamental reality of the world. As such, it bears a superficial resemblance to panpsychism. But this is misleading. Panpsychism, we recall, is the view that all things possess minds or have intrinsic mental attributes. This doesn't entail that all things *are* mind(s). One can be an idealist without being a panpsychist, taking Berkeley, Kant, and Hegel as cases in point. And clearly one can be a panpsychist without being an idealist. In fact, most panpsychists in history were not idealists in the metaphysical sense. Certainly there were idealist philosophers who were also panpsychists—Schopenhauer, Josiah Royce, Francis Bradley, and Tim Sprigge come to mind—but their idealism was supplemental to, not entailed by, their panpsychism. Thus, any attempted identification of panpsychism with idealism is inappropriate and unjustified.

1.3   The Question of Emergence

One of the strongest arguments for panpsychism today springs from the intrinsic weakness of its main competitor: emergentism. This requires some elaboration.

Even though they may not acknowledge it, nearly every contemporary philosopher of mind is an emergentist. They believe that, in the distant past, mind did not exist. Today, it does. Ergo, it must have emerged, in an absolute sense, from an organic milieu that was devoid of mind. Yes, they say, this must have happened; admittedly, they are not sure when or how, but self-evidently, it must have occurred. In any case, no further need for philosophers to ponder the matter. This is a question for paleontology or physiology, not philosophy. No important philosophical issues attach to it—or so they believe.

Panpsychists reply "Not so fast." When spelled out, the emergentist position is found to be rife with problems, questions, and profound implications.

Let me recount the emergentist position a bit more carefully. They believe, explicitly or implicitly, that there was a point in the past history of the Earth—say, a few hundred million years ago—when there were no mind-bearing organisms in existence. Before Homo sapiens, before mammalian life, before any "higher animals" at all, there were no experiencing beings on the planet. Biology ran strictly on unthinking, unperceiving, unfeeling instinct. There was no sadness, no happiness, no pain, no joy—anywhere at all on Earth. Hunger merely triggered a biological reflex to seek out food. A quenched thirst felt like nothing—rather, it was like the fuel gauge on a car: One drank, the needle "rose," the body was sated. When fleeing a predator, there was nothing at all like a sensation of fear; organisms simply ran, hid, or fought back. Sexual intercourse was in no sense enjoyable, but strictly a physical act that perpetuated the species.

Then, at some crucial point in organic evolution, the first enminded creature appeared. That is, *suddenly* appeared. Some first select species— and indeed, some first individual organism—suddenly "felt" the world. Suddenly, the light bulb went on. Suddenly, for the first time in the known universe, an entity actually experienced reality. Pleasures and pains actually felt a certain way. Fear, happiness, anger, jealously ... these actually now meant something. For the first time ever, it was something to be like a living organism.[10]

How, panpsychists ask, did this miracle happen? How could two parental organisms—which were not "slightly" or "proto" enminded but completely and utterly devoid of mind—give birth to an offspring that, for the first time ever, experienced the world? Was it a genetic fluke? A birth defect? A naturalistic miracle? And not just once—the same miraculous event must then have occurred over and over again, countless times, to many different sets of unminded parents. And then, later, to many other species—if we accept that enmindedness extends beyond our own. The end result is that, today, we and an indeterminate number of other species actually experience pain and pleasure, actually feel things, and thus are true ontological subjects.

The miraculous nature of such an event is hard to overestimate. Mind came from that which was utterly devoid of mind. Enminded children came from utterly unminded parents. Mentality, subjectivity, qualia, suddenly appeared, like a bolt from the blue, having never existed in the known universe. This is brute emergence. Panpsychists call brute emergence a miracle, and claim that miracles don't exist. Mind could never have emerged from no-mind. Therefore, it was there all along. And if it was there all along, panpsychism obtains.

Now, it is clear that this is not to say that *nothing* emerges. Emergence happens all the time, and it always has. In fact, nearly everything that we

10. With due credit to Nagel (1974).

see around us emerged. Every structured being in the universe—animals, plants, rocks, planets, stars—all, at some point, did not exist; now they do; therefore they did indeed emerge.

But not everything can plausibly do so. Time, for instance, seems inconceivable to have ever emerged from a timeless cosmos. So too with space; we simply cannot conceive how spatiality could have come into being in a universe that was non-spatial. Time and space must have always existed, everywhere. They are "pan" qualities of reality. Other entities likely fall into this non-emergent category. Mass/energy may be one. And certain subatomic qualities, like spin, charge, and quantum state, may be the same.

Panpsychists add one more item to the list: mind. Experientiality, subjectivity, qualia … the emergence of such things is inconceivable, from a universe utterly without them. If they did, it is a true miracle. And if we allow miracles, then anything is possible. Panpsychists prefer a rational, naturalistic, and non-miraculous universe. And in such a universe, mind must have always been present.

In addition to this historical emergence problem, there are two other forms. One is what we may call the phylogenic question: Among the organisms living today, which ones possess mind? Nearly everyone grants awareness and experience to the so-called higher animals, at least. And yet no one feels competent to define these fortunate creatures. Primates, dolphins, and whales? Surely. Dogs and cats? Probably. But mice? Goldfish? Earthworms? Fruit flies? Jellyfish? Amoeba? Sponges? We can see the problem. Again, conventional philosophers can declare this a non-issue, or simply relegate it to those exploring the fringe topic of "animal minds." But from a perspective of understanding the ontology of mind, we need to know: Where can we draw the line? And how can justify drawing it there? And if we can't justify it, perhaps the line doesn't exist. Perhaps all life, at least, is experiential.[11]

A third form of the emergence problem is ontogenic. Consider a developing human fetus. When, in the span of those nine months, does the fetus suddenly acquire a mind? For the emergentist, a fertilized egg is utterly mindless, whereas a newborn infant is (presumably) fully experiential. So the emergentist must ask, At what point in the process does the light

11. There are obvious implications here for environmental ethics and animal rights. As has been mentioned, panpsychism has important ethical consequences. Again, see Skrbina 2013 for one elaboration.

suddenly switch on? But any answer he gives will be deficient. No single moment in time, no specific number of cells, is necessary and sufficient to switch on consciousness or sentience. The emergentist has no plausible and defensible answer. The panpsychist thus has the stronger case: No sudden switch happens. There is no one magic cell, or one special moment, that turns on the light. The fetus is enminded and experiencing from Day 1— even if at an extremely low level.[12] For that matter, so are the unfertilized egg and every individual sperm cell.

The bottom line seems quite clear: One is either an emergentist, or one is a panpsychist. There seems to be no middle ground.[13] Either the early Earth—and the early universe—was mindless, or it was not. If we claim that it was originally mindless, we have an obligation to explain the miraculous, brute emergence of the experiencing subject. If we cannot explain it, the panpsychist case becomes all the stronger.

Now, all this is not to say that panpsychists don't have their own version of an emergence problem. If, say, our individual cells are experiential, how do their lesser minds relate to our one, unified, higher-order mind? Do they compose it? If so, how does this work?[14] Do they exist in parallel? Do we then in fact have many minds in our bodies? If so, why don't we sense this? And in any case, where does our higher-level mind come from? These are important problems that the panpsychist must address. But, I emphasize, these are lesser-order problems than that posed by brute emergence. It is intrinsically more difficult to explain the absolute appearance of some quality, than to explain how it complexifies. If one must have problems, one generally prefers that they are at least tractable. The complexifying, combinatorial nature of mind is a riddle, but we have analytic methods to address it. Brute emergence of mind is a miracle, and little more can be said.

1.4   Historical Approaches

The following chapters lay out the case for the role of panpsychism in the history of Western philosophy. It is no exaggeration to state that very few

12. There are obvious implications here for the abortion debate.

13. Of course, for philosophers there is *always* a possible middle ground. But in this case, it seems to be one that is exceptionally hard to articulate and defend.

14. This is the well-known "combination problem." I examine it in subsequent chapters.

philosophers today, even philosophers of mind, understand much at all of this lengthy and significant history. Most will know the concept of panpsychism, but when pressed to identify some prominent advocates, they will struggle to list more than half a dozen names. Furthermore, most find panpsychism vaguely embarrassing, and thus will rarely acknowledge its presence in their favored philosophers. Not uncommonly, many will explicitly deny that a certain individual was a panpsychist, despite clear textual evidence to the contrary. Often the topic is simply avoided, as being too troublesome or inconvenient.

My first task, therefore, is to establish and document the panpsychist views of the various philosophers. In nearly every case I draw from primary sources, though the use of secondary references will be necessary in some instances. The cases for many individuals are clear and explicit, but others are somewhat vague and open to interpretation. For each thinker I will marshal the strongest possible case for panpsychism, while considering counter-arguments as required.

Three issues stand out, when viewing the large historical sweep presented here. First, and surprisingly, many philosophers seem to almost take panpsychism for granted. They often view it as unexceptional, as something like a conventional stance, and as needing little defense. Some make brief passing comments supportive of panpsychism, and leave it at that. From a present-day skeptical standpoint, this is unsatisfactory; we are often left wanting to hear more of the arguments, the defense, and the implications. But we are frequently disappointed. Nonetheless, the views stated will typically suffice to establish the individual thinker as a panpsychist.

Second, there are varying degrees of commitment to the concept. This is due to the broad range of panpsychist theories of mind, and also to the scope of mental aspects under consideration. Some philosophers seem merely sympathetic, and stop short of endorsement. Others find the view compelling but also have significant concerns, such that, in the balance of pro and con, one doesn't know their final stance on the issue. In yet other cases we must rely on other, third-party accounts of an individual's philosophical outlook. Overall, most cases are quite clear, I believe, but some will demand a degree of subjective interpretation.

Lastly, in reviewing the many cases for panpsychism, one notices over and over again a striking fact: that there is almost no recognition of panpsychist predecessors. In other words, most philosophers cited here seem to operate in a vacuum; they appear to have no knowledge of the long and lustrous history of panpsychism. They typically cite no one—or at most, one or two individuals. They relate few relevant accounts of earlier panpsychist theories. In essence, they almost act as if they were the only panpsychist in history.

This seems odd to us modern philosophers, who are so steeped in careful research, precise citation, and a deep knowledge of our fields. But philosophers of the past were less concerned about such things. They wanted to convey penetrating insight, new ideas, and metaphysical visions. They saw little need to quote extensively, to show exactly how their ideas stacked up to their predecessors, or to demonstrate encyclopedic knowledge. There were exceptions, of course—Aristotle comes immediately to mind—but for the most part, the great thinkers of the past were concerned with imparting their own ideas, not those of others.

From a present-day perspective, this presents us with a fractured and disconnected story. We move from one individual to another, and from one era to the next, with seemingly little continuity. Theories and arguments appear at one time, vanish for awhile, recur in different form, vanish again, only to return in yet new garb later on. In my recounting of this history, I will try to fill in the gaps and provide the continuity that is lacking in our primary sources.

With this background in place, we can now begin to examine in detail the evolution of panpsychist thought from the time of the pre-Socratics through the present.

2 Ancient Origins

Modern theories of panpsychism have their roots in the mythology and spiritualism of the pre-classical world. For the Greeks, this worldview was embodied in the writings of Homer and Hesiod. Their work, combined with elements of Egyptian theology and Eastern philosophy, formed a potent context for the emergence of distinctively Western approaches to mind and reality. These precursors all contained aspects of animistic thinking, and thus Greek philosophy emerged from within a panpsychist milieu. We are not surprised, then, to find relatively blunt statements of panpsychism in the earliest Greek philosophers, and more subtle and sophisticated approaches in the later thinkers. Panpsychism remained strong into the Hellenistic era, and even found its way, indirectly, into early Christian theology.

2.1 Ancient Greece and the "Hylozoist" Tradition—the Pre-Socratics

The pre-Socratic era covered a range of roughly 200 years, from the emergence of Thales' philosophy circa 600 BC to the death of Democritus in 370 BC. There were a dozen or so major Greek philosophers in this time frame, and at least twice as many lesser ones; collectively they established basic framework of philosophical thinking that would be fleshed out by Socrates, Plato, and Aristotle. The panpsychist milieu into which these individuals were born shows itself in their clear and unambiguous statements. Some form of panpsychism seems to have been taken for granted by nearly all major pre-Socratics. Hence they provide not arguments for it but rather their own interpretations of it, using their uniquely personal terminology and concepts.

The very first philosophers were the Milesians: Thales (625–545 BC), Anaximander (610–540 BC), and Anaximenes (585–525 BC). They concerned themselves not with mythology and theology but rather with fundamental metaphysical questions: What are things ultimately made of? Where did things come from? What are the guiding principles of the cosmos? How can we account for such things as life, motion, and the psyche? Before these men, such questions were evidently never addressed in a systematic way.

At its most fundamental level, the world of the Milesians was composed of *things that move*. Hence among their most basic questions were "What is the essence of a thing?" and "What causes motion?" They seemed to have developed an intuitive view that the apparent plurality of things belied an underlying commonality or unity. This was a rational conclusion, given the fact that we live in a unitary cosmos and that things seem to be connected and even convertible into other things—as when wood burns and becomes fire, or when soil transforms into plant life, or when animals ingest and incorporate various foods and drinks. Also undeniable was the fact that certain things had the power of self-motion: humans, animals, some plants, stars, the moon, and various other astronomical objects. Finally, the cosmos seemed, upon reflection, to be much less arbitrary than portrayed by Homer and Hesiod. Events occurred not by divine mandate, but rather in a systematic and orderly manner. There were patterns of action in the universe, and these patterns indicated a kind of logic to things—to use their word, a *logos*. The flow of events in the world, furthermore, seemed to work in a specific direction, toward some undefined goal (*telos*). The apparently vast, diverse, and chaotic cosmos, then, was in reality a single moving substance in a diversity of forms, self-driven in some sense, guided by a higher logos, and moving toward a given end.

The Milesian worldview, therefore, possessed three fundamental qualities: (1) It reflected *a rational order*, governed by a logos, and thus formed a coherent and comprehensible system. (2) It was *evolutionary*, in the sense that things moved through the world and developed or changed over time, toward a telos or end. (3) It was *inherently animated*.[1] The rationality of their metaphysics was manifest as a materialist monism—they each sought to

1. Cf. Guthrie 1962–1981, volume 1: 140–145.

reduce the plurality of things to a single underlying substance or entity. This entity had certain definite characteristics, foremost of which was its capability of producing the movement, life, and soul that were apparent in the everyday world. If everything is ultimately one, and if that one yields spontaneity and life, then a reasonable conclusion is that everything possesses these qualities to some degree. For the Milesians, this was the most compelling and intuitive option. If one were to disagree, one would assume the burden of proof to show, at least, (a) why some things have life and other do not and (b) how such a phenomenon as life might plausibly emerge over the course of time from a lifeless substrate. Apparently no one in ancient Greece argued for such a position. For the Milesians, matter (*hyle*) possessed life (*zoe*) as an essential quality. Something like hylozoism was simply accepted as a brute condition of reality. As Guthrie (1962–1981, volume 1: 145) explains, "the union of matter and spirit in a material substance … is [for the Milesians] an assumption that raises no doubts and calls for no argument or defense."

Consider Thales, who was widely known for his panpsychist views. That he was also the first true Western philosopher demonstrates something of the significance of panpsychism in the early Greek worldview. Thales was famous for predicting a solar eclipse in 585 and for his theory that water was the cosmic *arche*, the fundamental principle underlying all material things. But of the few remaining fragments by him, two demonstrate his commitment to panpsychism. Both are found in Aristotle's *De anima*. First, we have the passage on the lodestone (magnet):

Thales, according to what is related of him, seems to have regarded the soul as something endowed with the power of motion, if indeed he said that the lodestone has a soul because it moves iron. (405a19)

Here we have two distinct ideas: that the soul (*psyche*) is defined as that which moves or produces motion, and that the lodestone itself has a soul because it can attract iron. Consider first the concept of *psyche*. In addition to its common interpretation as soul, it has other important meanings and associations, including spirit, life, breath, and mind. The *psyche* was connected with the life energy of living things, with the divine animating spirit that produced motion in physical objects, and with the activity of the mind. At this early stage in philosophy there was not yet the distinction between having a soul, being alive, and possessing a mind; all these were treated more or less as equivalent.[2] To the pre-Socratics, psyche was as much mind-like as it was soul-like. In the first book of *De anima* Aristotle takes pains to note that most everyone before him, including Plato, did not clearly distinguish between soul and mind (*nous*). For example, we find the following passage on the views of Democritus: "Soul and mind are, he says, one and the same thing." (405a10) And Anaxagoras "[only] seems to distinguish between soul and mind, but in practice he treats them as a single substance" (405a13). *Psyche*, then, is the energy that animates and produces movement in all things, including the movement of thoughts and ideas.

Humans and animals clearly possess *psyche*, and in a monist universe anything else that demonstrates the qualities of life—that is, to be self-moving or to cause motion—possesses it too. The lodestone clearly shows the power to move small bits of iron, a fact that must have been rather miraculous to the ancients. And yet the lodestone is obviously in many ways a rock like any other. That some rocks exhibit greater powers of *psyche* than others is comparable to the notion that humans are just animals of a certain type, and that they exhibit distinctive noetic powers. Apparently Thales concluded from this that all things possessed *psyche*, to a greater or lesser degree. We see this clearly in the second major fragment:

Certain thinkers say that soul is intermingled in the whole universe, and it is perhaps for that reason that Thales came to the opinion that all things are full of gods. (*De anima*, 411a7)

Aristotle, presumably following Thales, uses the word *theon*, which is translated as "gods." The power of *psyche* was seen as a god-like, divine power, or perhaps as the power of the gods themselves. But why say "full of gods" (*panta plere theon*) and not "full of soul'? We can only speculate. Perhaps it was a nod to the mythological language of Homer. Or perhaps it was a strictly linguistic issue; perhaps it was awkward and inappropriate to claim that things were full of soul. In any case, souls are divine, the gods themselves are spirits and souls, and thus, for Thales, the two concepts are deeply interconnected.

2. The rough equivalency of the terms 'mind' and 'soul' continued at least through the time of Lucretius, who wrote in *The Nature of Things*, "Be sure that under one name you join the two, and when ... I say 'the soul,' believe that the word will mean 'the mind' as well, since both make up a unit, a thing conjoint." (III, 420–425)

Or perhaps Thales was being more exact than we give him credit for. It would seem that an essential quality of a god is that it is a single being, a unitary presence, with a singular sense of identity and personality. *Psyche*, on the other hand, seems like a relatively amorphous, diffused power—especially conceived as a power to move something, rather than a power to think. It may be that Thales was pointing to singular sense of identity in all things, a mental being and personality, which could simultaneously act, perceive, and move.

If we attempt to construct a rational argument for panpsychism from these two fragments, it would go something like this: Material objects—humans, animals, wind, sea, magnets, heavenly bodies—have the power of motion; they move either themselves or surrounding things. The material object we know most intimately—our own body—possesses an energy, called *psyche*, that accounts for our power. Under the assumption that the world is rational and that humans are not ontologically unique, a reasonable conclusion is that all things with a motive power also possess *psyche*. And in light of the fact that we live in a connected, unitary cosmos, it is difficult to explain why only certain material objects are ensouled and not others. Therefore, a reasonable conclusion is that all things possess *psyche*, to a greater or lesser degree. I will call this the Indwelling Powers argument for panpsychism. It is the first of several that we find throughout history.

Like Thales, Anaximenes argued for a monist worldview, but with an underlying principle of air (*pneuma*). The word *pneuma* has an interesting array of meanings, some of which are strikingly similar to those of *psyche*. Besides "air," *pneuma* can also mean "breath," "soul," "spirit," or "mind." Whereas the primary meaning of *psyche* is "mind" or "soul," the primary meaning of *pneuma* seems to be "breath," as in "breath of life." For Anaximenes, the breath of life was the living, animating principle of all things. This again was a logical conclusion. In every animal, breath equals life: no air, no life; no life, no breath. And air seems to be everywhere, as does motion, and so it is not unreasonable to argue that *pneuma* is the underlying principle or *arche* of the cosmos.

Anaximenes, though, seems to offer a different kind of argument for panpsychism than Thales. He saw in air a principle of continuity throughout all things. If this substance can be argued to account for our soul/mind, and given that air is omnipresent, then a similar manifestation is likely to be present everywhere. I will call this the Argument by Continuity. Panpsychism is a natural and logical position to hold in a monistic worldview. In fact, to be a monist and dispute the Continuity argument demands either an explanation of the unique emergence of mind—no small matter—or a denial of mind altogether. That the Continuity argument differs from the Indwelling Powers argument of Thales is clear: Thales makes no connection between panpsychism and his *arche* of water, nor does water account for the existence of soul. Anaximenes, by contrast, fundamentally links his *arche* of air to mind/*psyche*. Both arguments, however, appeal to an analogy with basic human experiences of our own minds and selves.[3]

As it happens, Anaximenes also makes a kind of appeal to the concept of indwelling power. Air, in the form of soul, has a cohesive power in the world. It holds things together, animates them, and maintains their existence as discrete objects enduring over time. "As our soul … being air, holds us together and controls us, so does [breath] and air enclose the whole world."[4] But this is supplemental to, and independent of, his primary argument from continuity.

The concept of *pneuma*, inaugurated by Anaximenes, was seminal. It was taken up by Aristotle in his own quasi-panpsychist theory, and later, to a greater degree, by the Stoics. They gave it a precise elemental structure, and assigned it a specific animating role in the universe. Later still, it seems to have been the inspiration for the Holy Spirit of the Bible; as I will explain, in the original Greek of the New Testament, the term for "spirit" was *pneuma*.

Chronologically, the next major philosopher after the Milesians was the enigmatic Pythagoras (570–495 BC), who exerted much influence within Greek society generally. Unfortunately, little is known of him with certainty. He apparently lectured on mathematics, ethics, health, and metaphysics. Yet, like Socrates, he wrote nothing. His closest followers formed a secretive cult, and thus we have few direct accounts of him. Most of what

3. Some modern writers refer to "analogical" arguments for panpsychism. It is true that analogy is essential in many cases, but this designation is insufficiently precise. There are many forms of analogy at play, and we need to distinguish them.

4. Aetius (I, 3, 4), in Kirk et al. 1983: 158–159.

is known is indirect and anecdotal. Circa 50 BC, Cicero recounted that Pythagoras "held that mind was present and active throughout the whole universe, and that our minds were a part of it" (*On the Nature of the Gods*, I, 26–28). This "divine mind" or "pure spirit" was seen as "infused and imprisoned in the world." We also know that Pythagoras associated numbers with the cosmic *arche*. This is significant because, as Aetius informs us, Pythagoras "takes number as an equivalent for intelligence" (*Placita* iv.2).[5] Other reports attribute to Pythagoras the view that everything is intelligent, but this is difficult to confirm with much certainty. It seems clear that he held to a mystic, pan-spiritual view of the universe, and thus that he probably endorsed some variation of a panpsychist philosophy.

Parmenides (545–460 BC) developed ingenious arguments for the view that only Being is possible and therefore that only Being exists. This entails that Becoming, conceived as a change from non-being to being (or vice versa), doesn't exist—because non-being is not possible. The existence of change in the world is an illusion, he said; therefore motion, and even time itself, are also illusory. This was a radical view, as it directly contracted the centrality of the concept of motion within natural philosophy.

Also, since thinking was acknowledged by Parmenides to be an undeniable aspect of reality, it followed that thought, or mind, must be an essential aspect of Being. The otherwise homogeneous and unchanging Being has this unique, positive property, which apparently has a special ontological standing—perhaps due to its self-evident and undeniable nature. Parmenides concludes, then, not merely that Being "has" thought, but that Being *is* thought. There are two central fragments that explicitly make this claim, and both are subject to an unusually wide range of interpretations and translations. The first is fragment 3, transliterated from the Greek as *To gar auto noein estin te kai einai*. Among many translations, one finds the following:

For it is the same thing to think and to be. (Freeman 1948: 42)
What is ... is identical with the thought that recognizes it. (Lloyd 1959: 327)
For the same things can be thought of and can be. (Barnes 1987: 132)
Thinking and being are the same. (Reeve and Miller 2006: 13)

5. Cited in Guthrie 1988 (p. 310).

Parmenides is making an identity between thought and being, but it is a difficult matter to understand in what sense the two things are "the same." There are at least two interpretations. First is a sort of metaphysical idealism: that all being is of the nature of a thought, or a mental activity. In this sense it provides an interesting anticipation of the much later work of Berkeley. But there is a second, panpsychist interpretation: that all things can be said to think. But even this is problematic because, for Parmenides, it is not clear that there truly are distinct things in the world; rather, there seems to be only the one monistic Being. If all things, as a whole, think, then such a view would constitute a kind of pan-noetic ontology—something like a panentheism or world-soul, but without personality, just pure thought. This is arguably not panpsychism, which, as defined in chapter 1, requires things individually to possess mind. Parmenides' intentions on this point are vague.

Support for the second interpretation comes from Coxon (1986: 181), who remarks, regarding this fragment, that "the neoplatonic belief that Parmenides identified Being with Mind was well-founded." Additional supporting evidence comes from Xenophanes' assessment of God as a kind of cosmic mind; "[this] may also be regarded as suggesting that Parmenides envisaged Being as Intelligence." Xenophanes, incidentally, was a "panzo-ist," according to Cleve (1969: 21).

Long also argues for a strong "identity" reading of this fragment, one in which "being itself is or has a mind" (1996: 133). The non-identity reading, advanced by some, is untenable because it virtually eliminates mind from the cosmos. Confirming the near-universal stance on panpsychism at the time, Long adds that "no Greek philosopher prior to and immediately posterior to Parmenides treated reality as lifeless and mindless" (140).

The second fragment continues the same line of thinking, though with equally ambiguous results: *Tauton d' esti noein te kai ounechen esti noema* (fragment 8, line 34). Here we find no direct mention of *einai* ("being"), but rather a focus on *noein* ("thinking") and *noema* ("thought" or "consciousness"). The identification is made between thinking and the object of thought:

Therefore thinking, and that by reason of which thought exists, are one and the same thing. (Smith 1934: 16–17)

To think is the same as the thought that It Is. (Freeman 1948: 44)

Thinking and the object of thought are the same. (Cleve 1969: 537)

The same thing are thinking and a thought that it is. (Barnes 1987: 135)

Thinking and the thought that it is are the same. (Reeve and Miller 2006: 14)

Long says that this fragment, because it equates the object of thought (i.e., being) with thinking, "does give explicit testimony for the mind/being identity reading" (1996: 136).

Cleve is sensitive to the panpsychist implications in these two fragments. He observes that being, though technically unextended and incorporeal, is yet permeated by thought: "being itself ... is inextensive incorporeal thinking that is present whole and undivided in each and every part of seeming space" (1969: 536). He adds that "the only being is consciousness, noema, that, however, must not be split into act of thinking and content of thinking" (537). Thus it seems clear that thought permeates Being, and that anything that exists must also be said to be identical with thought. Since the metaphysical status of distinct things is unclear, we cannot determine the degree to which Parmenides' stance is true panpsychism. Yet in view of the "hylozoist" milieu into which he was born, it seems to be the most likely interpretation.

Parmenides' notion that thought is identical to being anticipates the discussion in *Sophist* in which Plato puts forth a similar view: that the Form of Being possesses the qualities of "understanding, intelligence, life, and soul" (249a). As we know, Plato held Parmenides in high regard, and thus it isn't surprising to find him incorporating elements of his predecessor's ontology.

In opposition to Parmenides' static world of pure Being, Heraclitus (505–450 BC) conceived a worldview in which change and motion were the essential reality. In a fitting manner, fire became his *arche*. To the ancient Greeks, fire was a form of pure energy, and it is interesting that Heraclitus developed a distinctively energeticist worldview some 2,300 years before it became fashionable in physics.

Fire, like the *pneuma* of Anaximenes, was associated with life-energy and hence spirit and soul. Significantly, Heraclitus referred to this fire not merely as *pyr* but as *pyr aeizoon*—ever-living fire. Consequently, this spiritual life-energy was seen as responsible for creating and sustaining everything. Diogenes Laertius reports in his *Lives of the Philosophers* that Heraclitus held to the view that "all things are full of souls and spirits" (IX: 5–12). Again, ensoulment is universal and associated with motion and change.

More specifically, the *pyr aeizoon* possesses a kind of intelligence or cognitive ability. In the only directly relevant fragment, Heraclitus says that "thinking is common to all" (fragment 113; Barnes 1987: 109). He evidently followed the logic of his predecessors in believing that, in a monist cosmos, intelligent spirit or life must exist in all things, if they exist anywhere. This is clearly Long's interpretation: "Heraclitus takes thinking … to be implicit in the things that are (the processes of nature)" (1996: 131). In sum, we have here a combination of the Indwelling Powers argument—in the energy of the *pyr aeizoon*—and the Continuity argument, in which *pyr* constitutes all things.

Heraclitus and Parmenides lived at about the same time, and their two opposing philosophies must have created something of a crisis in Greek intellectual circles. Each seemed independently plausible, yet they were profoundly incompatible. In response, Empedocles and Anaxagoras each sought, in different ways, to resolve this conflict. They concluded that the problem lay in the assumption of monism. Thus, each articulated a pluralist worldview with more than one fundamental substance. For Empedocles, it was the four elements, Earth, Water, Air, and Fire. For Anaxagoras, it was an infinity of substances. But both men were united in their panpsychist outlooks. As Long states, "Anaxagoras most forcefully and Empedocles more obliquely treat intelligent life as basic to reality" (131).

Anaxagoras, however, was evidently not content with postulating infinitely many substances of the world, and so he concluded that a single overarching principle was needed to provide unity to the whole system. This principle was *nous*, or mind. This introduction of the term *nous* into philosophy is evidence of a deepening distinction among the various meanings associated with *psyche* and *pneuma*. *Nous* is more related to the concept of mind in the sense of the human mind or reason, while remaining distinct from *logos*, which is also sometimes translated as "reason." *Nous* represents, furthermore, a kind of unity of thought—a unified entity, a mind, that is the subject of thinking.

Mind, for Anaxagoras, is ubiquitous, omnipresent, and even god-like:

Mind is something infinite and self-controlling … . For it is the finest of all things and the purest, and it possesses all knowledge about everything, and it has the greatest strength. … And mind arranged everything—what was to be, and what was, and what now is, and what will be … . (in Barnes 1987: 227–228)

The action of mind is analogous to a rotation or a turning: "And mind controlled the whole revolution, so that it revolved in the first place." Thus we see that mind causes motion, as it had for the earlier thinkers. But this motion is of a specific kind, namely circular. It furthermore is a creative force, bringing concrete things into existence.

Anaxagoras determined that mind, as a universal quality, existed in varying degrees: "All mind, both great and small, is alike." Here we see a form of pluralism that is tempered by a fundamental unity of the nature of the diverse minds. Mind is present in greater and lesser forms, yet they all share some common basis in *nous*. The lesser minds are not ontologically different than the greater. It is a question of degree.

Finally we have one further relevant citation, from Aristotle. In *Metaphysics* we find the following view attributed to Anaxagoras: "just as in animals, so in nature, mind is present and responsible for the world" (984b15). The mind that is ubiquitous is not just some amorphous, abstract mind; it is essentially like that of animals, i.e., an animated soul or spirit. Mind is present both in the whole of the cosmos and in the specific objects. This implies a multi-level system of mind, occurring distinctly in different levels of structured matter.

Cleve (1969) addresses this issue of individual minds in detail. Whereas some commentators see Anaxagoras' *nous* as existing only in a cosmic sense, Cleve sees it surrounding and penetrating all matter. On his view, the plural elements (*moiras*) never exist without some conjoining *nous*: "Anaxagoras, too, is a panzoist, i.e. one to whom body and consciousness are still a unity … . The notion of a 'matter without consciousness' … [does] not exist for [him]." (321) He adds that "every molecule is surrounded by *Nous* on all sides" (207). As to the question of distinct individual minds, he suggests that "a piece of *Nous* [could] be in a molecule—in the same sense as a fellow locked in a prison 'is in'" (269). In this interpretation, then, *Nous* surrounds all matter, and individual *nous* resides in at least some molecular elements. This is clearly a panpsychist metaphysic.

The pluralism of Empedocles (495–435 BC) was more modest. He argued that a small set of elements sufficed to explain the material nature of the world. Probably borrowing from his predecessors, he took water, air, and fire, added a fourth element, earth, and composed a four-part elemental scheme that held for nearly 2,000 years. As for Anaxagoras, Empedocles

believed that the elements required an overarching principle of organization. In his case it was not *nous* but rather a system of dual forces, designated
Philotes ("Love") and *Neikos* ("Strife"). Love was the power of attraction and
cohesion, and Strife it's opposite, namely, of repulsion and separation. It
was clear to Empedocles that both were needed; if there were only attraction in the universe, all matter would be drawn together into a formless
mass, something like a black hole. And if there were only repulsion, the
four elements would be driven apart, never to unite into structured objects.
He reasoned that there must be a balance of the two, in a kind of harmonic
tension.

From the perspective of modern physics, Empedocles' view is astonishingly accurate. His system was composed of matter and force or energy,
just as we believe today. Love has an obvious counterpart in gravity, and
physics has its own repulsive forces, namely, similar magnetic poles and
similar electric charges (Coulomb's Law). Even more surprising, physicists
have recently discovered a cosmic repulsive force generated by a mysterious
substance called "dark energy." This substance has only one salient feature:
a kind of anti-gravity force that serves to accelerate the expansion of the
universe. It seems that Empedocles was more correct than he could have
known.

Yet he was clearly no mechanistic materialist. Perhaps more than any
other pre-Socratic, he made panpsychism central to his worldview.[6] Guthrie
states that "it was in fact fundamental to Empedocles' whole system that
there is no distinction between animate and inanimate, and everything
has some degree of awareness and power of discrimination" (1962–1981,
volume 2: 233). The mere fact that Empedocles chose Love and Strife as
his two central forces is clearly suggestive of his belief that animate powers
were at work in the cosmos.

Explicit evidence of his panpsychism is found primarily in three fragments. In fragment 103 we read *"tede men oun ioteti tyches pephroneken
apanta"*—"Thus by the will of chance, all things think." (Barnes 1987:
178) This is an advance in philosophical reasoning. Earlier philosophers'
references to gods, souls, or spirit are absent, to be replaced by autonomous cosmic powers of attraction and repulsion, as we would have it

6. Trepanier (2004), for example, dedicates a lengthy section to "Empedoclean panpsychism."

today. The ability of all things to think is granted by *tyches*, interpreted either as the god Tyche or, more likely, as simply the process of chance or luck. Empedocles is saying, in effect, "By good fortune, all things are able to think."

The second important passage comes from Aristotle: "Empedocles [says that the soul] is composed of all the elements and that each of them actually is a soul." (*De anima* 404b11) The two relevant ideas here are (1) that souls (*psychein*) are material and composite, and (2) that each element, in itself, is ensouled. Clearly, if each element is a soul, and if these elements constitute the whole world, then all things are souls or soul-like. Empedocles thus seems view *psyche* in terms of mental activity and thinking rather than as a power of motion. Movement comes from the two central forces which, although animate, are apparently not *psychein*.

Third, we have a striking fragment recorded in Hippolytus' *Refutation of All Heresies* (ca. 210 AD):

If thou shouldst plant these things in thy firm understanding and contemplate them with good will and unclouded attention, they will stand by thee for ever every one, and thou shalt gain many other things from them; ... for know that all things have wisdom and a portion of thought. (fragment 110; Guthrie, volume 2: 230)

The final key phrase—*panta gar isthi phronesin echein kai nomatos aisan*—is, as usual, subject to varying translations. Barnes, for example, renders it as "for know that they all have thought and a share of mind" (163). Cleve offers this: "Do not forget, all things have mind and a share in cognition." (369) By contrast, Freeman translates *phronesin* as "intelligence" (1948: 64). In any case, we find here a poetic passage that is at once beautiful and insightful. Empedocles is indicating that a particular method of thinking, a way of approaching the world in a sympathetic fashion ("with good will"), will yield abundant fruit. He is clearly advocating a way of thinking about things with clarity and compassion, centered on the idea that, like ourselves, "all things have wisdom." Panpsychism is seen as the path to truth and lasting insight.

Empedocles thus relies on two variations of earlier arguments for panpsychism. First he employs the Indwelling Powers argument by claiming that everything has the power of thought. Mind is clearly an inherent part of his cosmic system, and as such it constitutes a kind of metaphysical first principle. The elements think, period. Thinking is a brute characteristic of matter and a power intrinsic to material reality. Second, he uses the

Continuity argument in a pluralistic fashion, appealing to an inherent soul-nature of the four elements that constitute all things.

Finally, consider the atomist theory of Leucippus and Democritus. On their view, all things in the world consist of imperceptibly small, indivisible atoms (*a-tomos*, "uncuttables") that move through otherwise empty space and interact via mechanical means to create large-scale material objects. Democritus claimed that not all atoms are alike, but that there are many different sizes and shapes, and that these differences account for the different physical properties of things.

It is sometimes believed that there is no place for mind or soul in the atomist universe. And in fact these philosophers did take the first steps away from a hylozoist interpretation. Cleve takes note of this point:

For the very first time, we have here the notion of "matter without consciousness." Democritus (or Leucippus) forms the notion of *atomoi apatheis*, of "unfeeling atoms," being the first to drop [in part] the idea of panzoism. (1969: 421)

However, these philosophers did not eliminate soul from the cosmos. Even though most kinds of atoms were completely unfeeling, one type—namely, that of spherical shape—was unique in that it possessed *psyche* and sensitivity. Aristotle explains that "those [atoms] which are spherical [Democritus] calls fire and soul" (*De anima* 404a2). The implied connection between soul and fire was evidently quite common in ancient Greece; both were seen as the most rarefied of substances, and often soul was considered to be made from elemental fire. The Democritean *psyche* was thus atomistic and material, like all things.[7]

The crucial question is this: Which objects, in addition to humans, contain the spherical soul atoms? Aristotle continues:

Spherical atoms are identified with soul because atoms of that shape are most adapted to permeate everywhere, and to set all the other [atoms] moving by being themselves in movement. (404a5)

If soul atoms are everywhere—and not just everywhere in the human or animal body—the apparent conclusion is that all things have souls (argument

---

7. Lucretius confirms this view: "[T]he soul is subtly built of infinitesimal atoms. ... Whatever is so mobile [as the soul] must be made of very round and very tiny atoms. ... Now since the soul has been revealed to be uncommonly mobile, we must grant it made of atoms very tiny, smooth, and round." (III, 175–205)

by Continuity). Consistent with earlier theories of soul, there are clear implications here that soul-atoms are omnipresent and are the ultimate cause of motion. Perhaps they are not *always* everywhere, and perhaps they are not the *only* source of motion—this we cannot tell. Consequently, it is difficult to clearly determine the extent of panpsychism in atomism. But the concept of a soul-atom had a great deal of influence, both on ancient atomists, including Epicurus and Lucretius, and on panpsychist philosophers generally, even through the late 1800s. Circa 1870, William Clifford and others put forth panpsychist theories of "mind-stuff" that recall the ideas of Democritus.

It bears noting that the "hylozoism" of the pre-Socratics was of a subtle and implicit form. Apart from Heraclitus, who explicitly referred to life (*zoe*), the others spoke in terms of *psyche*, spirit, gods, and motion. These terms were broadly and implicitly associated with the phenomenon of life, and thus, in a loose sense, the pre-Socratics were hylozoists. 'Hylopsychism' would be a more appropriate term for their view, or perhaps even 'hylotheism'. 'Hylozoism' carries a negative connotation in modern literature and is frequently used as a vague disparagement of aspects of Greek philosophy. But the term is misleading, and it is one more indication of the low regard—and poor understanding—of panpsychist philosophy. Surprisingly, the one ancient philosopher perhaps most deserving of the label 'hylozoist' is Plato, as I will now explain.

2.2   Plato

Socrates, Plato, and Aristotle collectively set philosophy forward on a new path of rationalism and logic. The consensus view that Plato was not a "primitive hylozoist" is typified by the following passage: "The hylozoism of the Milesians was no longer possible for Plato. Life (soul) and matter were not the same, and he sees soul as the self-moving principle which imparts its own motion to otherwise inert body, thus making it animate." (Guthrie 1962–1981, volume 4: 420) But this statement is misleading, and the implication is arguably incorrect. There is very strong evidence that Plato was in fact a panpsychist or even hylozoist of sorts—or at least that this is the most rational interpretation of his metaphysical scheme.

Certainly Plato broke new ground, but in some ways there was less divergence than is generally acknowledged or understood. Given the panpsychist views of Plato's esteemed predecessors, we should not be surprised to see elements of panpsychism in Plato himself. In fact he makes a number of statements that point toward such a view, even if he falls short of an outright endorsement. In the end, panpsychism seems to be the most plausible interpretation of his various beliefs.

First, though, I need to elaborate a bit on the status of the world-soul thesis. This concept, clearly and unambiguously held by Plato, is that the cosmos as a whole possesses a soul. This cosmic soul was constructed and set in place by the Demiurge, the creator god of the universe.[8] It is clear that a world-soul thesis doesn't entail hylozoism, panpsychism, or anything like this. Panpsychism demands that individual objects, in themselves, be ensouled; a cosmic soul has an uncertain relation to any lesser souls. But a world-soul hypothesis is obviously compatible with such views. Of course Plato, like all ancient philosophers, took it for granted that humans possessed souls, and therefore that at least one sort of lesser being was also ensouled. A cosmos with both human souls and a world-soul is immediately in a strange situation: Two highly disparate entities are ensouled. This would seem to be a dubious and arbitrary metaphysical scheme. One would expect that other entities, perhaps many such, would also be ensouled. And in fact this is what we find in Plato.

I also note that my analysis is centered on Plato's late works as representative of his mature thinking. He seems to have modified his perspective on ensoulment somewhere between his middle and late periods. It is significant that he moved from an ambiguous stance to a more consistent and more universal view of ensoulment in his later years.

As an example of Plato's middle-period views, consider *Phaedrus*. In this dialogue he makes a distinction between things animate and inanimate. He notes, for example, that "every bodily object that is moved from outside has no soul" (245e), and that "all soul looks after all that lacks a soul" (246b). There would thus seem to be two distinct categories of things— those ensouled, and those without.

And yet at the same time Plato seems sympathetic to the view that something soul-like is present in, or associated with, apparently inanimate

8. This idea is most fully laid out in *Timaeus* (31–36), but reference to a world-soul also occurs in *Philebus* (28d–30a) and in *Statesman* (269–273).

things. Socrates lectures in an unusual setting—outside of town in the shade of a large plane tree—and this inspires him to reflect on nature. Near the end of the dialogue he makes the rather surprising claim that nature was the original source of philosophy, and that the rocks and trees might themselves "speak the truth":

> [T]he priests of the temple of Zeus at Dodona say that the first prophecies were the words of an oak. Everyone who lived at that time, not being as wise as you young ones are today, found it rewarding enough in their simplicity to listen to an oak or even a stone, so long as it was telling the truth ... . (275b)

On the one hand this can be read as a breaking away from the "simplicity" of the earlier, hylozoistic view. And yet there is a gentle chiding of the purported wisdom of the young philosophers; one senses a certain sympathy with the ancient ways of knowing nature.

Plato's more explicit references to panpsychism are found in his later writings. The four primary sources—*Sophist*, *Philebus*, *Timaeus*, and *Laws*—are generally regarded as among his last works. In these we find three distinct arguments pointing toward a panpsychic universe. The fact that these come in the later works implies that they represent Plato's final thinking on the matter and thus have a relatively strong degree of significance in his overall system of metaphysics.

I emphasize that these are *not* explicit arguments. Plato doesn't explicitly draw a panpsychist conclusion in any of these works. And yet his arguments are individually and collectively consistent with such a worldview. More than this, they logically entail panpsychism. Significantly, nowhere in his late works does Plato deny this implication, and he avoids making fundamental distinctions between obviously animate and obviously inanimate things.[9] All this is indicative of, if not an outright endorsement, at least a strong sympathy with panpsychism.

---

9. One finds a few scattered references in his later works to *apsychon*, or inanimate and lifeless things, but none of these conclusively show that inanimateness is a distinct ontological category. In fact Plato uses the term in a variety of contexts, sometimes simply indicating "non-animal," as we understand the term today; examples of this would include *Sophist* (220a, 265c) and *Laws* (782d, 873e). Other uses (e.g., *Laws* 896b) indicate that soul is historically prior to matter, and thus that matter is in this sense *apsychon*. But this fact, of course, doesn't prevent soul from inhabiting material objects, or driving their movements and changes.

For Plato, as for the pre-Socratics, the concept of soul was closely related to that of the mind. *Psyche* and *nous* are important concepts for him, and the difference in meaning between them is relatively small. Often they are used interchangeably, as if they were evident synonyms. A number of points support this view. Writing on Plato's treatment in *Phaedo*—which is a primary text on the theory of the soul—Guthrie (1962–1981, volume 4: 421) states plainly that "in its pure state it [soul] was identical with *nous*." Aristotle (*De anima*, 407a5) observes that "it is evident that Plato means the soul of the whole to be like the sort of soul which is called mind." This is consistent with Aristotle's overall discussion in book I of *De anima*, in which he argues that his predecessors have generally not distinguished between mind and soul. Plato himself, in *Philebus*, identifies soul as the necessary, though not sufficient, condition for mind: "no wisdom and reason without soul" (30d). In *Timaeus* we learn that "it is impossible for anything to come to possess intelligence apart from soul" (30b). All this is consistent with his famous tri-partition of the soul: rationality, spiritedness, and desire. The rational faculty is an intrinsic aspect of the soul, and thus we cannot speak of one without the other.

Now let us turn to the four primary texts. In *Sophist*, Plato investigates the nature and meaning of "being" in its entirety: "that which wholly is." At the start of a somewhat complicated passage near the middle of the dialogue, the Visitor relates being to *dynamis* ("power" or "capacity"): "My notion would be, that anything which possesses any sort of power to affect another, or to be affected by another … has real existence; and I hold that the definition of being is simply power." (247e)[10] Some lines later, the Visitor elaborates that being is "an active or passive energy, arising out of a certain power" (248b). This identification of being with power, or a "potent capacity," recalls the *pyr aeizoon*, the ever-living fire, of Heraclitus; both refer to the energy inherent in all extant things. The Visitor then contrasts being (essence) with becoming (generation). The initial thought is that being is something static and fixed, whereas becoming is motion and change. Ultimately (249d), however, it is decided that this is misleading, and that one must "include both the moveable and the immoveable in his definition of being." The moveable aspect of being reflects both its ability to act upon

---

10. Original: *tithemai gar horon horizein ta onta hōs estin ouk allo ti plēn dynamis.* For *Sophist* I use Jowett's translation. White (in Cooper 1997) is somewhat less clear in these passages.

other things and to be known—a process that demands some change in the thing known. Consequently, "being" here must include both the realm of the changeless Forms and the dynamic phenomenal world as well; it refers to the sum total of reality.

This power of being—the movability and capability for active, dynamic change—draws on Plato's notion that such power of self-originating motion is indicative of the presence of psyche. This idea recurs later in *Laws* (below), where Plato equates life and soul/mind with self-motion. But the important conclusion is this: If being has the power of self-generating motion, then such complete or perfect being (*to pantelos on*) must have not only an inherent psyche but also life and mind:

O heavens, can we ever be made to believe that motion [*kinesi*] and life [*zoe*] and soul [*psyche*] and mind [*phronesi*] are not present with perfect being? Can we imagine that, being is devoid of life and mind, and exists in awful unmeaningness an everlasting fixture? —That would be a dreadful thing to admit. (249a)

Plato insists, very explicitly, that all three things—life, mind, and soul— inhere in being. As if to reinforce the point, he then immediately emphasizes the issue again. He considers three different possibilities, dismissing all of them as "irrational": that "[being] has mind and *not* life," that "both [mind and life] inhere in perfect being, but that it has no *soul*," and that "being has mind and life and soul, but although endowed with soul remains absolutely unmoved." Reality itself—"that which wholly is"— thus necessarily possesses life, mind, and soul. This constitutes a first argument for the concept of ubiquitous soul, arising from metaphysical first principles.

This conclusion is not without difficulties. If everything possesses life, mind, and soul, then it would seem that all things possess such abilities as the power of self-motion and the power of thought. Plato doesn't openly acknowledge these aspects of being. Yet it is certainly possible to expand the concepts of self-motion and thought so that they might encompass all material things. As we know, many of Plato's predecessors did precisely this. All things respond dynamically and change in the face of external stimuli. They perceive; they sense; they are aware of what is going on around them. Even the very process of becoming can itself be seen as a kind of self-motion. Thus the argument is stated, and the implicit conclusion remains. Since neither the panpsychist conclusion nor its denial is addressed, we are left with an open question, at least in this dialogue. But in the absence of a clear denial, and especially in light of the other passages below, the panpsychist conclusion seems the more compelling.

In *Philebus*, Plato returns to the structure of his earlier Socratic dialogues. In the passages of interest—29a through 31b—Socrates and his two interlocutors are debating the relative standing of knowledge and pleasure as they relate to the good. In the process, they seek to place each of these two qualities into the proper metaphysical category.[11] The relevant passage comes with their discussion of knowledge, which is also referred to as intelligence, wisdom, and reason; we can infer that these qualities are closely related to the concept of psyche in general.

Socrates asks whether the structure of the universe was created by chance or by "order of a wonderful intelligence." The answer comes that "reason arranges it all" (28d). He then explains that our human bodies are composed of the four elements—fire, air, water, and earth—as are all things in the cosmos, as is the cosmos as a whole. Therefore we may speak of the ordered universe as a whole as constituting a "body." Our human body possesses a soul (*psyche*); therefore the "body of the universe" must also possess a soul. In Socrates' words, "the body of the universe which has the same properties as our [body], but more beautiful in all respects ... possesses a soul" (30a). As an argument for the world-soul, the passage is clear enough. The cosmos is argued to possess a soul on the basis of its intelligent ordering of the elements, its regularity, and its beauty. But again, the concept of the world-soul, in itself, doesn't qualify as panpsychism. It can be seen simply as a form of theism, or of panentheism. Neither of these implies panpsychism. Panpsychism requires that each individual thing, in itself, possess a soul- or mind-like quality.[12] That the combination of all things collectively has a mind is a different proposition.

On the other hand, the concept of a universal mind or a world-soul is likely to be a part of any panpsychist cosmos. Virtually any system that sees mind in all individual things will see it in the whole. Panpsychism implies a world-soul, but not vice versa. Thus we need further elaboration from Plato to determine if his view is only that of a world-soul or whether it is something more, perhaps true panpsychism.

11. The four categories are limit, unlimited, mixture of limit and unlimited, and cause of the mixture.

12. Some authors emphasize this fact by using the term 'pluralistic panpsychism'.

In fact, we find in this part of *Philebus* the second of three arguments for a panpsychist cosmos. This is a variation of the Continuity argument, and it is quite similar to that used by Empedocles. Plato relies heavily on analogy: A non-human object is argued to be similar in content to the human body, and thus is claimed to possess at least one essential characteristic of humans, namely a *psyche*. In simplified form, Plato's Continuity argument is as follows:

(1) All physical objects, from the human body to the cosmos as a whole, are entirely composed of the four elements.
(2) The human body possesses a *psyche*.
(3) The human *psyche* is entailed by the body's composition of the four elements.

Therefore,

(4) the cosmos possesses a *psyche* (world-soul).

Then, with the further implication that

(5) *psyche* is a general quality of objects composed of the four elements,

one may conclude that

(6) every object possesses a *psyche*.

The weakest link in this argument is the third point: that somehow *psyche* is logically entailed by the fact that our human bodies consist of the four elements. Plato makes no argument here for that claim, but importantly, he does so later on in *Laws*; at 895c he refers to the elements "alone" and, given their capacity for self-generating motion, they must be counted alive. If the elements individually are alive, it is plausible to conclude that anything composed of them—i.e., everything—is likewise alive. But again, the argument is only implicit here.

Plato's third argument, also put forth in *Philebus*, is a version of the well-known Argument by Design. This argument has of course been traditionally used by theologians and philosophers to argue for God's existence on the basis of the vast and supreme ordering that we see in the world. Plato argues not for God, but for universal mind, the world-soul. In the process, he also makes the argument for panpsychism.

In *Philebus* one of the metaphysical categories under discussion is "cause," meaning, ultimate cause—the cause of all things and events in the universe. Socrates notes that "this cause is recognized as all-encompassing wisdom" and, more important, that "cause [is] present in everything" (30b). At issue is the meaning of the latter phrase.

Elaborating on the first point, Socrates says that "cause" is that which "orders and coordinates the years, seasons, and months, and which has every right to the title of wisdom and reason [i.e. mind]" (30c). Two lines later we find Plato's close correlation of mind and soul: "no wisdom and reason without a soul." Then, from Socrates, "reason belongs to that kind which is the cause of everything" (30e). Thus mind, in the form of reason, wisdom, or intelligence, belongs to the metaphysical category of "cause of all things." This cause—mind, and the underlying *psyche*—is "present in everything." Clearly this can be read in two ways. It can mean that evidence of the world-soul is present in the overall ordering of the cosmos, or it can mean that wisdom and reason themselves, and the underlying *psyche*, somehow reside in things. Viewing this passage in isolation, one might presume the former. Viewing it in conjunction with the other late-dialogue passages, however, we can see reason to support the latter interpretation.

Granting these arguments in *Sophist* and *Philebus*, we are still left wanting evidence of explicit attribution of soul to things other than humans or the cosmos. Some such evidence is necessary to confirm the panpsychist conjecture. And in fact this evidence appears in the other two late works, *Timaeus* and *Laws*.

In *Timaeus* Plato offers more an exposition of rhetoric than a traditional philosophical dialogue. Socrates is again present, along with a number of other men, including the title character and Critias. The central character, Timaeus, gives an extended description of the creation of the world. He is seen as a philosopher of considerable importance; Socrates says that "he has, in my judgment, mastered the entire field of philosophy" (20a). Thus, nominally at least, Timaeus' views are to be held in high regard. Also, the dialogue was considered to be the central Platonic text throughout the Middle Ages and into the Renaissance. There was significant interest in Plato's view of creation and in his idea of the Demiurge, the god-like being who created the universe and used the Forms to give it order. Also of interest was Plato's depiction of the universe as alive, intelligent, and ensouled.

After some introductory words, Timaeus explains why the Demiurge created the world: He wanted "everything to become as much like himself as possible" (29e)—that is, brought from "a state of disorder to one of order."[13] The intelligent, ensouled, and "ordered" Demiurge sought to reproduce himself in the cosmos. Timaeus tells us that the Demiurge "concluded that it is impossible for anything to come to possess intelligence apart from soul," and that "guided by this reasoning, he put intelligence in soul, and soul in body, and so he constructed the universe" (30b). Again we see the implied connection of body—meaning any physical object—with soul/mind. Timaeus sums up his point by saying that the "divine providence brought our world into being as a truly living thing, endowed with soul and intelligence" (30c).

Timaeus then informs us that "the universe resembles more closely than anything else that Living Thing of which all other living things are parts, both individually and by kinds" (30c). The emphasis here is on both the individual things and the whole, which are said to share qualities of life and intelligence. Soul seems to exist in layers—in the "parts," in the "kinds" of parts, and in the cosmos as a whole. The Demiurge "made [the cosmos] a single visible living thing, which contains within itself all the living things whose nature it is to share its kind" (31a).

Continuing in his account of the creation, Timaeus describes the formation of the stars and others heavenly bodies. The stars are "divine living things" (40b). The Earth itself is a "god," "foremost [in the universe], the one with greatest seniority" (40c). As the Demiurge was preparing to create the stars, "he turned again to the mixing bowl, ... the one in which he had blended and mixed the soul of the universe." He concocted another "soul mixture," and then "divided the mixture into a number of souls, equal to the number of the stars and assigned each soul to a star" (41e). Here is clear evidence that Plato saw individual, nonhuman objects—apart from the cosmos—as endowed with *psyche*.[14]

Later in the dialogue (69c–70e), Plato elaborates on his tripartite theory of soul. He examines the three components: reason, spirit, and appetite or desire. These are discussed, significantly, in the context of *zoa*—animals,

---

13. Notably, the Demiurge did not create the universe *ex nihilo*, as did the Judeo-Christian God. He simply gave form to shapeless matter.

14. Star-souls are also discussed in *Laws* (898d) and in *Epinomis* (981e–983e).

or living things. *Zoa* have, by definition, one or more of these soul-types. Humans have all three, each located in a different part of the body. Celestial objects such as the Earth and the stars have only the highest soul-type: reason.

Some lines later he addresses the potentially problematic issue of plants. Plants are clearly alive, and yet they are different than animals; they have very limited means of self-motion, they have no obvious sense organs, and they function in the world in a very different manner. But they do seek out water and sunlight, and grow in such as way as to fulfill their biological potential. Plants do not seem to reason or to possess any spiritedness *per se*, but they do evidently have wants and desires, at least. And they are sensitive to their environmental conditions, and thus would appear to have positive and negative sensations about the world—something like pleasure and pain. Plato thus has good reason for ascribing them soul:

We may call these plants "living things" on the ground that anything that partakes of life has an incontestable right to be called "a living thing." And in fact, what we are talking about now partakes of the third type of soul. ... This type is totally devoid of opinion, reasoning, or understanding, though it does share in sensation [*aisthêsis*], pleasant and painful, and desire. (77b)

Plants thus possess the appetitive soul, which apparently includes both the intentional characteristic of desire and the qualitative ability to sense pleasure and pain.

Left unstated, however, is the possible existence and nature of other soul-types, which may apply to lower-order objects such as rocks. Clearly it would not do to attribute appetite to a rock. And yet some rocks— lodestones, in particular—have an undeniable ability to move things. How does Plato assess the nature of the lodestone? Unfortunately he gives it only passing treatment in *Timaeus*, treating with disdain the idea that a lodestone exerts a true force of attraction (80c). But in the one substantial reference to the subject, in the early dialogue *Ion*, he likens the stone's magnetic power to that of the gods (533d–536a). Poets act as conduits of a "divine power"; thus, they are like the lodestone, which, through a chain of iron rings, passes along its attractive force. One is left with the implication that the power of the lodestone is itself divine, driven by a god or spirit, and thus, in a way, a marker of ensoulment.

In any event, the stock of ensouled entities has grown: humans and other animals,[15] individual elements, the cosmos, stars, the Earth, plants. Again, these are consistent with the arguments in *Sophist* and *Philebus*. Such arguments provide something of an ontological theory establishing why all things may be considered as ensouled. If one were to disagree with this conclusion, then one might reasonably expect to find something in Plato's ontology that would explain why the above set of objects is unique, why they alone are ensouled, and everything else is not. Such an explanation is lacking in his later writings, and thus panpsychism is the more reasonable conclusion.

Plato's longest and last work, *Laws*, is primarily known for its description of the structure of the ideal, constitutionally based state. In the process, the issue of punishment arises as an important concern. The theory of punishment depends on the existence of gods, and book X provides an extended argument proving their existence. The argument revolves around the concept of "self-generating motion," which is seen as primordial and as "the source of all motions." Any object exhibiting such motion has the further quality of being alive. The character Clinias offers this observation: "When an object moves itself, [we are] to say that it is 'alive.' [And furthermore] when we see that a thing has a soul, the situation is exactly the same. ... We have to admit that it is alive." (895c) Furthermore, we have the identification of self-movement with soul. The Athenian asks "What's the definition of the thing we call soul?" and answers "Motion capable of moving itself." (896a) Clinias reiterates the point: "The entity which we all *call* 'soul' is precisely that which is *defined* by the expression "self-generating motion." Thus, we end up with a three-way identification between life, soul, and self-movement.

Plato then makes a series of statements arguing that soul is primordial in the cosmos, is older than matter, and in fact is the mover of matter: "Soul, being the source of motion, is the most ancient thing there is. ... Soul is the master, and matter its natural subject." (896b–c) Next comes a restatement of the position, brought out in *Philebus*, that soul is the cause of all things (896d) and "controls the heavens as well" (896e).

The Athenian then addresses whether there is only a single world-soul or multiple souls. The initial answer is clear enough ("more than one"), but

15. The case for animals is not explicitly called out, but rather taken as self-evident. One finds in *Phaedrus*, for example, reference to souls in wild animals (248d, 249b).

he is not confident as to the exact number. Some lines later, he asks, "If, in principle, soul drives round the sun, moon, and the other heavenly bodies, does it not impel each individually? Of course." (898d) The Athenian then supports this contention by referring to the sun:

Everyone can see [the sun's] body, but no one can see its soul—not that you could see the soul of any other creature, living or dying. Nevertheless, there are good grounds for believing that we are in fact held in the embrace of some such thing though it is totally below the level of our bodily senses, and is perceptible by reason alone. (898d)

In this remarkable statement, Plato not only adds the sun to the list of ensouled objects—significant insofar as the sun wasn't recognized as just another star—but also makes clear that the soul of a nonhuman object is not empirically knowable. Rather, it is to be grasped solely by means of the intellect.

Then we have a final passage, arguably definitive, that indicates Plato's view of the possibility that all things, individually, possess *psyche*. After acknowledging once again that "soul manages the universe" (899a), he writes:

Now consider all the stars and the moon and the years and the months and all the seasons: what can we do except repeat the same story? A soul or souls ... have been shown to be the cause of all these phenomena, and whether it is by their living presence in matter ... or by some other means, we shall insist that these souls are gods. Can anybody admit all this and still put up with people who deny that "everything is full of gods"? (899b)

The last phrase, of course, is a nod to Thales and his famous declaration of panpsychism, examined earlier. Souls exist throughout the cosmos, driving and coordinating all movement and change. They are likely to be manifest as a "living presence in matter." And they are knowable not empirically but through reason alone.

One may object to the phrase "a soul or souls." It is almost as if Plato is unsure or ambivalent about whether the world-soul acts alone in the cosmos or in conjunction with the manifold individual souls. Yet all other passages suggest multiple souls, acting independently of and contemporaneously with the world-soul. An alternate rendering of this phrase might be "a world-soul, and the multiplicity of other souls, have been shown to be the cause ..."

The case for panpsychism in Plato is strong but indirect. The list of ensouled entities is impressively long and diverse. And there are others not mentioned above. For example, in *Timaeus* we read that our bones are ensouled: "next [the god] implanted in the marrow the various types of soul" (73c); "all those bones that had more soul than others" (74e). This is significant because it implies layers of soul within the human being—paralleling, perhaps, the structure of the cosmos.

Then in *Republic* we find an account of the polis that suggests that it too possesses a soul. The polis is shown to have a three-part structure, one that parallels the tripartition of the human soul. The structures are the same, and the moral virtues are the same in each. The polis is "courageous" (429b), "has good judgment and is really wise" (428d), is "just" (435a); generally, "everything else that has to do with virtue [is] the same in both" (441c). Indeed, the parts of the polis come from the people themselves; "where else would they come from?" (435e) Similar structure and similar effects imply a similar embodiment of soul, in human and polis alike.

One final piece of supporting evidence comes from Plotinus, circa 250 AD. In the only known explicit reference to panpsychism in Plato, Plotinus writes the following: "Plato says there is soul in everything of this [earthly] sphere" (*Ennead* VI, 7, 11). That Plotinus is referring not merely to Plato's world-soul but to a soul or intelligence in all things individually is clear from the context.

Perhaps the final question to ask is this: What consistent metaphysics of the soul could include all the above-mentioned entities and yet not include everything? Can we imagine Plato constructing a vastly complex and seemingly arbitrary theory of the soul that includes humans, plants, stars, bones, elements, Being itself … and nothing else? Surely this is unlikely. No conceivable theory would pick out just those objects for ensoulment. The list is too broad and too diverse not to include every individual object in the cosmos. And this view finds independent support from the arguments listed above. Considering all the evidence, one has a hard time comprehending Guthrie's bold claim that "hylozoism … was no longer possible for Plato."

Thus Plato makes subtle use of three distinct arguments for panpsychism. They occur in four of his last major works, and therefore likely represent his mature thinking on the matter. This panpsychist vision is consistent across these works, each mutually supporting the other. And it is in line with the generally panpsychist milieu. By any reasonable assessment, Plato was a panpsychist.

There are several reasons why a panpsychist interpretation of Plato's metaphysics is neither well known nor examined. First, some commentators simply assume that he is speaking poetically or metaphorically in these passages. This is difficult to prove either way, but in any case it is a problematic feature of much of his writing. To argue this way on the issue of panpsychism is a convenient and simplistic denial. By this tactic, we could dismiss much of substance in Plato's philosophy. The panpsychist statements are too explicit and too wide ranging to all be argued away as metaphor.

Second, panpsychism seems to be refuted by passages in the early and middle works. Such passages, however, are rare and ambiguous. They do not rule out a broader panpsychist scheme, even if they emphasize the human soul. Nothing in the earlier writings explicitly denies panpsychism. It is more likely that Plato shifted his focus from the human soul to soul generally as he matured. And of course there is the possibility that he himself changed his opinion, from one of uncertainty or unconcern to something approaching a more affirmative stance.

Third, panpsychism doesn't figure prominently in the overall corpus of Plato's thinking—at least, not explicitly. This, however, is true not only of him but also of many other major panpsychists. And, of course, this is no basis for denying its existence. The relevant passages must be judged as a whole and in light of any potentially conflicting passages elsewhere. There appear to be no passages anywhere in his writings that explicitly deny the panpsychist conclusion. And there are no implications that would demand a larger role for it.

Fourth, on this issue Plato tends to make relatively flat statements of fact, without supplying much rationale. Elaborate and extended logical arguments are lacking. The arguments that do exist are indirect and implicit. This might suggest that the matter of panpsychism was more of an intuitive view for Plato, grounded perhaps in the so-called hylozoism of his predecessors. Or that argumentation was unnecessary on this point, perhaps because it could not lead to a decisive conclusion. Without detailed and intricate arguments, it is easy for present-day analytical commentators to overlook the matter entirely.

Fifth, for at least two centuries philosophy has been dominated by mechanist interpretations of nature, and writers have been reticent about acknowledging aspects of panpsychism in *any* major historical philosopher, let alone Plato. We see the same phenomenon with respect to Aristotle and several other prominent thinkers. This is especially true in the last hundred years or so, as hostility to panpsychism became mainstream within analytic philosophy.

This is not to say that no one has addressed the topic. One notable case in point is Ian Crombie. The chapter on Plato's philosophy of mind in Crombie 1962 addresses his "animism." The use of that term suggests a hostile treatment, and that is precisely what we find. Focusing on the later dialogues, Crombie writes:

> For here we find Plato apparently maintaining, in all the dignity of metaphysical language, something almost indistinguishable from the animism of primitive savages. ... So odd is it to find such a doctrine in such an author that one is forced to wonder whether, in ascribing souls to self-moving objects, Plato is really maintaining an animistic doctrine, or whether the better account may not be simply that he is evacuating the word 'soul' of all content except 'self-activation.' (325)

Concluding a lengthy analysis of the soul-theory in *Phaedrus*, Crombie writes: "The lesson then of the Phaedrus myth is that all apparent self-activation in physical things is to be ascribed to the presence in the living body of a genuinely self-activating thing, or in other words of a soul." (328–329) Even if true, of course, this is something less than panpsychism; not every object in the universe is a self-mover. He then gives a brief and unfocused account of the souls of celestial objects, plants, animals, and parts of the human body.

Crombie's rambling analysis concludes by asking "How are we to interpret the animism of the *Phaedrus*, *Timaeus*, and *Laws*?" (337) After stating that "this is not a simple question to answer," he proceeds to consider both "figurative" and "literal" interpretations. On the former view, celestial souls are not really minds or spirits but rather a shorthand notation for the fact that "they conform to the requirements of [abstract and non-personal] reason." 'Soul' merely reflects the evident fact that the cosmos is well ordered and follows consistent and rational patterns. Of the latter, literal view, "we need not waste many words." Crombie does his best to defend the case for the figurative view but is forced to concede, in the end, that "this interpretation is really untenable" (339). In other words, we are stuck with the literal view: true animism or panpsychism. Precisely what this means, Crombie concludes, "is a question I should not like to answer" (341). Apparently he cannot bear to contemplate the possibility that Plato might actually have been a panpsychist.

There are many unanswered questions here. For example, what is the relationship between the myriad individual souls and the world-soul? Are the individual souls truly distinct entities, or are they merely aspects of the one Soul? If they are distinct, they must still stand in some relation to the larger world-soul, which would seem to have a special status among all the souls of the cosmos. One could speculate on answers to these questions, but there is little in Plato's writings to justify any particular conclusion. He seems to have simply left such matters open. And in any event such questions are not unique to the panpsychist interpretation, nor do they undermine it in any way. Indeed, one might ask if it really matters whether there are many souls or only one Soul with many manifestations. I take it as self-evident that it does matter. It would seem that one's self-conception, and one's vision of the self in the world, must be vastly different in each case. It's hard to imagine that Plato was unconcerned with this distinction. But it's not hard to imagine him struggling with issues of personhood and the relationship between soul and Soul, ultimately reaching a consistent view of soul as pervading the universe.

2.3   Aristotle

Aristotle is perhaps the last ancient philosopher who would be expected to put forth panpsychist views. His notion of mankind as alone, among living beings, in possessing a rational, separable, and immortal soul is in line with the traditional Cartesian view. His emphasis on analytics, logic, and classification aligns him with present-day materialist science. And his denial of the Platonic Forms makes him more of a conventional realist. Thus, it is in his case that we find perhaps the most surprising evidence of panpsychist thinking. Much of the groundwork along this line was done by A. L. Peck and by John Rist. Rist's insightful analysis in his 1989 book *The Mind of Aristotle* is a standout among recent writings on Aristotle's conception of mind and soul.

By way of background, we know that Aristotle viewed the *psyche* or soul as "the form of living things." Like Plato, he posited three degrees of soul:

nutritive, sensitive, and rational. These incorporate five "psychic powers": in ascending order, nutritive/generative, appetitive, sensory, locomotive, and rational. Each level encompasses and contains those below it.

Like Plato, Aristotle accepts that plants are ensouled. A typical statement is found in *De anima*: "It seems that the principle found in plants is also a kind of soul; for this is the only principle which is common to both animals and plants." (411b27) Plants, as the lowest order of living things, possess only a nutritive capacity. All animals have, at least, nutritive and sensitive powers; higher animals have additional powers; and man alone possesses all five psychic powers.[16]

At issue, then, are the non-living things. According to Aristotle they have no soul—hence, technically, he is no panpsychist. But the question remains whether non-living things have something soul-like in them. From early on, Aristotle seems to have been open to such a view:

Nature proceeds little by little from things lifeless to animal life in such a way that it is impossible to determine the exact line of demarcation, nor on which side thereof an intermediate form should lie. (*History of Animals* 588b4–6)

And again in the late work *Parts of Animals*:

For nature passes from lifeless objects to animals in such an unbroken sequence, interposing between them beings which live and yet are not animals, that scarcely any difference seems to exist between two neighboring groups owing to their close proximity. (PA 681a11–15)

Indeed, this continuity is an almost god-like quality of the world: "All things have by nature something divine in them." (*Nicomachean Ethics* 1153b33) The lack of a firm ontological distinction between living and lifeless things suggests, or at least leaves open the possibility, that there may be some common soul-like quality shared among all things.

As a part of his broader inquiry into the natural world, Aristotle sought to explain the puzzling phenomenon of the generation of living, ensouled beings. As he saw it, there are two ways in which this can occur: sexual reproduction and spontaneous generation. The former is challenging enough to understand, and he spends considerable effort explaining the nature and action of male and female reproductive organs. On his final view, sexual reproduction occurs because the male supplies the (rational) soul in his

16. The rational soul is of a different order than the others; it alone survives the body, and is immortal.

semen, which shapes and forms the raw material—the "menstrual blood"—in the female's uterus. Thus he offers something of a scientific account. Spontaneous generation, on the other hand, is very problematic. Plant and animal life appear out of inanimate matter. How is that possible?

First, we note that there is the clear presence of an evolutionary and teleological imperative in Aristotle's thinking. That is uncontroversial. He envisions all of nature as continually striving toward a final goal or end (*telos*), namely "the good," "the better," or "the best":

Nature creates nothing without a purpose, but always the best possible in each kind of living creature. (*Progression of Animals* 704b15)

There is something divine, good, and desirable ... [that matter] desire[s] and yearn[s] for ... . (*Physics* 192a18)

For in all things ... nature always strives after the better. (*On Generation and Corruption* 336b28)

All existing things ... seek [their] own special good ... . (*Eudemian Ethics* 1218a30)

All the operations of nature ... are for a final cause and for the sake of what is best in each case. (*Generation of Animals* 789b3)

By 'better' or 'best' Aristotle has in mind certain specific qualities; he comments that being is better than non-being, life better than non-life, and soul better than matter. Thus, as Rist points out (1989: 123), there is a meaningful sense in which "the whole of the cosmos is permeated by some kind of upward desire and aspiration"—upward in the sense of toward form, life, and soul.

Spontaneous generation is therefore explained in part by the upward striving of matter that Aristotle articulated throughout his writings. Given that striving or desire is typically seen as an intentional mental property, this in itself displays a tendency toward a kind of panpsychism. But Aristotle went further, describing the actual means by which such a tendency or striving became manifest as soul.

At the beginning of book 2 of *Physics*, he distinguishes things that come about "by nature" from those created "by cause":

Of things that exist, some exist by nature, some from other causes. By nature the animals and their parts exist, and the plants and the simple bodies (earth, fire, air, water)—for we say that these and the like exist by nature.

All the things mentioned plainly differ from things which are *not* constituted by nature [e.g. artifacts]. For each of them [i.e. the natural things] has within itself a principle of motion and of stationariness ... . (192b9–15)

Animals, plants, and even the four elements are here seen as possessing an inherent "principle of motion" that is related to the essential nature of all natural objects. Aristotle then begins the final book of *Physics* with a question regarding this universal motion: Has such motion always existed in the cosmos, or was there a time when all was still? After some brief consideration of the alternatives, he concludes that absence of motion is impossible. Thus he provides an affirmative answer to the question "Is [motion] in fact an immortal never-failing property of things that are, a sort of life as it were to all naturally constituted things?" (250b12) This "sort of life" that all things have is consistent with the view of universal striving that we see in the earlier portions of the same work, and in the related passages quoted above.

The "sort of life" in matter was no idle concept; it was directly connected to the process of spontaneous generation. Aristotle put it as follows in one of the last-written books of *Metaphysics*: "Those natural objects which are produced ... spontaneously, are those whose matter can also initiate for itself that motion which [in sexual reproduction] the seed initiates." (1034b5) The life in matter initiates the generative process, thus bringing biological life, and soul, into being.

Remaining to be explained are (1) the exact nature of this life or striving that all natural things possess and (2) precisely how this life or striving activates a process such as spontaneous generation. Clearly this life-property is not equivalent to *psyche*, as Aristotle consistently confines soul, in its three forms, to plants, animals, and humans. Rist argues that in the early Aristotle this quality is as much mind-like as soul-like. As evidence he cites a passage from Cicero's *On the Nature of the Gods*: "In one place [Aristotle] attributes divinity to mind only; in another he says that the universe itself is God." (book I, 30–33) The reference is to Aristotle's lost early work *On Philosophy*. Rist reads into this a three-way identification among the cosmos, mind, and God—the concept of the world-mind.

The identification of these three entities is supported by the ideas that all things have "a sort of life" and that "matter desires form." It is also supported, indirectly, by passages in the roughly concurrent work *De caelo*, at the beginning of which Aristotle reiterates that the four elements, or simple bodies, "possess a principle of movement in their own nature" (268b28). That is, the natural movement of fire and air is upward, whereas that of earth and water is downward. The heavens, however, contain the "primary body," or ether, which is fundamentally different from the four elements and whose natural movement is circular. Ether moves endlessly in a circle, accounting for the perceived circular motion of the stars and planets. Importantly, the ether exhibits *self*-movement, and thus is ensouled: "If it moves itself, it must be animate." (275b25) The self-moving ether is both "immortal" and "divine" (284a4). It contains all limited, finite, earthly motions within it. It is, in essence, the medium and the means by which all other movement occurs in the universe.

Book II of *De caelo* opens with a discussion of symmetry in the heavens, and again repeats the conclusion: "we have already determined … that the heaven is animate and possesses a principle of movement" (285a28). The self-moving ether drives the motion of the celestial bodies, thus endowing them with a kind of life: "We think of the stars as mere bodies, and as units with a serial order indeed but entirely inanimate; but we should rather conceive them as enjoying life and action." (292a19–21) Hence, "we must, then, think of the action of the stars as similar to that of animals and plants" (292a32). The motions of all things, from stars to elements, exhibit a degree of rationality, and rationality is a hallmark of mind. Mind is in all things to the extent that its action is manifest in them via a cosmic source of rational movement.

Aristotle evidently came to see the world-mind as insufficient, and so, shortly thereafter, he introduced the concept of the Unmoved Mover, which stood alone and apart from the natural world and, on Rist's view, operated in conjunction with the world-mind (1989: 129). Mind was immanent, and the Mover was transcendent. Aristotle also began to more clearly distinguish things with souls from those without. Plants, animals, and the ether fell into the former category; all other things, including the four elements, were relegated to inanimate status.

Yet even after the introduction of the Unmoved Mover and the separation between the animate and inanimate, Aristotle still had to account for both spontaneous generation and the natural tendency (*dynamis*) of the elements to move toward their natural resting places—fire upward, earth downward, and so on. Furthermore, there was the open status of the fifth element, the ether. Rist argues that Aristotle ultimately attached the notion of mind to the Unmoved Mover, removing it from immanence in the cosmos. But some agent of the Mover would have to remain in the natural world.

Aristotle then supplemented the notion of the ether with a new concept: that of the *pneuma*. Perhaps borrowing from Anaximenes, he installed the *pneuma* in a preeminent role in nature. It appears prominently in the last three of his biological works (*Parts of Animals*, *Motion of Animals*, and *Generation of Animals*). And it neatly ties together the issues of *psyche*, generation, and celestial and earthly motion—and panpsychism.

Just as the ether is the heavenly bearer of mind and motion generated by the Prime Mover, the *pneuma* is the earthly bearer; it is the "vehicle of Soul" and its "immediate instrument" (Peck 1943: lix), the "bearer of soul" (Rist 1989: 131). *Pneuma* is not mind; that was reserved for the transcendent Mover. Nor is it soul, as soul resides only in those animate beings. It is, rather, "soul-like." As Aristotle writes in one of his last works, *Generation of Animals*, it is the "faculty of all kinds of soul," the "vital heat" (*thermoteta psychiken*), the "principle of soul" (736b29ff). As such, *pneuma* shares much in common with ether; they are, as he says, "analogous." Both are intermediaries to the Prime Mover, and both convey its rationality and soul. Neither is explicitly mind or soul; each is only the carrier of such. Furthermore, both share a vital power or a generative capacity. Both bring soul to natural objects, and thus in a sense account for the life in them. This brings us back us to the problem of spontaneous generation versus sexual reproduction. In sexual reproduction it is the soul-heat of the *pneuma* in the semen that conveys life to the embryo. In the case of spontaneous reproduction—which works best in decomposing matter sitting out in the hot sun—it is the heat of the solar ether, manifest on Earth as the *pneuma*, that conveys life. Regarding this vital heat, Aristotle writes:

This is not fire nor any such force, but it is the *pneuma* included in the semen and the foam-like, and the natural principle in the *pneuma*, being analogous to the element of the stars [i.e. ether]. (GA 736b35)

The soul-like *pneuma* is ubiquitous in the natural world, penetrating and informing all things. Not only does it bring soul to the embryo and to the spontaneously generated creatures; it also accounts for the general property of matter, its desire for form and for the good. Aristotle is explicit and unambiguous that all things are inspirited by the *pneuma*:

Animals and plants come into being in earth and in liquid because there is water in earth, and *pneuma* in water, and in all *pneuma* is vital heat, so that in a sense *all things are full of soul*. (762a18–20; emphasis added)

The final striking phrase of this passage from *Generation of Animals* is unique in Aristotle's corpus. The text is emphatic: *hoste tropon tina panta psyches einai plere*. Echoing panpsychist thinking from Thales to Plato, Aristotle apparently came to the conclusion that something soul-like, of varying degrees, inhered in all objects of the natural world. Peck (1943: 585) referred to this passage as Aristotle's "startling admission," arguing that such a conclusion is justified in part by the fact that animated beings arise out of nature (*phusis*), and that "as we know, *phusis* never acts idly but always with a telos [end] in view." "Regarded in this way," Peck continues, "'matter' ... might be looked upon as considerably more than mere lifeless, inert material; and in *Generation of Animals* Aristotle does in fact ascribe even the possession of *psyche* to it." Peck seems taken aback by this "startling admission," and appears unwilling or unable to place it in the larger context of Aristotle's conception of life and mind. It is in the latter step—the elaboration of the larger role of *pneuma* in Aristotle's theory of mind—that Rist makes a significant contribution.

Pneuma is thus the universal link among all things, and it provides a common ontological dimension. It makes the distinction between animate and inanimate relatively superficial. Through the *pneuma*, Aristotle avoids an unacceptable and unexplainable dualism between things that are ensouled and those that are utterly soulless. Granted, he still has the problem of explaining just how *pneuma* becomes manifest as full-blown soul in certain objects, such as plants, animals, and humans. But this is more a difference of degree than of kind, and thus it is less difficult metaphysically. It is unfortunate that, as far as we know, Aristotle never addressed it fully.

As might be expected, panpsychist readings of Aristotle are as rare as of Plato. Thomas Aquinas cited this possibility in his *Summa* (part 1a, question 18; see discussion below). Apart from Peck and Rist, very few recent writers have commented on it. De Quincey (2002: 118–119) suggests that it is inherent in Aristotle's theory of hylomorphism. Several years earlier, Charles Hartshorne argued obliquely for a similar view:

Aristotle's statements that the soul ... is all things, that all things are moved by God as the lover by what he loves (implying that all things love, and thus are sentient ...), that a soul is the form of any organized, self-moving body (implying that if ...

nature consists entirely of more or less organized, self-moving bodies … then nature consists entirely of besouled constituents). (1950: 443)

Hartshorne was on the right track, but the details are sorely lacking. Apart from these few cases, recent literature on Aristotle is utterly vacant on this matter. Gill and Lennox (1994), for example, include eight chapters on Aristotle's theory of self-motion, and yet the *pneuma* concept appears not once. Freudenthal (1995) has an extensive discussion of vital heat and the *pneuma* but completely overlooks the panpsychist implication. As to why recent scholars fail to address the *pneuma* theory, a knowledgeable colleague remarked that "they simply don't know what to do with it."

As elaborated above, we can see a clear picture of a quasi-panpsychist cosmos in Aristotle—a cosmos in which everything has either soul or, at least, a soul-like presence, the *pneuma*, which confers an evolutionary, life-like impulse upon all things.

2.4 Epicurus and the Atomic Swerve

Epicurus was the founder of one of the three great Hellenistic philosophical systems—Stoicism and Skepticism being the others. Epicurean physical theory relied heavily on the atomism of Democritus and followed his central thesis of material reality as composed of atoms moving through the void. On this view, atoms possess only the primary qualities of size, shape, and mass or inertia; they interact and combine to form the large-scale objects of the world around us. It was a thoroughly materialistic and modern approach to physical theory.

As a theory, atomism had a unique problem: how to account for the soul in a materialistic and atomistic universe. As we saw, Democritus' solution was to posit a special class of atoms—small, round, smooth—that were the bearers of soul. Light, fluid, and self-moving, the soul-atoms penetrated everywhere and set the other atoms into motion. Because they were omnipresent, the action of the *psyche* was presumably also found everywhere.

The atomists also believed that atoms had a natural "downward" motion through the void, something like that of falling raindrops. For Democritus and Leucippus, the motion of these atoms, soul-atoms included, was of a deterministic nature: "Nothing happens in vain, but everything for a reason and by necessity." (in Barnes 1987: 243) Aristotle confirms this view: "Democritus, however, neglecting the final cause, reduces to necessity all the operations of nature." (GA 789b3) If everything, including the action of the soul, occurs deterministically, then there is no room for anything like free will in a Democritean universe.

That was problematic for Epicurus, whose ethical system required free will. He therefore kept the Democritean atoms but discarded the determinism. He argued instead that the motion of atoms resulted from three sources: weight, mechanical collisions, and a new third factor that he called "swerve"—in Greek, *parenklisis*, meaning a deflection or turning aside. In effect, the atoms occasionally "chose" to deflect from their normal downward flow. This was effectively seen as a small amount of free will exhibited by the atoms. The swerve was a crucial process in nature because it caused collisions and combinations with other atoms, leading to a cascading of action that resulted in the formation of large objects. Without swerve, atoms would fall smoothly through the void, unfettered by atomic collisions and interactions, and thus no complex structures would ever develop. And it also provided the root source of human will.

Very few of Epicurus' original writings have survived, so we rely primarily on later doxographers—primarily Cicero, Lucretius, and Diogenes Laertius. Lucretius' *De rerum natura* (On the Nature of Things), written around 50 BC, contains the best sympathetic account of the atomic swerve. The basic statement of the view is found near the beginning of book II:

> Though atoms fall straight downward through the void by their own weight, yet at uncertain times and at uncertain points, they swerve a bit. ... And if they did not swerve ... no clashes would occur, no blows befall the atoms; nature would never have made a thing. (II: 215–225)

The willful swerving of the atoms is the basis for our own free will: Out of the swerve "rises ... that *will* torn free from fate, through which we follow wherever pleasure leads, and likewise swerve aside at times and places" (II: 255–260). Human free will cannot arise *ex nihilo* ("since nothing, we see, could be produced from nothing"; 287) and hence must be present in the atoms themselves. "Thus to the atoms we must allow ... one more cause of movement [namely, that of free will]—the one whence comes this power we own." (284–286)

Cicero, in *On Fate*, adds a similar but more critical account:

Epicurus thinks that the necessity of fate can be avoided by the swerve of an atom ... . [He] introduced this line of reasoning because he was afraid that if an atom always moved by its natural and necessary heaviness, we would have no freedom, since our mind would be moved in such a way that it would be compelled by the motion of atoms. (in Inwood and Gerson 1997: 47–48)[17]

Thus the swerve serves two important purposes: It accounts for the complex physical structure of objects and, independently, it provides the basis for human freedom of will. Epicurus used the swerve to simultaneously solve two potentially serious problems for his atomic worldview.

The second purpose, in fact, also provides a new approach in arguing for panpsychism. Epicurus' argument can be reconstructed as follows: Humans clearly exhibit will. Will is a fundamental quality of existence and cannot plausibly emerge from non-will. Therefore will is present in the elemental particles of the cosmos, and hence, potentially, in all things. This is an Argument by Non-Emergence. If certain psychic qualities are not emergent, then they are necessarily present in at least some of the ultimate or most fundamental particles.[18] This particular argument has proved to be one of the more enduring and more important arguments for panpsychism, and it is still employed today. I examine this argument in detail in the chapters to follow.

Given that atoms have a will, this does *not* imply, according to Lucretius—and presumably Epicurus—that they possess sensitivity or other mental powers. Lucretius allows for certain qualities to emerge from nothing, including life and sentience. The ability to sense is evidently viewed as an emergent phenomenon, unlike the power of will. Thus, atoms are said

17. In the same essay we read that the swerve acts with a certain minimal interval called *elachiston*. This is a remarkable anticipation of quantum theory, which states that atoms can only change energy states by certain discrete or "minimal" amounts.

18. It is an open question whether all atoms swerve or only certain ones. Epicurus seems to have abandoned the idea of the special soul-atom, and so the implication is that all atoms swerve. But this was apparently never clearly spelled out. Cicero notes this ambiguity: "For if it is by natural necessity that atoms move [downward] ... then it is also necessary for certain atoms (or, if they prefer, all atoms) to swerve naturally." (in Inwood and Gerson 1997: 49) Arguably, if only some atoms swerve willfully, then this is not panpsychism—unless all objects have some minimal quota of swerving atoms. I will set this issue aside for now.

to possess will but not sentience: "Now all that we know [of] is composed of insensate atoms ... in every case." (864–846) And it is permissible to "rightly conclude that sense comes from non-sense" (930). The atomic swerve has no connection to human sensate qualities such as joy, happiness, or pain; atoms "must not, then, be endowed with sense" (972). This is a plausible claim. A non-emergentist need not hold that nothing emerges; that would be a ludicrous and indefensible position. Even today, the physical realm is held to consist of certain fundamental, non-emergent entities which then combine into more complex structures. The same could well be true for the mental realm.

In concluding this section, I must mention recent scientific developments that seem, surprisingly, to confirm the existence of an atomic will. The mathematicians John Conway and Simon Kochen argue in two papers (2006, 2009) that "if indeed we humans have free will, then elementary particles already have their own small share of this valuable commodity." Sounding rather like modern-day Epicureans, they explain: "Our [Free Will Theorem] asserts that if experimenters have a certain freedom, then particles have exactly the same kind of freedom. Indeed, it is natural to suppose that this latter freedom is the ultimate explanation of our own." (2009: 230) The technical details of their theorem are beyond the scope of this book, but Conway and Kochen note that the phrase "the particles make a free decision" is more accurately stated as "the Universe makes this free decision in the neighborhood of the particles" (2006: 1456). Quantum theory decisively refutes a deterministic universe, they say. The strangeness of quantum experiments can best be explained by atomic choices that we cannot predict.[19] Once again, ancient metaphysical ideas find confirmation in modern science.

By attributing will to atoms, Epicurus made explicit the implicit panpsychism of Democritus. Neither Cicero nor Lucretius expanded on the panpsychic implications, nor did they discuss freedom of will in ordinary inanimate objects—which seems to be a logical consequence.

---

19. As to the notion that particles simply behave randomly, Conway dismisses this idea: "Randomness doesn't help. If the action of each particle were a predetermined function of its past plus a random string of bits, then we might as well suppose that this string of bits was produced just before the universe was created, and this is excluded just as well as totally deterministic behavior." (Schleicher 2013: 570)

2.5   Stoicism and the *Pneuma*

Zeno of Citium, a contemporary of Epicurus, founded his own school of philosophy in Athens around 325 BC. Because Zeno spent much time in the *stoa* (covered portico) of the agora, his school came to be known as Stoicism. Zeno, along with successors Cleanthes and Chrysippus, pieced together the various lines of Stoic thought and constructed a comprehensive philosophical system. Stoic philosophy was highly influential in the ancient world, even more so than the views of Plato and Aristotle. It vied with and largely surpassed Skepticism and Epicureanism for influence, and it maintained a dominant position for nearly 500 years. Panaetius and Posidonius carried on the tradition through the pre-Christian era, and the Roman Stoics—Seneca, Epictetus, and Marcus Aurelius—continued it until nearly 200 AD.

Stoicism can be divided into the three traditional parts of philosophy: physics, logic, and ethics. These were not three isolated branches of thought; they all addressed the presence of reason in the cosmos. As Tony Long says (1974: 119), "the subject matter of logic, physics, and ethics is *one* thing, the rational universe." Reason (logos) is embodied alike in mankind and in the cosmos. "Cosmic events and human actions are ... not happenings of two quite different orders; in the last analysis they are both alike consequences of one thing—logos." (108) Thus, according to the Stoics, one cannot learn about mankind without learning about the rational cosmos, nor can one learn about the cosmos without gaining an understanding of humanity.

The Stoic universe consisted of two central principles: the Active and the Passive. The Passive is "primary matter," the unformed substance of the world, constituted by the four Empedoclean elements of fire, air, water, and earth. These elements are not equally passive, however. Fire and air are relatively active, earth and water relatively passive.

The Active is rather more complex, and it has a number of interpretations. In general it gives form and order to all physical objects. Owing to this capacity, it is equated with the logos of the universe, the rational principle governing all things. The logos, in turn, is seen as the supreme organizing power and thus is equated with god: "the Active is the rational principle [logos] in [the universe], i.e. god."[20] Because it was the highest of cosmic divine powers, it sometimes took the name Zeus. And because of its ability to control the destiny of all things, it functioned as a kind of providence or fate. Thus we read that "God and mind and fate and Zeus are one thing, but called by many different names."[21]

Also central to Stoicism, and intimately related to the Active principle, was the concept of *pneuma*. As a material compound, *pneuma* had to have an elemental structure; its active, energetic, and refined nature led to the conclusion that it was a joint composition of fire and air. The importance of these two elements was seen in our own human bodies, wherein warmth and breath were the two primary indicators of life. These two elements, when conjoined as *pneuma*, served as the omnipresent life energy of the universe. Citing the Stoic Posidonius, Sandbach (1975: 130) writes that "a 'life-force' could be recognized everywhere."

Furthermore, since all things have form, and this form is given to inert matter by the Active, and the Active is effective through the *pneuma*, it is clear that *pneuma* is present in all things. There are, of course, strong affinities here to Aristotle's theory. Aristotle died just as Zeno was reaching maturity, and his views would certainly have circulated among Zeno and his followers in Athens. By all appearances, Zeno adopted Aristotle's late development of the *pneuma* and elevated it to a central cosmic force.

Pneuma is—like fire—active, energetic, and inherently in motion. It is a fire that gives form and order; it constructs and builds, rather than destroys. In the words of Zeno, *pneuma* is a *pyr technikon*—a "creative fire"—that creates and animates the natural world. We find a number of interesting discussions of the *pyr technikon* in the literature. Sandbach (1975: 73) calls it "the god that makes the world" and "fire that is an artificer." Seneca, in the *Epistles*, refers to it as "creative reason" (Long 1974: 165). Inwood and Gerson (1997: 138) translate the phrase as "craftsmanlike fire." Then there is this famous and beautiful passage in Diogenes Laertius: "Nature is an artistic fire going on its way to create."[22] In *On the Nature of the Gods*, Cicero

20. Diogenes Laertius, cited on p. 132 of Inwood and Gerson 1997.

21. Inwood and Gerson 1997: 133.

22. Long 1974: 147.

cites the same passage, informing us that this, in fact, was Zeno's definition of nature.[23]

This creation of the world is clearly intelligent and mindful, and it demonstrates the god, or logos, in nature. Thus we see a linkage of several terms—Active, logos, god, mind, *pneuma*, fire, *pyr technikon*—which together paint a picture of the cosmos as, in the words of Diogenes Laertius, "an animal, rational and alive and intelligent" (Inwood and Gerson 1997: 135)—as well as divine. Sambursky sums up this idea nicely:

Pneuma became a concept synonymous with God, and either notion was defined by the other. ... Natural force (i.e. *pneuma*) was seen as endowed with divine reason, and *pneuma* was given epithets like "sensible" or "intellectual," thus alluding to its god-like nature. ... [Conversely] God was identified with the all-pervading *pneuma*, being totally mixed with shapeless matter, and divine reason was defined as corporeal *pneuma*. (1959: 36)

In addition to its cosmic role, *pneuma* has a number of important physical functions, each of which supports one aspect of Stoic panpsychism. First, *pneuma* acts as the cohesive force of the universe. Cicero tells us that "there is, therefore, a nature [*physis*, i.e. *pneuma*] which holds the entire cosmos together and preserves it."[24] This recalls Anaximenes' view, cited earlier, that "our souls ... being air, hold us together." Importantly, *pneuma* acts not only on the cosmos but also on individual objects. Referring to its cohesive force, Long (1974: 156) writes: "This function of *pneuma* in the macrocosm is equally at work in every individual body." The cohesive force exists in three distinct degrees of intensity, or tension (*tonos*). At the lowest level—that which holds all objects together, including inorganic objects such as stones and tables—it is called *hexis*, meaning a condition, state, or tenor. At a higher level, that of living organisms, it is called *physis* (nature). At the highest level, that of animals and humans, it is *psyche*. All are *pneuma*, though existing in varying degrees of *tonos*. Pseudo-Galen explains it as follows:

There are two forms of the inborn *pneuma*, that of nature [*physis*] and that of soul [*psyche*]; and some [the Stoics] add a third, that of *hexis*. The *pneuma* which holds things is what makes stones cohere, while that of nature is what nourishes animals

23. "Zeno, then, defines nature thus: he says it is a craftsmanlike fire which proceeds methodically to the task of creation." (Inwood and Gerson 1997: 150)

24. Inwood and Gerson 1997: 146.

and plants, and that of the soul is that which, in animate objects, makes animals capable of sense-perception and of every kind of movement. (in Inwood and Gerson 1997: 171)

Clearly, soul is not attributed to all things, only to animals. Unlike the pre-Socratics, the Stoics had differentiated soul from mind, equating mind and reason with the *pneuma*, which was in all things. Thus we do not find statements like "soul moved all things"; rather, we see an intelligent universal force that accounts for all motion. Consequently, the Stoics were panpsychists, but of a different type than Plato and the earlier philosophers. And their identification of *pneuma* with the rational mind was a step Aristotle was unwilling to take.

In a related role, *pneuma* not only holds things together; it also makes them one. It accounts for the unity of being. The unity of a thing is described as that which rules over the object and determines its character. This ruling unity, another important concept in Stoic philosophy, is given a special name: *hegemonikon*, from *hege* ("lead") and *monos* ("alone," "single"), often translated as "the leading part of the soul." The *hegemonikon*, like the *pneuma*, is present at all levels of existence. Cleanthes argued that the sun was the *hegemonikon* of the cosmos. Cicero explained the concept as follows:

There is ... a nature [i.e. *pneuma*] which holds the entire cosmos together and preserves it. ... For every [natural object] ... is joined and connected with something else, [and] must have in itself some "leading part," like the mind in man and in a brute beast something analogous to mind which is the source of its desires for things; in trees and plants which grow in the earth the leading part is thought to reside in their roots. By "leading part" I mean that which the Greeks call *hegemonikon*; in each type of thing there cannot and should not be anything more excellent than this.[25]

Something mind-like was thus seen as the unifying force in all objects: "The vital function of the *hegemonikon* [is] as the central seat of consciousness." (Sambursky 1959: 22) It was therefore central to the mind-body relationship.

It is important to clarify the Stoics' view of the mind-body relationship. In one sense they were mind-matter dualists. *Pneuma* and the four elements were matter; mind was something else, something immaterial. Mind was the Active, the form, that impressed itself upon matter and created

---

25. *On the Nature of the Gods* (2, 29), in Inwood and Gerson 1997.

individual objects. Long (1996: 228) describes it well: "All things in the Stoic universe are combinations of god and matter, stones no less than humans ... . The entire universe is a combination of god and matter, and what applies to the whole applies to any one of its identifiable parts." Their dualism is thus perhaps best seen as a kind of dual-aspect monism: There is only body, and it expresses itself both as matter, on the passive side, and mind, on the active side.

The Stoic fragments help to elaborate this view. Diogenes Laertius informs us that "mind penetrates every part of [the cosmos] just as soul does us. But it penetrates some things more than others."[26] This is an interesting observation, as it indicates that mind exists in different degrees, depending on the nature of the thing penetrated. Regarding the things in themselves, Cicero explicitly states that "the parts of the cosmos ... contain the power of sense-perception and reason" (146)—a clear statement of pluralistic panpsychism. And Cicero reiterates the view, which began with Plato, that the stars individually have souls:

Now that we have seen that the cosmos is divine, we should assign the same sort of divinity to the stars. ... They too are also said quite correctly to be animals and to perceive and to have intelligence. [And furthermore], the sun too should be [considered] alive. (148–149)

As to the Stoic rationale, Cicero informs us that the "orderliness and regularity of the heavenly bodies is the clearest indication of their powers of sense perception and intelligence," for "nothing can move rationally and with measure except by the use of intelligence." The Stoics thus had hard empirical evidence to support their claim.

Collectively, then, the Stoics employed several extant arguments for panpsychism. The psychic *pneuma* provides a cohesive force that acts as the seat of consciousness (Indwelling Powers). *Pneuma* exists in all things, human or otherwise (Continuity). It is the embodiment of the Active principle, and it accounts for such physical qualities as unity of form and orderliness of motion (Design). The Stoics were thus thoroughly panpsychist in their outlook on the world, and they developed a theory of the cosmos that was perfectly compatible with that outlook.

As has already been mentioned, Stoicism held a dominant position in both Greek and Roman society for centuries. The late period of Roman

26. Inwood and Gerson 1997: 133.

Stoicism peaked with the work of Seneca (1–65 AD) and Epictetus (55–135 AD) and reached a pinnacle of sorts with emperor and philosopher Marcus Aurelius (121–180 AD). Unfortunately, that occurred just as Stoicism's influence began to wane, and so the vision of a true Stoic society went largely unfulfilled. Upon the death of Marcus Aurelius, the Empire began to fall into decline, and Stoicism yielded to a resurgent interest in the Platonic and Aristotelian philosophies, especially in the form of Neo-Platonism. Ultimately those philosophies would be displaced by the emerging monotheistic religious worldviews, Christianity most of all.

2.6   Echoes of Panpsychism in the Christian Era

Throughout the entire pre-Christian era, people acknowledged the presence of spirit and mind in nature. But this began to change with the Judeo-Christian worldview. Christianity took spirit out of nature and placed it largely, and ambiguously, within the monotheistic figure of God. But when it did so, it carried along much of the terminological baggage that was associated with the idea of spirit. It is therefore interesting and relevant to briefly examine the concept of spirit in the Biblical tradition, particularly as it pertains to the panpsychist ideas of the Greek philosophers.

A central precept of Christianity is the Trinity: the Father (God), the Son (Jesus), and the Holy Spirit.[27] It is striking that in both the original Greek of the New Testament and the original Greek translation (from Hebrew) of the Old Testament[28] the word for Spirit is *pneuma*. Virtually every reference

27. Though, oddly, this concept is all but nonexistent in the Bible. The only plausible reference is in 1 John 5:8, and this is very tenuous at best: "There are three witnesses, the Spirit, the water, and the blood; and these three agree."

28. The origins of the Old Testament may go back to 1000 BC or even further, but the majority of it probably was first written down, in Hebrew, during the period 400–200 BC—just about the time that Stoicism emerged. The oldest extant texts of this Hebrew bible are the Dead Sea Scrolls, which were probably created during the period 200 BC–0 AD. The translation of the OT from its original Hebrew into Greek occurred over the period 250–50 BC, during the height of Stoic influence. This translation is known as the Septuagint (or LXX), and it is the source of all modern-era Christian texts of the Old Testament—the oldest surviving example being the Vatican Codex of 350 AD. '*Pneuma*' of the Septuagint was translated from the Hebrew word '*rû(a)h*', and it appears nearly 300 times in the OT. Thus, even though the original term '*rû(a)h*' may have predated Stoicism, its translation into '*pneuma*', and

to spirit or Spirit is either *pneuma* or some close variant, such as *pneumatos* or *pneumati*. Spiritual things are *pneumatika*; the spiritual man is a *pneumatikos*. This suggests a connection to Stoic and Aristotelian philosophy, and also to panpsychism. If there were such a connection, one would expect to find not just the occurrence of the word itself, but also that its usage would be consistent with Stoic principles. For example, one might expect to find such things as (1) the word '*pneuma*' in reference to both air and fire, (2) *pneuma* as God, (3) *pneuma* as a creative force in the cosmos (recall *pyr technikon*), (4) *pneuma* as intelligence or mind, (5) *pneuma* as life-giving, and (6) *pneuma* as omnipresent and as filling or penetrating things.

In fact, there are references to all these Stoic concepts in the Bible.[29] In particular, these are characteristics of the Holy Spirit itself.

(1) There are passages in which '*pneuma*' plays on its multiple meaning of wind, breath, and spirit: "The wind (*pneuma*) blows wherever it pleases. ... So it is with everyone born of the Spirit (*pneumatos*)." (John 3:8) "The Spirit of God has made me; the breath of the Almighty gives me life." (Job 33:4) Regarding reference to fire, we have the following: "For the Lord your God is a devouring fire." (Deuteronomy 4:24) "Do not put out the Spirit's fire." (1 Thessalonians 5:19) There is also the incident of the burning bush in which God first speaks to Moses: "And the angel of the Lord appeared to him in a flame of fire." (Exodus 3:2) Wind and fire are combined in Psalm 104: "He makes winds his messengers, flames of fire his servants."

(2) The most explicit identification of God and spirit is found in John 4:24: "God is spirit (*pneuma o theos*), and his worshippers must worship in spirit (*pneumati*) and truth." *Pneuma* is also equated with deity in Acts 5:3–4 ("a lie to Spirit equals a lie to God") and in 2 Corinthians 3:17–18 ("The Lord is the Spirit"). Additionally, one finds that *pneuma* has a

---

accompanying conceptual language, was certainly subject to Greek philosophical influences. Appearances of the various forms of *pneuma* are even more numerous in the New Testament, which dates from the first and second centuries of the Christian era. It is in this Testament that we find the most fully developed articulation of the Spirit; and perhaps not surprisingly, the clearest association with Stoic ideas.

29. Except where another version is specified, the following passages are taken from the New International Version.

number of God-like attributes and powers; it is omnipresent (Psalm 139:7ff.), self-existent (Romans 8:2), and involved with the Creation (Genesis 1:2) and the Resurrection (Romans 8:11).

(3) *Pneuma* as creative force is found in Genesis 1:2; at the first moment of Creation, we read that "the Spirit of God moved upon the face of the waters" (KJV).

(4) The Holy Spirit has a number of qualities related to intelligence and mind: "The Spirit searches all things, even the deep things of God. ... No one knows the thoughts of God except the Spirit of God." (1 Corinthians 2:10–11) Furthermore, it teaches ("the Holy Spirit ... will teach you all things"—John 14:26), and it intercedes in prayers ("We do not know what we ought to pray for, but the Spirit himself intercedes for us. ... He who searches our hearts knows the mind of the Spirit, because the Spirit intercedes for the saints." —Romans 8:26–27). Also, the Spirit can control the human mind ("the mind controlled by the Spirit is life and peace"—Romans 8:6).

(5) The Spirit gives life; note again the passage in Job cited above: "The Spirit of God has made me; the breath of the Almighty gives me life." And in John 3:6 we have "the Spirit (*pneumatos*) gives birth to spirit (*pneuma*)."

(6) Psalm 139 contains passages that describe the omnipresence of the Spirit: "If I go up to the heavens, you are there; if I make my bed in the depths, you are there. If I rise on the wings of the dawn, if I settle on the far side of the sea, even there your hand will guide me." (Psalm 139:7–10) There are numerous references to the Spirit "dwelling in" or "filling" the believer: "the Spirit of God lives in you" (Romans 8:9); "God's Spirit lives in you" (1 Corinthians 3:16); "the Holy Spirit, who is in you" (1 Corinthians 6:19). The Bible also says that believers will "walk in the Spirit" (Galatians 5:16).

Thus there appears to be good justification for claiming Stoic influence in the Bible, at least within the figure of the Holy Spirit, which has always had an odd and troubling status within a monotheistic system. It is perhaps not surprising, then, that this influence is widely ignored by Christian theologians.

Furthermore, the Bible acknowledges the existence of numerous other spiritual beings in the world: Satan, the angels, and others, not to mention the many distinct human souls. At the beginning of 1 John 4 we find the following: "Dear friends, do not believe every spirit (*pneumati*), but test the spirits (*pneumata*) to see whether they are from God." The spirits that fail the test are naturally those "of the Antichrist," and they must be defeated. So the Bible does convey a world of numerous spirits even as it puts forth a single God. But the spirits are otherworldly, and they are not connected with physical things—except, of course, human beings. Any conception of individual and independent spirits "in things," not to mention in *all* things, is decidedly anti-Christian.[30] Predictably, theologians typically dismiss all references to panpsychism as heathen or pagan primitivism.

One last point on the connections to Stoicism: It is not only *pneuma* that carries over into the Bible. There are also references to *logos* that resonate with Stoic principles. Recall that *logos* refers to reason or intelligence. In the Greek of the New Testament, we also find the word '*logos*', and it is translated as "Word," as in "the Word of God." At the start of John 1, we learn that "in the beginning was the Word, and the Word was with God, and the Word was God." This phrase, which is problematic from a traditional Christian standpoint, makes perfect sense as a carryover from a Stoic system in which *logos* ("Word") is God. In his study of Stoic philosophy, Sandbach (1975: 72) states unequivocally that "God is logos." Other connections between God and *logos* occur at John 1:14, 2 Timothy 4:2, 1 John 1:1, and Revelation 19:13. Again we seem to have an important biblical concept that was borrowed from the panpsychist Stoics.

Early Christian theology merged with Platonic, Aristotelian, and Stoic ideas to create a number of new perspectives on philosophy, most notable of which was Neo-Platonism. The third-century-AD founder of this school, Plotinus, combined notions of an ideal Realm of Forms with a monotheistic system in which the One was the divine and mystical source of all existence. The One exhibits a logos or reason-principle as it creates and sustains the natural world.

30. There is a lingering and problematic sense in which Christian theology does allow for a weak form of panpsychism. If God is omnipresent, then he is obviously in all things; this points toward panentheism. If a portion of God is in a thing, and if this portion assumes any sense of independent individuality or autonomous existence, then this could qualify as a "monistic panpsychism." Renaissance philosophers exploit this issue, as I will show.

Plotinus' major work, the *Enneads*, contains a number of scattered and cryptic references to a panpsychic cosmos. The most relevant of these, as was mentioned earlier, is Ennead VI, 7, in which we find Plotinus' enigmatic discussion on life and soul as existing in all things, both in the physical world and in the "higher realm" of Platonic Forms. Furthermore, he explicitly cites Plato as holding the same view:

[I]n the plant the Reason-Principle ... is a certain form of life, a definite soul. ... The growing and shaping of stones, the internal molding of mountains as they rise, reveal the working of an ensouled Reason-Principle fashioning them from within. ... The earth There [in the Platonic realm] is much more primally alive, ... it is a reasoned Earth-Livingness. ... Fire, similarly, with other such things, must be a Reason-Principle established in Matter. ... That transcendent fire, being more truly fire, will be more veritably alive; the fire absolute possesses life. And the same principles apply to the other elements, water and air. ... It is with this in mind that Plato says there is soul in everything of this [earthly] sphere. ... It is of necessity that life be all-embracing, covering all the realms, and that nothing fail of life.

In itself, the fact that "Plato says there is soul in everything of this sphere" could simply be a reference to the world-soul. Yet it is clear from the context that Plotinus sees everything individually as alive—the Earth, fire, water, air, and the other elements. And he clearly attributes the same view to Plato. Plotinus' reference is thus a further confirmation that Plato himself adopted a subtle form of panpsychism, a fact that evidently had some effect on the Neo-Platonist worldview.

Apart from the indirect biblical references to *pneuma* and *logos*, Christianity had little use for panpsychism. In fact, as has already been mentioned, it was positively opposed. The Bible attributes soul to man and to nothing else in nature. Only man is in God's image, and only man was given dominion over the soulless Earth. Humanity is unique, different, and better than everything else in the world. And yet Christian thinkers valued the insights of the Greeks, and in their attempts to incorporate Greek ideas they inadvertently picked up hints of panpsychist metaphysics.

A case in point is Augustine. In *The City of God* (ca. 410 AD), he appropriated and further developed Aristotle's ideas on matter. Recall that Aristotle held that each of the elements endeavors to move to its natural place: fire and air upward, earth and water down. In *Physics*, for example, he writes that it is "the property of fire to be carried upwards" (193a1). And in *De caelo* we read "For if the natural motion is upward, it will be fire or air, and if downward, water or earth." (269a16) Augustine accepted this view, believing that all natural objects sought their appropriate station in this world in order to preserve and protect themselves:

[E]ven the lifeless bodies, which want not only sensation but seminal life, yet either seek the upper air or sink deep, or are balanced in an intermediate position, so that they may protect their existence in that situation where they can exist in most accordance with their nature. (book XI, chapter 27)

This wanting or desiring that is present in all natural things is a manifestation of love:

If we were stones, or waves, or wind, or flame, or anything of that kind, we should want, indeed, both sensation and life, yet should possess a kind of attraction towards our own proper position and natural order. For the specific gravity of bodies is, as it were, their love, whether they are carried downwards by their weight, or upwards by their levity. (book XI, chapter 28)

Augustine evidently believed that God's love was somehow impressed into all things made by him, such that they themselves were also able to love.[31] Again, though, the panpsychist implications seem to have been lost on Augustine and his followers.

At least one Christian thinker, however, openly embraced the implications: Francis of Assisi. Francis (1181–1226) saw the presence of God in all parts of nature, and thus he viewed all things as enspirited beings. He is famous for his love of animals, but he also held insects, plants, and even rocks in highest regard. One of his earliest disciples, Thomas of Celano, wrote of Francis:

When he found many flowers growing together ... he would speak to them and encourage them, as though they could understand, to praise the Lord. It was the same with the fields of corn and the vineyards, the stones in the earth and in the woods, all the beauteous meadows, the tinkling brooks, the sprouting gardens, earth, fire, air and wind. ... He was wont to call all created things his brothers and sisters. (in Armstrong 1973: 9)

Armstrong further refers to Saint Bonaventure's accounts in *The Mirror of Perfection* as evidence of Francis' "being caught up in ecstatic contemplation of inanimate as well as animate things of God's creation" and "thus [treating] even inanimate things as, to all intents and purposes, children of God" (10). Others came to the same conclusion. In his quest for a Christian solution to the environmental crisis, the historian Lynn White Jr.

31. For an elaboration of this aspect of Augustine, see O'Brien 1958.

(1967: 1207) observes that "[Francis'] view of nature and of man rested on a unique sort of panpsychism of all things animate and inanimate." White cites as evidence Francis' "Canticle of the Sun," an ode to the Sun, the Moon, Wind, Air, Water, and Fire in which each of them is treated as an animate "Brother" or "Sister" and the planet is called "Mother Earth." Nature, Francis seems to say, is like us: ensouled, God-created, and capable of worshipping the divine.

Francis was apparently the first religious figure to explicitly employ a belief in the Christian God on behalf of a form of panpsychism. This strongly anticipated the work of Tommaso Campanella, who argued from a similar basis for his panpsychic beliefs.[32] But Francis did not lay down a systematic philosophy of spirit in nature, and so it is more correct to attribute such a theological argument for panpsychism to Campanella.

By the thirteenth century, Christian theology dominated Western philosophical views. Francis' beliefs notwithstanding, panpsychist or pantheist ideas were largely pushed from the mainstream. If the matter was given any consideration at all, it was rather abruptly dismissed.

Aquinas did precisely that. His *Summa Theologiae* (circa 1260) contains just a single brief discussion of the question "What things have life?" (question 18, part Ia) Summarizing the hylozoist position—and appropriately citing Aristotle—he presents three distinct arguments:

For Aristotle says that motion is a kind of life possessed by all things that exist in nature. But all natural objects participate in motion. Therefore all natural objects participate in life.

Further, plants are said to live because [they undergo] growth and decrease. But local movement [i.e., locomotion, or physical displacement] is more perfect than that. ... Since, then, all natural bodies have in themselves a principle of local movement, it would seem that all natural bodies have life.

Further, among natural bodies the elements are the less perfect; but life is attributed to them: e.g., we speak of "living water." Therefore *a fortiori* other natural bodies have life.

"On the other hand," Aquinas then cites Pseudo-Dionysius as saying that "plants live with life's last echo," interpreting this to mean that nothing lower than plants is alive. He completes his discussion by defining life much as Plato defined soul: as self-generating motion. Animals and plants have this power and thus are alive. Inanimate natural bodies, such

32. Campanella's views are elaborated in chapter 3.

as flowing waters and moving stars, have only the "appearance of self-movement." They are in fact moved by something else—"the cause which produces them"—not "from themselves." Hence, we call inanimate moving objects "living" only "by a metaphor," or "by analogy." This is clearly approaching a modern definition of life. And Aquinas is committed to the Christian view of the soul, something only humans possess. God, furthermore, is not a world-soul but a supernatural deity. Thus he sees no reason to accept any view approximating panpsychism. This, then, is the standard Christian position, essentially unchanged for the subsequent 800 years.

3 Developments in the Renaissance: Sixteenth- and Seventeenth-Century Europe

3.1 Transition to the Renaissance

From about the third century AD onward, Christian monotheism grew steadily in power and influence. Stoic, Roman, and other Greek influences were gradually buried beneath a growing orthodox theology. The faith-based Christian worldview first competed with and then surpassed the older Greek worldview, which was based primarily on reason and logic. Monotheism was in direct conflict with panpsychism, and thus it effectively suppressed any advances in panpsychist philosophy. The Christian worldview, along with select aspects of Aristotelian natural philosophy, dominated Western intellectual thought for about 1,300 years.

A new worldview emerged at the time of the Renaissance. The religious worldview had reached its peak, and its position as the leading social influence began to wane. The newly emerging worldview was a system based not on divine scripture but on empirical observations of nature and on rationalist introspection of reality. It saw the world once again as regular, rational, and knowable. It applied new techniques in mathematics to natural phenomena, and perceived a new kind of order in the universe. The regularity and predictability led to a new phenomenon: mankind's inclination to control and manipulate nature. This new vision of the cosmos has come to be known as the Mechanistic Worldview. Its central metaphor was the cosmos as a clockwork mechanism, a machine—consistent, predictable, comprehensible, and controllable, even though (perhaps) constructed by a Supreme Creator whose nature was necessarily of an entirely different sort.

Throughout the emergence and rise to power of this new worldview, there was a persistent countercurrent of thought that was non-mechanistic.

That line of thinking saw the universe as animated—as possessing mind, sensitivity, and awareness. It was explored, developed, and promoted by some of the greatest thinkers of the time. Empirical science did nothing to dissuade panpsychist philosophers from that view, and more often served to support it. Even some of the founders of mechanistic philosophy—the thinkers we most associate with advancing this new worldview—harbored doubts about viewing matter as inherently lifeless, inert, and insensate.

In the sixteenth and seventeenth centuries, several major philosophers advocated or were strongly sympathetic to panpsychism, including Paracelsus, Cardano, Telesio, Patrizi, Bruno, Campanella, Henry More, Margaret Cavendish, Spinoza, and Leibniz. In that era, when the dominant worldview was moving from Christianity to mechanism, panpsychism found sympathy in neither sphere. To the leading theologians it was heresy, and to the founders of mechanism it was largely irrelevant. Advocating views that were fundamentally opposed to mechanism and (especially) to Christianity was hazardous; it could mean anything from a sullied reputation to personal ruin, imprisonment, or death. Thus a panpsychist position had to be well thought out and deeply held. Only those most committed to it dared to speak out.

The Renaissance was both a rebirth and a reawakening of philosophy. The religious worldview had begun to play itself out as the dominant interpretation of the universe, even as the new mechanical philosophy was emerging. While still important in personal, cultural, and governmental matters, religion was proving increasingly unable to explain the events of the natural world. Marsilio Ficino kept God in his hierarchical system, but placed soul at the center and described it as radiating out into all aspects of reality. Similarly, other central thinkers, especially in the sixteenth century, denied not God but rather religion's claim to be the sole purveyor of truth.

This was particularly true of Ficino's star pupil, Giovanni Pico della Mirandola (1463–1494). For Pico, nature was an interconnected whole, living and ensouled. Cassirer (1942: 338) calls this system "universal vitalism"; it is a view in which a world-soul inhabits, moves, and even constitutes all matter. Thus Cassirer adds that "for Pico therefore it is certain ... that nature can be regarded and interpreted only as the first stage of spirit," a kind of unconscious mentality. Commenting on Pico's system, Dulles (1941: 88) notes that "if the lower forms of life are material, it must be true, conversely, that all matter is, in a sense, alive." In his *Conclusiones*, Pico writes: "Nothing in the world is devoid of life. ... Wherever there is life, there is soul; wherever there is soul, there is a mind."[1] We may therefore count Pico as among the earliest panpsychists of the Renaissance, even though his natural philosophy assumed a secondary role in his larger system.

Though working from faulty premises, the alchemists of the fourteenth and fifteenth centuries made considerable progress in revealing the capabilities and powers of material substances. While not denying God, they relied primarily on new empirical procedures that demonstrated the potency and energy inherent in elemental matter itself. Of particular note is the work of Paracelsus (1493–1541). Equal parts alchemist, physician, and philosopher, his view of the macrocosm-microcosm analogy imputed all properties of the one to the other. Mankind, having life and intelligence, was thus seen as reflected in the larger natural world. Paracelsus seems to have held to a form of spirit-matter parallelism in which all things possessed a life spirit that was connected with elemental air:

None can deny that the air gives life to all corporeal and substantial things. ... The life of things is none other than a spiritual essence, an invisible and impalpable thing, a spirit and a spiritual thing. On this account there is nothing corporeal but has latent within itself a spirit and life. (1894: 135)

Paracelsus' panpsychist or hylozoist view accounted for variations in spirit by the corresponding variations in physical nature: "it is evident that there are different kinds of spirits, just as there are different kinds of bodies." These different spirits accounted for the differing "lives" of material substances. He gives a lengthy account of the life of various things, including salts, gems, metals, minerals, roots, "aromatic substances," "sweet things," resins, fruits, herbs, wood, bones, and water (136–137). Walter Pagel elaborates on precisely this point:

Life to Paracelsus is "virtue" and function. At the same time it is ... something not merely spiritual but of finest corporeality. It comes to us from and through the air—for "air gives all things their life." There is nothing corporeal that has not a "spiritual thing" hidden in itself. Hence to Paracelsus, all things are alive ... . (1982: 117)

Here again we find an explicit form of hylozoism.

This kind of spiritual empiricism established the background for the emerging philosophy of the Italian Renaissance, typically referred to as

1. Dulles 1941: 89.

Renaissance naturalism. The first five panpsychist philosophers of that era—Cardano, Telesio, Patrizi, Bruno, and Campanella—were Italians. All were born in the sixteenth century, and all were among the leading intellectual figures of their time. All disdained the standard theology, all opposed the dominance of Aristotelianism and scholasticism, and all looked to nature for insights into reality.

3.2 Four Italian Naturalists: Cardano, Telesio, Patrizi, and Bruno

Girolamo Cardano (1501–1576) was the first of the Italian naturalists to put forth an unambiguous panpsychist philosophy. Spending most of his life in Milan and northern Italy, he was a renowned mathematician and physician, a prolific writer and inventor, and a diligent student of ancient philosophy. Stoicism affected both his metaphysical and his ethical beliefs. He studied Plato and Aristotle, ultimately siding with the Platonists in rejecting the Aristotelian picture of the universe.

Cardano's conception of panpsychism is spelled out primarily in *De natura* (On Nature) and *De subtilitate* (On Subtlety), works in which he describes his theory of soul and its central role of maintaining the unity of all bodies. Soul is one of five universal qualities: "There are five principles of natural things: matter or 'hyle,' form, soul, place, and motion." (1560/2013: 53) But soul clearly has a central role: "[Bodies] come into being from matter and form. But they are controlled by the soul, which in the more noble beings is mind ... ; in bodies it is the principle of life." (54) Here we see the Aristotelian influence both in the emphasis on form and in the distinction between mind and soul; all things have soul, but only the higher forms—such as humans—have mind. Cardano furthermore takes pains to emphasize the universality of soul: "Matter is everywhere, but cannot exist without a form, hence form too must be everywhere. But also a soul, whether because there is to be generation everywhere, or ... because in every body there is evidently a principle of motion." (27)

Cardano's other Greek influences also reveal themselves in his writings. First there is his theory of the "active" (heat) and the "passive" (prime matter in *De natura*, and moisture in *De subtilitate*), which recalls the Stoic system. Stoic influence is also found in his reference to the *pneuma*, the "vital spirit" that circulates in the animal body and gives it life. Empedocles' two forces of Love and Strife are reflected in Cardano's "sympathy" and "antipathy."

According to Fierz (1983: xvii), "the main principle underlying [hidden] relationships is the sympathy and antipathy of all things, which partake in a common life." Cardano does make a slight break with the Greeks in arguing against the designation of fire as an element. To him fire is heat, the active principle, which acts on the passive—matter and moisture—to produce form. This is a general ontological principle, and hence for Cardano "all permanent bodies, including stones, are always slightly moist and warm and of necessity animate" (66).

The animation of inorganic objects covers a striking list of properties, such that the usual distinctions are blurred. In *De subtilitate* Cardano writes extensively about compound or "mixed" substances—that is, things that are not pure elements. Such things are intrinsically alive:

The basis of growth and nutrition—and indeed of generation—is almost the same; there processes take place from the soul. In fact it is a task for the soul alone to be capable in this fashion of thinning out and then uniting and transmuting. If indeed there is anything devoid of life that could do this, it would above all be fire ... yet it cannot. ... And so all mixed things must be alive or have been so. (292)

Later he recaps this point: "We have shown previously that things that are mixed are alive; this is especially appropriate for stones. They are not simply alive, but also undergo diseases, old age, and later also death." (366) Near the end of the work, he adds this:

Then it should be said, on comparable reasoning, that while a stone is in motion, it moves sideways by violence, and towards the center by nature, and thus on a middle line, because this would occur through recognition by the stone thus deliberating (*deliberantis*). (741)

Apparently a stone set in motion, subject to both impulsive and gravitational forces, is able to calculate, or deliberate on, the net force and to move in that direction.

Cardano seems not to have left much of an immediate philosophical legacy. His contributions are acknowledged today; however, Renaissance philosophers don't appear to have been directly influenced by him, as we see little citation of his work. Such was not the case with Bernardino Telesio (1509–1588). Born eight years after Cardano, Telesio left a lasting imprint on Western philosophy, primarily through Bruno, Campanella, Bacon, and Hobbes. Hoeffding (1908: 92) called Telesio's work "the greatest task undertaken by thought in the sixteenth century," in large part because it

forcefully struck out against the dominance of Aristotle and the Scholas-
tics. Even more so than Cardano, Telesio relied on insights from nature to
form his philosophy. Experience became a crucial aspect of inquiry and the
cornerstone of all true knowledge.

Telesio's philosophy is encapsulated in his magnum opus, the nine-
volume *De rerum natura* ("On the Nature of Things"). The first edition, published in 1565 under a slightly different title, was revised in 1570 and then
enlarged for a third and final release in 1586. In it Telesio overthrew the
Aristotelian emphasis on matter and form, replacing it with an Empedoclean (and modern) conception of matter and force. Like Empedocles, Telesio saw two fundamental and opposing forces at work in the universe: Heat
(an expanding and motive principle) and Cold (a contracting principle).
These forces act on and shape the "third principle": passive matter, which
is associated with the earth. Thus, for Telesio all things consist of an active
energy component, in the heat principle, and a mass component, in the
passive matter of the earth: "All things [are] made of earth by the sun; and
that in the constitution of all things, the earth and the sun enter respectively as mother and father." (1586/1967: 309)

In addition to acting as material forces, Heat and Cold have the remarkable quality of perception. They necessarily tend to preserve themselves,
particularly in the face of the other. Heat, insofar as it tends to stay hot,
must somehow sense and know Cold, and repel it. And likewise with Cold.
Ultimately we find a kind of balance or stalemate between the two principles, each existing in a state of dynamic tension (*antiperistasis*). Heat
and Cold must possess the power to sense, to perceive, or else they simply
could not exist. "It is quite evident that nature is propelled by self-interest."
(304) Self-preservation demands sensation (*sensus*). More than this, as an
active principle of self-awareness, heat combines with matter to create a
spiritual entity, a *universitas spiritus* that pervades the cosmos. This cosmic
spirit is not only universally present, it is fully self-aware and thus aware of
everything—a true *spiritus omniscius omnino*. It is a kind of world-soul, but
one that derives from the inner nature of reality rather than as installed
from without by some Demiurge.

In sum, all material objects embody the active principles of Heat and
Cold. Therefore, all things must contain the power of perception. This is
the basis for Telesio's panpsychism. More properly, we refer to his position as *pansensism*—the view that everything is capable of sensation. As

Giglioni says, "We can therefore say that Telesio understands *sensus* as the primordial sense of "being affected" pervading the entire universe. ... [It] is an undivided and seamless process in which feeling, appetite, and motion mutate into each other." *Sensus* is necessarily self-awareness, "and nature is accordingly conscious nature" (2010: 72–73).

Telesio effectively used the Non-Emergence argument to support his pansensist view. He claimed that it was inconceivable that mind should emerge from within matter unless it already had been there to some degree. Hoeffding (1908: 97) informs us that Telesio maintains "the impossibility of explaining the genesis of consciousness out of matter, unless we suppose matter to be originally endowed with consciousness." Emergence is impossible, and therefore mind or soul is seen as inevitably present in the very structure of the cosmos—and in particular, in the fundamental active principles of Heat and Cold.

Telesio, like Cardano, was strongly influenced by Stoicism. Giglioni writes that "Stoic themes and their role in shaping his thought cannot be downplayed" (71). In addition to the active/passive distinction, his conception of the soul has many affinities to the Stoic *pneuma*. Like the *pneuma*, Telesio's soul is corporeal, existing as a substance of "extreme tenuity and subtlety" (1586/1967: 305). Soul, like the *pneuma*, pervades all things, and both are embodiments of the active principle. That both Telesio and the Stoics should have reached a panpsychist conclusion, then, is not surprising.

But there is one important difference: Soul "possesses, besides sensation, the faculty of memory or retention" (Kristeller 1964: 100). This is significant because it is the first instance of memory playing a role in a metaphysical system—thus setting the stage for the later developments of Hobbes, Bergson, Russell, Bohm, and others. Unfortunately it is unclear how Telesio intends us to take his conception of memory: as merely a kind of persistent *record* of past experiences or, in a stronger sense, as an ability to *recall* past experiences. Regardless, it is an important milestone in panpsychist thinking.

Telesio's heat and cold principles furthermore seem to find confirmation in modern physics. On some readings of cosmology, as the early universe began to cool after the Big Bang, a temperature differential emerged between radiation and matter. This thermal gradient supplies the universe with free energy that allows it to create order and structure in matter—everything

from stars and planets to plants, animals, and people. In a sense, all material objects embody this thermal gradient, and owe their very existence to
it. In the present context, we may note that the gradient occurs between
the relatively hot radiation and relatively cool matter. Telesio's "heat" and
"cold," understood as *relative* concepts, closely align with this modern conception. So conceived, heat and cold do in fact account for the existence of
all order in the universe. And if we allow that our minds also emerged by
this process of natural evolution, heat and cold also account for our sentience, self-awareness, and consciousness. Telesio seems to have been not
far from the mark.[2]

Francesco Patrizi (1529–1597), like the other Italian naturalists, professed
a deep dislike of Aristotelian philosophy and sought to place Platonism
on at least an equal footing. In 1578, in recognition of his efforts, he was
appointed to the world's first chair of Platonic philosophy, at Ferrara.
Patrizi, also a humanist and a poet, exchanged several philosophical letters
with Telesio. His lyrical view of the world is reflected in his most important
philosophical work, *Nova de universis philosophia* (New Philosophy of the
Universe), in which he introduced the term 'panpsychism' (*pampsychia*)
into the vocabulary of Western philosophy.

The *Nova philosophia* is a wide-ranging metaphysical treatise that lays
out Patrizi's theories of light, the soul, and the first principles of the cosmos. It is organized in four sections: Panaugia ("The All-Light"), Panarchia
("The All-Principles"), Pampsychia ("The All-Souls"), and Pancosmia ("The
All-Cosmos"). The third section is of primary interest here, as it focuses on
his interpretation of the world-soul and its particular manifestations in the
natural world. In Patrizi's cosmological hierarchy there are nine levels or
grades of being; from highest to lowest: unity, essence, life, intelligence,
soul, nature, quality, form, and body. Soul, notably, takes the middle and
thus central role in the scheme, much as it did for Cardano. Furthermore,
the nine levels of being are all fundamentally interconnected in what Brickman (1941: 34) describes as a deeply participatory process:

These nine grades are linked by a process of "partaking of one another"—*participatio*.
This "partaking" Patrizi describes as an "inter-illumination," through which beings

---

2. For details on the cosmic energy differential and the implications for universal
evolution, see Skrbina 2015 or Chaisson 2001.

are illuminated, come into existence, and are known. ... Every grade partakes of each of those above it ... and is also partaken of by each grade below it according to the capacity of the latter. Each grade ... is [at once] a "partaker" (*particeps*), and is "partaken of" (*participatus*).

Patrizi echoes the language of participation as found in Neo-Platonism, especially in the work of Proclus and Pseudo-Dionysius. Such terminology builds on Plato's original use of the concept as the means by which the phenomenal world interacts with the Forms.[3]

Soul, at the center of this participatory hierarchy, plays a major role in mediating between the upper spiritual grades and the lower earthly realms. At a minimum, it is clear that soul, in the form of the world-soul, penetrates all levels of being. The question, as before, is whether the individual objects of the world possess souls in themselves—i.e., true panpsychism— or whether they are merely extensions of the one world-soul. Patrizi clearly opted for the pluralistic view. He saw soul as a manifold entity, present both as distinct individuals and as united in the comprehensive world-soul. Kristeller (1964: 122) writes that "Patrizi does not treat the individual souls as [mere] parts of the world soul, but believes, rather, that their relation to their bodies is analogous to that of the world soul to the universe as a whole." In the words of Brickman (1941: 41), soul is "both [unity and plurality], with the many contained in the one."

Patrizi was the first to directly attack Aristotle's logic regarding panpsychism, a position that would be reiterated later by both Bruno and Gilbert. All three men focused their criticism on Aristotle's definition of *psyche*; and they all seem to have been unaware of his broader theory of the *pneuma*. As I noted, Aristotle believed the stars and heavenly bodies were animate, but he granted *psyche* to nothing in the earthly realm save plants and animals. Patrizi saw this as a logical inconsistency. On the one hand, the Peripatetics defined soul as the motive force behind a living, organic body. On the other, Aristotle himself stated that stars were ensouled even though they were not organic. One of the two positions must be wrong. Taking Aristotle's implicit definition, Patrizi argues that an organic structure is not a prerequisite for having a soul, and so it is certainly possible that the cosmos as a whole, as well as the basic elements of matter that constitute it, also have souls.

3. See, for example, *Parmenides* (129–132) and *Phaedo* (100–101).

Patrizi then runs through a series of brief arguments in support of his panpsychism: (1) How do we know that the elements do not have organs of some sort, and thus are "organic"? If they do, then this is a further argument on behalf of their souls (Design argument). (2) The cosmos is clearly the most perfect thing there is, and any perfect thing must have a soul or it would be less than perfect; therefore the world-soul exists (Design argument). (3) The elements give life and soul to all beings which have it, and nothing can be in the effect that is not in the cause; therefore, the elements must have souls (Non-Emergence). (4) All parts of the world experience birth, change, and destruction, yet they still have the power to hold together and persist; this cannot happen without soul (Indwelling Powers). These themes were developed by later philosophers, and Patrizi's participatory ontology thus set the stage for the advances made by his immediate successors.[4]

Apart from Telesio, the other great philosopher of southern Italy was Giordano Bruno (1548–1600). Bruno's philosophical system was rooted in his cosmology. The standard picture of the cosmos in the sixteenth century was essentially the same that Aristotle developed nearly 2,000 years earlier, and the same that Ptolemy had formalized in the second century AD: The universe was a finite space with the Earth at the center, and the stars and other heavenly bodies circulated around us on the celestial spheres. Throughout the centuries, a few thinkers had speculated otherwise, namely that the universe might actually be infinite. As early as 300 BC, Epicurus reasoned that the universe must be limitless: "The totality of things is unlimited ... and having no limit, it must be infinite and without boundaries." (*Letter to Herodotus*, 41–42) In the first century BC, Lucretius wrote:

The All that Is, wherever its paths may lead, is boundless. ... There can be no end to anything without something beyond to mark that end. ... Nor does it matter at which point one may stand: whatever position a man takes up, he finds the All still endless alike in all directions. (1977: 23; book I, 957–967)

4. For another, somewhat oblique view on Patrizi's panpsychism, see Leinkauf 2010: 215: "Since the powers [of things] are conceived in accordance with the paradigm of the psychical, and the soul ... functions as the *forma universalis* of the world, Patrizi's cosmology ... must be understood as affirming a universal ... presence of the psychical, in the sense that all that exists is permeated by processual-dynamic structures."

Closer to Bruno's time, the neo-Platonist philosopher Nicholas of Cusa (1401–1464) also discussed the possibility and significance of an infinite cosmos. Then came Copernicus' *De revolutionibus*, published upon his death in 1543, which placed the sun at the center of the cosmos and the Earth in orbit around it. But Copernicus still maintained that the universe was finite, and that the celestial spheres circled around the solar system; in that sense he was less revolutionary than is commonly believed.

Bruno gathered these insights from Epicurus, Cusa, and Copernicus and pieced together a strikingly modern picture of the cosmos. His universe was an infinite space composed of infinitely many solar systems like our own. He was one of the first to use modern terminology, reserving 'world' for the Earth and other planets and using 'universe' to mean the whole infinite cosmos. Bruno saw neither the Earth nor the sun as the center of the universe; like Lucretius, he realized that, in an infinite cosmos, every place would appear as the center. Bruno said: "The Earth no more than any other world is at the center ... . The Earth is not in the center of the universe; it is central only to our own surrounding space."[5]

From this cosmology he drew important philosophical and metaphysical implications. First, he realized that there was an aspect of relativity to the cosmos. If the universe was, in a sense, the same throughout, then the same rules must apply everywhere. Hoeffding stated that, in Bruno's cosmology,

every determination of place must be relative ... . From the relativity of [place and] motion follows the relativity of time ... . Nor have the concepts of heaviness and lightness any ... absolute significance ... . Nature is everywhere essentially the same [and] the same force is everywhere in operation. (1908: 124–126)

This "universality" of the universe meant that any physical or metaphysical conclusions arrived at here on Earth must of necessity apply throughout all existence.

Bruno's panpsychism followed directly from his metaphysics. Nature has two internal constituent principles: form and matter. He takes this Aristotelian orthodoxy and interprets it in a Platonic or Plotinian manner. In particular, form is to be considered as produced by soul, i.e., the world-soul: "Bruno asserts that ... every form is produced by a soul. For all things are

5. Bruno (1584b), cited on p. 58 of Singer 1950.

animated by the world soul, and all matter is everywhere permeated by soul and spirit." (Kristeller 1964: 133)

Bruno develops his panpsychism primarily in *De la causa, principio, et uno* (Cause, Principle, and Unity) and in *De l'infinito universo et mondi* (On the Infinite Universe and Worlds). Both were published in 1584, just after his visit to Oxford. Both were written in dialogue form, in the fashion of Plato.

It is in *De la causa* that Bruno states his view most clearly. In the second dialogue, the characters are elaborating on the animated nature of the cosmos. Adopting the language and concepts of his opponents, Bruno notes that, even within the old paradigm, the universe was ensouled: "There is no philosopher enjoying some reputation ... who does not hold that the world and its spheres are animated in some way." (1584a/1998: 42) Perhaps this is an exaggeration, yet he rightly acknowledges that panpsychism runs deep in Western philosophy. He then emphasizes the central aspect of ancient and medieval panpsychism: It is not only the world-soul that is animate, but all things individually are animate too. This view is reiterated in *De magia* (On Magic), in which the souls of individual things are at once distinct yet connected to the universal soul:

It is manifest ... that every soul and spirit hath a certain continuity with the spirit of the universe. ... The power of each soul is itself somehow present afar in the universe [and is] exceedingly connected and attached thereto. (in Singer 1950: 90–91)

In *De la causa* Bruno explicitly and concisely summarizes his view that "not only the form of the universe, but also all the forms of natural things are souls" (1584a/1998: 42). Thus he generalizes Aristotle's idea—that soul is the form of living bodies—to all physical bodies.

Interestingly, Bruno then acknowledges the unconventionality of this view. The character Dicsono says "Common sense tells us that not everything is alive. ... Who will agree with you?" Teofilo, speaking for the author, replies "But who could reasonably refute it?" In the manner of Patrizi's criticism, Bruno offers a "proof" that focuses on the world-soul and the parts of the universe that are possessed by it. Again, Aristotle attributes soul to the stars and other heavenly bodies. Bruno, like Patrizi, considered it terribly inconsistent to hold that certain parts of the cosmos are privileged to have a soul and others are not. Thus, in keeping with his rule that the same laws apply throughout the universe, he logically concludes that all things, all "parts," must be animated: "There is nothing that does not possess a soul and that has no vital principle." (43)[6]

A skeptical Polinnio retorts "Then a dead body has a soul? So, my clogs, my slippers, my boots ... are supposedly animated?" Teofilo (Bruno) clarifies his position by explaining that such "dead" things are not necessarily to be considered animate in themselves, but rather as containing elements that either are themselves animate or have the innate power of animation:

> I say, then, that the table is not animated as a table, nor are the clothes as clothes ... but that, as natural things and composites, they have within them matter and form [i.e. soul]. All things, no matter how small and minuscule, have in them part of that spiritual substance. ... For in all things there is spirit, and there is not the least corpuscle that does not contain within itself some portion that may animate it. (44)

This distinction anticipates the views of both Leibniz and the twentieth-century process philosophers—Whitehead, Hartshorne, Griffin, et al.—who also deny mind to inanimate material objects but grant it to atoms, molecules, cells, and other so-called "true individuals."[7]

Bruno's line of thinking hints at the Indwelling Powers argument of Plato and the pre-Socratics. Matter either is animate outright or has the power of animation. We get a further indication of this standpoint when Bruno speaks of "the spirit, the soul, the life which penetrates all, is in all, and moves all matter." As with the Greeks, soul has the power not only of animation but also of motion. This power is visible in the motion of the Earth, the stars, and other worlds, which have souls and are moved by them. In pressing his case that the Earth is ensouled, he even makes a passing reference to a version of the Continuity argument when he compares the structure of the Earth to that of a human being: "it is evident that waters exist within the earth's viscera even as within us are humors and blood" (1584b/1950: 315).

Two other aspects of Bruno's thought are relevant here. The first is his concept of the monad. He clearly was an atomist, and he believed that there existed some ultimately small and simple element of matter; he referred to these variously as atoms, *minima*, or monads. Unfortunately, he was not

---

6. Bruno followed the ancient Greeks in equating "alive" and "ensouled."

7. There are difficulties in defining a true individual. I examine this issue at length later in the book.

entirely clear or consistent in his definitions of these ultimates. Sometimes the monads are material entities ("the substance for the building of all bodies is the minimum body or the atom"—*De minimo*, in Singer 1950: 74). Other times they are something more ephemeral and mysterious; Singer describes them as "a philosophical rather than a material conception" and says that they "have in them some of the qualities of the whole" (72). Hoeffding (1908: 138) states that monads are "also active force, soul, and will." The monad is not only an ultimate element of smallness; it is more generally a *unity*, and may equally apply to large-scale objects. Hoeffding elaborates: "[T]he sun with its whole planetary system is a minimum in relation to the universe. Indeed, even the whole universe is called a monad. ... The world-soul too, even God himself, is called a monad." (138–139) Bruno is sometimes credited with creating the concept of the monad, but the philosophical usage of the term goes back at least to Plato—'monad' derives from *monas* ("unity"). Plato's younger contemporary Xenocrates made the monad a first principle of metaphysics, and identified it with a self-contemplating intellect or *nous*.[8]

The other important topic is Bruno's theory of matter. He saw matter as a single substance that exhibited two modes: *potenza* ("power") and *soggetto* ("subjectivity"). The power aspect of matter is revealed in its potential to act—that is, to exist or to be. Being is power, and power is the material aspect of matter—a clear connection to the concept of energy. Bruno's other mode, subjectivity, can be seen as a manifestation of the soul in matter. Subjectivity determines the inherent nature of a thing, and distinguishes it uniquely from all other things. In short, *potenza* and *soggetto* represent the physical and mental modes of matter, respectively. Such a dual-aspect ontology is again a form of dualistic panpsychism, and it anticipates the later developments of Campanella, Spinoza, Schopenhauer, and others.

Bruno had a substantial influence on subsequent philosophers. Leibniz is a clear successor, particularly with his own conception of monads that so closely resembles Bruno's.[9] Spinoza, Goethe, Herder, and Schelling all were influenced by Bruno's system.[10] Even his implication of the will as an aspect

8. See also Aristotle, *De anima* 404b22: "Mind is the monad."

9. The influence of Bruno on Leibniz is hotly debated. Leibniz makes only scattered references to the Italian; see the discussion on Leibniz below.

10. Cf. Singer 1950: 194; Kristeller 1964: 138; Calcagno 1998: 39.

of the monad anticipated the important advances of Campanella, Leibniz, Schopenhauer, Hartmann, and Nietzsche.

3.3 Gilbert and the Soul of the Magnet

Renaissance naturalism was not the only development in panpsychist philosophy in sixteenth-century Europe. Also of significance was *De magnete* (On the Magnet), by William Gilbert (1540–1603). Often deemed the first modern scientific work, *De magnete* is a detailed and technical study of magnets and their properties. In it he sought to summarize and clarify all previous knowledge of lodestones, from the time of Thales on. He introduced the concept of magnetic poles and showed how they align with the poles of the Earth. Most of Gilbert's experiments were performed on a spherical lodestone that he called a *Terella*, or "little Earth." He demonstrated that this little Earth duplicated the properties of the real Earth, and he correctly argued that the lodestone was given its power by the Earth— the natural field of the Earth magnetizes certain iron ores in the crust. Galileo was much impressed by Gilbert's work, calling it "great to a degree that is enviable."[11]

From a panpsychist point of view, the most striking thing about *De magnete* is Gilbert's Thalesian attribution of soul and other mental traits to magnets. Writing on the attractive power, he refers to the "friendship of iron for the lodestone" (1600/1958: 50). In noting that a magnet can magnetize a neutral piece of iron—in fact, limitless pieces—by mere contact, Gilbert refers to it as an awakening: "the dormant power of one is awakened by the other's without expenditure" (62). He sees the powers of the magnet as evidence of "reason" in a stone, just as the Greeks saw reason as guiding the movements of planets and stars. In possessing reason, the magnet is something akin to the human being:

[I]f among [material] bodies one sees [anything whatsoever] that moves and breathes and has senses and is governed and impelled by reason, will he not, knowing and seeing this, say that here is a man, or something more like man than a stone or a stalk? (66)

Near the end of *De magnete*, Gilbert makes his view clear: "the magnetic force is animate, or imitates a soul; in many respects it surpasses the

11. Gilbert 1600/1958: xii.

human soul" (308). Furthermore, just as the magnetic force is transferrable, he believed that soul was likewise given by one body to another—that the soul of the Earth was transferred to all earthly objects, whether animal, plant, or mineral. In the end, he characterizes the magnetic force as the single clear piece of scientific evidence that all objects, especially planets and stars, have souls and minds: "we deem the whole world [universe] animate, and all globes, all stars, and this glorious earth, too" (309). For this reason, Gilbert, like Bruno and Patrizi, assailed the logical inconsistency of Aristotle. The Aristotelian cosmology was a "monstrous creation, in which all [celestial] things are perfect, vigorous, animate, while the earth alone, luckless small fraction, is imperfect, dead, inanimate, and subject to decay."

Gilbert doesn't provide much more in the way of philosophical argumentation for his view, evidently believing that the amazing powers of magnets and the magnetic force are sufficient proof. But he does briefly touch on some of the standard arguments. He cites the ancient notion that "not without a divine and animate nature could movements [of stars and planets] so diverse be produced." He claims that the celestial bodies are perfect and must therefore necessarily have souls because "nothing is excellent, nor precious, nor eminent, that hath not a soul." He notes that the Earth and the sun can give their magnetic soul power to other objects, and consequently "it is not likely that they can do that which is not in themselves; but they awaken souls, and consequently are themselves possessed of souls" (Non-Emergence). And the mere fact that one magnet has the power to magnetize and thus ensoul another piece of metal is a form of the Indwelling Powers argument. It is significant that Gilbert, acknowledged as one of the first modern scientists, relied on panpsychist ideas in formulating his explanation of empirical phenomena.[12]

3.4 Campanella and the Seventeenth Century

Moving into thought that is more representative of the 1600s, we find an emerging scientific and objectivist worldview competing with the naturalistic and panpsychic theories of the Renaissance. The early rationalism and empiricism led the departure from Scholasticism and Church orthodoxy.

12. For a further discussion of Gilbert's theory of the magnet and his "animism," see Henry 2001.

This new rationalism of the sixteenth century was still open to panpsychist interpretations of the cosmos. But by the seventeenth century it began to harden into an objectivist and mechanistic worldview.

With respect to philosophy of mind, the 1600s were dominated by two of the most notable panpsychist philosophers in history, Spinoza and Leibniz. Additionally, I will examine the question of pansensism as discussed by Bacon and Hobbes. Also of note are the ideas of some lesser-known yet important figures, including Margaret Cavendish and Henry More. Even Locke and Newton made some interesting statements along panpsychist lines. The beginning of the seventeenth century was marked, though, by the culmination of Renaissance naturalism in the philosophy of Tommaso Campanella.

Campanella (1568–1639) was perhaps the last great Renaissance philosopher. His philosophy was marked by a strong opposition to Aristotle and an equally strong embrace of Telesio. His two major works—*De sensu rerum et magia* (On the Sense in Things and Magic), written in 1590 but not published until 1620, and *Metafisica*, published in 1638—both contained detailed and explicit arguments for panpsychism. Like the other Renaissance naturalists, Campanella emphasized an empirical approach to knowledge, but not in the restricted sense of the British empiricists. Rather, he combined experiential knowledge of nature with metaphysical first principles to form a complete philosophical system that was centered on his theory of the three "primalities" that were at the core of his panpsychism. That doctrine, one of the more original elements of his philosophy, pervades his entire system of thought. It claims that the essence of being consists of three fundamental principles: power, wisdom (or knowledge, or sense), and love (or will). Such characteristics had long been attributed to God—in the form of omnipotence, omniscience, and omni-benevolence. Campanella was the first to make them universally applicable. For him, they are aspects of all things, from God on down to the humblest bit of stone.

Power (*potentia*) has three connotations: the power to be (*potentia essendi*), the power to act (*potentia activa*), and the power to be acted upon (*potentia passiva*). The power to be is the first and the foremost of these, as it is the source of all existence. Without the *potentia essendi* a thing simply would not exist. Furthermore, existence demands the ongoing presence of this power in order to allow persistence through time. The powers to act and to be acted upon are related to Campanella's theory of knowledge, and involve the ability to communicate the likeness of one thing to another, as will be discussed below.

The notion that power is the preeminent principle of existence is an advance from the Telesian conception of Heat and Cold, but it retains the essential reference to the idea of energy. And energy and power were virtually synonymous in the sixteenth century, long before power was defined as the rate of change of energy over time. Also, the *potentia essendi* anticipates certain very recent aspects of systems theory, particularly the idea of a "dissipative structure" as an entity that requires power, or energy expenditure, to maintain its existence.

The second primality, wisdom or knowledge, is explicitly mental. Campanella argues that, because all things sense, they can be said to know, and consequently to possess a kind of wisdom. First and foremost, things know themselves. Each thing knows of its own existence and its own persistence over time: "All things have the sensation of their own being and of their conservation. They exist, are conserved, operate, and act because they know."[13] Hoeffding (1908: 153) explains it this way: "Every individual being has an 'original hidden thought' of itself, which is one with its nature." The same idea is explicit in the lengthy subtitle of Campanella's *De sensu rerum*:

A remarkable tract of occult philosophy in which the world is shown to be a living and truly conscious image of God, and all its parts and particles thereof to be endowed with sense perception, some more clearly, some more obscurely, to the extent required for the preservation of themselves and of the whole in which they share sensation. (1620; in Bonansea 1969: 156)

This "remarkable" subtitle captures many aspects of his philosophy in a single sentence.

Campanella offered a number of arguments in support of his primality of wisdom and the attendant panpsychism. Several tend to take the form of definitional arguments or an appeal to first principles—for example, that knowledge is required for self-preservation, and hence all things must have active power—but he also employed the ancient Non-Emergence argument:

[I]f the animals are sentient ... and sense does not come from nothing, the elements whereby they and everything else are brought into being must be said to be sentient,

13. Campanella (1638), in Bonansea 1969 (p. 156).

because what the result has the cause must have. Therefore the heavens are sentient, and so [too] the earth ... . (1620; in Dooley 1995: 39)

Campanella did, however, introduce a new form of the Design argument for panpsychism, one that explicitly incorporates theology. He claims that, in the words of Bonansea,

all beings ... carry within themselves the image or vestige of God and are essentially related to one another ... . [God clearly possesses sensation and wisdom, and so] sensation is therefore to be extended to all beings. (1969: 157)

It is significant that Campanella saw all things as participating in God, and thus sharing his qualities. In fact, the theological argument applies to all three primalities: "Campanella holds that God ... in effusing Himself into creatures, communicates to them power, knowledge [wisdom], and love, so that they may exist." (145) It is interesting that Campanella, a devout Christian, looked to God as justification for his panpsychism. Perhaps he thought this would placate the Inquisition. Unfortunately for him, it did not. The Church was beginning to feel the pressure of the new naturalist philosophy, and so it struck back hard. At about the same time that Bruno was burned alive, Campanella, at the age of 32, was imprisoned by church authorities; he served 27 years for his beliefs. Fortunately he was able to continue writing, and even to smuggle out some complete manuscripts.

Campanella's third primality, love, is a consequence of the primality of wisdom; things love existence, and such love follows naturally from self-knowledge. He explains it in *Metafisica*:

Beings exist not only because they have the power to be and know that they are, but also because they love [their own] being. Did they not love [it], they would not be so anxious to defend it ... . All things would either be chaos or they would be entirely destroyed. Therefore love, not otherwise than power and wisdom, seems to be a principle of being ... . (1638, in Bonansea, 162)

Thus it is clear that the three primalities are intimately linked. The primality of knowledge, for example, acts through the primality of power. The power to be acted upon represents the reception of an essence, the transfer of something from the object to the knower. The object is able to surrender this essence by its power to act. This essence is captured by the knower, is incorporated into its being, and is thereby changed. It is this change that constitutes knowledge. "Every sense," says Campanella, "is a change in the sentient body" (1620, in Dooley 1995: 49). This change is not arbitrary. By incorporating an essence of the object, the knower becomes like the object. Assimilation occurs. Thus, knower and known merge, at least in part. To know something is to become like it.

Cassirer (1927/1963: 148) noted that such an epistemology entails a joint sharing of a common essence, and that furthermore a panpsychist theory of mind naturally follows:

> [T]his unity [of knower and known] is only possible if the subject and object, the knower and known, are of the same nature; they must be members and parts of one and the same vital complex. Every sensory perception is an act of fusion and reunification. We perceive the object, we grasp it in its proper, genuine being only when we feel in it the same life, the same kind of movement and animation that is immediately given and present to us in the experiencing of our own Ego. From this, Panpsychism emerges as a simple corollary to [Campanella's] theory of knowledge ... .

Campanella has been revered throughout history as a man of powerful intellect and insight. In his own time he was acknowledged for his depth of thought. Battaglino called him "one of the rarest geniuses of Italy," and Brancadoro exclaimed that "in him all fiery and most subtle powers are glowing and excel in the utmost degree." Leibniz ranked him with Bacon, Hobbes, and Descartes.[14] He remains, along with Bruno, an outstanding exemplar of Renaissance naturalism, and together they mark the turning point from a medieval, dogmatic, theological worldview to that of modern science and rationalism.[15]

3.5   The Early Scientific Philosophers

Campanella lived at precisely the time when scientific philosophy was first being formulated. Nearly the same age as Bacon (b. 1561) and Galileo (b. 1564), he created his naturalistic vision contemporaneously with their materialist and objectivist philosophy. Some intellectuals were able

14. See Bonansea 1969: 35–36.

15. For an elaboration on Campanella's pansensism, see Ernst 2010: 262–263: "Thanks to sense, every being is endowed with the capacity to distinguish between that which benefits its existence and that which is harmful. ... Every being shares in life and in sense, according to various degrees and in specific forms: some, such as the heavenly bodies and light, are endowed with a sense that is much more acute than that of animals, while others, such as minerals and metals, are endowed with a sense that is more obtuse and darker ... ."

to accommodate both. Gilbert, as I have shown, integrated science and panpsychism. Johannes Kepler (1571–1630) saw soul as the force behind the movements of the celestial bodies, at least for the better part of his life. His first substantial work, *Mysterium cosmographicum* (1596), held to "the traditional conception of force as a soul animating the celestial bodies" (Jammer 1957: 82). The somewhat later *De stella nova* (1606) includes this comment:

Those motive powers of the stars share in some way in the capacity of thought, so that, as it were, they understand, imagine, and aim at their path—not of course by means of ratiocination like us human beings but by an innate impulse implanted in them from the beginning of Creation. (in Jung and Pauli 1952/1955: 173)

In 1609, Kepler published *Astronomia nova*, in which he discussed the "true doctrine of gravity" and noted that, wherever the Earth moved in space, heavy objects were always attracted to the Earth's center "thanks to the faculty animating it" (85). He likened this animating force of gravity, which he called a *species immateriata*, to the animate force of magnets. In 1610 he claimed that gravity was identical to the magnetic force: "The planets are magnets and are driven around by the sun by magnetic force." (89)

These themes continued in Kepler's *Harmonies of the World* (1618). The epilogue (section 10) contains passages relating to the solar mind. He believed that the periodic and rational movements of the planets were "the object of some mind" (1618/1995: 240). He noted that "it is not easy for dwellers on the Earth to conjecture … what mind there is in the sun" (240–241). Yet, he asserted, mind in the sun followed as a necessary explanation of the "solar harmonies of movements":

For as the sun rotating into itself moves all the planets by means of the form emitted from itself, so too … mind, by understanding itself and in itself all things, stirs up ratiocinations, and by dispersing and unrolling its simplicity into them, makes everything to be understood. (244)

The solar mind is the source of the harmonies: "there dwells in the sun simple intellect, *pyr noeron*, or *nous*, the source, whatsoever it may be, of every harmony."

In 1621, at the age of 50, Kepler changed his mind. He decided that 'force' was a better term than 'soul'. He concluded that gravitational attraction was something physical rather than supernatural:

Formerly I believed that the cause of the planetary motion is a soul. … But when I realized that these motive causes attenuate with the distance from the sun, I came to the conclusion that this force is something corporeal, if not so properly, at least in a certain sense. (90)

This is a remarkably frank and revealing admission. Because gravity decreases (regularly but non-linearly) with distance, it is a function of spatial dimension, and therefore it is of the physical world—hence, it cannot be soul. There is a deep implication here: Any entity that exhibits regularity in space or time must be physical in nature, and therefore cannot be mental or spiritual. In Kepler's day, soul and mind were by definition mysterious and immaterial, lacking all tangibility and regularity. Any phenomenon that would admit to mathematization must necessarily be natural, physical, corporeal. This is in striking contrast to the view of the ancient Greeks. They saw regularity of motion as a clear indication of reason at work, and hence of soul in the cosmos. Kepler took the very same empirical phenomenon and came to the opposite conclusion: that mechanistic forces were the causal factors.

This, then, was the beginning of the mechanistic worldview—the mathematization of natural phenomena. Galileo took this up in earnest, and greatly advanced scientific philosophy. The natural philosophers, emboldened by their successes, soon sought mathematical descriptions everywhere. As a consequence, they began to push spiritual explanations to the sidelines. Materialist and mechanistic philosophy began to dominate Western thinking.

Two of the first materialist philosophers of the modern era were Francis Bacon (1561–1626) and Thomas Hobbes (1588–1679). Both lived during the transition from naturalistic panpsychism to scientific materialism. Both were born in the sixteenth century, but their writing and thinking were more allied to the seventeenth. Bacon was seven years younger than Campanella and was certainly aware of the panpsychist and pansensist philosophies that were circulating on the Continent, and of Gilbert's *De magnete*.

Bacon could not abide the view that all things sense. For him, that ability was something that only livings things possessed. However, he was willing to admit that everything had some ability to perceive the local environment and to feel (though he did not use that word) temperature and force. Perception was, for him, a quality that all material objects possessed. Such a pan-perceptivist philosophy comes notably close to pansensism, and Bacon took care in spelling out his view in his *Natural History* (also called *Silva Silvarum*). In the early 1620s, near the end of his life, he wrote the following in introducing section IX of the aforementioned work:

It is certain that all bodies whatsoever, though they have no sense, yet they have perception; for when one body is applied to another, there is a kind of election to embrace that which is agreeable, and to exclude or expel that which is ingrate; and whether the body be alterant or altered, evermore a perception precedeth operation; for else all bodies would be alike one to another.

And sometimes this perception, in some kind of bodies, is far more subtle than the [human] sense; so that the sense is but a dull thing in comparison of it: we see a weatherglass will find the least difference of the weather in heat or cold, when men find it not. And this perception is sometimes at distance ... as when the lodestone draweth iron. ... It is therefore a subject of very noble inquiry, to inquire of the more subtle perceptions; for it is another key to open nature, as well as the [human] sense; and sometimes better. ... It serveth to discover that which is hid.

Clearly, perception is a quality that is comparable to human sense, though "more subtle" and more mysterious. It clearly merits study, but Bacon seems not to know how to tackle the issue. He is not so bold as to predict that all phenomena will yield to materialist interpretations.

Hobbes, also aware of the pansensist philosophers, takes up their challenge in his 1655 work *De corpore* (On the Body).[16] He first defines sense as "motion in some of the internal parts of the sentient; and the parts so moved are parts of the organs of sense." This is a relatively accurate description of some sort of stimulus, such as light or sound, impinging on a sense organ and generating a nerve signal that moves through the body to the brain. He then confines sensation to living organisms: "The subject of sense is the sentient itself, namely, some living creature." Then in section 5 he writes:

But though all sense, as I have said, be made by reaction, nevertheless it is not necessary that everything that reacteth should have sense. I know that there have been philosophers, and those learned men, who have maintained that all bodies are endued with sense. Nor do I see how they can be refuted, if the nature of sense be placed in reaction only. And, though by the reaction of bodies inanimate a phantasm [sensation] might be made, it would nevertheless cease, as soon as ever the object [causing the sensation] were removed. For unless those bodies had organs, as living creatures have, fit for the retaining of such motion as is made in them, their sense would be such, as that they should never remember the same ... . For by

16. See part IV, chapter XXV.

'sense', we [mean] ... the comparing and distinguishing [of] phantasms. ... Wherefore sense ... hath necessarily some memory adhering to it.

Thus, like Bacon, Hobbes confronted the doctrine of pansensism that was associated with Telesio and Campanella.

Not uncoincidentally, it was also in *De corpore* that Hobbes first used the concept of *conatus*, meaning "striving" or "endeavor," to refer to "all motion in general" (Herbert 1989: 64). If conatus is taken as an intentional quantity, then something mind-like inheres in all motion, and thus in all matter. But the degree to which Hobbes held that view is unclear.[17]

Hobbes recognized that the validity of pansensism hinges on the definition of "sense." If sensing means only reaction, then he concedes that all things sense—this much is obvious. But he adds an additional condition: To sense requires memory, something only living organisms are presumably capable of. That qualification recalls Telesio's claim that memory, along with sensation, is central to a proper conception of the soul.

However, the concept of memory may not be as transparent as Hobbes suggests. He seems to refer to a humanistic conception of memory, but there is no logical reason why the concept cannot be extended to general physical systems. A generalized conception of memory has at least two components: the ability to record experiences and the ability to replay or project them into the future. Humans record experiences through morphological changes in the brain, and then are able to replay them internally and to relate them externally via muscular action and language. Generalized memory requires, first of all, a permanent—or at least temporally persistent—change in the sensing body. That such a change occurs to all physical objects seems clear. Everything degrades and wears down to some extent, depending on the forces experienced. Ancient documents, fossils, rocks, and even planetary fragments can be dated with reasonable precision because of the permanent, cumulative record that all things acquire. This is a form of memory.

Furthermore, since physical objects do not communicate in the human sense, one may say that a form of memory exists if the record of experiences is present and available to an outside observer. Humans clearly can detect

17. The philosophical use of conatus was taken up by Leibniz and, especially, Spinoza, both to panpsychist ends. For more on Hobbes' use of the term, see Herbert 1989: 25–62.

and measure physical changes over eons, and thus in this way the record of experience is replayed. Many changes are more subtle and may not be detectable with present technology. But this doesn't alter the fact that all experiences are recorded and can theoretically be recovered.

Other thinkers have observed that inanimate objects can in fact display a kind of memory. William James, commenting on Fechner's analysis of natural events, wrote:

[T]he event works back upon the background, as the wavelet works upon the waves, or as the leaf's movements work upon the sap inside the branch. The whole sea and the whole tree are registers of what has happened, and are different for the wave's and the leaf's action having occurred. (1909: 171–172)

Henry David Thoreau's book *Wild Fruits* contains a similar observation of the apple:

It will have some red stains, commemorating the mornings and evenings it has witnessed; some dark and rusty blotches, in memory of the clouds and foggy, mildewy days that have passed over it; and a spacious field of green reflecting the general face of Nature … . (2000: 87)

Bertrand Russell made comparable remarks in his *Outline of Philosophy* (1927b). After stating that memory is "the most essential characteristic of mind" (153), he cited an example of memory in "inorganic matter":

A watercourse which at most times is dry gradually wears a channel down a gully at the times when it flows, and subsequent rains follow [the same] course. … You may say, if you like, that the river bed "remembers" previous occasions when it experienced cooling streams … . (155)

Logically, even other, more subtle perceptions—such as a gentle breeze, or the shadow of a hand on a leaf—also affect the system of a tree permanently, though such changes may be utterly undetectable. Henri Bergson further elaborated the philosophy of memory, defining it as the decisive factor in the graded transition from matter to mind; for an extended discussion, see his *Matiere et Memoire* (1896). Given a generalized conception of memory, then, it seems that a Hobbesian argument could support a pansensist or panpsychist view.

A final clue to Hobbes' beliefs comes from the autobiographical essay *The Prose Life* (1677). Recalling an earlier episode in which he was challenged about the nature of sensation, he remarks: "From that time, [I] devoted [myself] to determining the nature of the senses, disputing whether corporeal body and all its parts were inert, or in a state of continuous movement, and (in consequence) totally sensate."[18] The passage is ambiguous but suggests that sensation is an intrinsic property of motion. But again, if the sensation is lost because of a lack of memory, it can have no functional value.

The last great philosophical figure born in the sixteenth century was René Descartes (b. 1596). His ontological dualism of mind and body, arising from his technique of methodical doubt, set the emerging scientific, mechanistic worldview on a track that it would follow for the next 400 years and beyond. The Cartesian system was rationalist to the core and pragmatic in intent. The non-human world was utterly aspiritual, without mind and without reason. Humanity was radically different from the other objects of the material universe, and stood alone in an isolated sphere, privileged in the eyes of God. Nothing close to panpsychism was conceivable in such a world.

Henry More (1614–1687) is perhaps the best-known of the "Cambridge Platonists," a group that included Ralph Cudworth. A theist and an idealist, More came of age just as Cartesianism and the scientific philosophy began to implicitly threaten the philosophical standing of Christian theology. He was concerned that Descartes' dualism implied a mechanistic universe that could operate without any intervention from God. At the same time, the pantheistic philosophy of Spinoza arose—a radical monism in which a non-Christian, non-personal God was immediately present everywhere. Neither of these options was acceptable to More.

More's response was to suppose the existence of an intermediary force, the "Spirit of Nature," that animated all matter on behalf of God.[19] Matter in itself was inert, but the universal presence of the Spirit of Nature—which More described as "the vicarious Power of God upon Matter"—endowed all things with an internal animating principle. "The primordials of the world are not mechanical but spermatical or vital ... , which some moderns call the Spirit of Nature." Following Aristotle, this Spirit was seen to give form to all material things. It relieved God from the burden of continuous intervention and it saved the cosmos from an atheistic mechanism. It had numerous powers, including "self-penetration, self-motion, self-contraction and

18. Gaskin 1994: 253.

19. Compare this with Cudworth's notion of the "plastic nature."

-dilation, and indivisibility,"[20] but the power of thought or reason was not among them.

Hence, More's position qualifies as a quasi-panpsychism. It is interesting and relevant because it served as a direct spiritual response to the emerging materialist worldview and because More relied on theological arguments to support his view of spirit in matter, in a way comparable to Campanella. It also reflected the continuing influence of Plato and the concept of the world-soul.

Ultimately, More's theory failed, largely because it attempted to defeat science on its own terms. As Greene says (1962: 461), "it becomes increasingly obvious that More's attribution of function to the Spirit of Nature is highly arbitrary, and that it is a catch-all for the inexplicable." Robert Boyle, famous for his attacks on the Cambridge school's fuzzy metaphysical notions, complained that

[such agents] as the soul of the world, the universal spirit, the plastic power ... tell us nothing that will satisfy the curiosity of an inquisitive person, who seeks to know ... by what means, and after what manner, the phaenomenon is produced. (1674, in Bonifazi 1978: 68)

Finally, two of More's contemporaries merit brief discussion. One of them is the physician Francis Glisson (1599–1677). Though most of his work was on medicine and human physiology, Glisson wrote a significant philosophical monograph, *Treatise on the Energetic Nature of Substance*, in 1672. Henry (1987: 16) calls it "one of the most original systems of philosophy" of the time and "one of the most profound attempts to develop a monistic solution to the mind-body problem." And for present purposes, it makes the case for a strongly panpsychist ontology.

Glisson developed a theory of matter as composed of atom-like particles called *minima naturalia*. When coming together to form large-scale objects, these *minima* "communicate with each other" in a deliberate and conative manner; they "strive to adhere to each other due to a certain intrinsic property." Employing explicitly panpsychist language, Glisson writes:

The particles, by perceiving the utility through which they enjoy their communion amongst themselves, love and desire this communion, and consequently they strive to maintain it—that is, they strive to adhere to each other in such a way that internal cohesion itself is nothing other than a movement or striving resulting from

20. More (1668), in Bonifazi 1978 (pp. 59, 64).

continuity, through which nature strives to conserve itself. Therefore, by means of natural perception and appetite, the cohesion is firstly based on continuity. (in Giglioni 2002: 250–252)

The various parts of objects thus seek to retain their connection and whole-ness: "Here again we see nature perceiving the usefulness of its own parts, and loving them and striving (*conatur*) to defend them with all its strength." As Giglioni sees it, this is a more modern and sophisticated form of panpsy-chism; for Glisson,

Substance is alive because it is capable of perceiving ... . Therefore, if substance is essentially activity, activity is essentially perception, but *natural* perception ... . Natural perception ... founds the life of nature (*vita naturae*) without falling back again into the traditional aporias of animism and anthropocentrism. (2002: 254)

There is no divine Spirit of Nature at work here; matter is intrinsically perceptive and aware. God plays no role at all. It is a fundamentally natu-ralistic panpsychism.

The other person of note for purposes of the present discussion is Marga-ret Cavendish, Duchess of Newcastle (1623–1673). A poet and playwright, Cavendish also produced three major works on natural philosophy: *Philo-sophical Letters*, *Observations upon Experimental Philosophy*, and *Grounds of Natural Philosophy*. She advocated a form of materialism in which the cos-mos was an organic whole composed of organic and animate parts. Her organicist materialism was offered in response to purely mechanistic mate-rialism of the sort that Hobbes and Descartes had articulated.

Cavendish followed the thinking of the Stoics and the Renaissance natu-ralists in arguing that all of nature was alive and intelligent: "there is life and knowledge in all parts of nature, ... and this life and knowledge is sense and reason" (Letter 30, 1664/1994: 26). She distinguished between two types of matter, the animate and the inanimate, which were mixed together in all material objects: "my opinion is, that all matter is partly ani-mate, and partly inanimate, ... and that there is no part of nature that hath not life and knowledge, for there is no part that has not a commixture of animate and inanimate matter" (25). Such properties were to be extended to the smallest portions of matter. As Perry recounts (1968: 185–186), Cav-endish "felt that the world could not be made of atoms unless each one had life and knowledge."

Animate matter was distinct from the inanimate in its capability for self-motion. It moved itself, and by physical connection it in turn moved the inanimate matter: "the animate moves of itself, and the inanimate moves by the help of the animate" (Letter 30: 26). Thus the motion of all physical objects was to be explained by reference to their animate portion. The intelligence in both forms of matter was realized as a kind of knowledge, initially in terms of self-knowledge and, ultimately, as a knowledge of God:

All parts of Nature, even the inanimate, have an innate and fixt self-knowledge, [and] it is probable that they may also have an interior self-knowledge of the existency of the Eternal and Omnipotent God, as the Author of Nature. (1655/1991: 8)

Cavendish's metaphysical system was more poetic than analytic, but she established new standards for intellectual women of the seventeenth century. Her depiction of a compassionate and animate world provided inspiration to later feminist philosophers[21] and complemented the work of her male contemporaries.[22]

3.6 Spinoza

Baruch Spinoza (1632–1677) sought a holistic interpretation of the cosmos. He created a unified ontology in which all phenomena, including the mental and the physical, are bound together in a single comprehensive picture. In this sense he reflected the inclinations of the Renaissance naturalists Cardano and Bruno. However, he lived in an era of new rationalism, led by Descartes—who was 36 years his senior—and in an era of emerging scientific materialist philosophy, led by Bacon, Galileo, and Hobbes. In addition, the religious theology of the day still held considerable influence and affected the thinking and writing of many intellectuals. Spinoza's approach to unity took on aspects of all these influences; in *Ethics* (1677),[23] he built a logical, even mathematical case for the unity of God and nature, and of mind and matter—a case that incorporated the concept of the universal law.

21. See, for example, Merchant's *Death of Nature* (1979: 270–272).

22. On other, relatively obscure panpsychists of the time, including John Comenius and Jan Marek Marci, see Giglioni 1995.

23. Unless otherwise noted, the following citations refer to that work as published in Spinoza 1677/1994.

Spinoza's approach in *Ethics* was "geometrical" in the sense that it relied on a system of arguments patterned after mathematical formalism. Such a methodology was novel in philosophy, largely owing to the influence of Cartesian thinking.[24] But beyond pure methodology, Spinoza believed that mathematics could lead to true insight into the nature of reality. Mathematical formalism, he believed, reflected ontological formalism.

In his view, all of reality consists of a single substance, called "God" or "Nature" depending on the context and circumstances. Resurrecting the ancient pantheism of Plato and the Stoics, Spinoza saw God as the sum total of physical reality, the universe and everything in it constituting the substance of God. God was not a transcendent being, not a personal being, not a moral being, but simply the totality of existence.

This radical monism has to account for the apparent plurality of things in the world, and especially for the classes of things that we commonly call mental and physical. Spinoza proposes that the one substance, God/Nature, possesses infinitely many attributes. As limited beings, humans can perceive only the two primary attributes—those that he labels 'extension' (physical) and 'thought' (mental). Individual physical or mental entities, then, are considered modes or modifications of these attributes. A particular physical thing, such as an apple, is a "mode of extension," and any specific mental event, such as a feeling of pain, is a "mode of thought." The one substance God/Nature reveals itself to us through these two aspects. Hence Spinoza's theory is appropriately described as a dual-aspect monism.

The two knowable attributes of extension and thought are distinct yet intimately related, as is to be expected in view of the underlying monism. They have, in fact, a very specific and fundamental connection: Every physical thing has a corresponding mental aspect, which Spinoza calls an "idea." Conversely, every mental idea has a corresponding object, or thing. This is his unique brand of unity, known as psycho-physical parallelism: To every physical thing or event there corresponds an idea of that thing or event.[25]

24. The general structure of *Ethics*, though, was closely anticipated some 1,200 years earlier by Proclus; see his *Elements of Theology*.

25. For a good discussion of this system and its implications, see Bennett 1984: 125–143.

As the chain of physical events progresses in the world, there exists a parallel chain of mental events. These two chains of events track each other identically, one to one, and run forever in parallel. "The order and connection of ideas is the same as the order and connection of things." (IIP7) Why? Because the thing and the corresponding idea are really *the same thing*—there is only one substance, after all:

[T]he thinking substance and the extended substance are one and the same substance, which is now comprehended under this attribute, now under that. So also a mode of extension [i.e. a particular thing] and the *idea* of that mode are one and the same thing, but expressed in two ways. (IIP7S)

It is incorrect to say that the chain of physical events causes the chain of ideas, or that the ideas cause changes in the physical events. There in fact is no causal connection between the two series at all. Causality is not even possible, because they are only two aspects of a single substance. There is no interaction, and hence no Cartesian interaction problem. This is a virtue of any monistic system.

Consider the special case of the human body. It is a particular physical thing, and thus a mode of extension. Corresponding to this mode, as to all modes, is an idea. The idea of the human body is not just some arbitrary mental entity; it is in fact *the mind* of that person: "The [physical] object of the idea constituting the human mind is the [human] body, or a certain mode of extension which actually exists, and nothing else." (IIP13) Mind is the *idea* of body, and body is the *object* of mind.

Since the two aspects have no causal relationship, mind cannot affect body and body cannot affect mind. This is clearly stated in IIIP2: "The body cannot determine the mind to thinking, and the mind cannot determine the body to motion, to rest, or to anything else." Yet for every body there is an associated mind. As the body changes, the mind changes in a corresponding way. They change together without causal interaction: "the mind and the body, are one and the same individual, which is conceived now under the attribute of thought, now under the attribute of extension" (IIP21S). So we see in Spinoza a metaphysical system in which we have a new way of comprehending the two realms of physical and mental. Each physical thing has an idea associated with it; conversely, every idea has a corresponding physical thing.

It is natural to think in terms of human beings, but Spinoza tells us that his method is "completely general." His use of 'body', in fact, refers not just to a human body but to any physical object whatsoever. Hence the idea of any physical thing at all is in reality the mind of that thing. Every mode of extension has its corresponding mode of thought—or, in the simplest terms, every thing has a corresponding mind. Thus we arrive at Spinoza's panpsychism. This is spelled out explicitly in the Scholium of proposition 13 in part II:

> From these [propositions] we understand not only that the human mind is united to the body, but also what should be understood by the union of mind and body … . For the things we have shown so far are completely general and do not pertain more to man than to other individuals, all of which, though in different degrees, are nevertheless animate.

He then goes on to explain what he means by "different degrees":

> I say this in general, that in proportion as a body is more capable than others of doing many things at once, or being acted on in many ways at once, so its mind is more capable than others of perceiving many things at once.

Spinoza's argument for panpsychism is often seen to rest solely on the Scholium of proposition 13, but this is not the case. There are at least three other claims for it. First, it is a logical consequence of propositions 3 and 11. Proposition 3 states that "in God there is necessarily an idea … of everything which necessarily follows from his essence," i.e., all extant things. Hence all real things have ideas. Proposition 11 tells us that these ideas are minds. It does so not in general but by reference to the specific case of the human mind. Our mind is "nothing but the idea of a singular thing which actually exists," i.e., some extant thing. (Proposition 13 informs us that this thing is nothing other than our body.) But it doesn't matter what the particular singular thing is; what is relevant is that mind is the idea of some real thing. If minds are ideas, and all real things have ideas, then all real things have minds.

Further evidence can be found in proposition 1 of part III ("On the Affects"), where we find not so much an argument as a simple recognition that other things beside humans possess minds. Spinoza elaborates on the fact that humans have both "adequate" and "inadequate" ideas in their minds, and that either kind of idea is, however, adequate in God/ Nature because "he also contains in himself, at the same time, the minds of other things." Clearly the "other things" are non-human objects, and without reason to limit them, one must conclude that this covers all extant things.

Finally there is Spinoza's doctrine of conatus, or striving. Part III observes that all things display a kind of effort or power toward maintaining existence—much along the line of Campanella's *potentia essendi*. Like Campanella, Spinoza saw this striving as evidence of a vital or animate energy in things. The definitive passage is proposition 6: "Each thing, as far as it can by its own power, strives to persevere in its being." Proposition 7 adds that this striving "is nothing but the actual essence of the thing." And proposition 8 says that it is not merely occasional or sporadic but exists for "an indefinite time"; thus, striving is an eternal and essential aspect of any existing thing. In an earlier work—*Descartes' "Principles of Philosophy"*—Spinoza defined life as "the force through which things persevere in their being." Assuming that he maintained such a view through the *Ethics*, one can read the conatus doctrine as a form of hylozoism. This again would be consistent with a generally panpsychic outlook.

One further passage from Spinoza is worth mentioning here, though its status as a basis for panpsychism is unclear. In his 1674 letter to G. H. Schuller (letter 58), he elaborates on his theory of free will and determinism. By way of example, he cites the case of a stone that is "set in motion" through the air, as when thrown by someone. A stone set in motion is not unlike, say, a human set in motion; each moves through the world, reacting to various impulses and forces. Spinoza writes:

> Next, conceive now, if you will that while the stone continues to move, it thinks, and knows that as far as it can, it strives to continue to move. Of course since the stone is conscious only of its striving, and not at all indifferent, it will believe itself to be free, and to persevere in motion for no other cause than because it wills to. And this is that famous human freedom which everyone brags of having … . (1674/1994: 267–268)

It is not clear whether he means to say that the stone *does* think and *is* conscious or whether this is merely a hypothetical example. His point here, of course, is to refute the notion of free will, not to examine the mind of a stone. But it is a suggestive passage nonetheless.[26]

In view of the controversial status of panpsychism, it is perhaps unsurprising that many scholars have denied that Spinoza's view is panpsychist. This is particularly true of commentaries published in the early and the middle years of the twentieth century. Of the early commentators, Joachim

---

26. Schopenhauer found some significance in this letter for his own panpsychist thinking. See Schopenhauer 1819/1995: 58 or Schopenhauer 1819/1969: 126.

(1901) is the most neutral. But we find clearly hostile readings in Wolfson 1937 (ideas are really just "forms," not minds), in Fuller 1945 ("ideas can scarcely be regarded as individual psychical entities, like souls or minds"), in Hampshire 1951 ("only humans have minds"), in Parkinson 1953 (that all things are animate is merely an inconsequential "curiosity"), and in Curley 1969 (ideas are just "true propositions"). Interestingly, though, later commentaries display a clear trend toward greater sympathy for the panpsychist interpretation. Pro-panpsychism readings are found in Harris 1973, in Bennett 1984, in Delahunty 1985, in Allison 1987, and in Curley 1988. Even Hampshire (2002) seems to have turned toward a more sympathetic interpretation.[27] Curley (1988: 64) seems to go so far as to argue for a kind of super-panpsychism in Spinoza, in which not only do extended, physical things have minds, but so too do modes of all the other unknowable attributes. Few Spinoza scholars seem to acknowledge this large-scale shift toward a panpsychist interpretation.

3.7   Locke and Newton

John Locke and Isaac Newton played central roles in advancing the materialist and mechanistic worldview, but both appear to have had lingering doubts about the relationship between matter and spirit. Apparently neither seemed completely confident that pure materialism could account for the phenomena of the natural world. Both seemed to be open to the possibility that matter might possess an intrinsic mental aspect.

Locke (1632–1704) is perhaps best known for his empiricism—especially as expounded in the *Essay Concerning Human Understanding* (1689), in which he lays out his views on morality, knowledge, and humans' abilities to comprehend the world. The final book of the *Essay* contains a controversial passage on the relationship between mind and matter. Locke inquires into the question of how the human body, as a material object, is able to think. A point of interest to him is whether the material body has some kind of innate ability to think or whether divine intervention is necessary.

27. Donagan (1989) is perhaps the only dissenter from this trend, but his dissent is mild and ultimately he yields to a grudging acceptance: Panpsychism is a "doctrine to which [Spinoza] is committed." (129) But "[the mind of] a grain of sand … will not be cognition, and will be barely distinguishable from inanimateness" (130).

Locke seems to have recognized the possibility that former position could lead to a version of panpsychism, and to have attempted to clarify the issue. In section 6 of chapter III of book IV ("The Extent of Human Knowledge") he writes:

> We have the ideas of *matter* and *thinking*, but possibly shall never be able to know whether any mere material being thinks or no; it being impossible for us ... to discover whether Omnipotency has not given to some systems of matter, fitly disposed, a power to perceive and think, or else joined and fixed to matter ... a thinking immaterial substance. ... We know not wherein thinking consists, nor to what sort of substances the Almighty has been pleased to give that power. ... For I see no contradiction in [that God] should, if he pleased, give to certain systems of created senseless matter ... some degrees of sense, perception, and thought. ... [No one can] have the confidence to conclude [that God] cannot give perception and thought to a substance which has the modification of solidity.

On the surface, this passage can be seen as an argument for the omnipotence of God: God can do anything at all and therefore can certainly grant the power of thought to mere matter, any matter. Locke doesn't want to be seen limiting the power of God.

There is no obvious endorsement of panpsychism here. Locke makes no clear statement that "matter thinks," or that "anything besides humans think." On the other hand, he speaks of "matter," and not, say, the "human body." He sees "no contradiction" in the possibility that "certain systems of matter," presumably including non-human ones, may have "some degrees of sense, perception, and thought."

Locke is clear that matter has no *inherent* ability to think: Elsewhere in the same chapter, he claims that matter "is evidently in its own nature void of sense and thought," and thus thinking, wherever it may occur, must come from God, who after all can place it anywhere he likes. So who is to say that God has not given other material objects, or even *all* objects, some degree of thought?

Locke seems to avoid committing himself to a position. Near the end of section 6 he claims agnosticism, stating that the issue of understanding how any material object can think is "a point which seems to be put out of reach of our knowledge" and that "we must content ourselves in the ignorance of what kind of being [the "thinking substance" in us] is ... . [For after all], what substance exists, that has not something in it which manifestly baffles our understandings." As a classical empiricist, Locke recognizes the impossibility of investigating the internal perceptions of the non-human mind. This is perhaps an indication that rationalist approaches are the more promising.

Newton (1642–1727) was not only a great scientist but also a philosopher of science. His *Principia* (1687) described the laws of gravity and the basic equations of force and motion. But he was concerned not only how to describe the actions of nature in terms of universal laws but also how to grasp the underlying meaning. He sought explanations as much as descriptions.

In the so-called Newtonian worldview, inert material objects move about under mechanistic forces in a clockwork fashion. Such a universe is commonly understood to be non-spiritual, if not outright atheistic in its physical dimension. However true this may be of modern depictions, it was certainly not the view of Newton, as he was a profoundly religious and spiritual man. His belief that God was immanent in the universe and actively involved in its state of affairs is one of the few consistent threads in his philosophy.

Furthermore, Newton had serious doubts about viewing matter as dead and inert. In fact, he seems to have had a strong inclination to view all matter as living, and even as possessing mind-like qualities. McRae (1981) conducted a brief but interesting study along this line, based largely on a detailed investigation by McGuire (1968) of Newton's post-*Principia* writings. McRae states very directly that "Newton had no objection to hylozoism [and] indeed, appears to have been powerfully attracted to [it]" (191). The basis for this can be found in a draft variant of Query 22 in the 1706 work *Optice*:

For Bodies ... are passive ... . They cannot move themselves; and without some other principle than the *vis inertiae* [inertial force] there could be no motion in the world ... . And if there be another Principle of motion there must be other laws of motion depending on that Principle ... . We find in ourselves a power of moving our bodies by our thoughts ... and see [the] same power in other living creatures but how this is done and by what laws we do not know ... . It appears that there are other laws of motion ... [and this is] enough to justify and encourage our search after them. We cannot say that all nature is not alive. (in McGuire 1968: 170–171)

The final sentence is fairly astonishing, especially in view of Newton's traditional mechanistic image.

Other passages confirm this hylozoist inclination. As early as the *Principia* Newton acknowledges the existence of two states of force (later, two principles): passive (or "resistance") and active (or "impulse"). This apparent connection with Stoic philosophy is no coincidence; he had studied ancient philosophy and was undoubtedly influenced by Stoicism.[28] Definition III of book I of the *Principia* discusses the *vis inertiae*, or inertial force of a static body. When experiencing an external force, he writes, the *vis inertiae* exerts itself in two ways:

as both resistance [passive] and impulse [active]; it is resistance so far as the body ... opposes the force impressed; it is impulse so far as the body, by not easily giving way to the impressed force ... , endeavors to change the state of that other.

The *vis inertiae* actively exerts an effort; it acts back on the force, and attempts to change it. There is an implied notion of will or agency here.

Stoicism associated life, mind, and soul with the active principle. Newton seems to have done likewise. In the *Optice*, in draft Query 23, he challenges the notion that nature has only a passive inert principle:

[T]o affirm that there are no other [laws beside "passive"] is to speak against experience. For we find in ourselves a power of moving our bodies by our thought. Life and Will (thinking) are active Principles by which we move our bodies, and thence arise other laws of motion unknown to us.

[I]f there be an universal life, and all space be the sensorium of a immaterial living, thinking, being, ... [then] the laws of motion arising from life or will may be of universal extent. (in McGuire 1968: 171, 205)

For Newton it was not only the *vis inertiae* that animated matter. Some time after 1706, he hit upon the idea that electricity might be the main force acting at small distances. Further, he felt that in this might lie a new universal principle, which McGuire describes as "an electrical *arche* connecting mind with matter" (176). Newton made this clear in Quest 25:

Do not all bodies therefore abound with a very subtile, active, potent, electric spirit by which light is emitted, refracted, and reflected [by which] the small particles of bodies cohere when contiguous ... and regulate almost all their motions amongst themselves. For electric [force] uniting the thinking soul and unthinking body.

28. See the note on p. 204 of McGuire 1968. Also see the passage, quoted on page 196 of the same work, in which Newton directly observes that "the Stoics taught that a certain infinite spirit pervades all space ... and vivifies the entire world."

As McGuire notes (177), "Newton was speculating on the possibility of uniting under one principle, life and nature, vitality and matter"—hardly what one would expect from the West's greatest mechanistic scientist.[29]

3.8 Leibniz

The panpsychism of Gottfried Leibniz (1646–1716) was rooted in his conception of the monad. Yet even before his development of that concept he found reason to see all things as animate. Some of Leibniz's earliest philosophical writings date from the mid 1680s, when he was about 40 years old. In *Primary Truths* he asserted, with emphasis, that "*every particle of the universe contains a world of an infinity of creatures*" (1686a/1989: 34). The same year, in a letter to Arnauld, he defined soul as "substantial form" and attributed it to all things with a "thoroughly indivisible" unity: "I assign substantial forms to all corporeal substances that are more than mechanically united." (1686b/1989: 80) The extent of such objects is presumed to be widespread but is left unspecified.

Leibniz seems to have had at least two reasons for thinking this way. The first was Leeuwenhoek's recent (ca. 1660) invention of the microscope and his discovery of "animalcules" in apparently clear drops of water. This was dramatic empirical evidence that hitherto unseen forms of life resided in unsuspected places. A plethora of life implied a plethora of souls. Leibniz admitted as much in a 1687 letter to Arnauld: "[E]xperience favors this multitude of animated things. We find that there is a prodigious quantity of animals in a drop of water." (1989: 88) Second, Leibniz found theological reasons for this belief. An ensouled universe was more nearly perfect than one in which only mankind possessed soul, and thus was more in line with the perfection of God. It is, he wrote, "in conformity with the greatness and beauty of the works of God for him to produce as many [true] substances as there can be in this universe" (1687/1989: 87). It is "a perfection of nature to have many [souls]."

Leibniz did not make detailed reference to the notion of the monad until 1698, and did not develop the monad theory fully before *Principles of Nature and Grace* (1714a) and *Monadology* (1714b). However, even his

29. For a further discussion of these ideas relative to Aristotle's views, see McGuire 1994.

writings leading up to the concept of the monad indicate that he associated the soul or substantial form with an atomic or point-like entity. As early as 1671, at age 25, he wrote that "the soul, strictly speaking, is only at a point in space" (in Hoeffding 1908: 335). In 1695 he wrote of "true unities" underlying reality:

[I]n order to find these *real unities*, I was forced to have recourse to a *real and animated point*, so to speak, or to an atom of substance which must include something of form or activity to make a complete being. (1695: 139)

Here again we see the association of animation with a point-like entity. Leibniz continues:

I found that [the atoms'] nature consists in force, and that from this there follows something analogous to sensation [i.e. perception] and appetite, so that we must conceive of them on the model of the notion we have of *souls*.

Like Bruno's, Leibniz's monad was a point-like, atom-like entity that constituted all extant things. The monad was the true substance of the world, and all other things were simply collections or aggregates of these monadic substances: "These monads are the true atoms of nature, and, in brief, the elements of things." (1714b, section 3) Monads, he writes, have the rather paradoxical quality of being at once absolutely simple and "without parts" and yet being absolutely unique. In fact every monad is a kind of focal point for its own perspective on the universe, and is internally as complex and ordered as the entire cosmos:

[T]here must be a plurality of properties and relations in the simple substance [i.e. monad], even though it has no parts. (1714b, section 13)

[E]ach monad is a living mirror ... which represents the universe from its own point of view, and is as ordered as the universe itself. (1714a, section 3)

And these simple yet complex monads have other relevant characteristics. First, they are "windowless"—they have no direct interaction with the outside world or with each other, and they are exempt from physical causality. Second, and more to the point, monads have two primary capabilities: perception and appetite. Perceptions are the states that monads pass through as they continually reflect their ever-changing perspective on the universe. The appetite, or desire, "brings about the change or passage from one perception to another" (section 15). The importance of these two qualities cannot be overestimated. All mind, Leibniz says, even the simplest, possesses at least the subjective property of perception—feeling—and the intentional property of will or appetite. This aligns well with much of present-day philosophy of mind, which holds that the mind seems to have two irreducible components, namely the qualitative and the intentional.

Monads thus serve as the theoretical basis for Leibniz's panpsychism. Consider this passage:

> I believe that ... it is consistent neither with the order nor with the beauty or the reason of things that there should be something vital or immanently active only in a small part of matter, when it would imply greater perfection if it were in all. And even if ... intelligent souls ... cannot be everywhere, this is no objection to the view that there should everywhere be souls, or at least things analogous to souls. (1698/1956: 820; section 12)

In *Monadology* (section 66) he reiterates this view: "we see that there is a world of creatures, of living beings, of animals, of entelechies, of souls in the least part of matter." Clearly panpsychism was a consistent and essential aspect of Leibniz's metaphysics.

Leibniz faced three perplexing and related questions: How can point-like entities combine to form apparently solid objects? How can a theory of monads account for the high-level soul or mind that is found in humans? Why do certain collections of monads (e.g., humans) possess high-level unified minds whereas others (e.g., rocks) do not?

The answers to these questions center on two concepts: that of the aggregate and that of the dominant monad. Throughout his philosophical career, Leibniz emphasized the distinction between mere collections or aggregates of monads and collections with a real and substantial sense of wholeness and unity. Aggregates include objects or systems that are loosely organized, such as a "heap of stones," an "army," a "herd," or a "flock." They furthermore include objects that are apparently solid and whole—rocks, tables, houses, shoes, and so on. In his theory of aggregates, Leibniz followed Democritus in asserting that aggregates only *appear* to be whole and unified.[30] Their unity is only in our minds, not in reality. This is clear in the cases of flocks and herds, less so in the case of a solid rock. Yet Leibniz saw them as on a continuum and as distinct from other objects—humans, other animals, plants, monads—that were truly integrated beings. Integrated

30. Democritus wrote "By convention (*nomos*) sweet and by convention bitter, by convention hot, by convention cold, by convention color: in reality, atoms and void." (in Barnes 1987: 252–253)

objects possess a "substantial unity" that demands "a thoroughly indivisible and naturally indestructible being" (1686b/1989: 79). But this issue is metaphysically controversial.

The substantial unity of true individuals is realized physically by the dominant monad. Of the countless monads making up a person's body, one monad somehow comes to dominate the others and to draw them together into cohesiveness.[31] This dominant monad, or "primary entelechy," is the soul of the person. The human body, in itself, is considered a mere aggregate; but together with the dominant monad or soul it constitutes a "living being":

[The dominant monad] makes up the center of a composite substance (an animal, for example) and is the principle of its unity, is surrounded by a *mass* composed of an infinity of other monads, which constitute the *body belonging to* this central monad. (1714a, section 3)

This again is the case for humans, animals, plants, and the microscopic animalcules in the droplets of water. Such things are in fact doubly ensouled: They consist of animate sub-monads and they possess a single unifying soul in the dominant monad. Aggregates, by contrast, are not animate in themselves, but of course are still composed of the soul-like monads. Therefore even aggregates are animate in a restricted sense. This is more or less identical to Bruno's view, but Bruno offered no theory as to why it should be the case. Leibniz at least proposed the outline of a theory, even though he left many questions unanswered—including how and why one monad comes to dominate and why this happens only in certain collections of monads.

These open questions point to an incompleteness in Leibniz's theory. He was never clear, for example, on whether large-scale objects or systems, such as the Earth, were to be considered "substantial unities." Only once, in an early letter to Arnauld, did he address this directly:

[I]f I am asked in particular what I say about the sun, the earthly globe, the moon, trees, and other similar bodies. ... I cannot be absolutely certain whether they are animated, or even whether they are substances. (1686b/1989: 80)

Leibniz later accepted plants as animated beings, but the general status of large-scale systems remained open for him throughout his life.

31. This role of the dominant monad is strongly reminiscent of the Stoic *hegemonikon*, discussed earlier in the present volume.

Two other points indicate Leibniz's uncertainty about the status of aggregates. First, his final two major philosophical essays—*Principles of Nature and Grace* and *Monadology*—rarely mention the subject. *Principles* doesn't discuss it, focusing instead on living beings and their dominant soul monad. *Monadology* actually reverses Leibniz's usual terminology; he divides reality into "simple substances" (monads) and "composite substances," wherein the composite "is nothing more than a collection, or *aggregate*, of simples" (section 2). Apparently, then, all living beings are to be considered aggregates. But the remainder of *Monadology* contains no further discussion of the soulless aggregates. That these two essays constitute a summary of Leibniz's metaphysical system is all the more significant.

Second, there is Leibniz's late (ca. 1712) introduction of the *vinculum substantiale* (substantial chain) as a kind of glue that bonds together the monads of a living being. He consistently affirmed that ordinary material objects, such as rocks, are mere phenomena and only appear to be unified beings. But this also holds for the body of an animal, which, apart from its dominant soul or mind monad, is also a mere aggregate. Concerned to differentiate the two, and knowing that "points can never form a continuum," he introduced a substantial chain to link together all monads of true living beings. This chain is both "real" and "substantial," and it is to be "added to the monads in order to make the phenomena real" (1716/1989: 203). In retrospect the whole concept of the *vinculum substantiale* seems an *ad hoc* construction to account for the differing properties of aggregates. It is in fact a whole new ontological category, distinct from the monads themselves. We are given no explanation of how this chain comes to exist, or of why it is present only in select aggregates and not in others.[32]

A final point of note concerns the influence on Leibniz of the earlier panpsychists. Bruno clearly impressed him, and Leibniz's use of the monad concept may well have been inspired, if only indirectly, by Bruno's work. Consider the passage in section 66 of *Monadology* cited above: "we see that there is a world of creatures, of living beings, of animals, of entelechies, of souls in the least part of matter." This seems to recall an earlier passage in which Bruno asserted that "there is not the least corpuscle that does not contain within itself some portion that may animate it." And there were surely other Renaissance influences. We know for certain that Leibniz had

---

32. For an extended discussion of the problem of aggregates, see Skrbina 2008.

read Campanella and thus was aware of Italian naturalism. He even seems to have picked up a central element of Campanella's ontology: *Monadology* contains a virtual word-for-word reiteration of Campanella's doctrine of the three primalities of power, wisdom, and love or will:

God has *power*, which is the source of everything, *knowledge*, which contains the diversity of ideas, and finally *will*, which brings about changes ... in accordance with the principle of the best. (section 48)

Just before he introduced the term 'monad' in the late 1690s, Leibniz corresponded with the philosopher Francis van Helmont and was "considerably influenced" by him.[33] Helmont was a close associate of the British philosopher Anne Conway, who in turn was a colleague of Henry More. More cited the term 'monad' in his Cabbalistic axioms.[34] It is entirely plausible that either Conway or More (or both) picked up Bruno's concept of the monad and incorporated it into their own writing. Thus, it may have been by way of More, Conway, and Helmont that Bruno's influence was felt. In the end, Leibniz seems to have adopted many ideas of the Italian naturalists, elaborating and articulating them in his own terminology.

33. See note on p. 227 of Leibniz 1989.

34. See Brown 1990.

4 Continental Panpsychism of the Eighteenth Century

Mechanistic philosophy made substantial progress in eighteenth-century Europe, gradually displacing theism as the dominant worldview. Scientific advances were seen as validating the presumption of a mechanistic cosmos. Judeo-Christian theology was superseded, first in intellectual circles and then later in society at large; its explanatory power faded, and its theistic imperatives grew impotent.

The ascendancy of mechanism was opposed both by theists (on the ground that the cosmos was not without Spirit) and by those who argued for a panpsychist, animated worldview (on the ground that matter was not lifeless and inert). Panpsychism in various forms emerged as a significant challenger to mechanism, at least within the bounds of rationalist philosophy. As it happens, most of the important developments of the century occurred on the Continent, primarily in France and Germany. Notable philosophers, including LaMettrie, Diderot, Herder, Goethe, Maupertuis, and Priestley, argued for a panpsychist view. Even Kant had some interesting observations on the matter.

4.1 French Vitalistic Materialism

From the late 1600s on, the leading metaphor for nature was that of the machine. Descartes inaugurated this tradition, and Leibniz extended the usage by speaking about living beings as machines. Leibniz couched it in pleasant enough terms, calling living creatures "divine machines" and emphasizing that natural machines were qualitatively different from man-made versions. Further, these divine machines were at root spiritual; mind and soul resided in the monad atoms that composed them. Living beings were more or less automatons whose actions flowed from the nature of monads and from the universal laws of nature. Shortly thereafter, other thinkers took the next logical step and began to ask whether the soul hypothesis was really necessary at all.

Among the most notorious of these philosophers was Julien LaMettrie (1709–1751). Author of the provocative and scandalous *L'Homme Machine*, LaMettrie was the first thinker to unabashedly—though anonymously—claim that man was purely a natural automaton and did not require an immaterial soul to account for his behavior. He had been trained as a physician, and his study of human anatomy, along with the scientific theories of the day, seemed to support such a view.

LaMettrie's brand of materialism ran against the grain of the time. Pure materialism had been out of favor for nearly 1,500 years, particularly since the rise of the Christian worldview. Virtually all philosophers and natural scientists after the Stoics had claimed that there was some non-material, incorporeal aspect to reality. Hobbes broke with this tradition in the middle of the seventeenth century and met with severe condemnation. Descartes unintentionally set the stage for LaMettrie when he removed the spirit from nearly all aspects of the physical world, save the human. To Descartes, animals were unfeeling natural automata, in a different class of existence than humans. And as science came to explain more about physical reality, the need for an active incorporeal realm lessened. Also, there was increasingly less reason, from a physiological standpoint, to distinguish between humans and other animals. By the early 1700s, LaMettrie could speculate that either the soul did not exist or, if it did, it was essentially identical with the workings of the human body. In openly denying the immaterial soul, he carried scientific philosophy to its logical limit.[1]

LaMettrie is also widely pronounced a mechanist; however, that characterization is not correct, and the distinction is quite important. The mechanistic view sees matter as fundamentally lifeless and inert. If one believes that motion and mind somehow arise purely through physical interaction

---

1. LaMettrie was not an outright atheist. Rather, he held more to an agnostic view. On his view, one could certainly continue to believe in God, but it was strictly a matter of faith. God had no role to play in the material world, and certainly no explanatory power over natural phenomena. Nonetheless, atheism was his preferred position, and he asserted that "the world will never be happy until it is atheist." (1747: 58)

of inert and lifeless atoms, then one is a mechanistic materialist. That approach follows directly from a Cartesian view of matter—pure extension, completely dead. To account for the human mind or soul, a mechanistic philosopher must resort to brute emergentism, supernatural dualism, epiphenomenalism, or eliminativism. Those were not viable options for LaMettrie. To him, mind was a very real entity, and clearly it was embedded in a material cosmos. An obvious solution, therefore, was to see matter itself as inherently dynamic, capable of feeling, even intelligent. Motion and mind derive from some inherent powers of life or sentience that dwell in matter itself or in the organizational properties of matter. That view, sometimes called vitalistic materialism, is the one that LaMettrie—and later Diderot—adopted.[2]

Commentators often portray LaMettrie as a mechanist because it is assumed that anyone who denies the spiritual realm must see all things, and in particular all living things, as products of dead matter. It is quite common, even today, to equate materialism with mechanism. But, as has been noted, the two are logically independent. In fact, LaMettrie's first philosophical work attacked the Cartesian notion of animals as unfeeling machines, calling such a position "a joke" (see below). Though he obviously adopted the term 'machine' in his *L'Homme Machine*, it was in a specifically vitalistic sense.

LaMettrie's writing demonstrates that he had quasi-panpsychist and hylozoist inclinations, which necessarily have no role in a mechanistic materialism. Vitalistic materialism sees some degree of life and mind in all things; it seeks a natural rather than a supernatural explanation. LaMettrie's man-machine was not a machine in the modern sense but rather a natural material object, one capable of self-motion and self-animation. As Vartanian (1960: 19) saw it, LaMettrie's "primary task was to vitalize the Cartesian 'dead mechanism.'" It was science that set the example: "Just as the inexplicable force of attraction [i.e. gravity] was proved empirically to inhere in matter, LaMettrie was encouraged to suppose by analogy that matter might also be capable of consciousness." (67)

2. Vitalistic materialism was anticipated by Cavendish in her theory of organicist materialism of the 1660s—recall the discussion in chapter 3. Both of these forms of panpsychic materialism ultimately draw from the Greek notion of a material cosmos pervaded by the *pneuma*.

LaMettrie's first philosophical work, *L'Histoire Naturelle de L'Ame* (Natural History of the Soul), was published in 1745.[3] It begins with a quasi-Stoic explanation of the soul viewed as the "active principal" of the body rather than as an immaterial substance that somehow interacts with it. Following Descartes, he then accepts that all matter possesses the attribute of spatial extension. Next he claims that matter has an inherent animating force that gives it the power of motion: "it is clear enough that matter contains the motive force which animates it and which is the immediate cause of all the laws of movement" (1745/1996: 49). Later in the work, LaMettrie carries out the full implications of this thought, arguing for a third general attribute of matter: feeling. But he is not entirely clear as to how we are to understand that faculty. At one point he informs us that it is a general property of matter, something that is clearly apparent in living organisms. Elsewhere we read that this faculty is not always manifest: "Here then is yet another faculty [i.e. feeling] which likewise seems to inhere in matter only potentially, like all the others." Furthermore,

We must nevertheless admit frankly that we do not know whether matter has in itself the immediate faculty of feeling or only the power of acquiring it through the modification or forms of which it is susceptible. For it is true that this faculty only appears [to us] in organized bodies. (51)

Feeling becomes apparent to us when matter is sufficiently organized, but it exists latently in all matter. This seems to be the logical conclusion.

At the same time, LaMettrie chastises the Cartesians for positing non-human animals as unfeeling machines—another indication of his anti-mechanistic position:

I am aware of all the efforts vainly made by the Cartesians to take [feeling] away from matter. ... They thought they could extricate themselves with the absurd system "that animals are mere machines." Such a ridiculous opinion has never been accepted by philosophers except as a joke. ... Experience proves that the faculty of feeling exists in animals just as much as it does in men. (50)

Science and physiology prove that there is a "perfect resemblance ... between man and beast," which philosophers ignore at their peril. Thus he places humanity firmly in the natural order and denies any categorical distinction.

LaMettrie doesn't offer a good explanation of how matter can be sentient. In the passage cited above, he admits that it is not known whether

3. This work was amended and republished in 1750 as *Treatise on the Soul*.

feeling is inherent in all matter or is acquired through the forms it takes on. "How," he asks candidly, "can we conceive that matter can feel and think? I admit that I cannot conceive it." (65) Yet it self-evidently does, in ourselves and other animals.

LaMettrie's strongest case for vitalistic materialism appears in *L'Homme Machine* (1747). He begins by criticizing Leibniz's monadology as "unintelligible," arguing that Leibniz went in the wrong direction: "he spiritualized matter rather than materialized the soul" (1747/1994: 27). Later LaMettrie reiterates his view that men are really no different from animals and in fact should be "honored to be ranked among them" (47). And he again defends his thesis that the organizational complexity of the human body accounts for the so-called faculties of the soul:

[T]hese faculties are obviously just this organized brain itself, there is a well-enlightened machine! [Even our conscience is] no more foreign to matter than thought is. ... Is organization therefore sufficient for everything? Yes, once again. (59)

Utilizing a form of the Continuity argument, he argues that it is the matter of the body itself that exhibits feeling: "Since thought obviously develops with the organs, why would the matter of which they are made not be susceptible to [for example] remorse once it has acquired in time the faculty of feeling?"

Near the end of *L'Homme Machine* LaMettrie reiterates his claim that mere matter can think, but he acknowledges once again that there is an epistemological problem here. If matter can think, that implies a thinking subject, albeit one that is inherently unknowable:

On the basis of these [previous] observations and truths, we can attribute the admirable property of thinking to matter even without being able to see the connection between the two, because the subject of that thinking is unknown to us. (75)

This is a modern perspective. The subject—that which does the thinking—is known only to itself. The inner subjective feelings of any material being are forever hidden from public view. Vartanian notes that "the growth of subjective reality from matter in motion remains, in LaMettrie's opinion, a metaphysical riddle lying beyond the competence of psychological [and philosophical] investigation" (1960: 23).

In his effort to unify nature, LaMettrie compared humans not only to animals but also to plants. In 1748, a year after *L'Homme Machine*, he published a short work, *L'Homme Plante*, in which he noted the many similarities in physiology between humans and plants (anticipating Fechner) and disputed the ancient notion (e.g., in Aristotle) of plant-souls; he also explicitly denied the concept of a world-soul. He did make one small adjustment to his organizational complexity thesis, arguing that mind is proportional not merely to complexity but more specifically to "needs," the demands that the organism makes on the environment: "man is neither entirely a plant nor yet an animal like the others. ... Because we have infinitely more needs, it follows necessarily that man must have infinitely more mind." (1748/1994: 90) The implication is that all beings possess mind proportionate to their need to maintain their existence. The mind of a plant, though "infinitely smaller" than that of a human, is not non-existent. Unfortunately, LaMettrie seems not to have pursued this line of thought.

LaMettrie's works, in particular *L'Homme Machine*, caught the attention of the scientist-philosopher Pierre-Louis Maupertuis (1698–1759). In 1751, Maupertuis published a collection of meditations on the philosophy of biology under the title *Systeme de la nature*. In an earlier work, *Venus physique* (1745), he had argued for the view that natural organisms were formed in the womb by particles of matter that were pulled together by a force of attraction, supplemented by a kind of memory that reminded them where to go. His reference to "attraction" derived from Newton's theory of gravitation and the universal attractive force that all matter exhibited.

Newton's use of the word 'attraction' to describe his universal force was controversial. The word has clear animistic overtones, a fact not lost on the scientists and philosophers of the day. It recalls Empedocles' notion of Love as the universal attractive force, not to mention Cardano's "sympathy" of all things and the corresponding panpsychist theories of the world. In the 1680s Fontenelle had warned that granting the power of attraction to matter could lead to further animistic—and therefore digressive—attributions.

In *Systeme de la nature*, Maupertuis did precisely that. He determined that attraction alone, or even attraction with a degree of memory, was not sufficient to construct the complex unity of a living creature. Somehow there had to be a form of intelligence in the matter itself: "it is necessary to have recourse to some principle of intelligence, to some similar thing like that which we call *desire, aversion, memory*" (in Beeson 1992: 209). Thus Maupertuis took the standard conception of the material world as consisting of extended matter, motion, and attraction and supplemented those qualities with intelligence. Beeson writes:

Extension and movement are [for Maupertuis] not sufficient to explain the reproduction of living organisms, and it is therefore necessary to ... abandon some simplicity in fundamental assumptions for the sake of closer agreement with observation. Maupertuis proposes the adoption of four concepts: extension, movement, attraction and intelligence, all viewed as essential properties of matter. (209–210)

Consequently, the smallest units of matter must be associated with some smallest units of intelligence or perception. Maupertuis referred to such units as "percipient particles," a notion that recalls both the soul-atoms of Democritus and the monads of Leibniz. Thus were the physical properties (extension, movement) supplemented with mental properties (intelligence). Here again we see a form of panpsychic dualism—or perhaps dual-aspect panpsychism—argued for on the basis of first principles. And these intelligent qualities are seen to account for the unified form and properties of a living organism (argument by Design).

Denis Diderot (1713–1784) is best known as a co-editor, with Jean Le Rond d'Alembert, of the *Encyclopedie*—a monument to rationalist, secularist, and humanist thought of the French Enlightenment. The central project in all his writing was to dispel supernatural and theistic superstitions and to ground all phenomena in naturalistic explanations. That this could lead to panpsychism is perhaps surprising.

Like LaMettrie and Maupertuis before him, Diderot grappled with a fundamental problem: Given that there is neither a God nor an immaterial soul, one must still account for motion, life, and mind. Each of those three men had a strong intuition toward unity and holism, and all wanted to integrate the human into the natural world. They rejected the purely mechanistic interpretation of a universe of dead matter pushed around by myriad forces, and instead sought solutions in which life and sensitivity were inherent in all things. It is not surprising that, given these conditions and the state of scientific knowledge at the time, they came to similar conclusions.

Rather than formalize things, Diderot prefers to address general themes of a holistic and evolving natural world. Of those themes, the two most relevant here are panpsychism and the unity of the self.

Diderot's panpsychist inclinations first appeared in his *Pensees sur l'interpretation de la nature* (Thoughts on the Interpretation of Nature), published in 1754. In section 50 he offers a sympathetic account of the "intelligent matter" hypothesis of Maupertuis.[4] Diderot elaborates on this new modification of matter, referring to the various noetic qualities as "desire, aversion, memory, and intelligence" (1754/1966: 79). He notes that Maupertuis accepts these qualities "as being present, in due proportion to their forms and masses, in the smallest particle of matter as well as in the very largest animal." Diderot, clearly impressed by that thesis, devotes a rather large section of *Pensees* to it. He does not, however, offer it up as his own theory, as he would do 15 years later.

The concept of "sensitive matter" is one of the central themes in *Le Reve de d'Alembert* (D'Alembert's Dream), perhaps Diderot's most important philosophical work. Written as a dialogue between the author, D'Alembert, and a few minor characters, it explores a wide variety of themes, touching on psychology, morality, biology, and cosmology. In the opening passage of the first section, D'Alembert challenges Diderot with the classic rebuttal to panpsychism: "if this faculty of sensation … is a general and essential quality of matter, then stone must be sensitive" (1769/1937: 49). Diderot's casual reply is "Why not?" The everyman D'Alembert answers "It's hard to believe." As the dialogue progresses, it becomes clear that there are two levels of sensitivity in matter: an active form, such as is found in organic beings, and a passive form, such as is found in rocks and inanimate objects. The passive becomes active when taken up in an organic body, as when it is consumed; plants consume minerals, for example, and thus make their sensitivity active.[5] And yet, even as Diderot distinguished degrees of sensitivity, it is clearly the sensitivity itself that is primary.

Throughout the dialogue there are repeated references to "the general sensitivity of matter." Later we learn that "from the elephant to the flea, from the flea to the sensitive living atom, the origin of all, there is no point in nature but suffers and enjoys" (80). Diderot seems to simply accept this panpsychism—or rather pansensism—as a fundamental aspect of nature, and doesn't work it into a comprehensive metaphysical theory.

4. Referred to with the pseudonym "Dr. Baumann, of Erlangen."

5. We see here a close connection to LaMettrie's distinction between "direct" and "potential" ability to feel.

This outlook recurs in his other writings. In *Elements of Physiology*, for example, we find the following passage:

Some day it will be demonstrated that sensitiveness or feeling is a sense common to all beings. There are already phenomena which suggest this. Then matter in general will have five or six essential properties: dead or living force, length, breadth, depth, impenetrability, and sensitiveness. (1774–1780/1937: 139)

Diderot thus effectively modified Maupertuis' four essential properties of matter, arriving at force, extension, impenetrability, and sensitiveness. His notion of force incorporated the three general categories of kinetic ("living") energy, potential ("dead") energy, and gravity.

A second theme, unity of the self, addresses the well-known combination problem of panpsychism: If each particle of matter is individually intelligent, how do they combine to form the single sense of being that we all feel? Leibniz solved it by creating the dominant monad. In *Le Reve*, Diderot points toward an amorphous notion of unity of being that occurs when the intelligent particles are sufficiently interactive. He makes an analogy to a swarm of bees: "This cluster is a being, an individual, an animal of sorts." (67) It is a unitary being because of the extremely tight interaction between parts, which pass from being merely "contiguous" to being truly "continuous." Strength of interaction determines the intensity of being; one might also say that intensity of exchange determines intensity of mind. The human body is not categorically different from a swarm of bees. The body is a collection of organs, which "are just separate animals held together by the law of continuity in a general sympathy, unity, and identity" (68). It is the "continual action and reaction" between parts that creates the unity. "It seems to me," Diderot writes, "that contact, in itself, is enough." (76)

4.2   Kant and Priestley

The forefront of panpsychist philosophy moved from France to Germany over the course of the 1700s. But before discussing the role of German Romanticism it is necessary to address two intermediate figures: Immanuel Kant and Joseph Priestley.

Kant's (1724–1804) thinking on the matter of hylozoism and panpsychism underwent an interesting progression over the course of his life, moving from early sympathies to a final analytic rejection. A little-known booklet published in 1766, *Traume der Geisterseher* (Dreams of a Spirit-Seer), focuses on Kant's interest in the spiritual realm and the possibilities of trans-physical phenomena. "I confess," he writes, "that I am very much inclined to assert the existence of immaterial natures in the world, and to put my soul itself into that class of beings." (1766/1900: 52) He adds in a footnote that whatever "contains a principle of *life*, seems to be of immaterial nature," and that "those immaterial beings which contain the cause of animal life ... are called spirits." He then addresses the idea of hylozoism or panpsychism:

For every substance, even a simple element of matter, must have an inner activity as the reason for its external efficiency, although I cannot specify in what it consists. (53–54)

Another footnote contains this fascinating and revealing comment:

Leibniz says that this inner reason ... is the *power of conception* [i.e. intelligence], and later philosophers received this undeveloped thought with laughter. But they would have done better if they had first considered whether a substance of the nature of a simple particle of matter is possible without any inner state. [If so, they would have to] think out another possible inner state than that of conceptions. ... Everybody recognizes [that] even if a power of obscure conceptions is conceded to ... matter, it does not follow thence that matter itself possesses power of conception, because many substances of that kind, united into a whole, can yet never form a thinking unit.

Kant thus views the combination problem as insurmountable, stating directly that many individually intelligent particles can never form a single intelligent entity. Beyond this, he doesn't absolutely rule out Leibniz's panpsychist thesis; he recognizes that the issue is not as clear-cut as many would suppose. We see further evidence of his sympathies in the following chapter:

[T]o which members of nature life is extended, and ... those [to which] degrees of it ... are next to utter lifelessness, can, perhaps, never be made out with certainty. Hylozoism imputes life to everything; materialism, carefully considered, kills everything. (57)

That materialism "kills everything" is quite a statement. Kant seems to recognize a danger in this ontological view.[6] He then cites Maupertuis' panpsychist theory, going on to observe that, as Newton argued, one cannot be sure that all things are not alive: "The undoubted characteristic of life

---

6. It is clear that he means mechanistic materialism.

[is] free movement ... , but the conclusion is not certain that, wherever this characteristic is not found, there is no degree of life." Though certainly not endorsing hylozoism, Kant is at least open to the possibility.

Fifteen years later, Kant's focus had shifted from hylozoism to something more akin to true panpsychism. In *Critique of Pure Reason* (1781) he famously argued that *das Ding an sich* is inherently unknowable, and thus almost nothing can be said of it. However, in one passage in book II of the Transcendental Dialectic—chapter 1, "Paralogisms of Pure Reason (B)"—Kant accepts that the thing-in-itself may share some essential characteristic or quality of mind. In a short section titled "Conclusion, In Regard to the Solution of the Psychological Paralogism," he claims that his arguments "supply a sufficient answer to this question [of] the communion of the soul [i.e. mind] with the body." He elaborates:

The difficulty peculiar to the problem consists, as is generally recognized, in the assumed difference [in nature] between the object of the inner sense (the soul) and the [material] objects of the outer senses. But if we consider that the two kinds of objects thus differ from each other, not inwardly but only in so far as one appears outwardly to the other, and that what, as *Ding-an-sich-selbst*, underlies the appearance of matter, perhaps after all may not be so different in character, this difficulty vanishes ... .

Thus he observes that if one assumes that the soul and the objects of the material world are fundamentally alike, i.e., of the same ontological class, then the mind-body problem is resolved. Kant's wording suggests that he would look favorably on such an assumption, though he clearly stops short of endorsing it. Still, the implication is that matter, of which we do not know the true essence, is somehow like our mind, of which we do know, intimately, the essence. We may be mistaken about the true nature of mind, but we certainly know it more directly than we know anything else in the universe. One reasonable conclusion, therefore, would be that all matter has a mind-like quality in and of itself.[7] This leaves us, Kant continues, with only the problem of "how *in general* a communion of [such] substances is possible." But he doesn't address this, saying that it lies not only "outside the field of psychology" but also "outside the field of all human knowledge."

Kant's *Critique of Judgment* (1790) presents his final analytical stance. He writes that there are two types of philosophical systems that can explain

7. Kant leaves open the possibility of a neutral-monist position, in which case something other than mind or matter would underlie both.

the "productive power" and "purposiveness" of nature: realism and idealism. Both of these can exist in two forms: physical and trans-physical. Physical realism, he tells us, "bases the purposes in nature ... on the *life of matter* (either its own or the life of an inner principle in it, a world-soul) and is called *hylozoism*" (1790/1951: 239). That option, unfortunately, is inconceivable:

[T]he possibility of living matter cannot even be thought; its concept involves a contradiction, because lifelessness, *inertia*, constitutes the essential character of matter. The possibility of matter endowed with life ... can only be used in an inadequate way ... , [and] in no way can its possibility be comprehended *a priori*. ... Hylozoism, therefore, does not perform what it promises. (242)

This seems to be Kant's final word on the matter. Unfortunately, he never pursued the suggestion mentioned in *Critique of Pure Reason*. For him, apparently, the conceptual weaknesses could not offset the potential explanatory power.

As it happens, Priestley (1733–1804) did not see things as Kant did. Priestley is best known for his discovery of oxygen (in 1774), but he was also an astute natural philosopher. He was concerned with the problem of mind and body, and in 1777 he wrote a rather lengthy treatise on the subject, titled "Disquisitions relating to matter and spirit," arguing for the idea that mind and matter are not incompatible Cartesian substances but rather share common qualities, and in fact can be seen as different manifestations of the same underlying entity.

Priestley begins by challenging the traditional view that matter is something defined by extension, inertness, and impenetrability. He accepts the first of these, but replaces the latter two with a pair of forces: "I ... define [matter] to be a substance possessed of the property of *extension*, and of *powers* of *attraction* or *repulsion*." (1777: 219) He argues that these three properties—extension, attraction, repulsion—are sufficient to account for all material phenomena.[8]

Priestley's ideas were anticipated already in 1758 by the Italian scientist and philosopher Roger (Ruggiero) Boscovich. Boscovich's *Theoria philosophiae naturalis* presented a thesis in which the forces present in matter were the ultimate ontological reality—a view that came to be known as

8. His use of the two opposing forces again recalls Empedocles' Love and Strife.

dynamism. Priestley accepted and expanded on that view, adding the quality of extension under the presumption that form or shape was also an essential quality of matter.

For Priestley, the overriding opposition between classical matter and spirit was that matter was solid and spatial whereas spirit was non-spatial and immaterial. That incompatibility was the source of the problem of mind-body interaction. He argued that by dematerializing matter—by making it penetrable (i.e., pure force)—he could remove that barrier. For him, mind was then completely compatible with matter and could in fact be seen as a particular mode of it:

[S]ince it has never yet been asserted, that the power of *sensation* and *thought* are incompatible with these [powers of attraction and repulsion], I therefore maintain, that we have no reason to suppose that there are in man two substances so distinct from each other as have been represented.

Priestley sought a materialist monism that shared some qualities with the views of LaMettrie and Diderot; in particular, it saw matter as fundamentally dynamic and animated, and mind as a function of the organizational qualities of matter. In short, Priestley sought to "prove the uniform composition of man" (220). For him, "*mind* ... is not a substance distinct from the body, but the result of corporeal organization; ... whatever matter be, ... mind is nothing more than a modification of it." Mind reduces to matter, but matter which is, in some sense, fundamentally mind-like. Matter "ought to rise in our esteem, as making a nearer approach to the nature of spiritual and immaterial beings" (230).

Nowhere did Priestley explicitly state that all matter possesses mind, but this implication can be seen to follow from his premises. He was an implicit panpsychist, and one who, in his time, fundamentally challenged the inert-matter view of the world.

4.3 German Romanticism and *Naturphilosophie*

By the late 1700s, philosophical opposition to mechanistic thinking had moved to Germany. Panpsychism continued to play a prominent role, particularly in the emerging views of Johann Herder, Johann Wolfgang von Goethe, and Friedrich Schelling.

Herder (1745–1803) was a dynamist who rejected the idea that such a view implied materialism. He sought a naturalistic non-reductive ontology in which mind and matter were different degrees of organization of a single underlying force or energy called *Kraft*. In denying conventional materialism and placing force in a unique ontological category, Herder was one of the first explicitly neutral monists of the modern era, though the designation would not be used until the time of Bertrand Russell.

In the late eighteenth century, science recognized many different forces in nature—gravity, magnetism, electricity, light, and motive force, among others. Herder sought to unify these forces as the singular *Kraft*, of which the various *Kräfte* were different manifestations. Furthermore, *Kraft* was to be seen not merely as physical force but as an animating energy in which the individual sub-forces were in themselves soul-like entities. He wrote of the universal *Kraft* in *On the Cognition and Sensation of the Human Soul*:

Quite generally, nothing in nature is separated, everything flows onto and into everything else through imperceptible transitions; and certainly, what life is in the creation is in all its shapes, forms, and channels only a single spirit, a single flame. (1778/2002: 195)

Thus all material things, in addition to the standard forces of physics, are unified and vivified by the universal *Kraft*. It is at once a life-energy, spirit, and mind—recalling the *pneuma* of the Stoics.

The passage above could be interpreted as expressing a pure, almost idealist monism. However, Herder's thinking was more of a panpsychist variety in which each thing has an interior life and experiential perspective. Nisbet (1970: 10) explains that, in an early 1769 manuscript, Herder discusses "how the human body, and by analogy, the planets, are formed by the action of an inner *Monas* [unity], *Kraft* [force], or *Seele* [soul or mind]." Herder's 1778 work refers to the Continuity argument and the process of analogical inference: "the more we thoughtfully observe the great drama of effective forces in nature, the less we can avoid everywhere feeling *similarity with ourselves*, enlivening everything with our sensation" (1778/2002: 187).

Later he became even more explicitly panpsychist. Nisbet (1970: 11) notes that Herder "represents the *Kräfte* of plants and stones as analogous to the soul. ... Each endowed with a different degree of consciousness." In the attempt to classify Herder's metaphysical view, Nisbet runs through a number of panpsychism synonyms, ultimately deciding that "pan-animism" is most appropriate.

The panpsychist theme continues in Herder's later writings. *Ideen zur Philosophie der Geschichte der Menschheit* (Ideas for the Philosophy of the History of Humanity; 1784–1791) includes, for example, this passage:

All active forces of Nature are, each in its own way, alive; in their interior there must be Something that corresponds to their effects without—as Leibniz himself assumed … . (book I, section XIII, in Clark 1955: 311)

Herder clearly saw such a panpsychist dynamism as an alternative to the reigning Cartesian mechanistic materialism, which he strongly opposed. This opposition is consistent throughout his philosophical writings. Nisbet notes that for Herder "the psychology of feeling tends to replace mechanical analysis … , and *Kräfte* increasingly supplant 'dead' matter." From 1769 on, Herder "consistently attacks mechanistic theories of nature" (133).

Herder shared many opinions with his contemporary and friend Goethe (1749–1832). Like William Blake, Goethe infused many of his literary works with philosophical insight. The exemplary German Romantic, he combined a poetic, mystical feeling for nature with a strong sense of unity and holism.

Elements of panpsychism are found only indirectly in Goethe. First there is his general identification of Nature with God: "I have at times to resort to pantheism to satisfy my being."[9] Then there is his frequent attribution of personal and human traits to the phenomena of nature. Sherrington notes that "in reading Goethe's science we are never left long without a reminder of his tendency to personify Nature."[10] Goethe expresses this sentiment when he notes that Nature "reflects herself … everywhere in a manner analogous to our mind."[11] And we find suggestive passages such as this: "it is the observer's first duty … to aim at the completeness of the phenomena … so that they will present themselves to one's observation as an organization manifesting an inner life of its own."[12] The "inner life" of natural phenomena suggests the presence of mind in nature.

9. Goethe (1824), in Sherrington 1949 (p. 33).

10. Sherrington 1949: 21.

11. In Vietor 1950 (p. 13).

12. In Naydler 1996 (p. 83).

The panpsychist and hylozoist Ernst Haeckel cited Goethe on multiple occasions in support of his own ideas. Haeckel held that mind and matter were inseparably linked, and he attributed the same belief to Goethe:

As even Goethe has clearly expressed it, "matter can never exist and act without mind, and mind never without matter." (1868/1876: 487)

Here we find a beautifully concise statement: no matter without mind, no mind without matter. There is no claim that mind is identical with matter, or that one can be reduced to the other; there is simply the statement that mind and matter are conjoined, that neither exists without the other. This is an essential feature of panpsychism.

Haeckel's citation comes from a letter Goethe wrote in 1828, near the end of his life. The original passage is enlightening. Goethe notes that there are "two great driving forces in all nature: the concepts of *polarity* and *intensification*" (1828/1988: 6). The former is associated with the material dimension of reality, the latter with the spiritual. He defines polarity in a very Empedoclean manner as "a state of constant attraction and repulsion," and characterizes intensification as an evolutionary imperative—a "state of ever-striving ascent." He continues: "Since, however, matter can never exist and act without spirit [*Seele*], nor spirit without matter, matter is also capable of undergoing intensification, and spirit cannot be denied its attraction and repulsion." Again, no matter without mind, no mind without matter.

Herder and Goethe articulated aspects of a holistic philosophy of nature, but its culmination in Germany was achieved in the *Naturphilosophie* of Friedrich Schelling. In Schelling's view, humans were deeply integrated into nature, physical forces were seen as manifestations of a single underlying force, and mechanism was soundly rejected. He unified these elements and created a comprehensive philosophical system.

For the most part, Schelling's case for panpsychism is implicit. His absolute idealism emphasizes Mind as the underlying unity of all things. Everything finds meaning and resolution in the Mind of the Absolute: "Nature is to be invisible mind, mind invisible nature."[13] His early work *Ideas for a Philosophy of Nature* (1797/1988) includes this remark: "[T]here is a hierarchy of life in Nature. Even in mere organized matter there is *life*, but a life

13. In Bowie 1998 (p. 509).

of a more restricted kind." (35) He understands matter as intimately connected to mind: "Matter is indeed nothing else but mind viewed in an equilibrium of its activities." (1800/1978: 92) In arguing that mind in nature reveals itself as a form of will, which is a "primal being," Schelling was one of the first modern German philosophers to emphasize the ontological importance of the will, following Bruno and Campanella and anticipating Schopenhauer, Hartmann, and Nietzsche.

Commentaries on Schelling's panpsychism are rare. Blamauer (2012) offers what may be the most detailed discussion. Rothschuh describes Schelling's system as essentially that of an evolving spirit: "Nature is spirit in the course of becoming."[14] Such a vision appears to describe a cosmos wherein all things possess an element of mind. Werner Marx (1984: 58) notes that for Schelling "nature is rather a spirit that, in a dynamic series of stages from inorganic matter up to consciousness, is similar to an ego." This evolving mind is therefore in some sense a subject, a personality, that is manifest in all levels of matter.

14. In Schnaedelbach 1984 (p. 242).

5 Panpsychism, Mechanism, and Science in Nineteenth-Century Germany

Germany remained at the center of evolving views on panpsychism throughout the nineteenth century, even as mechanistic philosophy became increasingly dominant. Paradoxically, new developments in science, physics, and mathematics allowed both mechanists and panpsychists to strengthen their cases. Among the major philosophers advocating or sympathizing with panpsychist views were Schopenhauer, Fechner, Lotze, Hartmann, Mach, Haeckel, and (controversially) Nietzsche. By the end of the century, Friedrich Paulson could compile the first substantial overview of panpsychist philosophy, one that acknowledged the many important German contributions.

5.1 Schopenhauer

The philosophical system of Arthur Schopenhauer (1788–1860) is conveniently summarized in the title of his most famous work, *Die Welt als Wille und Vorstellung* (The World as Will and Idea).[1] Reality is comprehended in two distinct but connected ways. "World as idea" is essentially equivalent to classical idealism, in which things are collections of sensory images. "World as will," however, is something entirely new; it completely and radically rewrites our metaphysical picture in panpsychist terms.

To elaborate: When we examine the world in a naïve or prima facie sense, what we perceive, fundamentally, is a patchwork of sensory impressions:

1. *Vorstellung* is sometimes translated as "Representation" (e.g., in the 1958 translation by Payne), and occasionally as "Presentation" (e.g., by McCabe in Haeckel 1904: 466). The translation as "Idea" is found in the 1883 translation by Haldane and Kemp and in the 1995 Berman translation, which I will follow here.

colors, shapes, sounds, scents, and textures. The mind, attempting to make sense of the world, immediately bundles these sensory impressions together into what we identify as individual objects. An apple, for example, is round-ish, of a certain size, has a reddish color, smells and tastes a certain way. It is precisely this unique bundle of impressions that allows us to call a certain thing an apple. And so it is with every object that we perceive.

From the time of Bishop Berkeley, sensory impressions had been thought of as ideas, and "things" as self-evidently collections of ideas. He contem-plated a further question: What are things, apart from the ideas? His answer was Nothing; things are only ideas, and they exist only in a perceiving mind or soul. Matter, or material substance, literally doesn't exist. This out-look, which came to be known as idealism, has traditionally been attributed to Berkeley and his work of the early 1700s.

Schopenhauer accepted the notion that things were bundles of ideas, but he emphatically rejected the thought that they were nothing more. If Berkeley were right, he said, the entire world would be intrinsically empty—a kind of phantom or dream. There would be no substance to real-ity. There had to be an inner nature to things, something substantial, in order to "objectify" or reify the world.

Various attempts had been made throughout history to determine this inner nature, the thing-in-itself of material objects. Descartes had famously determined that it was an "extended, flexible, changeable" substance of an otherwise indeterminate nature.[2] For Kant, it was some inherently unknow-able entity. To Schopenhauer, both answers were inadequate. Descartes, Kant, and Berkeley had failed to discern the truth because they neglected to consider the one object in the universe that they knew better than anything else: one's own body. Had they not neglected to consider it, they would have realized that the human body, most essentially, knows and feels its own wants, urges, needs, and desires—in sum, its will. For Schopen-hauer, the will was the ontological essence of the human being, our true inner nature.

Schopenhauer completed his argument by noting that the human being is simply an object like every other in the world, composed of the same elemental substances and subject to the same laws and forces. If the human was essentially will, then so too was everything else. He thus reasoned

2. Second Meditation (1641).

that all things, in themselves, were will. His overall conclusion was that the things of the world were both, and at once, idea from the outside and will from the inside: "For as the world is in one aspect entirely *idea*, so in another it is entirely *will*." (1819/1995: 5)

As has already been noted, the world as will directly challenges Kant's conception of a fundamentally unknowable *Ding an sich*. The difference between the two views, however, may not be as great as Schopenhauer presumed, if we recall Kant's speculation that the *Ding an sich* may be of a mind-like nature. Hartmann recognized this very point: "What Kant entertained as timid supposition, that the thing of itself and the active subject might be one and the same existence, Schopenhauer declared as categorical assertion, in that he recognized the will as the positive character of this essence." (1869: 236) For Schopenhauer, the will was clearly and unambiguously mental. He thereby thrust the concept of the will into a central ontological role. Will, for him, was not merely the equivalent of human desire but was more generally a universal force, a drive, something that impelled and sustained all things. Hamlyn (1980: 95) argues that this will was "a kind of force which permeates nature and which thus governs all phenomena." Magee (1983:145) describes it as literally force or energy—making Schopenhauer out to be a dynamist or energeticist—and argues that the developments of twentieth-century physics have "provided the most powerful confirmation that could be imagined" of his metaphysics.

Schopenhauer lends credence to the dynamist view in his own writing. On a number of occasions he equates will with the physical forces of nature. For example, he notes that "the force which attracts a stone to the ground is according to its nature, in itself, and apart from all idea, will" (1819: 38). In a later work, *Über den Willen in der Natur* (On the Will in Nature), he states that "generally every original force manifesting itself in physical and chemical appearances, in fact gravity itself—all these in themselves ... are absolutely identical with what we find in ourselves as *will*" (1836: 20).

But Schopenhauer goes further in his thesis that the world *is* will. He speaks of material things as literally "objectifications of will"—as physical manifestations, or solidifications, or tangible embodiments of will. Of the human body, he says that "the whole body is nothing but objectified will" and "the action of the body is nothing but the act of the will objectified" (1819: 33). His graphic explanations leave no doubt: "Teeth, throat, and

intestines are objectified hunger; the genitals are objectified sexual desire."
(41) Objectification occurs in varying levels or degrees throughout nature,
generally corresponding to the complexity of the object. The human being
is the highest grade of objectification; the physical forces are the basest.
"The most universal forces of nature present themselves as the lowest grade
of the will's objectification." (61)

Since the will is clearly and unambiguously mental, panpsychism is
a central feature of his metaphysics. Thus we can understand Popper's
quip "One can say that Schopenhauer is a Kantian who has turned panpsychist." (1977: 68) This aspect is particularly evident in Schopenhauer's
concept of will as manifest in inorganic objects. Book II of *World as Will
and Idea* focuses extensively on the identification of will with the forces
of nature:

> [T]he force which stirs and vegetates in the plant, and indeed the force by which the
> crystal is formed, that by which the magnet turns to the North Pole, the force whose
> shock [results] from the contact between different metals, the force which appears
> in the elective affinities of matter as repulsion and attraction, separation and com-
> bination, and, lastly, even gravitation, ... all these [are recognized] as in their inner
> nature as identical [to that] which is called *will*. (1819: 42)

This will in nature is, in principle, the same as the will in man:

> [The will] is manifest in every force of nature that operates blindly, and it is mani-
> fest, too, in the deliberate action of man; and the great difference between these two
> is a matter only of degree of the manifestation, not in the nature of what is made
> manifest.

One can see in this quotation a reflection of Spinoza's idea that "all
things are animate in varying degrees," and in fact Spinoza was highly
influential in Schopenhauer's thinking. *World as Will and Idea* refers explicitly to Spinoza's notion that all things, even stones, possess an aspect of
mentality:

> Spinoza says that if a stone which has been catapulted through the air had
> consciousness, it would think that it was flying of its own will. I add only that
> the stone would be right. That catapulting is for the stone what the motive is for
> me ... . (58)[3]

The point here is that the inner nature of both men and stones is the same:
will. Furthermore, it is a will that has the appearance of freedom to the

---

3. Letter 58, Spinoza to Schuller, dated 1674, cited on p. 267 of Spinoza 1677/1994.

subject. We feel free in our own actions, just as the stone (wrongly) would if it could contemplate such things. In any case, the essence of both is the same: "In people [will] is called character, while in a stone it is called quality, but it is the same in each."

Even though Schopenhauer denied consciousness to all but the animals, it is clear that the will was to be described in terms of the human personality, and as a psychic or mental disposition:

When we scrutinize [the forces of nature] closely, we observe the tremendous, irresistible force with which rivers hurry down to the sea, the persistence with which the magnet turns again and again to the North Pole, the readiness with which iron flies to the magnet, the eagerness with which in electricity opposite poles strive to be reunited, and which, just like human desire, is the more intense for being thwarted: … it will cost us no great effort of the imagination, even at so great a distance, to recognize our own nature. (50)

Human nature is a reflection of universal nature. That which we see in ourselves must apply to reality writ large.

Schopenhauer's panpsychism is reiterated in his other two major works, *On the Will in Nature* (1836) and *Parerga und Paralipomena* (1851). In the former he looks to developments in the natural sciences as confirmation of his ideas. He finds in inorganic nature "absolutely no trace of a consciousness of an external world," yet even such things as "stones, boulders or ice floes" are "affected by an influence from without … which one can accordingly regard as the first step toward consciousness" (1836/1993: 82). And plants, though likewise lacking true consciousness, can be seen as experiencing "an obscure self-enjoyment" and "a feeble analogue of perception." In examining the study of gravitation and astronomy, he notes with satisfaction that Herschel and Copernicus spoke of gravity in terms of "desire" and "will": In 1883 Herschel wrote that objects drawn to the Earth are "impelled to this by a force or effort, the direct or indirect result of a consciousness and a *will* existing somewhere," and in *De revolutionibus* Copernicus expresses a belief "that gravity is nothing but a natural *craving*" (85–86). And Schopenhauer claims, for the record, to have been "the first to say that a *will* is to be attributed to the inanimate, to the inorganic" (88).[4]

4. This is not true, as we have seen. Leibniz attributed appetite or desire to all monads, which is a form of will. Campanella granted will or love to all things, as one of his three primalities. And even Empedocles' concepts of Love and Strife can be seen as manifestations of will. But it is true that Schopenhauer was the first to explicitly declare the will as the essential reality of physical things.

This theme continues in Schopenhauer's late work *Parerga und Paralipomena*. In a notable passage near the end of that book, he decries the "fundamentally false antithesis between *mind* and *matter*" (1851/1974: 212). To the extent that one can speak of "mind" or "matter" in the real world—that is, the inner and outer manifestations of things—mind must be equally attributable to both the organic and the inorganic. Any two material objects, such as (to use his examples) the human body and a stone, have internal qualities that are of necessity alike. Both are driven by the same forces of nature, both have mass and volume, and both are thus describable in the same metaphysical terms. If in one case we find mind, so must we find it in the other:

Now if you suppose the existence of a *mind* in the human head, ... you are bound to concede a mind to every stone. ... All ostensible mind can be attributed to matter, but all matter can likewise be attributed to mind; from which it follows that the antithesis [between mind and matter] is a false one. (213)

In the same passage, Schopenhauer makes an important observation on the limitations of the mechanistic philosophy in comprehending such truths: The mechanist knows only the mathematically derivable effects of nature, not nature as it is in itself. For a mechanist, "the exertion of weight in a stone is every bit as inexplicable as is thought in a human brain," and, insofar as these natural phenomena are related, "this fact would suggest the presence of a mind in the stone."[5] The mechanistic account of

5. I note in passing that Ludwig Wittgenstein was significantly influenced by Schopenhauer's metaphysics, and two passages in *Philosophical Investigations* (1953) seem to refer to his notion that a stone has a mind. Both occur in book I. The first passage reads "Could one imagine a stone's having consciousness? And if anyone can do so—why should that not merely prove that such image-mongery is of no interest to us?" (section 390) Wittgenstein is clearly disparaging the entire notion. The second passage seems to at least suspend judgment on the matter: "Is my having consciousness a fact of experience?—But doesn't one say that a man has consciousness, and that a tree or a stone does not?—What would it be like if it were otherwise?—Would human beings all be unconscious?—No; not in the ordinary sense of the word. But I, for instance, should not have consciousness—as I now in fact have it." (section 418) He suggests that the consciousness of man and of tree or stone are necessarily of different types—that seeing stones as conscious would entail viewing humans as something else, as "unconscious." He seems unwilling to consider them as both possessing a common type of mentality, in any sense of the word. Thus he rejects one of Schopenhauer's main theses.

nature "is limited ... to determining its spatial and temporal qualities." Furthermore,

as soon as we go beyond what is purely mathematical, ... we stand before modes of expression which are just as mysterious to us as the thought and will of man, ... for [to the mechanist] unfathomable is what every natural force is.

All this is undoubtedly true, and is furthermore an important anticipation of the later and related thoughts by Bertrand Russell and Arthur Eddington. This insight, in fact, is the basis for the so-called Russellian monism, much discussed in recent years, which naturally lends itself to a form of panpsychism.

Schopenhauer explicitly acknowledges his debt to Empedocles, especially for the general concept of existence as a struggle between forces of will—specifically, Love and Strife: "Everywhere in nature we see strife, conflict, and the fickleness of victory. ... This strife may be seen to pervade the whole of nature; indeed nature ... exists only through it." (73–74) He cites Aristotle's commentary: "as Empedocles says, if there were no strife in things, everything would be one and the same" (cf. *Metaphysics*, 1000b1). Thus nature reflects a kind of law of the jungle, with each form of existence competing with all others to maintain and fulfill itself.[6]

Schopenhauer saw struggle and strife all around him, and that led to his notoriously pessimistic assessment of life in general. He was exceptional in that instance; most all panpsychist philosophers seem to have adopted sympathetic, compassionate, and optimistic worldviews. Most philosophers seem to have found wonder and transcendence in the fact that mind pervades the universe. Schopenhauer saw a world of objectified wills locked in an eternal, almost Darwinian struggle for dominance. Such a view was, in its own way, influential, especially through Nietzsche.

5.2 Fechner

Gustav Fechner (1801–1887) was, in a sense, the antithesis of the pessimist Schopenhauer. Fechner's vibrant, exuberant, life-enhancing perspective on the world was intimately and openly linked to his panpsychist philosophy,

6. This has clear ethical implications in the social realm. Schopenhauer (1819/1995: 74) notes that it speaks to a view in which *homo homini lupus*—man is a wolf to man.

perhaps more so than the perspective of any other major philosopher. And he was a first-rate scientist and mathematician. He virtually invented the science of psychophysics, and he discovered the principle that the perceived strength of a sensation is proportional to the logarithm of the intensity of the stimulus (which came to be known as "Fechner's Law"). His important philosophical works include *Nanna, oder über das Seelen-Leben der Pflanzen* (Nanna, or on the Soul-Life of Plants, 1848), *Zend-Avesta* (1851), *Über die Seelenfrage* (On the Soul-Question, 1861), and *Die Tagesansicht gegenüber der Nachtansicht* (The Daylight View as Opposed to the Night View, 1873). The fact that little of this material has been translated into English accounts in part for Fechner's relative lack of exposure and analysis in the English-speaking countries. Only two books published in English explore his metaphysical views. The first is a series of partial translations of his major works compiled under the title *Religion of a Scientist* (1946). The second is a relatively lengthy and sympathetic discussion by William James in *A Pluralistic Universe* (1909). James was impressed by Fechner, calling him "a philosopher in the 'great' sense" (149) and noting that the current state of knowledge of psychology, psychophysics, and religion had led to "a decidedly formidable probability in favor of a general view of the world almost identical with Fechner's" (309–310).

The most important aspect of Fechner's panpsychism is his conception of the world as composed of a hierarchy of minds or souls (*Seele*). There are souls "below" us in the plants, and there are souls "above" us in the Earth, the stars, and the universe as a whole. Humans are surrounded, at all levels of being, by varying degrees of soul. This is Fechner's "daylight view"—the human soul at home in an ensouled cosmos. He contrasted it with the materialist "night view" of humans as alone, isolated points of light in a universe of utter blackness.

Consider separately Fechner's discussions of the lesser (sub-human) and greater (super-human or collective) minds. The former consist almost entirely of discussions of plants, which he is sure possess minds. His case relies on a form of the Continuity argument and on an analogy with human beings,[7] though he employs at least four other arguments for panpsychism. The Continuity argument appears repeatedly in *Nanna*, for example in this passage:

7. For an analysis of Fechner's analogical arguments, see Woodward 1972.

If we take a cursory glance at some of the outstanding points, is not the plant quite as well organized as the animal, though on a different plan, a plan entirely of its own, perfectly consonant with its idea? If one will not venture to deny that the plant has a life, why deny it a soul? For it is much simpler to think that a different plan of bodily organization built upon the common basis of life indicates only a different plan of psychic organization. ... Whether it be a plant or an animal, the complexity of structure and process is so completely analogous, except that the cells are differently arranged ... . (1848/1946: 168–169)

Because we cannot directly know the inner life of a plant, scientific or logical analysis is useless; "in this field, one must remember, there is nothing we have to rely upon except analogy" (175).

Fechner's personal, intuitive feel for the plant-soul is abundantly evident throughout his writing. One finds passionate and poetic words, such as the following:

I stood once on a hot summer's day beside a pool and contemplated a water-lily which had spread its leaves evenly over the water and with an open blossom was basking in the sunlight. ... It seemed to me that nature surely would not have built a creature so beautiful, and so carefully designed for such conditions, merely to be an object of idle observation. ... I was inclined rather to think that nature had built it thus in order that all the pleasure which can be derived from bathing at once in sunlight and in water might be enjoyed by one creature in the fullest measure. (177)

Or consider this passage, in which he describes the glory of the daylight view:

With the abolition of the plants from the realm of souls how sparsely scattered would sensibility be in the whole realm of nature ... ! How different it all is, if the plants have souls and are capable of feeling! ... Is it not more beautiful and glorious to think that the living trees of the forest burn like torches uplifted towards the heaven? To be sure, we can only think this; we do not directly see anything of these soul-flames of nature; but since we *can* think it, why are we not willing to? (180)

We see here a culmination and synthesis of Goethe's poetic imagery and Schelling's *Naturphilosophie*; it is a rebirth of the religious view of nature, and perhaps one of the earliest forerunners of the ecological worldview that, in Skolimowski's words, sees "the world as a sanctuary."[8] We find even stronger evidence of this in Fechner's discussion of the earth-soul.

8. See, for example, Skolimowski 1990, 1992, and 1993.

According to Fechner, plant-souls are the most direct indicators of the overall panpsychic nature of the world. He explains this in *On the Soul-Question*:

[B]elief in the plant soul is just a little instance of the general situation ... , for in this whole question the least and the greatest things are closely connected. ... I considered that in the little soul of the plant I had found a little handle by which faith in the greatest things could be more easily hoisted to the big pedestal. (1861/1946: 138–139)

And, as he states in *Nanna*, "the decision as to whether the plants are animated or not decides many other questions and determines the whole outlook upon nature" (1848/1946: 163).

Of course, for Fechner this "whole outlook" is a panpsychic one in which every thing and every part of every thing is ensouled. Regarding plants, he argues that "there are as many individuals as there are leaves on the tree, nay, there are in fact as many as there are cells" (204). These individuals, whether cells or whole plants, are not simply part of some larger mind; they possess souls in their own right: "It is only an independent animate life we have in mind when we enquire about the souls of plants." (165) Each thing has its own unique view on the world and interacts with the world as a unitary mind.

Perhaps more important than Fechner's elaborations on the plant-soul was his discussion of what James called the "superhuman consciousness"— the mind of society, of the Earth, of the stars, and of the cosmos. Fechner was the first scientist-philosopher to examine these possibilities seriously and to regard them as actual features of reality. James provides an excellent summary:

In ourselves, visual consciousness goes with our eyes, tactile consciousness with our skin. ... They come together in some sort of relation and combination in the more inclusive consciousness which each of us names his *self*. Quite similarly, says Fechner, we must suppose that my consciousness [and yours, though] they keep separate and know nothing of each other, are yet known and used together in a higher consciousness, that of the human race. ... Similarly, the whole human and animal kingdoms come together as conditions of a consciousness of still wider scope. This combines in the soul of the earth with the consciousness of the vegetable kingdom, which in turn contributes ... to that of the whole solar system, and so on from synthesis to synthesis and height to height, till an absolutely universal consciousness is reached. (1909: 155–156)

So here is a view of mind as a nested hierarchy, reaching from the lowest forms to the highest. It is, as James said, "a vast analogical series, in which the basis of the analogy consists of facts directly observable in ourselves" (156).

Fechner's view is often described as a form of psycho-physical parallelism of the sort that Spinoza proposed. But Fechner went further, laying out an explicitly pluralist panpsychism. James embraced it wholeheartedly, while emphasizing that all these levels of hierarchy in the world possess, individually, their own minds:

The vaster orders of mind go with the vaster orders of body. The entire earth on which we live must have, according to Fechner, its own collective consciousness. So must each sun, moon, and planet; so must the whole solar system have its own wider consciousness, in which the consciousness of our earth plays one part. So has the entire starry system as such its consciousness ... . (152–153)

The limit in this sequence, the mind of the cosmos, Fechner took as God.

Of special interest is Fechner's emphasis on the Earth as a consciousness and spirit, an "angel" that supports all life. His vision would seem to draw from the Platonic notion of the Earth as a god, and it anticipated the Gaia concept of the 1970s, in which the Earth is seen as a living, sentient being. The idea of an Earth-soul was critical to Fechner: "Just as man is the starting point ... for belief in animate character of all other creatures, so is the animated earth the starting point ... for belief in the animate character of all other stars." (1861: 150) As with plants, he starts with a Continuity argument: "[I]s not the earth in its form and content, like our bodies, and like the bodies also of all animals and plants ... ?" (155) He then lays out four points in support of this view. First he notes that the Earth is a unified system, relatively closed and well defined. Second, it develops, like living organisms, from within; it is relatively self-sufficient, and it contains its own means for self-realization. Third, it is a complex being, vastly more so than any mere plant or animal. Last, it is a unique member of the class of planetary bodies, which constitute a kind of "species" of things.

Beyond these arguments, Fechner clearly adopted a spiritual and reverential attitude toward the Earth. It was not just some animated rock; it was his sacred home:

One spring morning I went out early: the fields were greening, the birds were singing, the dew glistening; ... it was only a tiny fraction of the earth, only a tiny moment of its existence, and yet, as I comprised more and more in the range of my vision, it seemed to me not only so beautiful but so true and evident that it is an angel, so rich and fresh and blooming, and at the same time so stable and unified, moving in the heavens, turning wholly towards heaven its animated face, and bearing me with it to that same heaven—so beautiful and true that I wondered how men's notion could be so perverted as to see in the earth only a dry clod ... . (1861: 153)

Such a divine being deserves our most profound reverence. As James said (1909: 153), Fechner "treats the earth as our special human guardian angel; we can pray to the earth as men pray to their saints."

Though relying chiefly on analogy, Fechner used a variety of arguments to make his panpsychist claims. Above we have seen a number of arguments by Continuity, but he employed at least four other arguments:

In-Dwelling Powers—Plants have the power to take ordinary matter and make it living, and in this sense they have more "vital force" than do animals. "Out of raw earth, water, air, and decaying substances the plant makes glorious forms and colors." (1848: 184)

Non-Emergence—The Earth must be sentient, because "animate beings cannot arise from inanimate" (1861: 156).

Design—The cosmos creates ensouled beings in order to attain full and complete enjoyment of existence. (Recall the passage on the water lily.)

Theological—Fechner admitted that there is an element of faith involved here, writing that "however we begin it or however we end, we shall not be able to discover and impart any exact proofs" (135). He noted that even in traditional theology the Spirit of God is everywhere: "If one concedes a God who is at once omnipresent, omniscient, and omnipotent, then in a certain sense the universal animation of the world by God is already admitted." (1848: 163–164)

In the end, Fechner was, after all, a hard-headed rationalist. He spoke not as a poet, not as an artist or mystic, but as an empirical scientist drawing reasonable conclusions about the world. He made clear that his entire philosophical system was intended as a literal truth of reality: "All this is not metaphorical, is not an hypothesis: it is a simple and literal statement of how things are." (1861: 153) Evidently it was a compelling vision, at least to certain prominent scientists. The Dutch physicist Hendrik Lorentz stated, in a letter of 1915, that he explicitly endorsed Fechner's psychophysical parallelism:

[T]he mental and the material are inviolably tied to one another, they are two sides of the same thing. The material world is a way in which the *Weltgeist* appears, since the smallest particle of matter has a soul, or whatever one chooses to call it. This is all closely tied to Fechner's views ... and I think that we have to assume something similar. (in Heidelberger 2004: 178)

Albert Einstein concurred, stating in a 1922 letter that relativity theory was fully compatible with Fechner's views: "To guard against the collision of the various sorts of realities' with which physics and psychology deal, Spinoza and Fechner invented the doctrine of psychophysical parallelism, which, to be frank, satisfies me entirely." (in Heidelberger 2004: 177)

5.3   Other Scientist-Philosophers of the Age

Among the German scientist-philosophers, Fechner was the outstanding proponent of a panpsychic worldview. However, a few other thinkers— important philosophers in their own right—merit discussion. They will be addressed here in the order in which their panpsychist views emerged.

R. Hermann Lotze (1817–1881), trained as a physician and a philosopher, saw merit in both mechanism and idealism, and yet he sought to avoid the more extreme claims of each. He saw that mechanistic materialism was coming to dominate the philosophical and cultural landscape, and he was deeply concerned about the loss of reverence and wonder in the world.

Lotze's major work, *Microcosmos* (1856–1864), describes his comprehensive views on mind and matter. He prefaces the entire discussion by describing the antipathy between "mechanical science" and "Philosophy of the Feelings." Here we find one of the first explicit acknowledgments of two competing worldviews, two completely divergent platforms from which to understand the cosmos. As the mechanical view came to dominate, its weaknesses became apparent. The proponents of this view were becoming increasingly bold, even arrogant, and they showed utter disregard for the spiritual aspects of life. As Lotze explains, these people "estimate the truth of their new philosophic views in direct proportion to the degree of offensive hostility which [this view] exhibits toward everything that is held sacred by the living soul of man" (1856–1864/1971: iii). They have forgotten that the true nature of intellectual inquiry is to ultimately provide "one meaning": "to trace an image of the world from which we may learn what we have to reverence as the true significance of existence" (ix). Mechanism disintegrates the harmony of the ancient cosmic order, and "the further advance of mechanical science begins to threaten with similar disintegration the smaller world, the *Microcosm of man*" (xv).

The mechanist philosophers seek to describe everything in terms of forces and laws, but they overlook that such things "are not the ultimate components of the threads that weave the texture of reality" (xii). The reality Lotze has in mind is a panpsychic reality, one rather similar to Leibniz's monadology. Early in the book he briefly recounts the history of animism and its attribution of personal spirits to nature; he also examines its role in satisfying a deeper spiritual need of humanity—the need to feel at home in the cosmos. Mechanistic philosophy, according to Lotze, has taken people completely away from this primitive worldview, and he slowly leads the reader back toward acceptance of just such a world. In part II he introduces the notion that all matter has "a double life, appearing outwardly as matter, and as such manifesting ... mechanical [properties, while] internally, on the other hand, moved mentally" (150). He speaks of this inner soul- or mental-life as an "absolute indivisibility" (157), and he proceeds to draw analogies between the soul and the indivisible atoms of matter.

In a very Leibnizian manner, Lotze proposes that in fact atoms are prime candidates for possessing an inner psyche: "We once again take for granted in the multitudinous connected atoms of the body that internal psychic life which ... must be attributed to all matter." (161) Lotze's full panpsychist view is finally laid out in part III, where he makes his bid for "a thoroughgoing revolt of the heart against the coldness of a theory that transforms all the beauty and animation of forms into a rigid physico-psychical mechanism" (344). His panpsychism is founded on the principle of the indivisibility of the atom. Matter as "infinitely divisible extension" is "an illusion" (354); rather, matter consists of point-like atoms structured in a cohesive pattern by their respective forces. It is precisely this point-like nature of the atom that permits us to see it as a single unifying center of experience, with its own psychic life:

The indivisible unity of each of these simple beings [atoms] permits us to suppose that in it the impressions reaching it from without are condensed into modes of sensation and enjoyment. [As a result,] no part of being is any longer devoid of life and animation. (360)

Like the ancient Greeks, Lotze accepts that motion is ultimately attributable to such a psyche: "We must ... in general allow and maintain that all motion of matter in space may be explained as the natural expression of the inner states of beings that seek or avoid one another with a feeling of their need." (363)

The psychic lives of atoms join together to create the soul of the body. For Lotze this occurs in a very specific and fundamental process of two-way interaction. He explains that bi-directional interaction is in fact the very basis of ontology, both physical and mental. Kuelpe (1913: 168) comments on this aspect of Lotze's philosophy: "We know real relations ... only in the form of reciprocal action. Consequently the whole problem of 'being' narrows down to acquiring an understanding of reciprocal relations." Lotze then claims that the soul, as a spiritual being, stands as an unchanging entity in relation to these changing reciprocal actions. Kuelpe adds this:

Consequently all things, whose unity we recognize and for which we presuppose real relations, must be considered after the analogy of our own inner being, as spirits or souls. According to this, our body is regarded by Lotze, as it was earlier by Leibniz, as a multiplicity of individual souls ... . (171)

Kuelpe proposes that this "theory of reciprocal action is the most original and most important point" of Lotze's metaphysics (173). It is undoubtedly a central aspect of his panpsychism, as it outlines an explanation for the combination problem that faces any monad-like ontology.

Lotze acknowledges the *prima facie* improbability of his view:

Who could endure the thought that in the dust trodden by our feet, in the ... cloth that forms our clothing, in the materials shaped into all sorts of utensils ... , there is everywhere present the fullness of animated life? (1856–1864: 361)

And yet this view fundamentally changes one's outlook on the world: "dust is dust to him alone whom it inconveniences." Ultimately it is the "beauty of the living form [that] is made to us more intelligible by this hypothesis" (366). And this, says Lotze, is precisely why we must accept his view. Science itself neither wants nor needs panpsychism; rather, it is needed by the human spirit, to make the nature of the soul comprehensible.

Eduard von Hartmann (1842–1906) further developed Schopenhauer's system of the world as will and idea, drawing in elements of Leibniz, Schelling, and Hegel into a doctrine of spiritual monism. In his most famous work, *Die Philosophie des Unbewussten* (Philosophy of the Unconscious), published in 1869, he articulates a view of the unconscious will as the cause of all things. The fact that matter is resolvable into will and idea leads Hartmann to conclude "the essential likeness of Mind and Matter" (1869/1950, volume 2: 81). Like Schopenhauer, he holds to a dynamist conception of matter, of the will as manifest in elementary atomic forces:

Hencewith is the radical distinction between spirit and matter abolished; their difference consists only in higher or lower forms of manifestations of the same essence. ... The identity of mind and matter [becomes] elevated to a scientific cognition, and that, too, not by killing the spirit but by vivifying matter. (180)

Hartmann continues by noting that previous attempts at monism were extreme: materialism denied spirit, and idealism denied matter. He sees his monism as a system that does justice to both.

Like Fechner, Hartmann sees each cell of the organic body as endowed with consciousness. The animal "has as many (more or less separate) consciousnesses as he has nerve-centers, nay, even as he has vital cells" (225). These individual consciousnesses are united through intimate communication:

Only because the one part of my brain has a direct communication with the other is the consciousness of the two parts unified; and could we unite the brains of two human beings by a path of communication equivalent to the cerebral fibers, both would no longer have two, but one consciousness. (224)

Communication and exchange thus resolve the combination problem, a view that recalls Diderot's claim.

Hartmann's work was prescient but unfortunately not very influential. His focus on the unconscious reappears, without credit, in the writings of Ernst Haeckel and Friedrich Paulsen. Generally speaking, his overall synthesis of ideas was underappreciated by later philosophers, in Germany and elsewhere.

The Austrian physicist Ernst Mach (1838–1916) was known primarily for his scientific advances, but he produced some important philosophical writings in the early 1880s. He made substantial contributions to the philosophy of science, and he was an early proponent of logical positivism. For Mach, the primary aim of science was to predict and describe, and only secondarily to explain. Epistemologically he was strongly empiricist.

Mach developed a neutral monist philosophy in which the primary substance of existence was neither mind nor matter but rather "sensations."

That led him rather suddenly to a panpsychist conception of reality. "In adolescence," Hamilton recounts (1990: 127), "Mach was a Kantian, but then he reacted against the thing-in-itself, experiencing a panpsychic epiphany in which (to quote Mach) 'the world with my ego suddenly appeared to me as one coherent mass of sensations.'" It was around this time, in 1863, that Mach wrote the following:

> Let's confess it straightaway! We cannot reasonably discover any external side to atoms, so if we are to think anything at all, we must attribute an internal side to them, an inwardness analogous to our own souls. In fact, how could a soul originate as a combination of atoms in an organism, if its germ were not already contained in the atom? (in Heidelberger 2004: 157)

This is a striking statement: Science reveals no "exterior" to atoms at all, only various fields of force. If they are to be real, then, they must have an interior, along the lines of our own mentality. And furthermore, since human minds cannot emerge from no-mind, it must reside in the atomic parts. Thus we find two compressed arguments for panpsychism in a single passage.

A decade later, Mach had apparently acquired something of an adverse reputation for such ideas. In his lecture notes of 1872, he cited a panpsychist statement by astrophysicist Karl Zöllner: "Sensitivity is a general attribute of matter, more general than mobility." Mach then added this: "I myself have been reproached for saying that." (in ibid.: 159)

Nonetheless, Mach persisted in his views, which were developed most fully in *The Science of Mechanics* (1883). "Properly speaking," he wrote, "the world is not composed of 'things' ... but of colors, tones, pressures, spaces, times, in short what we ordinarily call individual sensations." (1883/1942: 579) On first glance the view that all things are sensations recalls a conventional Berkelian idealism, but then it becomes clear that there is no observing mind involved. One might call it a pansensist view, but one clearly different from the pansensism of Telesio or Campanella; they held that all things do sense (i.e., have the power of sensing), whereas Mach holds that all things in themselves *are* sensations. But who or what is doing the sensing? Or are things simply subjectless sensations? At one time he accepted the idea of a personal ego, but eventually he dropped it. He thus seems to ultimately have argued for a theory of "objective sensations," independent of any so-called ego or subject.[9]

9. This was the view of Hamilton (1990: 117–118): "the 'given' ... was not to be construed as given *to* someone. 'Experience' was essentially subjectless."

If Mach is less than clear on the details of his pansensism, he is unambiguous about his monist ontology and its panpsychist implications. "The fundamental character of all these [human] instincts," he writes, "is the feeling of our oneness and sameness with nature; a feeling ... which certainly has a *sound basis*" (559). He goes on to characterize both mechanistic monism and animistic monism as inadequate worldviews:

[O]ur judgment has grown more sober. ... Both [the mechanical and animistic mythologies] contain undue and fantastical exaggerations of an incomplete perception. Careful physical research will lead ... to an analysis of our sensations. We shall then discover that our hunger is not so essentially different from the tendency of sulphuric acid for zinc, and our will not so greatly different from the pressure of a stone, as now appears. We shall again feel ourselves nearer nature, without its being necessary that we should resolve ourselves into a nebulous and mystical mass of molecules, or make nature a haunt of hobgoblins. (560)

Clearly Mach is sensitive to the close association between his view and primitive animism, and he wants to make nature sensate without introducing personal spirits. He seems to draw inspiration from Schopenhauer (note the comparison between "will" and "pressure of a stone"), if only implicitly, and we know from his other writings that he was highly influenced by Fechner. Mach equates the processes of nature with human inclinations and feelings, and his opposition to mechanistic ontology steers him toward a view of "nature as animate" rather than "human as mechanical." His particular form of pansensism led the way for the soon-to-follow developments of James (radical empiricism) and Whitehead (process philosophy).

One of the first major philosophers to embrace Darwin's theory of evolution was Ernst Haeckel (1834–1919). Haeckel, who developed the biogenetic law that ontogeny recapitulates phylogeny, quickly became known as the leading German Darwinist. He developed a monistic philosophy in which both evolution and the unity of all natural phenomena played major roles. His system was clearly panpsychist, even pantheist, and he strongly opposed the mysticism and irrationalism of Christianity.

Even in his first philosophical work, *The History of Creation* (1868), Haeckel vigorously promoted his monistic philosophy, using the theory of evolution as evidence. The unity and relatedness of all living things convinced him that all dualities were false, and especially that of body and mind. Furthermore, he argued, mind-body duality was a particular instance of the physical duality of matter and force (or energy), and hence that too was a false duality; body was equated with matter, mind was equated with energy, and all were intimately connected:

[B]ody and mind can, in fact, never be considered as distinct, but rather that both sides of nature are inseparably connected, and stand in the closest interaction. ... The artificial discord between mind and body, between force and matter, ... has been disposed of by the advances of natural science. (1868/1876: 487)

Science had now achieved what philosophy alone could not: compelling proof of the monist worldview. Truth was to be found in nature, and it was therefore "necessary to make a complete and honest return to Nature and to natural relations" (496). Natural science had proved the truth of evolution, and this theory promised great things for humanity: "[In the future] mankind ... will follow the glorious career of progressive development, and attain a still higher degree of mental perfection." (495)

Haeckel was explicitly panpsychist by 1892. In an article for *The Monist* he wrote: "One highly important principle of my monism seems to me to be, that I regard *all* matter as *ensouled*, that is to say as endowed with *feeling* (pleasure and pain) and *motion*." (1892: 486) Here he offers one argument for panpsychism, namely that "all natural bodies possess determinate chemical properties," the most important being that of "chemical affinity." This affinity, Haeckel says, can be explained only "on the supposition that the molecules ... mutually *feel* each other" (483). Elsewhere he employs evolution on behalf of the Continuity argument, claiming that evolution shows "the essential unity of inorganic and organic nature" (1895: 3). Evolutionary monism strikes at the heart of both the religious worldview and the mechanical philosophy: "Our conception of Monism ... is clear and unambiguous; ... an immaterial living spirit is just as unthinkable as a dead, spiritless material; the two are inseparably combined in every atom." (58)

Haeckel's most famous work, *The Riddle of the Universe* (1899), was meant to be a popular book that would explain the essentials of the monistic view to the general public. It succeeded in becoming a best-seller in Europe— rare for a work of natural philosophy. Drawing on the latest developments in physics, Haeckel presented the case for his monism, then claimed that science had proved the conservation of mass, the conservation of energy, and the equality between matter and energy. In the end he arrived at a neutral-monist position in which his ultimate reality was "substance," which possessed two simultaneous attributes: matter and energy. He embraced the term "force-matter," which was functionally identical to our present-day "mass-energy." This was something of a milestone in the history of monistic philosophy. From the earliest days of philosophy, when Empedocles argued that all reality was composed of four elements (fire, air, water, earth) and two forces (Love and Strife), philosophers had sensed that things like mass and energy were of fundamental importance, but the monists perennially had difficulty explaining just how these two entities were to be unified. Haeckel saw in evolutionary monism the resolution to many age-old problems in philosophy.

The specific resolution that Haeckel envisioned was equating mass with body and energy with spirit, then uniting these two pairs in an explicitly Spinozan manner. He made this case throughout *The Riddle of the Universe*: All living creatures, microbes included, possess "conscious psychic action." The inorganic world also possesses an inherent psychic quality, though he took care to emphasize that this is "unconscious" rather than "conscious" mentality. This applied even to the atoms: "I conceive the elementary psychic qualities of sensation and will, which may be attributed to atoms, to be *unconscious*." (1899/1929: 179)

One of Haeckel's last major works, *The Wonders of Life* (1904), is primarily an elaboration of his previous ideas. In it, though, he refers to himself for the first time as a hylozoist, apparently fearing—unnecessarily—the connotation of consciousness with the term 'panpsychism'. "Monism," he writes, "is best expressed as hylozoism, in so far as this removes the antithesis of materialism and spiritualism (or mechanism and dynamism)." (88) And it is in this work that he first proposes a third fundamental attribute to his one substance—to matter and force he adds *psychoma*, or "general sensation." This is his response to the charge that mere matter and force/energy are not in themselves "psychic" enough to account for mind. Paraphrasing and expanding on Goethe, he summarizes his view as follows: "(1) No matter without force and without sensation. (2) No force without matter and without sensation. (3) No sensation without matter and without force." (465)

During Haeckel's lifetime, philosophy and science had diverged to the point that he could be criticized by professional philosophers as a "mere scientist." The conflict was exacerbated by his bold claims that natural science had solved problems that traditional philosophy found intractable. He drew the ire of major philosophers of the day, most notable among them Friedrich Paulsen (1846–1908). Paulsen was a panpsychist who had advocated a view that was substantially in agreement with Haeckel's.[10] The root of the conflict seems to have lain in the fact that Haeckel's primary training had been in biology and science, and that he had come rather late, but with spectacularly success, to philosophy—especially with *The Riddle of the Universe*. Paulsen disliked both Haeckel's claim that evolutionary theory was the key to philosophical progress and his belief that religion and classical metaphysics had been defeated by natural science. The criticisms have some merit, but Paulsen's disagreements seem to center more on professional competition than on substantial philosophy.

5.4   A Survey of the Field

Paulsen is an important figure in his own right. His 1892 *Introduction to Philosophy* was the first work in history to present a detailed academic survey of panpsychism and the first to review and summarize a number of historically important positions. In that book Paulsen also articulated his own views on panpsychism—views that were substantially in line with those of Haeckel, Fechner, Schopenhauer, and Leibniz.

As a German philosopher, Paulsen's emphasis was, naturally, on German thought of the 1800s. In addition to Fechner, Schopenhauer, and Leibniz, he covered Lotze, Schelling, Wundt,[11] von Nägeli, and Zöllner,

10. For a good summary of Paulsen's criticisms, see DeGrood 1965: 57–64.

11. Wilhelm Wundt is occasionally cited as a panpsychist, but he seems to have been half-hearted at best. His primary treatise on psychology (1892) offers scant mention of the subject. He does oppose emergentism ("It is surely inadmissible to suppose that mental existence suddenly appeared at some definite point in the developmental chronology of life"—1892/1894: 443), which implicitly leaves him with some form of panpsychism. But the discussion that follows includes only a single passage that cautiously endorses it: "[W]e have every right to assume that primitive mentality was a state of simple feeling and sensing; while the possibility that this state accompanies every material movement-process … is still certainly not to be denied. At least, it looks very much more probable than the materialistic function hypothesis, if we accept the dictum 'Ex nihilo nihil fit' [out of nothing comes nothing]."

but he also referred to the panpsychist arguments of Spinoza, Hoeffding, and du Bois-Reymond. Paulsen's survey is far from exhaustive; he mentions early Greek thinkers only in passing, he makes no reference at all to Hellenistic philosophy, Renaissance naturalism, or French vitalist materialism, and he inexplicably ignores the work of Hartmann and Mach. Despite these weaknesses, *Introduction to Philosophy* is an important book, presenting virtually every extant argument for panpsychism. Panpsychism is not the entire focus of the book, but it is clearly a central theme, forming the core of chapter 1 and persisting as a primary theme throughout. Many of Paulsen's formulations of existing arguments are still advocated and debated today, and thus it is worthwhile to examine his general case for panpsychism in some detail.

Paulsen begins by attacking the basis of materialism. He claims that the materialistic theory—characterized as the theory that "all reality is corporeal or the manifestation of corporeality"—is a fundamentally inadequate conception. He immediately adopts an idealist standpoint: "Bodies have [only] phenomenal existence. ... Their entire essence is a content of perception." (1892/1895: 75) He then attributes to materialist philosophers two possible views: that "states of consciousness are effects of physical states" (reductive materialism) and that "states of consciousness ... are nothing but physical states of the brain" (identity theory). He dismisses the second view, that "thoughts are movements in the brain," by claiming that such a statement has no meaning. One is then obliged, he argues, to consider that the physical and the psychical bear some sort of relationship to one another. This relationship must be either interactionist (and hence causal) or parallelist (and therefore acausal). Materialism, Paulsen claims, typically opts for the former. But this involves a "transformation of motion or force into thought," resulting in a "destruction of energy" in the physical realm—a recognized impossibility. Similarly, a transference from the psychical to the physical would appear as "creation out of nothing" and hence also impossible. Thus, one is forced to conclude that a form of parallelism must be true.

Parallelism, or acausality, logically assumes that the mental doesn't affect the physical, and conversely that the physical doesn't affect the mental. The first condition leads one to the view that "the living body is an automaton" (87), albeit a complex and sophisticated one. Of the second condition, Paulsen states that psychical events, such as a particular sensation, must have a cause. Since the cause cannot be physical—under the conditions of parallelism—it must be psychical. In other words, mental events are caused only by preceding events of a like nature.

Paulsen concludes, along with Spinoza and Fechner, that physical events move along in corporeal causal chains, and mental events move along in psychical causal chains. The two chains simply proceed together; they are "concomitant." Furthermore, Paulsen claims that, of the two chains, the psychical is the more fundamental, because it is "the representation of reality as it is by itself and for itself" (92). He attributes this advance to Leibniz. And it justifies his claim that such a view is a form of idealism.

Paulsen then addresses the question of panpsychism: In which physical structures does this parallel chain of events exist? Like Schopenhauer, he begins introspectively. Each person is directly aware of his own mental states. He then extends this by analogy to other human beings and deduces the existence of others' mental states. The crucial question is "How far may this inference be extended?" The commonly accepted view of the time was to include all animals, but he notes that there is no sharp dividing line between animals and plants, and that therefore the rational conclusion is that plants possess an inner life as well. He notes additional similarities between animals and plants: in aspects of nutrition, cellular structure, genetic reproduction, development and death, even language. In considering whether such a position constitutes a proof of the plant-soul, Paulsen quickly turns the tables on the materialist: "To deny that there is [a plant-soul], would, to say the least, require some proof." (96) "The burden of proof," he argues, "rests on him who denies the validity of the analogical syllogism. He must show why it is not valid here, otherwise his negation is arbitrary." (98)

Eventually Paulsen arrives at the main point of contention: the inorganic world. In brief, his arguments are the following:

(1) There is "no difference in substance" between organic and inorganic bodies; they are "composed of the same ingredients" (the Evolutionary Continuity argument). Developments in biology and chemistry had confirmed this by the late 1800s, and the theory of vitalism—that living beings are composed of some unique material or substance—was becoming discredited. "The same forces act in inorganic as well as in organic bodies." (104)

(2) The question "Whence did psychical life arise?" (100) raises the classic
     emergence issue. The sudden appearance of a mental realm "would be
     an absolute 'world-riddle'; it would mean a creation out of nothing."
     This Non-Emergence argument is supported by natural science. Since
     scientists accept that organic beings are formed out of inorganic mate-
     rial, and hence no new "vital substance" appears, they should accept
     the same reasoning and allow that psychical life of the higher organ-
     isms is composed of lower elements of inorganic mentality. And within
     the realm of living beings, the theory of evolution supports this view:
     "The process of psychical evolution runs parallel with the evolution of
     organic life." (143)

(3) Paulsen addresses the argument that living beings exhibit "spontane-
     ous activity," and that this is an indication of an inner sense. He points
     out that chemistry and physics demonstrate that even the smallest
     and simplest pieces of matter are active, self-organizing, and respon-
     sive (the Indwelling Powers argument): "Your inert, rigid matter ... is a
     phantom that owes its existence, not to observation, but to conceptual
     speculation. ... Modern science has utterly discarded that idea of such
     absolutely dead and rigid bodies. Its molecules and atoms are forms of
     the greatest inner complexity and mobility." (101–102) This, of course,
     is true, and aligns with our current thinking.

(4) Schopenhauer's Continuity argument, based on first principles, holds
     that all things appear to us as sensations or sensory phenomena—that
     is, as ideas. But, like humans, things must also have an inner nature.
     Thus, Paulsen informs us, "that which appears to us as a body must be
     something in and for itself" (105). We know firsthand that human bod-
     ies have an inner sense, and logically "analogous phenomena point to
     analogous inner being." Therefore, "to every body which ... appears as
     a relatively complete system of phenomena and activities, [the logical
     thinker] ascribes a relatively complete inner life like his own."

Like Fechner, Paulsen applied similar reasoning to large-scale systems
such as the Earth, concluding that it is clearly reasonable to ascribe them an
inner life as well. Ultimately he acknowledged that such arguments stand
on a different plane than conventional scientific or materialist ones: "these
thoughts are not matters of scientific knowledge. ... This is no place for
real scientific work." (109) "Still," he continued, "they have their value."
The world-soul, which he saw as a logical necessity, can serve as a kind of

non-religious deity, arrived at by reasoning rather than ancient theological texts. More important, "this view destroys the negative dogmatism of a purely physical view of the world" (110). Conversely, the hallmark of an "empty and low life" is the development of "a nihilistic conception of life, [and] a loss of reverence for moral and spiritual greatness" (69). Inevitably, "such a nihilistic view of life naturally tends to a materialistic philosophy" (70). For Paulsen, materialism was an indicator of weakness and deficiency; panpsychism was a sign of greatness and depth.

5.5   Nietzsche and the Will to Power

No philosopher placed more emphasis on the philosophy of greatness than Friedrich Nietzsche (1844–1900). If Paulsen saw panpsychism as the path to greatness, Nietzsche strode that path with the utmost flair and conviction. The foundational concept of this approach was his ultimate metaphysical principle, *der Wille zur Macht*—the will to power. In humans, according to Nietzsche, this power is manifest as the consummate life-affirming drive, an inclination to achieve dignity, mastery and greatness. But it is also the ground-source of the flourishing of life generally, and most broadly, the force by which all things in nature exert and expand their claim on existence. A strong argument can be made that the will to power was ultimately a form of panpsychism, but one that he developed only cautiously.

The evolution of Nietzsche's thinking on panpsychism constitutes a fascinating study of the emergence of one of his central themes. It seems that he was strongly predisposed to something like panpsychism from his teenage years, though initially it was more a version of classical pansensism than a system based on the will. From late 1865, when Nietzsche was 21 years old, the influence of Schopenhauer's panpsychist metaphysics became pronounced, ultimately looming over of all of his writings. Parallel to his thinking on panpsychism was his development of the will-to-power thesis. For several years these two concepts existed side by side; not until in 1884, when he was 40, did they become unified.

The strikingly hostile reception to Nietzsche's panpsychism among recent commentators is directly relevant to the present study. His view is denied, defamed, denigrated, and ignored—despite considerable evidence to the contrary. Indeed, this is a case study in present-day attitudes toward panpsychism generally.

Let me begin by presenting the evidence for Nietzsche's panpsychism in his own words. It is extensive, but most of his statements on the topic occur not in his published works but in the *Nachlass*, his unpublished notebooks. Consistent with their unpublished status, they are also unpolished—often mere sentence fragments, and cryptic ones at that. This is perhaps the critics' strongest point; had he truly been committed to panpsychism, they say, he surely would have emphasized it in his published books. But I do not find that argument very compelling. Nietzsche's primary concern seems to have been humanity—specifically our values, our religious beliefs, our societal norms, and our human condition. His metaphysics is developed primarily as it applies to human beings and their place in the world. At least toward the end of his short productive life, he seems not to have developed a systematic metaphysics of reality in general—at least, not to the point where he was ready to compose a book on the subject.[12] With more time, he might have tackled the subject directly. As it is, we must reconstruct his thinking largely on the basis of the notebook entries.

His earliest known reference to panpsychism comes from 1861, when Nietzsche was only 17 years old. In an autobiographical essay, he notes in passing that "the 'spiritless' [*Geistlose*] cannot exist—all that is, lives."[13] One may be inclined to dismiss such a passage as mere youthful hylozoistic musing, but it does indicate a general sympathy to the idea, and from an early age.

More than a decade passed before Nietzsche's next series of comments on the subject. In his notebooks of 1872 we read the following:

Is there such a thing as an unconscious inference? Does matter *infer*? It has feelings and it strives for its individual being.

What if thoughts were the essence of things? What if memory and sensation were the *matter* of things?

The impact, the influence of one atom upon another is likewise something which presupposes *sensation* [*Empfindung*].[14] Something which is intrinsically alien can

12. Early in 1889, when he was only 44 years old, Nietzsche suffered a severe mental breakdown that ended his productive life. The cause is unknown; it has been variously attributed to syphilis, manic-depression, meningioma, stroke, and early-onset dementia.

13. *Denn alles, was ist, lebt* (Nietzsche 1954, volume 3: 89).

14. *Empfindung* is usually translated as "sensation," but it can also mean "feeling" or "perception."

have no effect upon anything else. What is difficult is not awakening sensation, but awakening consciousness. Yet this is nevertheless explicable if everything is sensate. [In this case,] whether larger or smaller, these sensation complexes would be called 'will'.[15]

Notable here is his recognition that a pansensist universe would solve the emergence problem. Also significant is his connection, already at this early date, between the sensation-complexes and the will.

In the same year, 1872, Nietzsche published his first major work, *The Birth of Tragedy*—a book that contains some suggestive though ambiguous passages relating to panpsychism. He writes of the "omnipotent art impulses" in nature, and notes that the more closely he perceives them the more he is "impelled to the metaphysical assumption [of] the truly existent primal unity" which is "eternally suffering and contradictory" (section 4). A few lines later he speaks of "suffering, primal and eternal, the sole ground of the world." These thoughts recur in section 5, where the "primal unity" is said to experience "pain," and the "heart of the world" is portrayed as "primordial contradiction and primordial pain, together with primordial pleasure." All this points to a kind of sensitivity at the core of being. Also suggestive is Nietzsche's extended quotation of Schopenhauer's panpsychist masterpiece *The World as Will and Idea* in the same section.[16]

In the following year, 1873, we find this notebook entry: "I have nothing but sensation [*Empfindung*] and idea [*Vorstellung*]. ... That which is, is sensation and idea." (KGW 26[11])[17] Three years later, in 1876, we find the first mention of the phrase *Wille zur Macht* (will to power) in the notebooks (KGW 23[63]); it would not appear in published form until *Thus Spoke Zarathustra* in 1883. As was noted above, there was no initial linkage between will to power and anything like panpsychism.

The will-to-power thesis was slow to develop. A second appearance in the notebooks would not occur until 1880 (KGW 4[239]), some four years after its debut. But related terms did gradually emerge. *Daybreak* (1881), for example, includes several mentions of a "feeling of power" (*Gefühl der*

15. Nietzsche 1979: 35–36.

16. And again, at even greater length, in section 16. The English translations of passages in *The Birth of Tragedy* given here are Kaufmann's.

17. KGW refers to *Kritische Gesamtausgabe Werke* (Colli and Montinari 1967). The German text is available at http://www.nietzschesource.org/ under "Posthumous fragments."

Macht).[18] *The Gay Science* (1882) includes a reference to "the doctrine of the feeling of power" in section 13, and in section 310 Nietzsche examines "will and wave," in which the crashing ocean waves exhibit many signs of purposive activity.[19]

In *Zarathustra* (1883) we find the first publication of the phrase "will to power": "A tablet hangs over every people. ... Behold, it is the voice of their will to power." (1883/1954: 170) Later in the work there is an implied connection to Schopenhauer:

Where I found the living, there I found will to power. ... Only where there is life is there also will: not will to life but—thus I teach you—will to power. (226–227)

Schopenhauer's notion of the world as will is elaborated in his primary work as a specific form of will, namely will to *life*: "And since what the will wills is always life ... it is all one and a mere pleonasm if, instead of simply saying 'the will,' we say, 'the will to life'" (1819/1995: 177).[20] Nietzsche rejected this qualification, even as he initially found will to power only in living things. Life wills *power*, not merely more life.

Had this been his final word on the matter, we would have had will to power as a strictly organic phenomenon; in *Zarathustra*, only living things will power. In recent literature, this interpretation is called the "biological will-to-power." Some current commentators believe that this was always Nietzsche's view, or even that he only ever meant it to apply to human beings ("anthropocentric will-to-power"). My claim here, by contrast, is for *ontological* will-to-power[21]: will to power as an essential feature of reality. Only this suffices to demonstrate a panpsychist outlook.

Up to *Zarathustra*, we have no evidence of ontological will-to-power in the writings of Nietzsche. But a contemporaneous notebook entry suggests that something comparable is forthcoming. In an important 1883 entry, Nietzsche comments on the lack of grounding for the assumption that

18. See sections 23, 113, 189, 204, 348, and 356.

19. "How greedily the wave approaches, as if it were after something! ... It seems that it is trying to anticipate someone. ... And now it comes back ... with excitement; is it disappointed?—But already another wave is approaching ... and its soul, too, seems to be full of secrets and the lust to dig up treasures. Thus live waves ... ."

20. Of course, this will to life is embodied in all things, non-living included. Evidently, for Schopenhauer even inorganic substances have a will to life.

21. Also called cosmological or metaphysical will-to-power in the literature.

matter is non-experiential: "Substance devoid of feeling is only a hypothesis! No experience [of this]! Sensation [*Empfindung*] is thus a property of substance: there are sensitive substances." (KGW 24[10]) Then in the next year, 1884, we find a decisive and unambiguous notebook entry: "reduction of generation to the will to power (it must also be present in the appropriated inorganic matter!)" (KGW 26[274]). This is our first indication that a shift has occurred; will to power is now seen as residing in matter itself. If the will is now an ontological feature of reality, as it was for Schopenhauer, then a form of panpsychism obtains.

In 1885, several of Nietzsche's notebook entries confirm the ontological view. Consider this clear and explicit statement from *Writings from the Late Notebooks*: "that it is the will to power which guides the inorganic world as well, or rather, that there *is* no inorganic world" (Nietzsche 2003: 15). Most of the relevant entries from that year, though, appear in the posthumous book *The Will to Power* (1906/1967):

The only force that exists is of the same kind as that of the will. (section 490)

The victorious concept of "force" ... still needs to be completed: an inner will must be ascribed to it, which I designate as "will to power." (section 619)

We cannot think of an attraction divorced from an *intention*. (section 627)

The drive to approach—and the drive to thrust something back are the bond, in both the inorganic and the organic world. The entire distinction is prejudice. (section 655)

There is absolutely no other kind of causality than that of will upon will. (section 658)

Perhaps the most dramatic such statement appears in the final entry in the book (still from 1885):

This world is the will to power—and nothing more! And you yourselves are also this will to power—and nothing more! (section 1067).

But there is nothing on the ontological will-to-power thesis in Nietzsche's published works until *Beyond Good and Evil* (1886), wherein we find the extended and hotly debated section 36, in which he seems to endorse the ontological view. But his tone raises questions, providing an opening for his critics. He writes in provisional language ("Suppose ... ") and speaks of an "experiment": What, he asks, if "the so-called mechanistic (or 'material') world" held the same rank as "a more primitive form of the world of affects in which everything still lies contained in a powerful unity" before

it became "organic"—"as a kind of instinctive life," as a *"pre-form* of life."[22]
If the will has causal power, he writes, "then we have to make the experiment of positing the causality of the will hypothetically as the only one. ...
In short, one has to risk the hypothesis whether ... all mechanical occurrences are not, insofar as a force is active in them, will force, effects of will."
The section concludes as follows:

Granted finally that one succeeded in explaining our entire instinctual life as the development and ramification of *one* basic form of will—as will to power, as is *my* theory—[then] one would have acquired the right to define *all* efficient force unequivocally as: *will to power*. The world seen from within, the world described and defined according to its "intelligible character"—it would be "will to power" and nothing else.

I won't relate here the many alternate interpretations of this section.[23] On my view, the suppositional form and the "experimental" language do not alter the basic commitment to the message. It is rather like an atheist saying "Suppose there were no God" and then laying out his case. It is a rhetorical tactic, nothing more.

We find two other clues later in *Beyond Good and Evil*. Section 186 speaks assertively of "a world whose essence is will to power"—a relatively clear and explicit phrase. But then we have section 259, which has been used by some proponents of biological will-to-power, and against the ontological view. Nietzsche writes that "life simply *is* will to power," and of "the will to power, which is after all the will of life." But this is no contradiction: On the ontological view, everything, life included, is will to power. If on certain occasions he emphasizes this fact, it doesn't exclude the notion that nonlife is also will to power. He doesn't say that *only* life is will to power. He simply observes that life, like everything, is such a will at its core.

A second published reference to the ontological view appears in *On the Genealogy of Morals* (1887). The primary passage comes in the second essay, but early in the work we read that "a quantum of force is equivalent to a quantum of drive, will, effect—more, it is nothing other than precisely this very driving, willing, effecting" (34). Nietzsche then cites an inorganic

22. This recalls Aristotle's "sort of life" in all things, discussed in chapter 2 of the present volume.

23. For a flavor of the debate, see Clark 1990: 212–218; Clark and Dudrick 2012: 229–243; Endres and Pichler 2013; Hill 2007: 77–87; Janaway 2007: 154–157; Loeb 2015; Stack 2005: 197–201.

example—lightning—to press his point, followed by references to the scientific concept of force, the atom, and the thing-in-itself. The main passage, though, comes in section 12 of the second essay:

… all aims, all uses are merely *signs* indicating that a will to power has mastered something less powerful than itself and impressed the meaning of a function upon it in accordance with its own interests. So the entire history of a "thing," an organ, a custom may take the form of an extended chain of signs … . (58)

The meaning of this becomes clearer as we progress:

I emphasize this central perspective of historical method all the more since it is fundamentally opposed to the prevailing instincts and tastes of the time, which would rather accommodate the absolute arbitrariness, even mechanistic senselessness of all that happens, than the theory of a *will to power* manifesting itself in all things and events. (59)

The "senselessness" of mechanistic philosophy derives from the fact that it posits nothing, no motive force, at the center of material reality. There is no interior at all. This notion is reflected in the contemporaneous book 5 of *The Gay Science*, in which Nietzsche says "an essentially mechanical world would be an essentially *meaningless* world" (section 373).

The year 1887 also continued the string of relevant notebook entries. In *The Will to Power* we read:

"Being" as the universalization of the concept "life". … Being—we have no idea of it apart from the idea of "living."—How can anything dead "be"? (sections 581–582)

In *Writings from the Late Notebooks* (Nietzsche 2003) we find this: "what appears to be 'purposiveness' … is merely the consequence of the *will to power* played out in everything that happens" (156). And this: "the 'will to power' expresses itself in the *interpretation*, in the *way* that *force is consumed*" (199). Will to power seems to be a primordial aspect of the world: "the 'will to power' cannot have become" (207). And further: "all 'purposes,' 'goals,' 'meanings,' are only modes of expression and metamorphoses of the single will that inheres in all that happens, the will to power" (217).

Into his last productive year, 1888, Nietzsche continued such observations with unwavering consistency. In one of his final published works, *Antichrist*, he virtually defines will to power as the ultimate good: "What is good? All that enhances the feeling of power, the Will to Power" (section 2). *The Will to Power* contains several reiterations of the ontological view:

Every atom affects the whole of being. ... That is why I call it a quantum of "will to power." (section 634)

The will to power not a being, not a becoming, but a *pathos*—the most elemental fact from which a becoming and effecting first emerge. (section 635)

[E]very center of force—and not only man—construes all the rest of the world from its own viewpoint, i.e. measures, feels, forms, according to its own force. ... My idea is that every specific body strives to become master over all space and to extend its force (—its will to power) ... . (section 636)

[A]ll driving force is will to power, that there is no other physical, dynamic or psychic force except this. (section 688)

The will to accumulate force. ... Should we not be permitted to assume this will as a motive cause in chemistry, too?—and in the cosmic order? (section 689)

[L]ife is merely a special case of the will to power. (section 692)

[T]he innermost essence of being is will to power ... . (section 693)

And then the last such entry (2003: 259):

That will to power in which I recognize the ultimate grounds and character of all change ... .

Such is the evidence. Objectively considered, the case for ontological will-to-power—that is, for panpsychism—seems clear enough. Nietzsche's lifelong sympathy, the extensive notebook entries (documented over the final five years of his productive life), and the occasional published references all point to this conclusion. His general acceptance of Schopenhauer as his "great teacher"[24] is another clue, as is his high regard for the panpsychist pre-Socratic philosophers. Galen Strawson (2015b) is certainly sympathetic to this conclusion; that Nietzsche held that "reality is suffused with—if it doesn't consist of—mentality in some form or sense" he calls "very probably true" (11). On the strength of the primary evidence, it would be difficult to come to any other determination.

Or so one would think. Somehow, though, mainstream thinking on Nietzsche disagrees—and strongly. A review of the recent literature exposes the striking fact that nearly every recent commentator opposes the ontological view, and dismisses any talk of panpsychism in the strongest possible terms. This phenomenon is highly revealing as a statement on panpsychism generally.

24. Preface to *On the Genealogy of Morals*.

The tone was set in 1950, when Walter Kaufmann, in an influential book titled *Nietzsche: Philosopher, Psychologist, Antichrist*, concluded that "the projection of the will to power from the human sphere to the cosmos is an afterthought—an extreme conjecture which is not substantiated by the evidence and at variance with Nietzsche's own critical principles" (367). Later, in his entry on Nietzsche in *The Encyclopedia of Philosophy*, Kaufmann put it even more bluntly: "As a metaphysical theory about the universe or ultimate reality, the doctrine need not be taken seriously, not even in an effort to understand Nietzsche." (1967/1972: 510) Nehamas (1985: 75) clearly agrees, calling the ontological view "horrible," a "wildly implausible picture," and "unflinchingly obscure." By 1990, Maudemarie Clark was ready to launch an all-out attack, arguing that the ontological view is not "worthy of serious consideration" (209), that there is "overwhelming reason to deny that Nietzsche accepts" the view (213), and that Nietzsche himself "pretty much admits [that it is] only interpretation" (221). Poellner (1995: 286) simply states that "this [ontological] model is itself not a coherent one."

Things did not improve in the new millennium; in fact they got worse. Richardson (2000: 114) finds the "vitalist" ontological view "unbelievable," something that "involve[s] a confused projection of human cognitive powers into places they simply can't be." Williams (2001: 77) states, flatly, "I interpret will to power nonmetaphysically, noncosmologically, and nonontologically." For Moore (2002: 43), ontological will-to-power is "anthropomorphic" and "reminiscent of Leibniz's pan-animism." Bittner (2003: xxi) castigates Nietzsche for being "somewhat cavalier" and writes that the ontological view represents a kind of "mummification" of thought; it is "really sunk" and has "no chance of being true." For Richardson (2004: 51), it is merely a "useful fiction," a "metaphor or image." The literal view is "incredible" and an "apparent absurdity" (64). Stack (2005: 198) finds the crucial section 36 of *Beyond Good and Evil* to be "a completely suppositional *Gedanken-experiment*" that lays out a "deliberately constructed exoteric myth." It is "an elaborate, cleverly devised deception" and "cunningly misleading." Porter (2006: 551) finds the ontological view "deeply anthropomorphic" and "too fantastical even to imagine." Mincing no words, Janaway (2007: 153) calls it an "appalling embarrassment," asserting that defenders of the panpsychist interpretation have "a virtually impossible task" and that section 36 is "not really a literally meant argument at all."

The past few years have brought more of the same. Young (2010: 545) says there is "nothing more anthropomorphic" than the ontological view, calling it "obviously false." Clark and Dudrick (2012: 237) declare the view "a nonstarter," "laughable," and "obviously implausible." For Endries and Pichler (2013: 105) the "supposedly central 'doctrine'" is "purely virtual." Leiter (2013: 594) calls the ontological view "silly," "unimportant," and (four times on the same page) "crackpot." Loeb (2015) at least tries to be objective, writing that the widespread "interpretive hostility" to the ontological view "derives from a misunderstanding of this concept as panpsychist" (!). Surprisingly, Loeb asserts that section 36 of *Beyond Good and Evil* is "actually ... a refutation of panpsychism" (85), merely a "counterfactual thought experiment" that involves a "confused projection of human psychology" (72). In the end, he writes, "Nietzsche's naturalistic methodology commits him to rejecting panpsychism as an anthropomorphic falsification of nature and reality." (76)[25]

What can we say about such statements? What thinking is operating behind such evidently deficient assessments?[26] I think we can reconstruct an implicit argument here: (1) Panpsychism is a ludicrous and discredited thesis. (2) No philosopher of any merit would hold such a view. (3) Nietzsche is among the greatest philosophers in history. Therefore, (4) Nietzsche was not a panpsychist. And then the analysis proceeds from there. The evident bias is clear. Undoubtedly all the above commentators know little or nothing about the history or arguments for panpsychism; if such were not the case, they would not dismiss it out of hand as "crackpot," "laughable," or a "nonstarter."

The situation with Nietzsche today is comparable to that with Spinoza in the middle years of the twentieth century, when nearly all commentators were hostile to panpsychism. It took 30 or 40 years for the consensus opinion to shift to a panpsychist reading. By all accounts, a comparable shift on Nietzsche's views will take as long.

25. Strawson (2015b) gives one of the few sympathetic treatments. Parkes (1994) and Hill (2007) are relatively neutral on the matter. Reginster (2012) declares himself "agnostic."

26. As evidence of this deficiency, the reader is invited to review any of the critical sources mentioned above and then determine how many of the relevant Nietzsche passages are cited there.

6   The Anglo-American Perspective

Near the end of the 1800s, the focus of panpsychism shifted again, this time to the Anglo-American philosophers. In the early years of the twentieth century, panpsychist views appeared in the writings of Charles Sanders Peirce, William James, Francis Bradley, and Josiah Royce. Since that time the majority of works addressing panpsychism have come from British and American thinkers. The century was also marked by the emergence of several prominent scientist-philosophers who either sympathized with or directly advocated panpsychist views; they will be discussed in chapter 8.

6.1   Anglo-American Panpsychism of the Late Nineteenth Century

English panpsychism, largely absent since the time of Henry More and Margaret Cavendish, was reestablished in 1874 by the physicist and philosopher William Kingdon Clifford (1845–1879). That year, he published an article, titled "Body and Mind," in which he claimed that science had bridged the gap between the organic and the inorganic. By then it was known that the same chemical elements and same laws of physics applied to both realms, and hence the laws of the organic were "only a complication" of the inorganic. Clifford then proceeded to explore whether there was a basis for believing that a similar bridge had been built between the Science of Physics and the Science of Consciousness.

Beginning introspectively, Clifford notes that, for him, "there is only one kind of consciousness, and that is to have fifty thousand feelings at once, and to know them all in different degrees" (1874/1903: 46). This state of consciousness is "an extremely complex one," a complicated unity arising from a multiplicity of sensations. As a singular state of consciousness, it is something completely non-physical and non-material: "We have no possible ground ... for speaking of another man's consciousness as in any sense a part of the physical world of objects or phenomena. It is a thing entirely separate from it." (53) Clearly he is referring to a naturalistic yet non-material mind, and not arguing for an immaterial soul in the traditional sense. If the mind is immaterial, it cannot be reduced to force, as others have argued, because force is clearly physical and observable. The conclusion then must be a form of parallelism—"the physical facts go along by themselves, and the mental facts go along by themselves."

The view Clifford arrived at was a form of Spinozan parallelism that incorporated elements of LaMettrie's and Diderot's vitalist materialism. Clifford regarded the human body as "a physical machine," but "not *merely* a machine, because consciousness goes with it" (57). In making his case for panpsychism, he applied the Continuity argument: As we move down the chain of living organisms,

> it is impossible for anybody to point out the particular place in the line of descent where [absence of consciousness] can be supposed to have taken place. ... Even in the very lowest organisms, even in the Amoeba ... there is something or other, inconceivably simple to us, which is of the same nature with our own consciousness, although not of the same complexity. [Furthermore] we cannot stop at organic matter, [but] we are obliged to assume, in order to save continuity in our belief, that along with every motion of matter, whether organic or inorganic, there is some fact which corresponds to the mental fact in ourselves. (60–61)

Echoing Fechner, Clifford then notes that his doctrine "is no mere speculation, but is a result to which all the greatest minds that have studied this question in the right way have gradually been approximating for a long time."

Four years later, Clifford expanded on his views in the journal *Mind*, advocating a monist philosophy in which the basic constituent of reality is "mind-stuff."[1] Mind-stuff is neither mind nor consciousness, but rather the elements that combine together to form "the faint beginnings

---

1. The concept of a mind-stuff theory did not originate with Clifford. It was anticipated as far back as Democritus and his idea of the soul-atom. Leibniz's monads are another, more developed precursor. And in Herbert Spencer's *Principles of Psychology* (1855) we find this: "There may be a single primordial element of consciousness, and the countless kinds of consciousness may be produced by the compounding of this element with itself ... in higher and higher degrees." (1855/1897: 150) Clifford was, however, the first to explicitly promote a panpsychist mind-stuff theory.

of Sentience."[2] Mind is viewed as composed of "mental atoms" that exist in parallel with physical atoms and which combine in an analogous manner. "A moving molecule of inorganic matter does not possess mind, or consciousness; but it possesses a small piece of mind-stuff." (1878: 65) Intelligence and volition emerge only in higher-level complexes of mind-stuff, but a kind of proto-consciousness seems to be present in all things.

Clifford's mind-stuff theory was vulnerable to the combination problem. He offered no answer, and his untimely death a year later precluded any chance for resolution. This unresolved issue led certain philosophers to "reject decisively every form of mind-stuff."[3] Others, including William James, were fascinated by it. James dedicated an entire chapter of his 1890 book *Principles of Psychology* ("The Mind-Stuff Theory") to it. After acknowledging the power and attraction of such a theory, he rejected it for essentially the same reason: Mental atoms cannot combine, because to do so they would have to be combined "upon some entity other than themselves" (158)—i.e., something non-mental.[4]

The next important development occurred in a work by the noted British author Samuel Butler (1838–1902). More a novelist than a formal philosopher, Butler nonetheless offered speculations on philosophical and metaphysical matters, and was an ardent supporter of evolution. He discussed his panpsychist views in his 1880 book *Unconscious Memory*

Like many other thinkers of the time, Butler noted that scientists had determined that the nature of the organic was the same as that of the inorganic, that vitalism had been largely disproved, that organic matter had been shown to be identical with inorganic, and that the same forces were everywhere present—views that hold to this day. The logical conclusion, then, was that certain essential characteristics of the living must inhere, in

2. This is very similar to the modern notion of "proto-mind" or "proto-consciousness," in which certain basic elements of reality are not themselves mental, but in combination give rise to mind.

3. Stout 1919b/1952: 212–213.

4. For the early James, "mental combination" is impossible, whether for mental atoms or for individual people; the so-called group mind doesn't exist. James responds to the challenge of mind-stuff by proposing his own alternative: "polyzoism" or "multiple monadism," which is just as strongly panpsychist as the theory of mind-stuff. By 1907 James had revised his view to allow for the possibility of mental combination and group mind.

some form, in the non-living. "If we once break down the wall of partition between the organic and inorganic," Butler writes,

the inorganic must be living and conscious also, up to a point. ... It is more coherent with our other ideas, and therefore more acceptable, to start with every molecule as a living thing ... than to start with inanimate molecules and smuggle life into them; ... what we call the inorganic world must be regarded as up to a certain point living, and instinct, within certain limits, with consciousness, volition, and power of concerted action. (23)

At the conclusion of *Unconscious Memory* Butler reiterates his perspective, suggesting that it is the morally enlightened view: "I would recommend the reader to see every atom in the universe as living and able to feel and to remember, but in a humble way. ... Thus he will see God everywhere." (273) That a moral perspective is engendered by panpsychism is perhaps not obvious: "True, it would be hard to place one's self on the same moral platform as a stone, but this is not necessary; it is enough that we should feel the stone to have a moral platform of its own." (275) This is one of the earliest commentaries, along with those of Fechner and Paulsen, to cite the moral relevance of panpsychism. It indicates an emerging ecological value system in which objects of nature have intrinsic moral worth.

Gregory Bateson, apparently inspired by Butler, cited him on a number of occasions. But Bateson disagreed with the principle of attributing life and mind to atoms; rather, he adopted more of a qualified panpsychism in which all things *except* atoms possess minds—because they have no parts.[5]

In an 1884 article titled "Religion: A Retrospect and Prospect," the noted evolutionist Herbert Spencer (1820–1903) retraced the evolution of religion, discussed the origins of primitive animism, and observed that the spirits of nature gradually became more powerful, more unified, and more abstract. The concept of God, he asserted, lost more and more of its anthropocentrism, eventually becoming a kind of pure consciousness or spirit.

Spencer argued that the concept of God-as-First-Cause was a necessary and real aspect of the world, and that this God, stripped of all superfluous characteristics, was nothing more than pure mind. He saw force and consciousness as two distinct entities, but since "either is capable of generating the other, they must be different modes of the same [thing]" (1884: 9). He

5. Bateson's ideas are discussed in more detail in chapter 8 of this volume.

concluded from this that "the Power manifested throughout the Universe distinguished as material, is the same power which in ourselves wells up under the form of consciousness." Science, he noted, had confirmed that view. He then went on to claim that physics had revealed the "incredible power" of brute matter, as with the ability of simple materials to transmit sounds over wireless airwaves. And so too "the spectroscope proves ... that molecules on Earth pulsate in harmony with molecules in the stars." The man of science, Spencer wrote, was forced to conclude that

every point in space thrills with an infinity of vibrations passing through it in all directions; the conception to which [the enlightened scientist] tends is much less that of a Universe of dead matter than that of a Universe everywhere alive: alive if not in the restricted sense, still in a general sense. (10)

In 1885, Morton Prince published *The Nature of Mind and Human Automatism*, in which he presented a naturalist, Schopenhauerian metaphysic that he characterized as a form of materialism in which the inner essence or thing-in-itself of matter was, following Clifford, mind-stuff. Prince's was not a dual-aspect theory; it was more of an idealist monism that opposed the inert view of mechanism: "matter is no longer the dead and senseless thing it is popularly supposed to be" (1885/1975: 163). Evolution suggested the unity of all phenomena. As a consequence, he wrote, "the whole universe ... instead of being inert is made up of living forces; not conscious [but] pseudo-conscious. It is made up of the elements of consciousness." (164)

Charles Strong wrote approvingly of Prince's book, calling it "an extremely clear and forceful statement of the panpsychist hypothesis" (1904a: 67). He noted that Prince was "entitled to an honorable place among [panpsychism's] earliest discoverers and defenders." In fact Prince and Clifford were the first two philosophers to articulate systemic and explicit panpsychist theories strictly as theories of mind, rather than as adjuncts to larger metaphysical systems. Prince drew on both Schopenhauer and Clifford, and reinterpreted their theories in an evolutionary vein.[6]

6. Prince summarized his theory and responded to some criticisms in his 1904 essay "The Identification of Mind and Matter," and he also explicitly stated that "consciousness and the brain process are identical" (447), which made him one of the first identity theorists of his era in England. Prince's view also emphasizes the close connection between identity theories and panpsychism. (See the discussion of Herbert Feigl in chapter 9 of the present volume.)

6.2   William James

In 1890, William James (1842–1910) published his first major work, the aforementioned *Principles of Psychology*. In it he examined the mind-stuff theory in detail, noting that the essence of the mind-stuff approach is that, as with the monads, higher-order consciousness is compounded of simpler, atomic mental entities. The theory of evolution, along with other scientific advances, offered a strong line of reasoning in favor of a pan-psychist mind-stuff theory; if complex material bodies could evolve from simpler ones, why couldn't the same happen for psychical entities? From an evolutionary-psychological viewpoint, James wrote, "if evolution is to work smoothly, consciousness in some shape must have been present at the very origin of things. ... Some such doctrine of atomistic hylozoism ... is an indispensable part of a thorough-going philosophy of evolution." (1890/1950: 149)

James appears to have implicitly agreed with this statement but doesn't seem to have been convinced that mind-stuff was the proper interpretation. As has already been noted, the combination problem was for him an insurmountable barrier to the mind-stuff theory. On the ground that mental entities can only compound upon something non-mental, he called the compounding of consciousness "logically unintelligible." Further, he argued, such a sum exists only to an outside observer and not in itself. In support, he quoted Royce: "Aggregations are organized wholes only ... in the presence of other [external] things. ... Unity exist[s] for some other subject, not for the mass itself." (159) However, James commented in a footnote (162) that he was not opposed to combination *per se*, only to the intelligibility of combination within the assumptions of the mind-stuff theory. On his view, a combination resulted in something "totally new" and unlike that which composed it. Mind-atoms could combine not to form mind, but rather something completely different—though perhaps still mind-like. Thus the problem remained unresolved.

Upon rejecting the mind-stuff theory, James offered up the alternative theory of "polyzoism" or "multiple monadism." He claimed no original-ity for that view—which "has been frequently made in the history of phi-losophy"—but simply asserted that it was the most logically consistent and problem-free alternative. Consider the human brain. Under polyzoism, every cell in the brain has its own unique consciousness, which is distinct from and unrelated to the consciousnesses of the other cells. But the cells clearly interact physically, and their interaction is brought together in a unifying hypothetical entity that James calls the "central cell" or "arch-cell." Unfortunately science finds no evidence of any such central cell in the brain or any other organ. Furthermore, one cannot stop logically at the cell; one must extend the reasoning down to some ultimately small and simple units, arriving at a system much like Leibniz's monadology: "The theory [of polyzoism] must set up for its elementary and irreducible psycho-physic couple, not the cell and its consciousness, but the primordial and eternal atom and its consciousness." (180) Such a view is "remote and unreal" but nonetheless "must be admitted as a possibility"—and in fact "must have some sort of a destiny."

In 1890, James was only implicitly panpsychist. His soul-theory took on all the central features of Leibniz's monadology, including the universal presence of a central unifying point of mind—though he did not yet claim that all things have souls. Not until later would he argue more explicitly for what he called "pluralistic panpsychism." His panpsychist metaphysics is one of the few such systems to have been seriously discussed and debated in recent philosophical discourse; for a detailed treatment, see Ford 1982. I will summarize some of the most important points here.

James' metaphysical turn roughly coincided with the turn of the century. In 1901 and 1902 he presented his Gifford Lectures, which were then published as *Varieties of Religious Experience* (1902). In the book he clarified his conception of panpsychism without yet truly endorsing it. First he indicated his sympathy with a panpsychist or animist worldview:

How could the richer animistic aspects of Nature ... fail to have been first singled out and followed by philosophy as the more promising avenue to the knowledge of Nature's life? ... A conscious field PLUS its object as felt or thought of PLUS an attitude toward the object PLUS the sense of a self to whom the attitude belongs [constitutes a] full fact ... ; it is of the *kind* to which all realities whatsoever must belong." (392–393)

James' first explicit endorsement of panpsychism came in a series of lecture notes to a philosophy course taught at Harvard University in 1902–03. According to Perry (1935: 373), James announced that "pragmatism would be his method and 'pluralistic panpsychism' his doctrine."

The series of 1904–05 lectures that would become *Essays in Radical Empiricism* (1912) marks a further change in James' thinking, as he seems to move more toward a position of neutral monism. Here he suggests, after the manner of Mach, that "pure experience" is the ultimate reality. James seems to recognize that his view of radical empiricism is close to panpsychism, yet he defers an elaboration:

The "beyond" must of course always in our philosophy be itself of an experiential nature. If not a future experience of our own ... , it must be a thing in itself in [pan-psychists] Dr. Prince's and Professor Strong's sense of the term—that is, it must be an experience *for* itself. ... This opens the chapter of the relations of radical empiricism to panpsychism, into which I cannot enter now. (1912/1996: 88–89)

Later in the book, James again suggests that the problems of causality between mind and matter lead "into that region of pan-psychic and onto-logic speculation of which [panpsychists] Professors Bergson and Strong have lately [addressed] in so able and interesting a way. ... I cannot help suspecting that the direction of their work is very promising, and that they have the hunter's instinct for the fruitful trails." (189)

In his 1905–06 lecture notes, he once more steers toward panpsychism: "Our only intelligible notion of an object *in itself* is that it should be an object *for* itself, and this lands us in panpsychism and a belief that our physical perceptions are effects on us of 'psychical' realities." (in Perry 1935: 446)

James' 1907–08 Hibbert Lectures, published as *A Pluralistic Universe* (1909), not only furthered his commitment to panpsychism but also made clear his fundamental opposition to the attitude and logic of conventional materialism. There are, he said, two kinds of philosophers: the cynical and the sympathetic. The former inevitably develop materialistic philosophies; the latter develop spiritualistic ones. Here we see his recognition of the ethical imperatives that are built into one's worldview. Spiritualism may be either of the traditional dualist type or of the monist variety. The spiritual monists, furthermore, may be radically monist (e.g., absolute idealism) or may be more a "pluralist monism." James then places himself and his radical empiricism in the latter group. The monism resides in the fact that all things are pure experience, the pluralism in the fact that all things are "for themselves" (that is, are objects with their own independent psychical perspectives). Radical empiricism is thus not only sympathetic; it is a morally vital philosophy. Materialism, because it removes the intimacy between mankind and nature, is cynical and axiologically defective: "Not to demand intimate relations with the universe, and not to wish them satisfactory, should be accounted signs of something wrong." (1909/1996: 33)

As I have already noted, James devoted an entire lecture (chapter) to Fechner's panpsychism and gave a very sympathetic reading. The next lecture, "Compounding of Consciousness," offers his final solution to the combination problem. Formerly he had argued that any collective experience had to be unlike the constituent experiences; they had to be "logically distinct." The result, logically speaking, was that combination was impossible. Now he realizes that this situation is "almost intolerable" because "it makes the universe discontinuous" (206). Such logic forces one to conclude that the universe is a "contradiction incarnate." If analytic logic compels one to this view, "so much the worse for logic" (207). For James, logic is an intellectual tool of the cynical, materialistic philosophers, and he thus transcends it. He adds this: "Reality, life, experience, concreteness, immediacy, use what word you will, exceeds our logic, overflows and surrounds it." (212) Combination, therefore, is possible after all, and in fact it maintains the continuity of mind throughout the universe.

Here, too, James abandons his earlier soul-theory: "Souls have worn out both themselves and their welcome, that is the plain truth." (210) Individual minds and the hierarchy of lower- and higher-order mind constitute the reality of the cosmos: "the self-compounding of mind in its smaller and more accessible portions seems a certain fact" (292).

In the final lecture, James states his belief in a superhuman consciousness and speculates that "we finite minds may simultaneously be co-conscious with one another in a super-human intelligence."[7] Overall, he advocates "a general view of the world almost identical with Fechner's" (309–310). He foresees a new worldview, a fundamental change in philosophy, "a great empirical movement towards a pluralistic panpsychic view of the universe" (313).[8] This new system "threatens to short-circuit" the cynical worldview of the mechanistic materialists.

Not that we must abandon all present modes of thinking, or fall into mysticism or irrationalism. James holds out the hope that, in his new worldview, "empiricism and rationalism might [yet] strike hands in a lasting treaty of peace"; he implores thinking people to "seek together ... using

7. He comments that paranormal phenomena provide strong evidence for this view: "I find in some of these abnormal or supernormal facts the strongest suggestions in favor of a superior co-consciousness being possible." (299)

8. "Empirical," again, refers to his radical empiricism, in which everything is pure experience.

all the analogies and data within reach" to understand this new conception of mind and consciousness. "Why," he asks, "cannot 'experience' and 'reason' meet on this common ground?" (312) The new worldview is thus spiritual, sympathetic, even reverent. Following Paulsen, James notes that the greatest order of mind in the cosmos is that which we may call God. God is the mind of the cosmos, a kind of nouveau world-soul in which we all co-consciously participate. "Thus does foreignness get banished from our world. ... We are indeed internal parts of God and not external creations, on any possible reading of the panpsychic system." (318)

Others of James' later writings reinforce his final commitment to panpsychism. In the Miller-Bode notebooks of 1908 he writes that "the constitution of reality which I am making for is of [the] psychic type" (in Perry 1935: 764). His last writings include a series of essays meant to be a kind of philosophical text; they were eventually collected and published as *Some Problems of Philosophy* (1911a). In the last two of these essays he again addresses the problem of causation, considering both the conceptual and the perceptual views. The conceptualist or "intellectualist" approach consists of essentially a Humean negation of causality, something he derides as "confused and unsatisfactory." Preferable is a perceptualist view based on our own personal experience of the continuity of causality. This leads James into the mind-body relationship and its larger implications. He takes the experience of causal continuity as literally the stuff of causation—recalling his radical empiricism. Upon taking this view, "we should have to ascribe to cases of causation outside of our own life, to physical cases also, an inwardly experiential nature. In other words we should have to espouse a so-called 'pan-psychic' philosophy." (218) In the posthumously published *Memories and Studies*, James remarks:

[T]here is a continuum of cosmic consciousness, ... into which our several minds plunge as into a mother-sea or reservoir. ... Not only psychic research, but metaphysical philosophy, and speculative biology are led in their own ways to look with favor on some such "panpsychic" view of the universe as this. (1911b: 204)

Ultimately, he writes, what is important in philosophy is vision. "Philosophy is more a matter of passionate vision than of logic." (1909/1996: 176) Unfortunately, "few professorial philosophers have any vision," and "where there is no vision the people perish" (165). Pluralistic panpsychism seems to provide James with the vision he seeks.

Reaction to James' panpsychism is revealing. Despite the considerable evidence, most philosophers still argue that James only "toyed" with panpsychism. A few—among them Ford (1981, 1982), Kuklick (1977), Cooper (1990), and Sprigge (1993)—explicitly acknowledge his endorsement, Ford (1982) citing several examples to the contrary.

6.3   Royce, Peirce, and Other Sympathetic Thinkers

Four important panpsychist works were released in 1892. One was Friedrich Paulsen's *Introduction to Philosophy*, discussed in chapter 5. Another was "Panpsychism and Panbiotism," a notable article by Paul Carus, editor of *The Monist*. In the article, Carus offers some pro and con thoughts on panpsychism, proposing that the term 'panbiotism' be used in its place. "Everything," he argues, "is fraught with life; it contains life; it has the ability to live." (234) Surprisingly, he dismisses Ernst Haeckel's view that matter possesses mind or soul as "fantastic," and proceeds to develop his own definition of soul. One of the more interesting sections of Carus' piece is titled "Mr. Thomas A. Edison's Panpsychism." In a brief essay titled "Intelligent Atoms," Edison had stated that "every atom of matter is intelligent." Carus quotes him as follows:

All matter lives, and everything that lives possesses intelligence. ... The atom is conscious if man is conscious, ... exercises will-power if man does, is, in its own little way, all that man is. ... I cannot avoid the conclusion that all matter is composed of intelligent atoms and that life and mind are merely synonyms for the aggregation of atomic intelligence. (243)

Quite unexpected words from one of the world's greatest inventors and practical thinkers!

In *Spirit of Modern Philosophy*, Josiah Royce—an American philosopher well known for his pragmatism and absolute idealism—proposed a theory of the Universal Self (or Logos, or World-Spirit, or God) as the cosmic mind which is the reality behind all physical phenomena. Of this Infinite Self, according to Royce, we know little directly—only that it exists, is conscious, and is fundamentally One. The Self doesn't act on reality, precisely because it *is* reality: "He isn't anywhere in space or in time. He makes from without no worlds. ... The absolute Self simply doesn't *cause* the world." (1892/1955: 348)

Royce examines several dual-aspect theories of mind, including Clifford's mind-stuff concept; he finds them unsatisfactory in their original form, but "luminous and inevitable" when understood in light of the Self. Consider two people. Their bodies follow physical laws and may interact in causal ways. But their physicality is merely a manifestation of their underlying inner reality as conscious beings. In the non-physical realm, their two minds interact, communicate, and participate—and this results in true knowledge. "He and I," Royce claims, "have spiritual relations, think of each other, and do somehow indirectly commune together." (417)

Like many other thinkers of the time, Royce saw in evolution grounds for viewing all physical objects as subject to the same metaphysical principles. Since humans possess an inner mind and a distinct identity, then so too does everything. This is the "relation of the inorganic world to our human consciousness":

The theory of the "double aspect," applied to the facts of the inorganic world, suggests at once that they, too, in so far as they are real, must possess their own inner and appreciable aspect. ... In general it is an obvious corollary of all that we have been saying. (419)

[W]e ... know that there is no real process of nature that must not have, known or unknown to us, its inner, its appreciable aspect. Otherwise it could not be real. (427)

Royce counsels the reader not to view this as mere animism or anthropomorphism. It would be simplistic and misleading to presuppose that "stones or planets" have anything like a human inner life: "it is not ours to speculate *what* appreciative inner life is hidden behind the describable but seemingly lifeless things of the world." Yet we are certain that it exists, because "the Logos finds a place for it ... in the world of appreciation." The Logos is by definition timeless, and hence the cosmos has always had this inner life—before humans, before life, before the Earth.

Royce advances this line of thinking in *Studies of Good and Evil* (1898), displaying a deepening conviction that all things have inner lives with as much reality and intrinsic worth as those of humans:

[W]e have no sort of right to speak in any way as if the inner experience behind any fact of nature were of a grade lower than ours, or less conscious, or less rational, or more atomic. ... This reality is, like that of our own experience, conscious, organic, full of clear contrasts, rational, definite. We ought not to speak of dead nature. (1898/1915: 230)

The contrast is clear: The "dead nature" of mechanism is fundamentally challenged by the panpsychic worldview.

The final and perhaps most important articulation of Royce's panpsychism can be found in *The World and the Individual* (1899–1901). He asks the reader to "suppose that even material nature were internally full of the live and fleeting processes that we know as those of conscious mental life" (213). Drawing on recent science, he then introduces some new variations on the arguments for panpsychism, all based on "four great and characteristic types of processes" (219) that ordinary matter shares with "conscious Nature" (i.e., mankind). First Royce notes that both matter and mind exhibit irreversibility in their processes—a reference to the recently formulated second law of thermodynamics. Second, he notes that both realms display a tendency to communicate: Minds and ideas interact with each other, and likewise matter and energy exhibit field properties ("wave-movements") that indicate an interpenetration and communicative interaction. Third, both show tendencies toward a quasi-stable behavior, in spite of their irreversibility, that Royce—following Peirce—calls a "habit." Nature exhibits countless "approximate rhythms" that are repeatable and definite yet never absolutely fixed. Fourth, the process of evolution demonstrates the continuity of nature, from inorganic to organic to consciousness. These are all variations on the Evolution/Continuity arguments, employing the latest developments in science and physics.

From these arguments Royce concludes that a mental aspect of nature must exist, but that it operates so much more slowly than our human consciousness that we cannot perceive it:

[W]e have no right whatever to speak of really unconscious Nature, but only of uncommunicative Nature, or of Nature whose mental processes go on at such different time-rates from ours that we cannot adjust ourselves to a live appreciation of their inward fluency, although our consciousness does make us aware of their presence. (225–226)

The "very vast [mental] slowness in inorganic Nature," such as in a rock or a solar system, is no less extant that our own mentality. Time scale is entirely arbitrary, and therefore slower is not lesser. The Mind in nature is fully conscious. Hence, a mental life is to be found everywhere:

Where we see inorganic Nature seemingly dead, there is, in fact, conscious life, just as surely as there is any Being present in Nature at all. And I insist, meanwhile, that no empirical warrant can be found for affirming the existence of dead material substance anywhere. (240)

The fourth significant publication of 1892 was "Man's Glassy Essence," in which Charles Sanders Peirce (1839–1914) discussed the relation between the psychical and physical aspects of material things. This was the fourth of Peirce's five famous *Monist* articles on metaphysics, published in 1891–1893. The first three—"The Architecture of Theories," "The Doctrine of Necessity Examined," and "The Law of Mind"—laid the groundwork for the panpsychist vision he set forth in "Man's Glassy Essence."

"The Architecture of Theories" begins with a discussion of the "brick and mortar" of any viable philosophical system. That article, like all of the five, is very diverse in concepts; Peirce seems to dash from one topic to the next, only roughly forming a consistent overall theme. After discussing the relevance of evolution to philosophy of mind, he asserts that "the old dualistic notion of mind and matter ... will hardly find defenders today" (1891/1992: 292). We are thus compelled to a new form of monism—one that he designates, surprisingly, 'hylopathy', meaning the view that all matter "feels."

This monism must have one of three forms: neutralism (in which mind and matter are independent), materialism (in which the physical is primary), and idealism (in which the mental is primary). Peirce rejects neutralism because two independent entities are proposed where only one is required. He dismisses materialism as "repugnant to scientific logic" because "it requires us to suppose that a certain kind of mechanism will feel." Thus, we are left with idealism. Peirce has in mind a particular variation, "objective idealism":

The one intelligible theory of the universe is that of objective idealism, that matter is effete mind, inveterate habits becoming physical laws. (293)

Here Peirce refers to his so-called cosmogonic thesis in which the universe originates in a condition of pure, chaotic feeling, then becomes progressively crystallized into matter as this mind undergoes a kind of solidification through patterns of recurrence that he calls "habits." Mind is thus at the core of reality. It exists in varying stages of solidification (or "objectification," as Schopenhauer would have it), and can be seen in one sense as matter and in another as mind.

In "The Doctrine of Necessity Examined" Peirce rejects determinism, arguing instead for his own version of anti-necessitarianism ("tychism"). One of the reasons for his rejection is that necessitarianism requires an entirely unsatisfactory epiphenomenal view of mind: "Necessitarianism cannot logically stop short of making the whole action of the mind [sim-ply] a part of the physical universe. ... Indeed, consciousness in general thus becomes a mere illusory aspect." (1892a/1992: 309) Some small degree of tychistic freedom is required to "insert mind into our scheme."

Peirce returns to panpsychism briefly in "The Law of Mind." He observes that "*tychism* must give birth to an evolutionary cosmology ... and to a Schelling-fashioned idealism which holds matter to be mere specialized and partially deadened mind" (1892b/1992: 312). But he then diverts again to a different discussion. At the end of the article he reiterates that "what we call matter is not completely dead, but is merely mind hide-bound with habits" (331).

Coming now to the main piece, Peirce begins "Man's Glassy Essence" with a look at physics and chemistry, then goes on to discuss primitive life forms and the protoplasm inside all living cells. Of all the properties of protoplasm, the most important is that it "feels"—and what is more, it exhibits all essential qualities of mind. Sensitivity and sentience are inferred, Peirce tells us, by analogy: "[T]here is fair analogical inference that all protoplasm feels. It not only feels but exercises all the functions of mind." (1892c/1992: 343) Among the properties on which the analogy is based are reaction to the environment, ability to move, ability to grow, and ability to reproduce.

And yet, Peirce writes, protoplasm is simply complex chemistry, a partic-ular arrangement of molecules. Feeling cannot be accounted for by mecha-nistic laws; therefore, we are forced to admit "that physical events are but degraded or undeveloped forms of psychical events" (348). He then pre-sents his own dual-aspect theory of mind:

[A]ll mind is directly or indirectly connected with all matter, and acts in a more or less regular way; so that all mind more or less partakes of the nature of matter. ... Viewing a thing from the outside, ... it appears as matter. Viewing it from the inside, ... it appears as consciousness. (349)

The dynamic sensitivity of protoplasm necessarily results in an enhanced capability for feeling: "nerve-protoplasm is, without doubt, in the most unstable condition of any kind of matter; and consequently, there the resulting feeling is the most manifest" (348). Again, this sort of sensitivity is a general property of matter: "Wherever chance-spontaneity [i.e. unsta-ble sensitivity] is found, there, in the same proportion, feeling exists." Peirce thus effectively introduces a new argument for panpsychism, drawing on the correlation between a specific physical characteristic—dynamic sensitivity—and the mental property of feeling. All matter is dynamic to some degree, and thus must be associated with an "interior" that feels. I will designate this as the argument from Dynamic Sensitivity. Like the evolutionary argument, it incorporates forms of continuity and non-emergence, to which it adds a reference to the indwelling power of dynamical systems. Clearly Peirce was only sketching out his views in this essay, but certainly the lack of a developed theory of dynamical systems restricted his ability to articulate himself. With the advent of chaos theory and non-linear dynamics in the late twentieth century, we now have new ways of expanding on Peirce's insight—see, for example, Skrbina 2009b and chapter 9 below.

Later in "Man's Glassy Essence," Peirce elaborates on his notion of a "general idea." Individual ideas, he claims, spread out over time, influence one another, and become fused together into a general idea. As he wrote in his earlier article "The Law of Mind," such general ideas are "living feelings spread out" (1892b/1992: 327). Any general idea that comes to exhibit a pattern of regularity or recurrence is said to acquire a habit: "Habit is that specialization of the law of mind whereby a general idea gains the power of exciting [regular] reactions." In fact the general idea is rather the mind of the habit. This mind associated with the general idea is a unity—one that is, in some fundamental ontological sense, like a human personality:

The consciousness of a general idea has a certain "unity of the ego" in it. ... It is, therefore, quite analogous to a person; and, indeed, a person is only a particular kind of general idea. ... Every general idea has the unified living feeling of a person. (1892c/1992: 350)

Peirce recognized that his generalized theory of mind applied to larger-scale super-human structures as well as the smaller sub-human systems. People who interact strongly with one another produce a true group mind that is essentially like the mind of the individual. Personhood or personality results when the feelings (sub-minds) are "in close enough connection to influence one another." "There should be," Peirce continues, "something like personal consciousness in [collective] bodies of men who are in intimate and intensely sympathetic communion." In other words, degree of participation determines degree of mind. He adds that these ideas "are no mere metaphors" and that "the law of mind clearly points to the existence of such personalities."

After the *Monist* series, Peirce continued to articulate his cosmogony, albeit in a vague and indeterminate way. This outlook relates to his broader semiotic conception of the world, in which the basic architecture of reality consists of *signs*. "All this universe is perfused with signs, if it is not composed exclusively of signs." (1934: 302) Signs in general have a symbolic nature[9]; they represent an object to an interpretant. Signs or symbols are furthermore alive; they grow, expand, and reproduce. "[E]very symbol is a living thing, in a very strict sense that is no mere figment of speech." (1992b: 264) The symbol or sign is the most general conception of life, a "living general"; "it is of the nature of a sign to be an individual replica and to be in that replica a living general. … There can be no reality which has not the life of a symbol." (1992b: 324) Biological life is but a special case of "living general."

Peirce's cosmogony, in brief, is this: In the beginning there was a vast formless state, which he calls "the ovum of the universe." This ovum was not empty, but consisted of "a primeval chaos of unpersonalized feeling"[10]— that is, of subjectless, disembodied, undifferentiated feeling-qualities. This cosmic Feeling is alive, is sentient, and may even be consciousness *per se*: "every true universal, every continuum, is a living and conscious being" (1993: 162), and "whatever is First is *ipso facto* sentient" (260). Random reactions within this vast sea of feeling-qualities at some point gave rise to a first symbol—an original, living entity that marked the beginning of natural law or "habit." With the advent of symbols or signs came space, time, matter, and energy, all of which were emergent qualities. From these things the visible universe evolved. But the cosmos never lost its fundamental character as a composition of living, feeling signs. Halton (2005) refers to this metaphysical system as "Peircean animism."

Burks (1996: 343), however, had it more correct: "Peirce is a panpsychist, making feelings (psychological Firsts) the elementary building blocks of the universe." The primordial feelings are prior not only to mind and matter, but even to space-time: "As the ultimate atoms of the universe, panpsychic feelings (Firsts) are too simple to be related by space and time." (345) Indeed, it was from precisely such feelings that space and time emerged: "Objects and events are relational complexes of Firsts. … This is

9. Formally, symbols are merely complex signs.

10. Cited on p. 27 of Houser 2014.

the sense in which space and time have evolved … ." Burks dedicates an entire section of his paper to "Peirce's panpsychic firsts." In that section he explains that "objective idealism is a form of panpsychism, the view that all objects of the universe are constituted of basic feelings and their interactions" (349–350). There are even theological implications: "panpsychic feelings provide a mental basis for Peirce's panpsychic God" (352). In a related essay, Burks (1997: 531) offers a concise summary: "Peirce's cosmic theory of evolution was a panpsychism: the universe began as a chaos of primitive feelings and gradually evolved the material and mental laws and systems of today." Houser (2014: 29) evidently concurs: "This is a panpsychism." Without citing any history, Houser acknowledges its unconventional nature: "Clearly, though, Peirce's panpsychism is not at all ordinary, but it is a panpsychism all the same … ." And it follows directly from the ideas sketched out in the *Monist* essays.

Such views are in striking contrast to Peirce's more famous analytic work in logic and positivism. Yet it is clear that he read other panpsychist philosophers—he cites Fechner, Schelling, Clifford, Carus, Empedocles, Epicurus, Gilbert, James, Leibniz, von Nägeli, Royce, and the Stoics, all in contexts that would indicate familiarity with their theories of mind. Peirce's pragmatism, like James', thus seems to have been fully compatible with a panpsychist outlook. This fact may have influenced the later pragmatists John Dewey and Ferdinand Schiller, both of whom also articulated panpsychist views.

Anglo-American panpsychism of the late nineteenth century came to a close with the British idealism of Francis Bradley (1846–1924). In 1893 Bradley published the first edition of his major work, *Appearance and Reality*. His system of idealism was based on an absolute monism in which, as with Mach and James, the ultimate reality is pure experience. "Feeling, thought, and volition," writes Bradley, "are all the material of existence, and there is no other material, actual or even possible." (1893/1930: 127) Thus, this ultimate reality is not merely experience, but "sentient experience." His monism doesn't allow for separating subject from object, and as a result the subject himself is nothing more than experience—as was the case with Schopenhauer's "will." For both subject and object, "to be real is to be indissolubly one thing with sentience" (128).

Later in *Appearance and Reality* Bradley addresses the nature of the inorganic. In his absolute monism, all things are fundamentally one, and hence the inorganic shares essential qualities with the organic. This justifies an argument by analogy: "A sameness greater or less with our own bodies is the basis from which we conclude to other bodies and souls." (239) Where the sameness is clear, so is the imputation of psychical life. But even in the cases where it is not obvious, we have "no sufficient warrant for positive denial [of mind]." In our profound ignorance of the absolute, we must allow for the possibility that "every fragment of visible Nature might, so far as is known, serve as part in some organism not [obviously] like our bodies." He reaches a somewhat tentative panpsychist conclusion:

[Physical] arrangements, apparently quite different from our own, and expressing themselves in what seems a wholly unlike way, might be directly connected with finite centers of feeling. And our result here must be this, that ... we cannot call the least portion of Nature inorganic. (240)

If this is less than a ringing endorsement, Bradley at least concludes—in the absence of evidence to the contrary—that the intellectually prudent view is to assume that inorganic matter has its own center of feeling.[11]

11. Sprigge (1993: 546) argues that only a panpsychist interpretation of Bradley is intelligible.

7 Panpsychism in the Years 1900–1950

Vigorous discussion of panpsychism continued into the 1900s. William James, Josiah Royce, and Morton Prince published important new works (cited in the preceding chapter). A significant number of major philosophers—among them Henri Bergson, Ferdinand Schiller, John Dewey, Alfred North Whitehead, and Bertrand Russell—entered the debate, offering important insights on behalf of panpsychism. Additional support came from such diverse thinkers as Pierre Teilhard de Chardin, Charles Hartshorne, Samuel Alexander, Charles Strong, Nicholai Lossky, William Montague, and Leonard Troland.

7.1 Bergson and the Early-Twentieth-Century Panpsychists

In 1903, Charles Strong (1862–1940) published *Why the Mind Has a Body*, a work that continued the Schopenhauerian argument that things-in-themselves have a mind-like nature. Like Schopenhauer, Strong interpreted this as a fundamentally panpsychist ontology. James was impressed with the book; he called it "a wonderful piece of clear and thorough work—quite classical in fact, and surely destined to renown."[1]

Why the Mind Has a Body is presented as a kind of textbook on the state of philosophy of mind. It addresses various arguments for interactionism and parallelism, each in a variety of forms. As was usual at the time, Strong doesn't present an objective study but rather steers the reader toward a particular viewpoint: "psycho-physical idealism." In support of that viewpoint, he makes arguments by Continuity and Non-Emergence[2] (287–293).

1. James 1920, volume 2: 198.

2. He considers the latter "absolutely conclusive."

Though he doesn't explicitly mention the word 'panpsychism' until the very end, it is clear that he takes the panpsychist worldview. That "thought [is] to be extended to inorganic matter [thus] making mind omnipresent in nature" is said to be "precisely the conclusion at which we have arrived" (291–292). In closing the book, Strong admits that he has no "positive conception" of the mentality that underlies all things, and thus is in no position to effectively argue whether this mentality "consist[s] of as many separate feelings as there are atoms, or of one great feeling or consciousness, or of something between the two" (354).

The missing analysis of mind was addressed in Strong's next book, *Origin of Consciousness* (1918), in which he explicitly advocated a panpsychist outlook. Regarding the nature of the mental, Strong adopts and expands on Clifford's mind-stuff theory. Mind-stuff, he writes, has four central qualities: It is "in space," "in time," and "capable of change," and most important, it "possesses the psychic character." The last quality is "the core of the whole matter, without which our panpsychism would be merely materialism" (319). Manifest in humans as "attention," it is, more generally, an intensity or vividness of experience that varies with the nature of the material object—an "accumulation of energy in a psychic state" (320).

In *Origin of Consciousness* Strong also addresses a potentially major weakness of the mind-stuff view: the combination problem. Any mind-stuff theory, he observes, necessarily adopts an atomistic conception of mind. Innumerable "minute feelings" must fuse to create a single high-level psychic state. A human, as a large-scale organism, lacks the perceptive ability to differentiate these many atomistic feelings, and thus by default experiences them collectively as a whole: "The fact of the case ... is not that we [directly] perceive the unanalyzable feeling to be one, but only that we are unable to perceive it to be many. This, of course, in no way interferes with its actually being many." (310) Just as ordinary objects appear to us as solid only because we are unable to see the individual atoms, so too our subjective feelings feel as one only because we cannot differentiate its components. Hence Strong's novel solution: Combination is an illusion, owing to our cognitive limitations. It is an epistemological problem, not an ontological problem.

It was clear to contemporary readers that Strong "regarded a panpsychistic metaphysics as the key to the mind-body problem," writes Klausner (1967: 273). Also clear, unfortunately, was "the tremendous difficulty of presenting [this] in a convincing way." Strong explicitly admitted that, with a definite note of resignation: "The difficulty of making people believe that there is in suns and atoms anything of the nature of feeling is so mountainous that I sometimes wish I had devoted my energies to something else." (1937: 5) Nonetheless, Strong stands out as one of the more consistent and open advocates of panpsychism in the first part of the twentieth century.

In 1905, William Montague (1873–1953) wrote a short piece, titled "Panpsychism and Monism," in which he defended Strong's panpsychism against criticisms raised by Theodore Flournoy—the primary one being that panpsychism is "merely verbal" and thus "methodologically useless." This is a standard mechanistic critique. The inner mental experiences of non-human things are inherently unknowable, and thus unverifiable. They further seem to be epiphenomenal, having no causal effects in the physical world. Empirical evidence, such as a magnet's motive power, can be described without recourse to any intrinsic noetic abilities. Of course, panpsychism is "methodologically useless" only if one chooses to ignore the broader implications. Clearly there are many potential ways in which one's thoughts, actions, or values could be altered by adopting a panpsychist outlook.

In a 1912 article, "A Realistic Theory of Truth and Error," Montague contrasted materialism—or "panhylism"—with two forms of panpsychism: a positive view (all matter "has something psychical about it") and a negative view ("all matter is nothing but psychical"). After criticizing the negative or idealist version, Montague lays out his own theory, a positive variation of panpsychism that he calls *hylopsychism*. It is a brief and rather cryptic theory, but it attempts to make some interesting connections between time, energy, and mind.[3] He seems to be operating more on intuition than on formal reasoning, and this suggests that there must be a path allowing for all things to participate in mind without their being at root either pure mind or pure matter.

Montague continued his defense for decades. A late piece, "Human Soul and Cosmic Mind" (1945), further develops the connection between energy

3. For example, Montague defines consciousness under this theory as "the potential ... presence of a thing at a space or time in which that thing is not actually present."

and mind. In it he argues that the physical manifestation of mind occurs as potential energy—a scientific concept defined as any system capable of doing work, such as a compressed spring or an object raised up into the air. Potential energy is ubiquitous in nature, and if it is equivalent to mind then mind is universal: "If mental states are identical with forms of potential energy then the extent to which some sort of mental reality is present in the universe will be the extent to which potential energy is present—and that is everywhere." (1945: 60)

One of the most important and visionary philosophers of the turn of the twentieth century was Henri Bergson (1859–1941). His philosophical system is complex, insightful, and unusually difficult to categorize. His central themes of time and evolution tend to paint him as a process philosopher, but his discussions of mind, creativity, freedom, and numerous other themes make for an intricate, emotionally powerful, and often enigmatic philosophy.

One of the more striking features of Bergson's thought is his flirtation with panpsychism. At times he seems to believe that mind, consciousness, or life pervades the universe and animates all matter, and yet he always stops short of clearly advocating a fully panpsychist or hylozoist position. His suggestive writings began in the late nineteenth century, one of the first being *Matter and Memory* (1896). He wrote of a phylogenic continuum from matter to life, the latter culminating in the human species: "[W]e can conceive an infinite number of degrees between matter and fully developed spirit. … Each of these successive degrees, which measures a growing intensity of life, corresponds to a higher tension of duration." (221)

The concept of duration implies time, and in the realm of life this implies memory. As the complexity of organisms increases, so too does the corresponding element of memory. Humans have the greatest capacity for memory; matter has none, yet matter still possesses pure perception— that is, perception without memory. "Now," Bergson writes, "as we have shown, pure perception, which is the lowest degree of mind—mind without memory—is really part of matter, as we understand matter." (222) In the book's conclusion, he characterizes consciousness as a universal phenomenon that somehow counterbalances individual beings and minds, unifying them while allowing them their uniqueness. "No doubt," he says, "the material universe itself, defined as the totality of images, is a kind of consciousness, ... a consciousness of which all the potential parts ... recip-rocally hinder each other from standing out." (235) He refers repeatedly to the "confluence of mind and matter," of "seeing the one flow into the other"—again, with matter representing pure perception and mind repre-senting pure memory. Ultimately he concludes, in a manner not unlike that of the ancient Greeks, that movement itself is mind-like because it necessarily involves duration (i.e., continuation) and memory:

Only one hypothesis, then, remains possible: namely, that concrete movement, capable, like consciousness, of prolonging its past into its present, capable, by re-peating itself, of engendering sensible qualities, already possesses something akin to consciousness, something akin to sensation. (247)

Nature, on this reading, is a latent consciousness with the inherent power of mind.

We find similarly suggestive passages in Bergson's most famous book, *Creative Evolution* (1907). Recalling Schopenhauer, he calls "pure willing" the "current that runs through matter, communicating life to it" (260). In an almost hylozoistic manner he argues that both matter and life are like an "undivided flux," each interpenetrating the other. But he is silent on any further implications or articulations of panpsychism.

A lecture Bergson delivered in 1911 at the University of Birmingham was included, under the title "Life and Consciousness," in a volume pub-lished in French as *L'Energie spirituelle* and in English translation as *Mind-Energy*. In his preface to English edition, the translator, H. Wildon Carr, comments that just as the earlier conceptions of physical reality have been unified under the concept of energy, so too can the ultimate psychical real-ity be described as such: "[The] dynamic conception of psychical reality has replaced the older concept of mind [identified with awareness or conscious-ness], and the physical analogy suggests energy as the most expressive term for it." (in Bergson 1911/1920: vi)

In the published version of the lecture, Bergson argues for an identity between mind and consciousness, and posits memory—along with "antici-pation of the future"—as a leading feature of consciousness. *"In principle,"* he then claims, "consciousness is co-extensive with life." (11) As to whether inert matter has any aspects of mind, he claims that "matter is necessity, consciousness is freedom." Yet mind is an energy-form that somehow inserts itself into matter and animates it—something that can happen only if the two are fundamentally linked:

We may surmise that these two realities, matter and consciousness, are derived from a common source. If ... matter is the inverse of consciousness ... then neither matter nor consciousness can be explained apart from one another. (23)

Matter would not be receptive to life unless it had a preexisting and inherent tendency to it. "In other words, life must have installed itself in a matter which had already acquired some of the characters of life without the work of life." (26–27) Again, highly suggestive, but something less than outright panpsychism.

The last and perhaps clearest indication comes from *Duration and Simultaneity* (1922), which contains Bergson's strongest statement of his process philosophy. All space-time events proceed literally from moment to moment, each phase at once both something new and something old. Every event retains some aspect of preceding events; otherwise there would be no continuity to the world. Things persist in space and in time, energy flows continuously, and characteristics and qualities carry over from past into future. There are both novelty and stability in all aspects of reality. The aspect of stability, of the carryover of past into future, is, again, an aspect of memory. The future always remembers the past, if only to a small degree, even as it creates something new. Thus memory necessarily inheres in all things. Since memory is equated with mind, the obvious conclusion is that mind is in all things. Bergson is notably clear on this point:

What we wish to establish is that we cannot speak of a reality that endures without inserting consciousness into it. ... It is impossible to imagine or conceive a connecting link between the before and after without an element of memory and, consequently, of consciousness.

We may perhaps feel averse to the use of the word "consciousness" if an anthropomorphic sense is attached to it. [But] there is no need to take one's own memory and transport it, even attenuated, into the interior of the thing. ... It is the opposite course we must follow. ... Duration is essentially a continuation of what no longer exists into what does exist. This is real time, perceived and lived. ... Duration therefore implies consciousness; and we place consciousness at the heart of things for the very reason that we credit them with a time that endures. (1922/1965: 48–49)

Capek (1971: 302) calls this passage "the basis of Bergson's panpsychism," noting that it makes little difference whether we apply the term 'panpsychism', the description "organic view of nature," or the term 'proto-mentalism'. The net result is the same: "there is no question that [Bergson] regarded physical events as 'proto-mental'" (308).[4]

4. For another perspective, see Bjelland 1981.

In the end Bergson's panpsychism is still perplexing. The relevant passages are somewhat isolated, and the deeper implications seem to be unexplored. Bergson never explicitly mentions panpsychism, nor does he discuss other comparable theories, nor does he cite any of the extensive history on the matter. This is due in part to his writing style, but one is still left wanting further elaboration.

7.2 Schiller

A major milestone in the development of panpsychist philosophy occurred in 1907: the publication of Ferdinand Schiller's book *Studies in Humanism*. Schiller (1864–1937) is best known as a humanist and pragmatist, and his unique interpretation of these approaches was original and insightful. The four major pragmatist philosophers of the early twentieth century—Peirce, James, Dewey, and Schiller—all held panpsychist views. Yet this fact doesn't appear to bear directly on pragmatism, which traditionally includes the notion that truth is not absolute but depends in some sense on human interaction and the notion that the critical factor in a philosophical theory is its consequence, its implications in the real world. Perhaps openness to panpsychism is attributable to the flexibility of thought engendered by pragmatism—the willingness to repudiate standard or fixed notions of truth—and to a view of experience as an ongoing process that is in some sense constitutive of both subject and object.

Schiller took up the personal and subjective aspects of pragmatism and developed them in light of a deeply humanistic and panpsychic perspective. Even in his first major book, *Riddles of the Sphinx* (1891), he demonstrates an openly panpsychist worldview. The central idea of that book is that matter is driven by evolutionary forces toward an ever-greater form of spirit, and in fact is essentially a spiritual substance: "Matter ultimately [is] but a form of the Evolution of Spirit." (276) This is a striking interpretation of evolution, anticipating many of the ideas that Teilhard would take up some 40 years later. Schiller observes—as Teilhard would—that "the single process of Evolution is a correlated development of both [matter and spirit]" (288). He also anticipates Teilhard's thesis of complexity-consciousness: "the growth of the complexity of material organization should be the invariable accompaniment of the growth of consciousness."

Schiller's panpsychist idealism draws heavily on scientific ideas for confirmation. He reiterates the dynamist position that atoms are simply centers of force, and that force, as an ontological category, is to be interpreted as a spiritual or mental entity:

Force is a conception which inevitably implies the spiritual character of ultimate reality. Historically it is undeniable that Force is depersonalized Will, that the prototype of Force is Will. ... The [related] sense of Effort also ... is irresistibly suggestive of the action of a spiritual being. For how can there be effort without intelligence and will? (274)

The reference to Schopenhauer's system is clear. In the end, a form of intelligence exists in all levels of matter. The force-atoms can properly be thought of as monad-like spiritual things possessing proto-mental characteristics: "it is not very much more difficult to conceive of an atom as possessing rudimentary consciousness and individuality" (277).

Schiller observes that most contemporary forms of idealism are classically humanist, in that mind either requires or is reflected in human mentality. Evolution shows that the Earth existed long before humans, and critics have used this fact to argue that without spiritual beings there could be no idealism. His "evolutionary idealism" answers that objection by claiming that "material evolution is an integral part of the world-process, and obeys the same law as spiritual evolution." Thus we must rightly conceive of atoms as "spiritual beings," for "the material is but an earlier and less perfect phase of the spiritual development" (306).

These early themes are developed more fully in Schiller's 1907 book *Studies in Humanism*, in which the notions of truth and reality are central. He directly challenges the dominant mechanistic view of objective reality, of a reality unaffected by the thoughts and perceptions of the observer. Objective reality implies a notion of absolute truth, fixed and eternal, awaiting our discovery. For Schiller such ideas are nonsensical. Both truth and reality are literally created by human beings. Our minds, working on the raw chaos of the material world, condition and shape that which we ultimately call facts or reality. Humans are active participants in the world; the making of truth is "an active endeavor, in which our whole nature is engaged" (425). He is emphatic: "reality can, as such and wholly, be engendered by the consequences of our dealings with it" (428).

Schiller takes our "making of truth" and "making of reality" to be central to any acceptable epistemology. The mere act of knowing, of encountering and contemplating, changes both the knower and the known. The knower is affected by his encounter with any given object; his active selection of things and his reactive bodily states are the most direct ways in which he is changed. The object known is affected either by physical consequences of being known or by its sensitivity to the state of the knower—something like when an actor suffers stage fright as a result of "being known" by the audience. Since obviously both the knower and the known are aspects of reality, it is clear that reality is actually changed by the act of knowing.

One can perhaps see how humans or the so-called higher animals may be affected by the processes of knowing and being known. But what about the lower animals, or plants, or inanimate objects? Schiller is adamant that *all* objects are altered by such processes. He takes the standard example: a stone—an object that displays an "apparent absence of response" and seems utterly unconcerned about its environment. But this apparent unresponsiveness is illusory:

A stone, no doubt, does not apprehend us as spiritual beings. ... But does this amount to saying that it does not apprehend us at all, and takes no note whatever of our existence? Not at all; it is aware of us and affected by us on the plane on which its own existence is passed. ... It faithfully exercises all the physical functions, and influences us by so doing. It gravitates and resists pressure, and obstructs ... vibrations, etc., and makes itself respected as such a body. And it treats us as if of a like nature with itself, on the level of its understanding ... . (442)

The common world of knowledge, the common reality between a person and a stone, is clearly not the same level of complexity as that between two people, but it is no less real. It is a brute plane of existence, one of mass, force, and temperature; it is one in which the two objects, knower and known, come together with different histories and different sensitivities. The stone "plays its part and responds according to the measure of its capacity." Schiller responds to the charge that this view is "sheer hylozoism" as follows: "What if it is, so long as it really brings out a genuine analogy? The notion that 'matter' must be denounced as 'dead' ... no longer commends itself to modern science." (443) He then correctly notes that his outlook is best described as panpsychism—as seeing all things with a mind analogous to that of a human. This is why he emphasizes that his view is that of humanism. And it also is humanistic in the sense that it seeks to fully and deeply integrate the human into the universe. After all, the true end objective of any valid system of philosophy is "to make the human and the cosmic more akin, and to bring them closer to us, that we may act upon them more successfully."

Thus Schiller makes his case that, in the process of knowing, both the knower and the known are altered, changed, re-made. The critic may reply with the charge that this is not what one means by "making reality," but that is beside the point. Of course Schiller doesn't mean that we can create something out of nothing, or that we have some strange paranormal powers. We work with the stuff of the universe, which is meaningless and in a sense non-existent in itself until we act on it and make it something known, something real.

Schiller was the first to make the leap of understanding and to see that all things have an aspect of mentality after the manner of the human, and that therefore all things, not just humans, have some power to make reality. This is not merely panpsychism, but an articulated theory of mind as an active and universal quality. He is very explicit on this point: Humanism, as he conceives it, sees "the occurrence of something essentially analogous to the human making of reality throughout the universe" (437).

Such a theory of mind has gone completely unexamined by twentieth-century philosophers—predictably so, because it was in direct opposition to the positivism and realism that has dominated recent discussions. And yet, Schiller argued, something approaching a realist position is obtained, because of our common human physiology, culture, and history. Of course, the common world among humans will be different from the one that includes other animals, or the one with inanimate objects. Such a view might be called a qualified or conditional realism. Of recent philosophers, only Skolimowski (1994) has developed this line of thinking further.

Schiller maintained this overall philosophical outlook throughout his subsequent writings. In one of his last works, *Logic for Use* (1929), he reiterates many of the themes found in *Studies of Humanism*. In discussing the meaning of humans as makers of reality, he comments: "For what is real and true for us depends on our selecting interests: the answers we get follow from the questions we put." (445) He emphasizes his pragmatism and his thesis of action: "Real knowledge does not lie idle—it colours our life. We act on it, and act differently. So reality is altered, not only *in* us but *through* us." And he again points out that every object has some qualified power to make reality and to display dynamic sensitivity to the world:

[W]e can say that inanimate objects also are responsive to each other, and modify their behavior accordingly. A stone is not indifferent to other stones. On the contrary, it is attracted by every material body in the physical world. ... The stone responds, after its fashion, to our manipulation. Treat them differently, and they behave differently: that is as true of stones as of men. (447)

Thus all objects participate in a common world based on their own capacities and sensitivities. From Schiller's panpsychist perspective, this is the process by which things collectively create an inter-subjective world. Panpsychism is the true and only basis for a reified existence.

7.3   Alexander, Lossky, Troland, and Dewey

In 1914 Samuel Alexander (1859–1938) published an important article titled "The Basis of Realism." Alexander was, along with Moore, Russell, James, Holt, and Montague, one of the so-called new realists; they argued, among other things, that objects exist independent of the human mind, but not necessarily of mind in general. Alexander proposed a metaphysical system for an evolving universe in which there are six levels of emergent reality: space-time, primary qualities of matter, secondary qualities of matter, life, animal mind, and deity. This emergent hierarchy is significant for two reasons. First, it indicates his conception of an evolutionary universe, moving from space and time through matter, life, and on to God. Alexander was one of the first philosophers, along with Schiller, to envision such a grand sweep of evolution, and he thereby anticipated some of the more important ideas of Teilhard and Skolimowski.[5] Second, it emphasizes his unique dual conception of mind: mind in the ordinary human sense, and mind as a more ontological and panpsychist reality. On the latter view, mind is seen as representing the connection between levels in the hierarchy. In particular, each specific level functions as the mind of the levels below. At the level of space-time, space is seen as primary, time as secondary; thus Alexander can claim that "time is the mind of space." Similarly, life is seen, when viewed from below, as the mind of space, time, and matter. We humans are the "mind of life," and we tend to identify this mind as true mind only because it is our privileged point of view.

The central point of "The Basis of Realism" is that our cognitive relationship with things is essentially the same as the relationship between any two objects. Alexander (1914/1960: 189) first notes that "mind and things

---

5. Skolimowski's idea of "evolutionary God" as an endpoint of universal evolution is notable. See his 1993 work *A Sacred Place to Dwell*.

are continuous in kind." This continuity between knower and known is described as one of "compresence," or co-present existence. Thus, he writes, "our compresence with physical things ... is a situation of the same sort as the compresence of two physical things with one another" (191), or, more generally, "between any two existences in the world whatsoever."[6] The focus is on the comprehension of things of an equal or lower order in the ontological hierarchy:

Mind enjoys itself and contemplates life and physical things. The living being, the tree, enjoys itself and contemplates the air it breathes. ... The distinction may be carried further down ... and it may be carried up [to the realm of the divine]. ... The universe consists of distinct real existences of different order, compresent with each other and "knowing" each other in such measure as is possible to them at their various stages of development. (195)

He concludes the essay with an argument by analogy:

[M]atter receives much more [potency] than materialism credits it with. ... It is even possible that the union of body and mind which we find in the human person may turn out in the end to be typical of every form of existence from the lowest to the highest and perhaps of the universe as a whole.

Thus he argues on the basis of first principles for panpsychism, defining mind as integral to the very structure of reality.

In perhaps his most famous work, *Space, Time, and Deity* (1920), Alexander develops these ideas further, rejecting strict parallelism between the physical and psychical and opting to see mind as an emergent aspect of each level of existence. The standard response to anti-parallelism is, he says, some form of animism in which the psychical is present in all things but is independent of the physical (volume II: 12–13). Instead of animism, he proposes a panpsychist quasi-identity theory in which physical events are causal on the physical, mental events are causal on the mental, many physical events are identical to their corresponding mental events, but some physical events have no mental counterpart. Each emergent mental level is "expressible completely or without residue in terms of the lower stage" (67). The mind is therefore "equivalent only to a portion of [a] thing"; that is, it is a subset of the total entity. Alexander thus arrives at a hierarchical form of panpsychism, with higher levels of mind building on lower levels:

6. For a good discussion of this concept that "mind-object relations have analogues at each level of finite existence," see Brettschneider 1964.

For though matter has no life, it has something which plays in it the part which life plays in the living organism and mind plays in the person; and even on the lowest level of existence [i.e. motion], any motion has its soul, which is time. Thus matter is not merely dead as if there was nothing in it akin to life. It is only dead in that it is not as alive as organisms are. ... We are compelled to the conclusion that all finite existence is alive, or in a certain sense animated. (67)

The human mind is an emergent phenomenon of our lower levels of existence—our life, our matter, etc.—and this is a process that is repeated universally; "everywhere this result appears to be secured as it is in our own persons." Hence, "all existence is linked in a chain of affinity, and there is nothing which does not in virtue of its constitution respond to ourselves ... ; so there is nothing dead, or senseless in the universe, [even] Space-Time itself being animated" (69).

The early years of the twentieth century witnessed a minor wave of panpsychist thinking in Russia. Among the more notable philosophers in that vein was Peter Ouspensky (or Uspenskii) (1878–1947). In *Tertium Organum* (1912/1981) he elaborates a startlingly clear and explicit panpsychism; in places, it is unparalleled in its candor. Adopting a strong form of the Continuity argument, Ouspensky argues passionately that, since man is alive and enspirited and is an integral part of nature, these same phenomena must be omnipresent:

If intelligence exists in the world, then intelligence must exist in everything, although it may be different in its manifestations. ... There can be nothing dead or mechanical in Nature. If life and feeling exist at all, they must exist in everything. ... We must admit that every phenomenon, every object has a mind. *A mountain, a tree, a river, the fish in the river, drops of water, rain, a plant, fire*—each separately must possess a mind of its own. (1912/1981: 165–166)

Shortly after the release of *Tertium Organum*, Nicholai Lossky (or Losskii) (1870–1965) published an important book detailing a panpsychist ontology: *Mir kak organicheskoe tseloe* (*The World as an Organic Whole*) (1917/1928). Lossky was the most influential of the Russian neo-Leibnizians, a Christian-oriented movement that began in the 1880s with Alexey Kozlov. For his part, Kozlov envisioned a form of monadology in which the monads, unlike Leibniz's variation, had the essential ability to interact. These interacting, spiritual, conscious monads were conceived as the basis of all reality. Lossky elaborated on Kozlov's system in the 1901 article "Kozlov: His Panpsychism."[7]

Lossky called his system "intuitivism." It was more articulated and far-reaching than Kozlov's, incorporating a radical interpretation of Christian metaphysics. Aligned with both the new realism of Alexander and Montague and the classical idealism of Berkeley, intuitivism held that perception is reality—that is, that reality is identical to that which is presented in the mind of the perceiver. "Knowledge," Lossky writes, "is not a copy … but reality itself."[8] Following Leibniz, he argues that the world is composed of innumerable "substantival agents," each superspatial and supertemporal, each interacting with the entire cosmos, and each creating reality through cognitive acts. This is the basis for the vision elaborated in *The World as an Organic Whole*. All objects of the material world, including humans, other animals, plants, rocks, the Earth, are in fact just substantival agents in different stages of evolution. Natural processes, forces, and events are all the result of actions of such agents. This was Lossky's view even many years later:

[A]ll events, all processes—i.e. all real being—are created by substantival agents: the singing of a tune, the experiencing of feelings or desires is the manifestation of some self. Acts of attraction and repulsion and movements in space are produced by human beings and also by electrons, protons, etc., in so far as substantival agents also lie at their basis. (1951: 253)

These agents are to be conceived as spiritual entities, and thus the world is profoundly ensouled. Starchenko (1994: 661) explains that, on Lossky's view, spirituality "is spread throughout the world, even through material nature, but in discrete, strictly apportioned portions, so that even a small portion of rock crystal had a special 'indistinct soul' that aspired to a definite goal known only to it."

Substantival agents fundamentally reflect human personhood, and thus are to be considered as persons in their own right. These persons are structured in a hierarchical fashion, from subatomic particles up to the cosmos itself. Each level of being, and each object or system within those levels, is a "person of persons," both composed of lesser agents and a part of larger-scale ones. This is Lossky's doctrine of hierarchical personalism; it recalls

7. Lossky 1901.

8. Lossky, cited in Starchenko 1994 (p. 656).

both Cardano's and Fechner's hierarchical views of the world, but is more explicit and more articulated. Agents surrender a portion of their independence to enter into alliances, forming larger-scale beings:

The combination of several agents ... is a means of attaining more complex stages of existence. ... That results in such a hierarchy of unities as an atom, a molecule, a crystal, a unicellular organism, a multicellular organism, a community of organisms like a beehive or a nest of termites; in the sphere of the human life there are nations and mankind as a whole; further, there is our planet, the solar system, the universe. Each subsequent stage of unification possesses higher creative powers than the preceding and is headed by a personality on a higher stage of developments. (1951: 256)

The preceding passage suggests an elaboration of Leibniz's thesis of the dominant monad and of Whitehead's "organism of organisms" concept.

Lossky, however, denied that his view was a form of panpsychism, which he defined as making an identification between mental and physical processes. Mental and physical events are not identical but are related via a common basis in spirit. The net result, however, clearly fits the broader definition of panpsychism: "Since all matter is active and purposive in character, so that it is capable of progressing to higher levels of being, it must be recognized that there is no lifeless matter. ... Matter is living because the basis of it is spirit." (1917/1928: 171)

In 1918, Leonard Troland, a professor of psychology at Harvard University, argued for an analytical form of panpsychism that he called "paraphysical monism." Following Clifford's mind-stuff theory, Troland claimed that the psychic realm has elementary atomic particles that are counterparts of the physical atoms. At the time, physics recognized only two elementary particles, protons and electrons; thus he argued that there must exist "at most only two kinds of psychical atoms": "para-electrons" and "para-protons." All conceivable mental states and feelings, then, would be seen as combinations of these two psychical atoms.

Since physical atoms know only two forces, attraction and repulsion, Troland claimed by analogy that the psychical atoms feel only the corresponding psychical qualities, "pleasantness" and "unpleasantness"—yet another implicit reference to Empedocles' Love and Strife. Evolution in the physical world tends toward greater cohesion and integration, and therefore the parallel psychical realm tends toward ever-greater pleasantness or happiness in an objective sense of the word. He called this the "psychical law of hedonic selection" (1918: 58).

Troland revised and developed his thesis in a 1922 article, titled "Psychophysics as the Key to the Mysteries of Physics and of Metaphysics," in which he offers an early insight into the philosophical importance of relativity theory: that it implies active participation by the observer: "all three of the fundamental dimensions of physics [space, time, mass] are conditional for their objective significance upon the conditions of observation" (145).[9] Troland then notes that the parallelism between physics and the mental realm implies the existence of a certain regularity or law-like behavior between them—"psycho-physical bridging laws." He was one of few philosophers to argue that "consciousness is at least in part representable as a mathematical function of certain aspects of organic structure and activity" (148). This led him to conclude that a form of the identity theory must be true—that "there exists a point-to-point correspondence between the constitution of immediate experience and that of the cortical activity" (150). As a consequence, "we are required to treat mind as if it were a substance and to identify it with the reality of matter" (152). He called this new, revised view "psychical monism." He claimed that it had originated with Fechner in the mid 1800s, but he also cited Clifford, Prince, Strong, and Paulsen as advocates. In spite of these panpsychic references, Troland doesn't make it clear that psychical monism is necessarily panpsychism until the end of the article. He notes that psychical activity must be associated not only with the brain as a whole but with each level of structure, from individual neuron down to atom: "For every neuron in the nervous system and for every atom in each neuron there must be a real psychical fact which is related to my consciousness." (156) Thus, each person's individual field of consciousness must be "considered the focus of a vast psychical nervous system ... made not of protons and electrons but of atoms of sentiency." This is a straightforward application of the mind-stuff theory.

But, Troland continues, "you cannot stop here," because the continuity of physical nature compels us to envision a psychical universe "which corresponds point-for-point ... with all the constituents of my organism

9. It was this idea that observation (more generally "experience" or "sentience") was implicated in any valid concept of reality that John Wheeler later developed into his notion of the participatory universe.

and of my environment; indeed, with the totality of the physical universe" (157). He refers to this as "the panpsychic extension of consciousness" to all physical reality. Furthermore, he argues, this view, far from being inconsequential, suggests a new method of metaphysical research:

This new method ... consists simply in determining carefully the laws which link the factors of human consciousness with those of brain function and then generalizing these laws ... to any physical structure or process whatever. The possibility of doing this rests upon the continuity of nature and upon the belief that human consciousness is sufficiently complex to exemplify all of the elementary psycho-physical relationships. (161)

According to Troland, panpsychic "psychical monism" has great merit and "should be expected ... to take the philosophical world by storm" (153). That it has not done so is due, he says, to the "habitually fuzzy methods of thinking" of professional philosophers and psychologists.

In 1925, the fourth major pragmatist, John Dewey (1859–1952), published his most significant philosophical work, *Experience and Nature*. In examining the connection between body and mind, Dewey comments that medieval views of causality led to stark contrasts between the two; as a result, "there were no intermediates to shade gradually the black of body into the white of spirit" (1925: 251). He then compares the physical bases of organic and non-organic things, concluding that, when properly understood, both types of objects share in comparable "qualities of interaction." This continuity between organic and inorganic is the basis for his quasi-panpsychism.

Dewey explains that any living organism exhibits certain basic qualities that we typically associate with life: needs, efforts, and satisfactions. But these processes are not unique to life. He proceeds to define each of those qualities more closely: A need is a "condition of tensional distribution of energies" wherein a body is placed in an "unstable equilibrium," efforts are movements or changes that "modify environing bodies" in such a way that equilibrium is restored, and satisfaction is the actual restoration of that equilibrium (253). The need-effort-satisfaction process is a "concrete state of events" that is common to all things, including plants:

[T]here is nothing which marks off the plant from the physico-chemical activity of inanimate bodies. The latter also are subject to conditions of disturbed inner equilibrium, which lead to activity in relation to surrounding things, and which terminate after a cycle of changes ... .

There is, of course, a difference between a plant and something like an iron molecule, and the difference "lies in the *way* in which physico-chemical energies are interconnected and operate, whence different *consequences* mark inanimate and animate activity respectively" (254). The emphasis on consequences again displays Dewey's pragmatist orientation. A plant, he claims, actively seeks to maintain its original structure. An iron molecule, on the other hand, "shows no bias in favor of remaining simple iron; it had just as soon, so to speak, become iron-oxide." Yet, of course, an iron atom retains its structure even when bound with oxygen atoms in the form of rust. The interaction with oxygen becomes dominant, and thereafter the combined structure that we call rust is what acts differently than pure iron.

Dewey doesn't attribute mind or psyche to iron molecules. These are qualities of the specially organized forms that we call "life." And yet something like sensitivity may apply to iron, in that it has the power of selection in its interaction with the environment. Iron reacts only with oxygen (under normal circumstances), and thus discriminates in favor of it. "Discrimination," Dewey adds (256), "is the essence of sensitivity."

The critical issue then is the continuity between humanity and nature, and once again a Continuity argument tends toward panpsychism. In his 1940 article "Time and Individuality," Dewey elaborates this idea from the perspective of temporality. Adopting something of a process view, he observes that time-embeddedness is central to the meaning of the human: "Temporal seriality is the very essence ... of the human individual." (1940/1988: 102) Our life-history and progressive interactions with the world are the defining characteristics of our existence as individuals. Furthermore, science reveals that "temporal quality and historical career are a mark of everything" (104), from human beings to atomic particles. This, therefore, implies a kind of individuated personality in all things, including human individuals and non-human "physical individuals." Such a viewpoint, Dewey argues, "does not mean that physical and human individuals are identical, nor that the things which appear to us to be nonliving have the distinguishing characteristics of organisms. The difference between the inanimate and the animate is not so easily wiped out. But it does show that there is no fixed gap between them." (108)

Dewey sought to avoid supernaturalism, and in a unified, naturalistic universe a compelling case can be made for attributing mind-like or person-like qualities to all things. Putting it concisely, Hartshorne (1937: 40) says of his view that "if man is natural, then nature is manlike." For Hartshorne, such continuity logically and necessarily implies panpsychism: "Consistently carried out, [Dewey's] attitude here must, if I am not deceived, carry him all the way to a radical panpsychism, according to which all process has a psychic character." (40–41) And yet Dewey himself was apparently unwilling to embrace this logical conclusion. He has been justly criticized for his half-hearted stance. Rorty (1995: 1), for example, acknowledges that "[a] sort of panpsychism ... loomed large in ... Dewey's mind." He proceeds to construct a "hypothetical Dewey" who was "a naturalist without being a panpsychist," the point being "to separate ... what I think is dead in Dewey's thought" (3).[10] Of course, it is not the panpsychism itself that is dead, but rather, perhaps, Dewey's formulation of it.

Panpsychist ideas continued to draw attention throughout the 1920s. In *Mind and Its Place in Nature* (1925), the philosopher Durant Drake (1878–1933) advocated another mind-stuff form of panpsychism. He argued that the basic building blocks of matter—energy, force, electricity— must be understood as having noetic components: "these units of matter are psychic units" (94). Such an understanding supplements rather than

10. Rorty's bias against panpsychism comes out loud and clear. He calls "futile" any attempt to "invoke panpsychism in order to bridge the gap between experience and nature" (6). He sees the only valid approach as *contrasting* experience, consciousness, or mind with nature, not in seeking to understand their connection and overlap. This is a typical objectivist, positivist approach. He claims that Dewey "dodg[ed] hard epistemological questions" in viewing nature as continuous with experience. Rorty's answer is to create a break in continuity "between non-language-users (amoebae, squirrels, babies) and language users," assigning mind and cognition only to the latter. But this approach has at least three major problems. First, what is the definition of 'language'? Certainly any form of information exchange could constitute a kind of language. Second, at what point do babies acquire mind? Does mind gradually come into existence, or does it leap into being at some initial utterance? Either answer is fraught with difficulties. Third, one cannot help but feel that this distinction based on language is an even more arbitrary and indefensible break, a dodging of hard *ontological* problems. The most definitive evidence of Rorty's stance occurs in a footnote to the article cited above: "All I have to say about [panpsychism] is contained in 'The Subjectivist Principle and the Linguistic Turn'" (211). The 1963 article doesn't contain a single mention of the term 'panpsychism' or even any discernible reference to the concept.

challenges the scientific view. These psychic units, furthermore, are neither conscious nor aware, as those qualities are reserved for highly evolved
organisms. Thus, he writes, "it would be wrong to use 'mental' or 'feeling' to denote the stuff of which things are made" (98). Likewise with
the notions of thought, sensation, emotion, and will. Such "poetic and
fanciful" anthropomorphization would be an inaccurate portrayal.

Yet Drake sees the stuff of reality as intimately psychic. "The term
'panpsychism'," he writes,

may properly be applied to our theory; but we must understand that it is only mind-
stuff that is universal, not mind itself. ... The whole world is indeed, in a sense, alive.
... It is an enormously intricate pattern of psychic units, continually changing their
interrelations. (99)

Drake's main argument is based on continuity. Humans are made of the
same materials as all things. Hence, "we are therefore free to believe that
the stuff that is deployed in this or that order throughout the universe is
the same sort of stuff that composes us, sentient being that we are." Such
a worldview has no effect on science, but despite this it has a number of
virtues:

It does assert our thoroughgoing kinship with all the rest of the natural world. It
puts an end to the need of introducing such magical entities as "souls" or "entelechies," and ... explains consciousness in natural terms. It enables us to explain the
origin of minds [and] to see *how* matter affects mind, and how mind affects matter.
(100–101)

Panpsychism, for Drake, solves important philosophical problems and
offers an integrative worldview that places humans and the human mind
in a larger natural order.

Philosophers of science were becoming aware of panpsychist theories in the
late 1920s, and a long period of scientific interest in the topic was beginning
(as I explain in the following chapter). For example, the fields of psychiatry
and psychoanalysis were developing and branching away from philosophy,
and they too brought certain panpsychist concepts into their realm of discussion. The psychoanalyst Wilhelm Reich, following Hartmann, advanced
ideas connecting the unconscious with all of nature and thus leading to a
putative resolution of the mind-body problem.[11] According to Brown (1959:

11. See chapter 6 of Berman 1981.

315), the psychologist Sandor Ferenczi believed that a movement toward a "sophisticated" form of animism was useful in psychoanalysis:

Ferenczi saw psychoanalysis as marking a significant step forward in general scientific methodology, a step which he defined as "a return to a certain extent to the methods of ancient animistic science" and "the reestablishment of an animism no longer anthropocentric."

According to Ferenczi (1926/1950: 256), Sigmund Freud himself had supported such a move:

Naive animism transferred human psychic life *en bloc*, without analysis, on to natural objects. [Freudian] psycho-analysis, however, dissected human psychic activity, pursued it to the limit where psychic and physical come in contact ... and thus freed psychology from anthropocentrism.

The result was a "purified animism" that Freud employed to the benefit of his psychoanalytic technique.

7.4   Whitehead and the Emergence of Process Philosophy

The best-known and most controversial panpsychist of the twentieth century was Alfred North Whitehead (1861–1947). The nominal founder of process philosophy, Whitehead took the insights of Heraclitus, Bergson, James, and Russell and combined them with the revelations of the so-called new physics of the day to create an intricate and complex philosophical system. Process philosophy saw time as a fundamental ontological entity, something deeply implicated in the nature of being. Given that all matter is dynamic, and that space is more properly viewed as space-time, there is clearly a sense in which all things can be seen as "events"—that is, occurrences in space and time. On this view, the event is the fundamental reality of the world.

The importance of Whitehead's system and its continuing role in panpsychist thought demand a relatively detailed discussion of his ideas.

The third phase of Whitehead's philosophical career—the so-called metaphysical phase—began in 1924, when at age 63 he accepted a professorship in philosophy at Harvard. In the next year he published the first of a number of works that included either intimations or outright affirmations of panpsychism. His panpsychist theory of mind is relatively well known and has been widely discussed, most recently by Griffin (1998), De Quincey (2002), and Clarke (2003).

As the focal point of Whitehead's metaphysical system, events—also called "occasions" or "actual occasions"—constitute the substance of the world and hence are truly fundamental. They are the sole components of reality in a creative cosmos. Occasions are "the final real things of which the world is made up. There is no going behind actual [occasions] to find anything more real." (1929/1978: 18) They constitute everything from God down to "the most trivial puff of existence in far-off empty space." Though they differ greatly in intensity, importance, and functionality, all occasions are at root fundamentally alike. Most important for present purposes, these transitory actual occasions all embody an aspect of mind, namely as "experience": "these actual entities are drops of experience, complex and interdependent." If all real things are occasions, and all occasions are "drops of experience," then all things contain an experiential, and hence mental, quality.

Panpsychism is thus at the core of Whitehead's worldview, and even more so of his conception of mind. Human beings, as natural entities, experience a particularly high-grade sort of mind—one that includes consciousness, complex feelings, and analytic abilities. Our qualities of mind, which are unique to us, do not apply to other beings. In no sense would Whitehead attribute complex, human-like mental qualities to all things. But this fundamental mode of existence—experientiality, subjectivity—is, he says, built into the very fabric of the universe. Experience is inseparable from existence.

The first major book of Whitehead's metaphysical phase was *Science and the Modern World* (1925). Nominally a history of science, it also articulates a new conception of science based roughly on quantum wave theory. Quantum particles, as we know, can assume only discrete energy states. Energy is not infinitely divisible, but exists as multiples of certain minimal quanta, or quantum units. That may have been the idea that had led James to speculate that experience too, and even time itself, was likewise quantized into discrete units. Whitehead seems to have adopted the idea and developed it further. In addition, quantum particles are defined by temporally evolving probability functions, and hence must be viewed dynamically. Matter is not a substance, it is a *process*. "Nature is a structure of evolving processes. The reality is the process." (Whitehead 1925/1967: 72) He calls this approach the "new doctrine of organism" (36), offering it as a replacement for conventional materialism.

Processes are naturally defined in terms of events. Every event has a past, a set of contemporaries, and a future; thus each event has "anticipation"— a feeling or sense for its place in the sequence of the universe. This constitutes a kind of self-knowledge, not unlike the self-knowledge that each person has. We have a fundamental knowledge of our own "total bodily event"—of ourselves as whole organisms. And this knowledge is the model on which we must view all events:

I generalize by the use of the principle that this total bodily event is on the same level as all other events, except for an unusual complexity and stability of inherent pattern. The strength of the theory of mechanistic materialism has been the demand that no arbitrary breaks be introduced into nature. ... I accept this principle. But if you start from the immediate facts of our psychological experience, as surely an empiricist should begin, you are at once led to the organic conception of nature ... . (73)

And in "organic" Whitehead intends to include "the organic unities of electrons, protons, molecules, and living bodies." This is his first step toward panpsychism.

On the one hand Whitehead finds it "difficult to believe that the experienced world is an attribute of our own personality" (90), as subjectivism would have it; on the other hand, it is clear to him that mind or mentality is somehow intimately involved in the substance of reality. He explains that the more appropriate view of a provisional realism—or, following Peirce, objective idealism—is a combination of the other two views: "[T]he world disclosed in sense-perception is a common world, transcending the individual recipient. ... [But also], cognitive mentality is in some way inextricably concerned in every detail." This passage may be read more as a description than as an endorsement, but clearly Whitehead favors the approach it sets forth.

Later in the book he elaborates further: "A natural event is only an abstraction from a complete actual occasion." (170) More to the point, "A complete occasion includes that which in cognitive experience takes the form of memory, anticipation, imagination, and thought." Just as every event can anticipate, so can every event remember, imagine, and even "think" to some degree. These qualities seem to belong to all events, and to characterize their mentality, as it were. Using his infamously obscure terminology, Whitehead describes the situation as follows:

In each case there is one finite eternal object prehended within the occasion as the vertex of a finite hierarchy. This breaking off from an actual illimitability is what in any occasion marks off that which is termed mental from that which belongs to the physical event to which the mental functioning is referred. (171)

Hence it seems that, at a minimum, every occasion—that is, every event whatsoever—possesses both a mental and a physical aspect or dimension. This foreshadows his later assignment of mental and physical "poles" to all events.

A closing indication of panpsychist thinking comes in Whitehead's declaration that every occasion possesses experientiality: "Consider an occasion *a* ... . What *a* is in itself, is that it is a unit of realized experience." (174) At the very least, all this points to an advocacy of panexperientialism, which by most accounts is a form of panpsychism.

The dual mental-physical nature of occasions or events returns more explicitly in Whitehead's 1926 book *Religion in the Making*. He describes humans and animals as embodying a sequence of occasions obviously both mental and material; these proceed together "in the very closest connection" (1926a: 106). But "in the case of a bit of inorganic matter, any associate route of mentality seems to be negligible"—and by 'negligible' he means approaching, but not equal to, zero. Thus even something as small as an electron follows both mental and physical routes, even if the former are vastly outweighed by the latter. This point is emphasized a few pages later: "[T]he most complete concrete fact is dipolar, physical and mental. But ... the proportion of importance, as shared between the two poles, may vary from negligibility to dominance of either pole." (114) There is some latent ambiguity here, because in principle it is possible that not all occasions ("facts") are "complete" and thus not every occasion would necessarily have a mental pole. But in context it is reasonably clear that all occasions are dipolar in nature, and that panpsychism is the result.

Any remaining ambiguity is erased with Whitehead's short essay "Time," also published in 1926.[12] In it he writes that "each occasion is dipolar, and that one pole is the physical occasion and the other pole is the mental occasion" (303). He further explains that there is a relationship between the two poles: "the mental occasion supersedes the physical occasion." The suggestion here is that an occasion begins with a physical unification of past occasions, which are then prehended, or unified, into a mental experience.

12. Reproduced in Ford 1984. Citations are of that work.

This moment of experience then passes away and the occasion becomes "completed," ready to serve as the physical basis for future occasions. "With 'Time'," Ford writes (1995: 28), "panpsychism is clearly affirmed in the sense that every actuality has mentality."

By the time of his central work, *Process and Reality*, Whitehead is fully comfortable in referring to all occasions, in Jamesian fashion, as "drops of experience." "Each actual entity," he writes, "is a throb of experience including the actual world within its scope." (1929/1978: 190) Discussing the organic or "social" nature of all actual entities, he comments:

[The] development of mentality is characteristic of the actual occasions which make up the structured societies which we know as "material bodies." ... These material bodies belong to the lowest grade of structured societies which are obvious to our gross apprehensions. They comprise societies of various types of complexity—crystals, rocks, planets, and suns. (101–102)

Physical causality between material bodies is expressed in terms of feelings: "A simple physical feeling is an act of causation. ... [A]ll our physical relationships are made up of such simple physical feelings, as their atomic bricks." (236–237) Later Whitehead adds: "The physical theory of the structural flow of energy has to do with the transmission of simple physical feelings from individual actuality to individual actuality." (254) And elsewhere in *Process and Reality* we find further elaboration of the dipolar nature of actual entities (239), and of the notion of value as an expression of the subjectivity of an occasion (240–241, 248). Thus we see a multi-level reconfirmation of panpsychism, with mind and subjectivity present in all events.

Adventures of Ideas (1933) continues Whitehead's examination of persistence, a subject he had explored in great detail in *Process and Reality*. If the ultimate reality is the occasion of experience, and if that occasion somehow exists outside the scope of time, how do we account for such durable objects as molecules, human bodies, rocks, planets, and galaxies? Persistent objects are, on Whitehead's view, collections or "societies" of occasions that somehow share a close family relationship. Societies are thus the only material things that endure. "A society must exhibit the peculiar quality of endurance. The real actual things that endure are all societies. They are not actual occasions." (1933/1967: 204)

Societies, furthermore, are composed of individuals who are themselves societies. We thus arrive a picture of the world in which things are seen as nested hierarchies of social orders, from lowest to highest: "The Universe achieves its values by reason of its coordination into societies of societies, and in societies of societies of societies." (206) Certain of these enduring societies—such as human beings—attain a high-grade form. Others— among them cells, atoms, and electrons—achieve only very low-grade forms of mentality. Humans are therefore societies of mental subjects of varying degrees of complexity: "in a man, the living body is permeated by living societies of low-grade occasions so far as mentality is concerned" (208). All enduring things are constructed on the same general plan.

Thus, it is a mistake to posit an absolute distinction between minded and unminded entities on the basis of empirical observation. The distinction is illusory. "Nature suggests for our observation gaps, and then as it were withdraws them upon challenge." Whitehead makes this point explicitly in the late work *Modes of Thought*. The chapter "Nature Alive" includes this comment:

[T]his sharp division between mentality and nature has no ground in our fundamental observation. … I conclude that we should conceive mental operations as among the factors which make up the constitution of nature. (1938: 156)

The social or organismic structure of material reality thus accounts for the appearance of things around us, but Whitehead never lets us forget that the experiential occasions themselves are at the foundation of things: "The actualities of the Universe are processes of experience, each process an individual fact. The whole Universe is the advancing assemblage of these processes." (1933:1967: 197)

A final confirmation of Whitehead's generally panpsychist or pan-experientialist outlook comes from a late speech, published as "Immortality," in which he contrasts the universe as a place of great variety and differentiation ("World of Activity") with the underlying metaphysical unity of things at the level of process ("World of Value"). Things appear to be Many, but philosophically we know that they are ultimately One. Insofar as things are unified, they are all manifestations of occasions of experience, each an expression of intrinsic value. Insofar as things are manifold, they appear to separate into two groupings: the purely physical and the physical/mental. But again, this is a false distinction. "[T]here is no need to postulate two essentially different types of Active Entities, namely, the purely material entities and the entities alive with various modes of experiencing. The latter type is sufficient to account of the characteristics of that

World." (Whitehead 1941: 695) Experience, then, is the ultimate reality of existence.

Whitehead's process panpsychism has proved exceptionally fruitful. Russell and Hartshorne are among his more notable followers, but many others have found inspiration there. Even today it is one of the most active lines of metaphysical research, and is a direct beneficiary of more analytic defenses of panpsychism such as that offered by Strawson (2009). In one form or another, process thinking has been influential for more than 2,000 years; no doubt it has another millennium or two to go.

7.5   Russell

Whitehead's student and colleague Bertrand Russell (1872–1970), in the latter part of his career, held to a neutral monist process view in which events were the primary reality, comprising both mind and matter. In that sense he continued the line of thinking of Bergson and Whitehead. Russell's neutral monism was unique, however, in that he proposed that mind and matter each resulted from a set of causal laws; matter from physical laws of science, mind from "mnemic" laws that were not yet understood.[13] The relationship between these two sets of laws (if there was one) was not clear.

The connection between neutral monism and panpsychism is relevant and illuminating. If, for example, all things are composed of events, then an event is capable of giving rise to mind as well as matter. Therefore, either an event undergoes some kind of bifurcation that steers it in one of two fundamentally different paths, resulting in two fundamentally different modes of existence, or an event retains both a mind-like and a matter-like aspect. The former case presents a difficult ontological problem that Russell attempted to resolve with his two classes of causal laws. The latter is the more logically coherent alternative; this seems to have been the choice of Bergson and Whitehead, and even Russell appears to have endorsed it at times. It is this alternative that urges one toward panpsychism.

Passages suggestive of panpsychism appear early in Russell's work. One of the first can be found in the 1915 article "The Ultimate Constituents of Matter." Although the article preceded his neutral monist phase, in it

13. See Russell 1921: 25.

Russell offered up an alternative theory of matter in which sense data compose the ultimate reality of things; this thesis is a clear extension of Mach's idea that reality consists of sensations. As with Mach, the concept of sense-data seems to imply a psychological or mental aspect to reality, though at the time Russell apparently denied this interpretation.

Into the 1920s, and upon his acceptance of neutral monism, Russell argued that sensations belonged equally to mind and matter. In *The Analysis of Mind* he wrote: "I should admit this [neutral monist] view as regards sensations: what is heard or seen belongs equally to psychology and to physics. ... Sensations are subject to both kinds of [causal] laws, and are therefore truly 'neutral.'" (1921: 25–26) Sensation, then, is apparently part of the stuff of reality. This is not necessarily panpsychism, or even pansensism. Later in the book, however, Russell puts forth a kind of qualified pansensist position:

We may say generally that an object whether animate or inanimate, is "sensitive" to a certain feature of the environment if it behaves differently according to the presence or absence of that feature. Thus iron is sensitive to anything magnetic. (260)

But he is quick to add that this form of sensitivity doesn't even constitute knowledge, let alone intelligence. As such, it is a rather trivial form of pansensism—yet one that he apparently held for much of his life. He reiterated it nearly 20 years later: "Perceptive awareness is a species of 'sensitivity,' which is not confined to living organisms, but is also displayed by scientific instruments, and to some degree by everything." (1940/1949: 13)

In *The Analysis of Matter* (1927a) Russell reveals his process orientation, positing events as the neutral, ultimate elements of reality. He continues to narrow the mind-matter gap, characterizing matter as "less material, and mind less mental, than is commonly supposed" (7). As a consequence, "physics must be interpreted in a way which tends towards idealism, and perception in a way which tends towards materialism." Both matter and mind are "logical structures" composed of events. Significantly, these events are in themselves to be seen, as in Russell's earlier works, as sense data or "percepts": "As to what the events are that compose the physical world, they are, in the first place, percepts, and then [secondarily] whatever can be inferred from percepts." (386) "Mental events," he adds, "are part of that stuff [of the world], and ... the rest of the stuff resembles them more than it resembles traditional billiard-balls." (388) He concludes that "from the standpoint of philosophy, the distinction between physical and mental is superficial and unreal" (402). Again, this is highly suggestive but less than definitive.

Russell clearly rejected the mechanistic model of reality, but it is uncertain whether a form of panpsychism was implicated in the reason. He was, however, repeatedly willing to blur the distinction between mind and matter. In *An Outline of Philosophy* (1927b) he addresses that distinction directly, again in a way suggestive of panpsychism: "My own feeling is that there is not a sharp line, but a difference of degree [between mind and matter]; an oyster is less mental than a man, but not wholly un-mental." (209) One reason why we cannot draw a line, he says, is that an essential aspect of mind is memory, and a memory of sorts is displayed even by inanimate objects: "[W]e cannot, on this ground [of memory], erect an absolute barrier between mind and matter. ... Inanimate matter, to some slight extent, shows analogous behavior." (306) In the summary at the end of the book, he adds this:

The events that happen in our minds are part of the course of nature, and we do not know that the events which happen elsewhere are of a totally different kind. The physical world ... is perhaps less rigidly determined by causal laws than it was thought to be; one might, more or less fancifully, attribute even to the atom a kind of limited free will. (311)

Recalling the ancient Epicurean idea, this modern reference to an atomic free will is based on the newly discovered phenomenon of quantum indeterminacy. Notably, it even finds confirmation in recent physics; see Conway and Kochen 2006, 2009.[14]

Perhaps Russell's clearest articulation of panpsychism came near the end of his writing career, in the 1956 book *Portraits from Memory*. He asks a simple question: "What is the difference between things that happen to sentient beings and things that happen to lifeless matter?" (152) The common view is that inanimate things undergo many stimuli and reactions, but experience—as a mental property—is not one of them. Recalling his idea from *Outline of Philosophy*, he notes that the chief characteristic of experience is "the influence of past occurrences on present reactions," that is, memory. Memory is "the most essential characteristic of mind," and "using this word [memory] in its broadest sense to include every influence of past

14. Recall the discussion on Epicurus in chapter 2 above.

experience on present reactions" (153–154). As before, Russell points out that such a notion of memory must apply, properly speaking, to all physical objects and systems. He is explicit:

This [memory] also can be illustrated in a lesser degree by the behavior of inorganic matter. A watercourse which at most times is dry gradually wears a channel down a gully at the times when it flows, and subsequent rains follow [a similar] course. ... You may say, if you like, that the river bed "remembers" previous occasions when it experienced cooling streams. ... You would say [this] was a flight of fancy because you are of the opinion that rivers and river beds do not "think." But if thinking consists of certain modifications of behavior owing to former occurrences, then we shall have to say that the river bed thinks, though its thinking is somewhat rudimentary. (155)

This is as clear a statement as can be found in his body of writings. Yet his reticence about fully endorsing such a view is obvious. Later in the book he tends toward agnosticism with respect to any intrinsic mental nature in physical objects, stating that "we cannot say either that the physical world outside our heads is different from the mental world or that it is not" (164).[15]

Panpsychist readings of Russell are traditionally rare, though less so in recent years. Hartshorne (1937) thinks he is virtually there. Popper (1977) locates him very close to a Leibnizian panpsychism. Chalmers (1996) has placed him in the panpsychist camp; referring to *The Analysis of Matter* (without quotation), he writes: "Perhaps, as Russell suggested, at least some of the intrinsic properties of the physical are themselves a variety of phenomenal property [i.e. of sense-data]? The idea sounds wild at first, but on reflection it becomes less so." (154) And we know the reason it is wild: "There is of course the threat of panpsychism." Chalmers raises the issue because he is sympathetic to the view, as I explain in a later chapter.

Recently there has been focused interest in so-called Russellian monism, much of which touches on the question of panpsychism in Russell himself. *Consciousness in the Physical World*, an anthology edited by Alter and Nagasawa and published in 2015, includes numerous references to the topic. Galen Strawson (2015a: 203) notes that Russell is "open to panpsychism," if not already there. Leopold Stubenberg, on the other hand, argues that

15. Hartshorne (1937: 222) makes the same observation: "only sheer agnosticism separates Russell from panpsychism."

"Russell would want to resist his being classified as a panpsychist" (2015: 75) because the neutral elements of his neutral monism are conceivably non-mental. Thus Stubenberg says that, despite the arguments of some recent Russellian monists, it is "inaccurate" to "view Russell as a panpsychist" (82). Certainly Russell was reluctant to fully endorse the view, but on the basis of the passages quoted above it is clear that he was strongly oriented in that direction and deeply sympathetic to it.

7.6 Phenomenology

Phenomenology, as a loosely bound school of philosophical concepts that defies concise definition, is generally centered on the notion of mind and consciousness as a primary aspect of existence. Its development in the work of Edmund Husserl, Martin Heidegger, and Maurice Merleau-Ponty, and the related elaborations by Jean-Paul Sartre and Gabriel Marcel, seem to imply that mentality is a fundamental feature of the world, intimately bound up with any meaningful conception of being. This ontological essentialism has prompted some to suggest a connection with panpsychism. Hartshorne comments as follows—though without supplying clear evidence:

[Heidegger holds] that a cautiously positive form of anthropomorphism [i.e. panpsychism]—that which attributes to other creatures neither the duplication, nor the total absence, but lesser degrees and more primitive forms, of those properties exhibited in high degree, and more refined or complex forms, of those in us—is the only rational initial hypothesis for us to form. (1979: 52)

Abram (1996) also drew inspiration for his neo-animism from the work of Husserl and Merleau-Ponty. He depicts the phenomenological worldview as one in which "the sensible world … is described as active, animate, and, in some curious manner, alive" (55). But the passages Abram cites are obscure and indirect, with no clear correlation to any recognizable form of panpsychism. The statement by Hartshorne quoted above included a footnote reference to two vague passages in Heidegger, but, as with much of Heidegger's writing, neither is conclusive.

Generally speaking, the obscurity of most phenomenological writing makes it difficult to discern any clear connection to panpsychism. There are, however, certain ideas that, under the appropriate interpretation, are suggestive of it. For example, Heidegger's *Being and Time* (1927) attempts an analysis of being through the characteristics of *Dasein* (literally "being-there"). *Dasein* is typically taken as pertaining to the human essence, but is amenable to a broader interpretation of being or existence in general. Thus, Heidegger's conclusions about *Dasein* logically should pertain to all forms of being. The human "taking-account-of" and the relations such as "for-the-sake-of" and "in-order-to" seem to apply to all entities whatsoever, as Heidegger demonstrates no clear ontological distinction between humans and objects generally. Even simple physical encounters, such as a raindrop's hitting a leaf, can be seen as episodes of awareness or experience not unrelated to that of humans.

One study of Heidegger that suggests such a view is Graham Harman's *Tool-Being* (2002). Harman aims to extend Heidegger's insights, further than even Heidegger did, to reach their full logical conclusions. Harman sees the key to Heidegger's whole philosophical system in his analysis of tools. Heidegger related tools to human *Dasein*, but on Harman's view "the tool-analysis does not rely in the least on any priority of the human standpoint" (29). Any particular object may serve as a tool, and it stands in some relationship to every other object; using Heidegger's terminology, we may say that each entity exists "for the sake of" (*Um-willen*) any other thing that it encounters. In Harman's words, "the structure known as the 'for-the-sake-of' occurs even on the level of soulless matter" (30). If so, the presumed particularity of human consciousness in our everyday encounters is swept away. The network of relationality that we are embedded in, the "as-structure," is no longer the private domain of the human mind. "The ontological status of sentient awareness has been radically altered: it no longer has the entire as-structure to itself, and therefore has lost its previous ontological distinction." (225) Harman adds that "the as-structure of the human *Dasein* turns out to be just a special case of relationality in general. We ourselves are no more and no less perspectival than are rocks, paper, and scissors."

Yet Harman resists casting this interpretation in a panpsychist light. Discussing an example of a metal stove sitting on a frozen lake, he says: "I see no reason to accept the animistic claim that such a stove ... 'perceives' the lake in the usual sense." (223) He makes no explicit claim that his thesis of "pan-relationality" is any variant of panpsychism. Elsewhere he has stated that, even though he is "not inherently opposed" to panpsychism, he wants "to be careful in not jumping from the claim that all objects are involved in relations to the much more far-ranging claim that all relations are psychic relations."[16] Yet this raises the question of the precise nature of the relationship, if any, between "psychic relations" and relationality in general. And all this, of course, relates to Harman's own interpretation, not to Heidegger. According to Harman, "there is no real panpsychist tendency in Heidegger."

Likewise, Merleau-Ponty's *Phenomenology of Perception* (1945) appears to articulate a sympathetic relationship between perceiver and perceived wherein each actively apprehends the other. Merleau-Ponty imputes a kind of animate quality to the sensory world: "Hardness, softness, roughness and smoothness ... present themselves in our recollection ... as certain kinds of symbioses, certain ways the outside has of invading us." (1945/1962: 317) Elsewhere in the book (211) he describes this process as one of an active world taking possession of the body. But such references are rare, and are subject to various interpretations. Generally speaking, elements of panpsychism in phenomenology are faint at best. In Harman's opinion, "it's safe to say that there is no panpsychist strain anywhere in the phenomenological movement."

7.7 Teilhard de Chardin

There was perhaps no more visionary and exuberant panpsychist than Pierre Teilhard de Chardin (1881–1955). Teilhard—geologist, paleontologist, Jesuit priest, and philosopher—combined elements of Bergson's evolutionism and its transcendental ethos with a devout if radical interpretation of Christianity to produce a unique and visionary metaphysical system. The core of his thesis was an elaboration of an idea from Schiller and Lossky: the concept of "complexity-consciousness." This involved the notion that, as matter evolves into increasingly complex forms, so too does the corresponding dimension of consciousness that is attributed to it. Consciousness equals complexity; simple elements of matter possess a low-grade consciousness, and the more complex forms, like the human, possess it in great degrees. In Teilhard's words (1959: 301): "this particular involution 'of complexity' is experimentally bound up with a correlative increase in interiorisation, that is to say in the psyche or consciousness."

16. Personal communication, January 2003.

The Phenomenon of Man, Teilhard's masterpiece, was his first substantial work of philosophy. It was written over the course of several years and completed circa 1938 in the midst of a 20-year stay in China performing paleontological work. The book has many varied dimensions and implications, and panpsychism is only one aspect of Teilhard's comprehensive vision.

Early in *The Phenomenon of Man* Teilhard establishes his view that the realm of matter is driven by an evolutionary energy that carries it toward increasingly complex and intricate organization. This universal concept of energy presents itself in varying forms, including its different physical manifestations, but nonetheless is an energy that yields mind: "All energy is psychic in nature." (1959: 64) Teilhard argues that the evolutionary process results in matter that possesses, at all levels of complexity, an interior that is inherently mental or psychical. Much like Spinoza, he writes that "there is necessarily a *double aspect to* [matter's] *structure*," and that "*co-extensive with their Without, there is a Within to things*" (56). The process of evolution, in its most universal sense, is thus one of increasing articulation of mind and consciousness: "We regard evolution as primarily psychical transformation." (167) The natural result is a panpsychic worldview: "From the cell to the thinking animal, as from the atom to the cell, a single process (a psychical kindling or concentration) goes on without interruption and always in the same direction." (169) As he reiterates in the postscript,

[W]e are logically forced to assume the existence in rudimentary form ... of some sort of psyche in every corpuscle, even in those (the mega-molecules and below) whose complexity is of such a low or modest order as to render it (the psyche) imperceptible. ... The universe is, both on the whole and at each of its points, in a continual tension of organic doubling-back upon itself, and thus of interiorization. (301–302)

For Teilhard the *becoming of mind* is a monumental, universal process of unending progress from dim and unarticulated mentality to ever-greater depth of intensity and interiorization. This is the leitmotif—"noogenesis," as he calls it—that pervades his works.

In a 1941 essay titled "The Atomism of Spirit," Teilhard again emphasizes the continuity of psychic evolution in all things, from atoms to *Homo sapiens*: "[W]e do not immediately recognize in man the natural extension of the atom. Nevertheless ... it becomes clear that in each one of us the same movement [of interiorization] is being continued." (1970: 34) In a 1947 article, "The Place of Technology," he notes that "interiority, the rudiment of consciousness, exists everywhere; ... 'the within' is a universal property of things" (1970: 156). Three years later he argued that "matter and Spirit [are] two states or two aspects of one and the same cosmic Stuff," and that Spirit is on the ascension while Matter is on the decline (1950/1979: 26–27). And in one of his last pieces, "The Reflection of Energy" (1952), Teilhard discusses the universal complexification of energy with respect to the tendency of thermodynamic decay, or entropy. Evolution is driven by "some *powerful magnetic force, psychic in nature*" (1970: 334), and by this fact it overcomes entropic degradation.

Teilhard thus combined a kind of non-emergence argument with a panpsychist ontology based in first principles. For him, emergence of species and other forms of being was clearly possible, just as new and more complex forms of mind could emerge, but mind as an ontological category was present from the beginning of time. The evolutionary imperative of noogenesis was for him a central cosmological principle, and thus a fundamental metaphysical assumption.

Teilhard's philosophical legacy has been mixed. For some he has been immensely influential, but in an era dominated by materialistic, analytic, and secular philosophy he has typically been seen as too theological—or, worse, too mystical. Theologians have tended to look skeptically at his fundamental endorsement of evolution and his radical conception of God. In this sense he was very much like his panpsychist contemporary Charles Hartshorne—both men were radical theologian-philosophers who articulated visions too unconventional for either academia or religion.

7.8   Hartshorne and the Problem of the Aggregate

After Whitehead, the preeminent process philosopher of the twentieth century was Charles Hartshorne (1897–2000). A sort of counterculture figure in the world of philosophy, he was, to a significant degree, shunned by mainstream philosophers, both for his failure to embrace the analytic and linguistic tradition and for his open advocacy of panpsychism and theological philosophy. On the other hand, he was seen as too radical by conventional theologians, primarily because of his pantheistic process view of God. Though clearly in the vein of Whitehead's philosophy, Hartshorne's writing is in a sense its mirror image—he wrote clearly and elegantly, avoided abstruse technical phases, and was very direct and personal in tone.

Hartshorne was the first philosopher to extensively employ the term 'panpsychism' and thus may be credited with bringing the word into something approaching mainstream philosophical discourse. He was open and explicit about his panpsychist beliefs; panpsychism, he claimed, offers the only viable third way between mechanism and vitalism. It also treads a middle ground between "extreme materialism" (eliminativism) and Cartesian dualism. And it allows for a new, more naturalistic vision of God—approaching a form of pantheism. Writing very much like William James, with echoes of Empedocles and Campanella, Hartshorne argued that panpsychism offers a sympathetic view of the world, and in particular a sympathetic epistemology that holds great promise for society.

All these ideas were introduced in one of Hartshorne's first major works, *Beyond Humanism* (1937). The entire book is panpsychist in tone, but it is the central theme of two chapters: "Mind and Matter" and "Mind and Body: Organic Sympathy." The former begins with a critique of science and the scientific method, which, Hartshorne says, treats objects in nature not as individuals but as "crowds," "swarms," and "aggregates." Mind and sentience are not to be found in aggregates but only in true individuals, and thus science overlooks the possibility of panpsychism—interpreted as meaning that all true individuals possess minds. The latter chapter outlines a panpsychist epistemology in which the mind knows the body through "organic sympathy" with sentient cells.

The issue of "aggregates" versus "true individuals" is central to Hartshorne's interpretation of panpsychism. In fact some philosophers, among them David Ray Griffin, claim that this point is crucial to the entire process view, as it allows Whitehead's system to avoid potentially debilitating criticisms of standard dual-aspect panpsychism. It furthermore directly addresses a question that is central to virtually all panpsychist theories—the combination problem: How can a unified collective consciousness arise from the mental qualities of lower orders of matter, such as atoms or subatomic particles? This question requires further examination, beginning with a brief historical review.

There is a significant context to this issue of aggregates that the process philosophers have generally neglected, and thus they overlook essential weaknesses in their position. The problem relates to the notion of substance, which began with Democritus' atomic theory. Since Democritus held that only atoms and the void were real, he was compelled to argue that all ordinary large-scale objects only appeared to be solid substances. A rock, a tree, and a human being were only sophisticated aggregations of imperceptibly small atoms; their unity was real only in the sense that they appeared as singular objects. "The objects of sense are supposed to be real and it is customary to regard them as such, but in truth they are not."[17] The solidity of ordinary objects is taken strictly "by convention." Aggregates thus have no true unity; they are not true individuals.

Giordano Bruno read Democritus and embraced his ideas. Yet Bruno also believed in the world-soul and in a universe animated throughout all its parts. He wrote that "all the forms of natural things are souls," and that all things "possess life, or at least the vital principle" (1584a/1998: 44). As was noted earlier, he believed that so-called inanimate objects, such as a table or items of clothing, are not animate as wholes, but that "as natural things and composites, they have within them matter and form" and thus "part of that spiritual substance." This spiritual substance or vital principle is a kind of latent soul that becomes fully animate when absorbed into the body of a plant or an animal. Since the vital principle is present in the smallest portions of matter, Bruno concluded that all atoms, or monads, must be in some sense ensouled: "Here is the monad, the atom: and the whole Spirit extending hence upon every side." (in Singer 1950: 74) All things are made of monads, and therefore all things have, at least, this atomic soul in them. But the object as a whole, if it is "inanimate," possesses no unified higher-order soul.

Leibniz was also well acquainted with Democritus and cited him often. And he probably was familiar with Bruno's work, though he doesn't seem to have mentioned it. Like Democritus, he held that solidity of ordinary matter was only an appearance, an "accidental unity," a "phenomenon," something like a rainbow. Leibniz followed Bruno in attributing mental qualities to all monads, but that left him with some daunting problems. First, he had to explain why such things as rocks and tables, though composed of sentient monads, were not in themselves somehow animate. Bruno simply made a flat assertion that this was so, but offered no real argument. Leibniz had some ideas on how to solve that problem. A second and related problem, which Democritus and Bruno completely bypassed, was an accounting of the human soul, or mind: How could a single, large-scale, unified mind

17. Fragment 9 (Smith 1934: 40).

arise from monadic souls? That is, how can we account for the combination problem?

To his credit, Leibniz attempted to address both problems directly, arguing that objects were collections of monads and that some of these objects—those, such as animals and plants, with "a thoroughly indivisible and naturally indestructible being" (1686b/1989: 79)—possessed a unifying and dominant monad. This served as the soul or mind of the individual. Such individuals were considered both "living beings" and "composite substances." The other, non-dominant monads composed the body of the living being, and were linked to the dominant monad either by pre-established harmony or, in Leibniz' later theory, by the *vinculum substantiale*.

Yet it must be admitted that Leibniz never gave any explanation of how the dominant monad came to be, or why it appeared only in animals. His discussion of borderline cases is informative. Only once does he directly address the issue of larger-scale objects: "[I]f I am asked in particular what I say about the sun, the earthly globe, the moon, trees, and other similar bodies and even about beasts. I cannot be absolutely certain whether they are animated, or even whether they are substances." (1686b/1989: 80) His uncertainty about trees, and presumably all plants, apparently subsided soon thereafter; by 1687 he clearly included plants among the sentient. "I do not dare assert" he wrote, "that plants have no soul, life, or substantial form." (1687/1989: 82) Later he added this:

[I]t seems probable that animals, which are indeed analogous to us, and similarly plants, which correspond to animals in many ways, are not composed of body alone, but also of soul, by which the animal or plant, the single indivisible substance ... is controlled. (1690/1989: 104)

Near the end of his life, Leibniz observed that "the limbs of [each] living body are full of other living beings, plants, animals, each of which also has its entelechy, or its dominant monad" (*Monadology*, section 70). The issue of plants is relevant because Hartshorne, ignoring Leibniz and dubiously citing Whitehead, pointedly excludes them from the ranks of the animate.

Two hundred years later, Whitehead developed his theory of the organism as the model for reality, apparently employing some of Leibniz's ideas. But, like his predecessor, he had an ambiguous conception of the aggregate. Whitehead was faced with the same issue as the monadists: how to account for combination and unity of the human mind. In his system, point-like occasions of experience with both physical and mental poles were likened to "monads with windows"—that is, they were considered capable of interaction. But Whitehead did not say clearly how they were unified, or in what types of beings.

In Whitehead's last four major philosophical books—*Science and the Modern World* (1925), *Process and Reality* (1929), *Adventures of Ideas* (1933), and *Modes of Thought* (1938)—there is virtually no discussion of Leibniz's notion of aggregates. Leibniz's dominant monad theory is largely ignored, except for a few passing mentions in *Process and Reality*. This is rather surprising, especially in light of the generally high regard Whitehead seems to have had for Leibniz. Furthermore, the discussion of aggregates—or, as Whitehead prefers, societies—is sporadic and obtuse throughout. *Science* and *Adventures* make almost no mention of the topic. *Process and Reality*, by contrast, contains a lengthy discussion of the nature of a society. The one consistent theme is that all objects, from atoms to stones to humans, are in reality "societies of [point-like] actual occasions," much as Leibniz saw things as aggregates of point-like monads. However, Whitehead offers nearly a dozen different categories of society, including "electromagnetic," "corpuscular," "structured," "specialized," "stabilized," "living," and "subordinate." It is never clear which of those categories possess unified sentience and which do not.

A number of passages in *Process and Reality* are vague and conflicting. First, the critical passage on "the ultimate metaphysical principle"—the "advance from disjunction to conjunction," or, more succinct, "the many become one, and are increased by one" (1929/1978: 21)—seems to apply to any aggregate of occasions. Whitehead bears the burden of explaining why, though an ultimate principle, this advance to unity doesn't occur in all things.

Second, "structured societies" are those that have both "dominant" and "subordinate" sub-societies. The overall structure provides a protected environment that sustains the sub-societies. "Molecules are structured societies, and so in all probability are separate electrons and protons. Crystals are structured societies. But gases are not." (99) Elsewhere Whitehead includes "crystals, rocks, planets and sun" (102) in this list. Structured societies have two ways of creating a protective environment. The first is by "massive average objectification of a nexus," which would appear to apply to stones and such. However, "this mode of solution requires the intervention of mentality"; further, "this development of mentality is characteristic of the actual occasions which make up the structured societies we know as 'material bodies'" (101). Whitehead adds that "such mentality represents the first grade of ascent," possessing "some initiative of conceptual integration, but no originality in conceptual prehension." Apparently, then, there is a latent mentality in even the simplest structured society. The second way is "appetition," i.e., the ability to "originate novelty to match the novelty of the environment" (102). This ability ranges from "thinking" (in higher organisms) to "thoughtless adjustment of aesthetic emphasis" (in lower ones). Societies that act in this second way are deemed living or organic, the others inorganic. However, "there is no absolute gap between 'living' and 'non-living' societies." Thus, they seem to exist on a continuum of mentality—again, implying mentality in all.

Third, the standard view of post-Whitehead process philosophers is that atoms, molecules, and individual cells are included among the sentient. On the one hand, the above point suggests this. On the other, Whitehead explicitly notes that "a cell gives no evidence whatsoever of a single unified mentality" (104). Later he goes further: "In the case of single cells, of vegetation, and of the lower forms of animal life, we have no ground for conjecturing living personality." (107)

Fourth, and by contrast, Whitehead suggests elsewhere that all aggregates can be seen as individuals in their own right:

[T]here is the ... potential aggregation of actual entities into a super-actuality in respect to which the true actualities play the part of coordinate subdivisions. In other words, just as ... one atomic actuality can be treated as though it were many coordinate actualities, in the same way ... a nexus of many actualities can be treated as though it were one actuality. This is what we habitually do in the case of the span of life of a molecule, or of a piece of rock, or of a human body. (286–287)

Such is the case as presented in *Process and Reality*. One would have hoped for a clearer and more decisive account of this central issue.

In *Modes of Thought* we find other passages that conflict with the standard view. Whitehead initially informs us that "a vegetable is a democracy; an animal is dominated by one, or more centers of experience" (1938: 24). Unfortunately, he adds that "our statement is oversimplified" because "the distinction between animals and vegetables is not sharp cut. Some traces of dominance can be observed in vegetables, and some traces of democratic independence can be found in animals."

Whitehead continues by articulating four types of aggregations: the "lowest" or "nonliving," which is "dominated by the average"—though even here he allows that "flashes of selection" are possible, if only "sporadic and ineffective" (27); "vegetable grade," which "has added coordinated, organic individuality to the impersonal average of inorganic nature"; "animal grade," with "at least one central actuality"; and "human grade," with "novelty of functioning." He reiterates a similar sequence at the end of the book, again emphasizing "the aspect of continuity between these modes" (157). The conclusion would seem to be either that Whitehead was trying to articulate a tremendously complex theory of the aggregate or that he in fact saw some degree of mentality in all things *as wholes*, and not simply in the mental poles of their constituent occasions.

Reading Whitehead in light of Leibniz's monadology, Hartshorne claims that only things with a deep organic unity qualify as true or "genuine" individuals.[18] In the absence of a clear theoretic structure, Hartshorne concludes that precisely which objects qualify is not definable *a priori*, but is rather a function of empirical study.[19] Generally speaking, true individuals exhibit some—if even only a slight—degree of spontaneity and unpredictability, which is indicative of a unifying, dominant force. Aggregates, on the other hand, behave very predictably and mechanistically. They display absolutely no degree of unified action. Any inherent dynamics, such as those of the constituent atoms, are averaged out by the aggregate, leaving no net force to serve as a unified individual.

Based on his rough empirical assessment, and drawing from certain passages in Whitehead, Hartshorne determines that not only humans but all animals clearly display spontaneous unified behavior, even down to the level of one-celled creatures. At the level of the micro-constituents of matter, he includes molecules, atoms, and sub-atomic particles; their

18. Elsewhere Hartshorne called Leibniz's position "the first clear statement of panpsychist theory" (1950: 444), apparently overlooking all the developments after the early Greeks—most notably, Renaissance naturalism.

19. Interestingly, Plato flatly disagreed with this view. For him, the only way to determine anything about the psyche in apparently inanimate objects was via rational reflection. Recall the passage cited earlier, reflecting on the soul of the sun: "Everyone can see [the sun's] body, but no one can see its soul—not that you could see the soul of any other creature, living or dying. [Such a thing] is totally below the level of our bodily senses, and is perceptible by reason alone." (*Laws*, 898d)

unpredictability and their spontaneity had been confirmed by then-recent advances in quantum theory and by the probabilistic behavior of such particles.

At the higher end of the scale, Hartshorne jumps directly from humanity to the universe as a whole, including it among the ranks of animate beings. He explicitly excludes virtually everything else, including inorganic objects such as rocks, tables, and houses. Also excluded are all higher-order systems—e.g., a forest, a social group, or the Earth as a whole—even though these contain sentient parts. Even individual plants are excluded; apparently basing his view on Whitehead's "vegetables are a democracy" statement, Hartshorne sees plants as mere colonies of sentient cells rather than as truly integrated individuals. Hence, all aggregates, even though composed of sentient atoms, molecules, and perhaps cells, are not in themselves sentient. Only the genuine individuals, as determined empirically, are unified animate beings.

In this sense, process philosophy effectively advocates a dualistic theory of mind. Objects and structures classified as true individuals possess mind and have experiences; all others do not. Experience or sentience is posited as a fundamental, ontological characteristic of reality, and thus there exists a clear divide between the experiencers and the non-experiencers. Griffin (1998: 169–198) and some other recent writers attempt to downplay this distinction, characterizing it as upholding a form of monism because the aggregates are not "true beings." But the distinction is there nonetheless. There is no clear ontological separation between the mere aggregates and true individuals. This point is important because, as Griffin notes, it is presented as the way out of a number of critical attacks against process panpsychism.

Like Leibniz and Whitehead, Hartshorne doesn't offer much in the way of argumentation for his particular list of animate things. The reliance on empiricism is a matter of epistemological concern, but it says nothing about the theoretical and ontological basis for such a divide. Why should it be that only certain aggregates are blessed with mind and experience, while others are not? And what is the ontological basis by which a dominant or "regnant" monad takes control and serves as the mind? Are these to be taken as unfathomable mysteries? Are they simply brute facts of reality? One is led to suspect that process theory is significantly incomplete on this matter.

Ultimately this dichotomy between true individuals and aggregates seems entirely too arbitrary. If one postulates a fundamental distinction in nature, then one ought to have a compelling reason for doing so.[20] Both a rock and an animal are aggregates of sentient atoms, yet one is seen as sentient in its own right and the other is not—what is the difference? Of course they differ in many ways—internal complexity, dynamic relation to the environment, etc.—but they are alike in their constitution *as aggregates*. A living aggregate is clearly different from a non-living aggregate, but not in its aggregateness. The process view argues not merely that they are different in degree, but that they are ontologically different, different in kind; the true individuals are said to possess something real and fundamental that the others do not have. Even *a priori*, it seems that any two coherent and persistent structures of mass-energy should share certain core characteristics, and that (unless one is prepared to argue for eliminativism) mind is among them—which is essentially Schopenhauer's argument.

Apart from the problem of aggregates, Hartshorne tackles the issue of "proving" panpsychism. Rather than attempting to do so directly, he adopts Paulsen's tactic and turns the question around. First he asks whether science, which is in the business of proofs, can disprove panpsychism. He answers No, both because it treats things primarily in aggregate form and also because it cannot distinguish the fact *that* an object feels from *how* it feels. He goes on to explain that philosophical reasoning offers no inherent basis for rejecting panpsychism. On the contrary, there are "great philosophical advantages" (1937: 175) to panpsychism, including explaining the relation between sensation and feeling, and a deeper comprehension of the concepts of space and time. Relying on a Bergsonian argument for memory in all aspects of reality, he states that "the idea of time is unintelligible unless panpsychism is true" (174).

20. Griffin believes he has a compelling reason, in that the dominant monad preserves the freedom of action of the individual (1998: 97). The dominant monad both acts on and is acted upon by the body. On the process view, this two-way causality is the basis of freedom. There are at least two problems with this: (1) It assumes a fairly conventional view of freedom of the will, when in fact there are other ways to conceive this, apart from determinism. (2) Nothing Griffin says rules out the possibility that all things have a dominant monad. Simply because we see no apparent spontaneity in rocks doesn't mean it isn't there at some low level, or on some long time scale. This issue is discussed further below.

Hartshorne then argues that panpsychism has been damaged by its association with idealism. In the early 1930s, as the views of Kant and Berkeley were being discredited by the rising positivist philosophy, panpsychism too was disparaged. Moore and Perry were among the leading critics. Yet it should be clear, Hartshorne says, that panpsychism, while conceivably a form of idealism, is substantially different from a Berkelian or a Kantian position. Hartshorne associates it with the so-called idealism of Leibniz and Whitehead, which is almost a realist or even objectivist view.[21] The "absurdity of [traditional] idealism," he says, "has no bearing upon panpsychism" (177).

Hartshorne proceeds to claim that organic sympathy, and its accompanying panpsychism, is capable of resolving six major philosophical problems: mind-body, subject-object, causality, the nature of time, the nature of individuality, and the problem of knowledge. In short, the human mind results from a "sympathetic participation" or "sympathetic rapport" with the sentient cells of the body, whose sentience is itself a product of the rapport with the sentient atoms. The relation of subject to object is, similarly an exchange between enminded participants, without which knowledge would be impossible. More generally, all causality is manifested through such a resonance between two minds. Moments in time are a "sympathetic bond" between past and future, much as Bergson and Whitehead described. The "individual" is a result of a balance between the integrative power of sympathy and the disintegrative power of its opposite, antipathy; in the manner of Empedocles, Hartshorne asserts that pure sympathy would destroy individuality (by merging all into one), and that pure antipathy would not allow for any structure or knowledge at all.[22]

These ideas, and especially the emphasis on panpsychism, recurred frequently throughout Hartshorne's long career. They appeared in one of his discussions of freedom and free will,[23] and they were featured in his entry

21. Hartshorne was not entirely enamored of Leibniz's philosophy. He criticized his notorious mechanistic stance, and was fundamentally opposed to the mechanistic worldview in general: "mechanism and materialism are really two aspects of the same view—the view that the world is fundamentally dead, blind, uncreative, insentient" (1937: 180).

22. See Hartshorne 1937: 194–199.

23. Hartshorne 1949.

on panpsychism in *A History of Philosophical Systems* (1950: 442–453)—a woefully incomplete survey of the field, incidentally. Then, in the late 1970s, he published some important articles directly arguing for panpsychism. The most notable of these was "Physics and Psychics: The Place of Mind in Nature" (1977), in which he again presents panpsychism—now preferring to call it "psychical monism" or "psychicalism"—as a third way between dualism and materialism: "Psychical monism avoids the most obvious demerits of its two rivals. It is a monism, yet it is not a materialism." (1977: 90) He offers a straightforward case for panpsychism, beginning with four reasons why inanimate objects appear devoid of mind: apparent inactivity or inertness, lack of freedom and initiative, absence of a clear distinction between parts and the whole, and lack of purpose. He disposes of these four by recalling the distinction between aggregates and true individuals. Rocks and chairs are, he says, not sentient individuals but only aggregates of sentient atoms and molecules. Matter is not inert but is continuously active and dynamic at the atomic level. Quantum indeterminacy is a kind of freedom. And "purpose" probably is reflected over varying lengths of time, which may be exceedingly short or exceptionally long; it would require superhuman abilities to grasp the full range of temporality and to declare definitively that purpose was nonexistent.

On the positive side of the argument, Hartshorne asks "What are the advantages of giving up the notion of mere dead, mindless physical things?" He concedes that the advantages are mostly theoretical, but he argues that giving them up "enable[s] us to arrive at a view of life and nature in which the results of science are given their significance along with the values with which art, ethics, and religion are concerned" (92). In other words, spiritual and reverential values are strengthened by such a worldview. More specifically, Hartshorne cites some strictly philosophical advantages: (1) The problem of how matter produces mind is dissolved. (2) It supports the intuitive view that organic and inorganic substances lie along one continuum of existence. (3) The problem of causality is resolved by taking account of memory and perception or anticipation. (4) It provides the most satisfactory solution to the mind-body issue, describing it as "a relation of sympathy." (5) It solves the old problem of primary and secondary qualities by ascribing secondary or subjective qualities to all things. (6) It provides for an account of behavior of all things in psychical terms, relating to perception, emotion, memory, and so on.

In the final analysis, Hartshorne concludes that panpsychism or psychicalism has little direct bearing on matters of science *per se* but does profoundly influence our human attitudes, and consequently our actions. "For logical, aesthetic, and religious reasons our view of the general [panpsychic] cosmic status of quality (and value) influences our behavior, and in this sense its consideration is pragmatically significant." (1990: 397) It is, after all, the most viable ontology available to us—certainly preferable to an utterly unintelligible materialism: "[T]he concept of 'mere dead insentient matter' is an appeal to invincible ignorance. At no time will this expression ever constitute knowledge." (1977: 95)

8 Scientific Perspectives

From a scientific perspective, the human mind is an unexplained and perhaps unexplainable mystery. Mind that may exist elsewhere in nature is scientifically unintelligible and methodologically superfluous. Modern analytic philosophy generally concurs with the scientific outlook that non-human minds are incomprehensible or irrelevant. It furthermore accepts uncritically the scientific view that matter is intrinsically non-experiential. Both science and modern philosophy, therefore, generally find no credibility in panpsychist theories.

As I stated early in this book, virtually all present-day naturalistic theories of mind are forms of emergentism, arguing that mind is a rare and unique phenomenon that arises only in highly specialized circumstances. The standard versions of emergentism—including the identity theory, functionalism, and various forms of behaviorism—attribute mind to only those structures that have achieved sufficient biological or functional complexity.[1] They are, however, generally at a loss to explain either the criterion for this emergence or how the qualities of mind or consciousness are linked to such complexity. Emergentism, in all its forms, is thus profoundly incomplete at present. This fact alone suggests that panpsychist theories deserve greater attention.

8.1 Historical Arguments from the Scientific and Empirical Perspectives

The failings of emergentism constitute what might be called a negative argument on behalf of panpsychism. Yet there are many positive arguments,

---

1. It should be noted, though, that all of these, especially functionalism, can be interpreted as forms of panpsychism.

some from within the realm of science. Numerous scientist-philosophers (including Gilbert, Kepler, Leibniz, LaMettrie, Herder, Fechner, Haeckel, Mach, and Teilhard) found grounds for panpsychism in the fields of physics, chemistry, and biology. Their arguments were based not only on rationalism but also on empirical evidence and evolutionary principles. It is helpful to briefly retrace some of these older scientific arguments in order to set the context for the more recent developments.

Scientific arguments are traditionally based on a combination of empirical evidence and so-called scientific reasoning. Given a conjecture or proposed theory, evidence is sought that can confirm it. This raises two questions long known to philosophers of science: What counts as evidence? What qualifies as scientific reasoning? It is clear that any observed data about the world can be interpreted in many ways and may count for or against widely divergent theories. Scientific reasoning is roughly defined as a logical and empirically based process that leads to positive theories about some aspect of reality, and ideally to the truth about the world. Applying similar reasoning to issues of philosophy of mind has led some thinkers to panpsychist conclusions.

Consider Thales' evidence: that a magnet has a *psyche* because it can move metallic objects. He held to a theory of mind in which *psyche* was the source and cause of motion. On that definition, it is clear that a magnet must be ensouled. It was, then, a rational process that led Thales to consider whether *psyche* was shared only by humans, animals, and certain rocks (such as those from Magnesia) or was a universal property that was manifest in all objects by degrees.[2] We don't fully know Thales' rationale, but we know that he ultimately concluded that "all things are full of gods" and thus that panpsychism was true.

Anaximenes noted the commonly observed fact that living, ensouled beings must breathe, and that loss of breath was a fairly certain indication of loss of *psyche*. Furthermore, breath, in the form of air (*pneuma*), seemed to surround and permeate all things. Thus, a reasonable "scientific" conclusion was that *psyche* was present everywhere, in all things.

Plato saw *psyche* as the principal source of motion and, like Thales, held that where there was evident power of motion the presence of a soul had to

2. There is evidence that the Greeks also experimented with rubbed amber and the attractive force of static electricity. If so, that would have added further evidence of psyche in inorganic objects.

be inferred. He observed the regular motions of the heavens and concluded that only a world-soul could regulate such motions with orderly precision. As to the *psyche* itself, Plato stated the obvious: that it cannot be directly observed and is thus "perceptible by reason alone"—that is, on the basis of ultimate metaphysical principles.

Aristotle was confronted with the puzzling phenomenon of spontaneous generation of life out of heaps of decaying matter. To make sense of such generation, he was compelled to postulate a soul-like *pneuma* as pervasive in the physical world. *Pneuma*, as the earthly life-principle, was the analogue of the heavenly ether, which was thought to animate the stars and other celestial bodies. Only the ether could account for the appearance of life from a non-living substrate. Aristotle was wrong about spontaneous generation, but his methodology was logical and plausibly scientific.

Centuries later, Gilbert's study of magnets in the late 1500s considered two different empirical results. The first was his observation that a magnet can magnetize a previously nonmagnetic piece of metal. For him, this "power to confer power" was evidence of a magnet's *psyche*-like ability. Second, Gilbert documented the consistency and orderliness of the magnetic force: the repulsion of like poles, the attraction of opposite poles, inverse-square action with respect to distance, and so on. He saw this as evidence of "reason" in the magnet—a disputable but putatively scientific conclusion if one assumes that the *psyche* acts in an intelligent and orderly manner, much as Plato had assumed. The jump to panpsychism required additional presumptions, such as "whatever is in the effect is in the cause." Gilbert showed that the Earth was a large magnet, then rightly determined that magnetism was thereby bestowed on individual rocks. Since the Earth granted its magnetic *psyche* to the magnet, and (evidently) the animal *psyche* to humans and animals, it was reasonable to generalize that all Earthly things were endowed with a kind of animation.

Like Plato and Gilbert, Kepler saw soul as the motive force behind the planets—at least until 1621, when he decided that the rational orderliness of planetary motion was indicative of a corporeal, non-psychic force. Newton viewed gravity as an occult quality, something perhaps lifelike in nature. As I noted earlier, his theory of universal attraction had implicit panpsychist overtones. He understood that gravity could be quantified, but this did not explain its basis or its origin.

In the mid to late 1600s, various new scientific technologies began to emerge, some of which supported panpsychist theories. Leeuwenhoek's work with the microscope revealed tiny "animalcules" in ordinary water—a startling discovery that impressed a number of thinkers, including Spinoza, Leibniz, and LaMettrie. Suddenly there was indisputable empirical proof of life and sentience in the smallest portions of nature. Later discoveries of the cellular nature of plants and animals, and of the ubiquitous presence of microorganisms, only furthered this belief.

Fechner's work in the mid 1800s relied less on empirical data than on a scientific form of argumentation by analogy. He observed the functional similarities between animals and plants, and concluded that plants were animate. He then considered the Earth as a system, arguing that its internal dynamics and sentient components supported such notions as an Earth-soul. Empirical evidence of the Earth's ability to self-regulate did not appear until about 100 years later, with the work of Wright and Lovelock.

Advances in physics in the eighteenth and nineteenth centuries moved toward unification of physical forces. More important, with the dynamist and energeticist theories, even matter itself was seen as an ethereal, quasi-spiritual entity. This "spiritualization" of matter—in a scientific context—was important to the panpsychist theories of Priestley, Schelling, Herder, Lossky, and the early Schiller.

Darwin's theory of evolution (1859) initiated a series of new scientific arguments. Even before *On the Origin of Species*, the early anticipations of Maupertuis, LaMettrie, and Diderot suggested that an evolutionary perspective would entail some form of panpsychism. After Darwin, it became evident that all life shared a common ancestry, and that conscious humans had no claim to ontological uniqueness. This was further supported by chemical analyses that showed human bodies to be composed of the same elements that existed in other life forms, in the Earth, and even throughout space. These scientific facts supported the Continuity arguments of Haeckel, Spencer, James, Teilhard, and others. Evolution was not empirical *per se*, but empirical evidence supported it and indirectly served as a form of confirmation for certain panpsychist theories.

8.2   Panpsychism in Twentieth-Century Science

Into the twentieth century, further developments in physics, biology, and mathematics were presented as scientific evidence in favor of panpsychist claims. The equation of mass and energy furthered the notion that the underlying nature of matter was something vaguely spirit-like. Quantum mechanics emerged as an accepted theory of atomic and subatomic particles; its bizarre, indeterminate implications led a number of scientists to panpsychist conclusions, beginning with John Haldane in 1932 and continuing with Jeans, Sherrington, Wright, Rensch, Walker, Cochran, Dyson, Bohm, and Hameroff. More recently, concepts in mathematical analysis, especially cybernetics, state-space analysis, and chaos theory, have been employed on behalf of panpsychism.

To many scientists of the early twentieth century, panpsychism was uncomfortably close to the recently discredited theory of vitalism. As a result, they largely avoided discussing it. But there were exceptions. The first notable scientist to tentatively put forth panpsychist views was the British astronomer Arthur Eddington, who concludes his book *Space, Time and Gravitation* (1920) with the observation that physics only addresses the surface structure of matter and energy and doesn't have anything to say about the inner content of reality. Arguing roughly in the manner of Schopenhauer, Eddington claims that the inner content of reality must be like the inner content of the human, i.e., consciousness:

In regard to the nature of things, this knowledge [of relativity] is only an empty shell—a form of symbols. It is knowledge of structural form and not knowledge of content. All through the physical world runs that unknown content, which must surely be the stuff of our consciousness. Here is a hint of aspects deep within the world of physics, and yet unattainable by the methods of physics. (200)

This somewhat vague passage can be read either as a form of pure idealism or, in the manner of Schopenhauer, as a panpsychic idealism.[3]

Eddington's 1928 book *The Nature of the Physical World* contains a section titled "Mind-Stuff" in which Eddington, explicitly acknowledging the views of Clifford, bluntly states:

The universe is of the nature of a thought or sensation in a universal Mind ... . To put the conclusion crudely—the stuff of the world is mind-stuff. ... The mind-stuff of the world is something more general than our individual conscious minds; but we may think of its nature as not altogether foreign to feelings in our consciousness ... . (276)

3. It also anticipates the soon-to-follow work of Russell and his quasi-panpsychist neutral monism. That concept—the basis for what is today called "Russellian monism"—is discussed in chapter 9 of the present volume.

Again we are lacking in details, but the statement seems to support a panpsychist form of idealism.

Eddington's quasi-panpsychism appeared for a third time in 1939, leaning more toward conventional idealism and arguing that physics "abolishes all dualism of consciousness and matter" (150). Dualism, he claimed, contains a logical inconsistency: "Dualism depends on the belief that we find in the external world something of a nature incommensurable with what we find in consciousness." Since physics shows that all reality is structurally the same, it must all be commensurate with consciousness—that is, it must be of the nature of a mental sensation:

Although the statement that the universe is of the nature of "a thought or sensation in a universal Mind" is open to criticism, it does at least avoid this logical confusion. It is, I think, true in the sense that it is a logical consequence of the form of thought which formulates our knowledge as a description of the universe. (151)

Eddington's reference to a universal Mind is somewhat Berkelian—matter as consciousness only with respect to an observing mind, not as a mind in itself. His argumentation comes across as a bit confused, but his intention seems to be to argue that the unified view of physics supports a belief that the content of mental reality is comparable and even equivalent to the content of mind.

The biologist John (J. B. S.) Haldane speculated on mind in nature in the early 1930s, and he addressed the thorny problem of the emergence of life and mind from inanimate matter: "It is clear that aggregates of a certain kind do manifest qualities which we cannot observe in their components." (1932: 113) This is an important and subtle observation; Haldane doesn't say that emergent qualities do not exist in their components, but rather that we cannot see them there. The problem is epistemological, not ontological. In fact, if consciousness were not present in matter, that would imply a theory of strong emergence that is fundamentally anti-scientific. Such emergence is "radically opposed to the spirit of science, which has always attempted to explain the complex in terms of the simple." Haldane rejected this thesis, and hence was driven to the conclusion that life and mind exist to some degree everywhere:

We do not find obvious evidence of life or mind in so-called inert matter, and we naturally study them most easily where they are most completely manifested; but if the scientific point of view is correct, we shall ultimately find them, at least in rudimentary form, all through the universe. (113)

Two years later Haldane offered thoughts on the philosophical implications of quantum mechanics. In "Quantum Mechanics as a Basis for Philosophy" (1934) he proposes that mind is a "resonance phenomenon" that is associated with the wave-like aspect of atomic particles. This is a reasonable assertion, he claims, because the characteristics of mind are comparable to those of atomic particles: Both arise from dynamical systems, both exhibit a continuity and wholeness, both are at once localized yet spatially diffused. For example, the wave nature of an electron allows it to penetrate through an insulating barrier; this is the so-called tunneling effect. Haldane interprets this as a primitive variety of "purposive behavior." He offers the suggestion that "man also has a 'wave system' which enables him to act with reference to distant or future events, this system being his mind" (89). Anywhere this resonance phenomenon occurs, there we must accept the presence of mind. He speculates that this may happen even inside stars:

It is not inconceivable that in such [stellar] systems resonance phenomena of the complexity of life and mind might occur. ... It is conceivable that the interior of stars may shelter minds vastly superior to our own, though presumably incapable of communication with us. (97)

Haldane had previously cited Plato, and one cannot help but suspect that he had Plato's "star-souls" in mind.[4]

The physicist and astronomer Sir James Jeans was likewise drawn to philosophical speculations on mind. Like Eddington, he saw evidence for mind as present throughout nature, concluding that a form of idealism must be

4. Interestingly, scientists have discovered that the sun does in fact have an internal "resonance phenomena" that is surprisingly complex. The sun exhibits at least two modes of resonance: a 16-month cycle of increasing and decreasing rotation near the solar equator (see Howe et al. 2000) and a series of up-and-down surface vibrations, about 2,000 kilometers in magnitude, centered on a period of 5 minutes (see Friedman 1986 or Lang 1995). These "solar heartbeats" point to an internal structure and complexity of a high order, and through the associated sun-spot activity they have a non-trivial effect on the Earth. The sun has a number of other fascinating mysteries about it, not the least is the sudden and dramatic rise in the temperature of its atmosphere, from around 6,000°K at the surface to around 1,000,000°K at a height of 100,000 km above the surface; this astonishing increase has no known cause, and in fact appears to violate the second law of thermodynamics. Such physical complexity indicates, if nothing else, that our understanding of a body as complex as the sun has significant gaps. We should thus not be too quick to dismiss the possibility of yet other unacknowledged aspects of its existence.

true: "the universe can be best pictured ... as consisting of pure thought" (1932: 168). Jeans was clear that this conception undermines the mechanistic worldview: "[T]he universe begins to look more like a great thought than like a great machine. Mind no longer appears as an accidental intruder into the realm of matter." (186) In a later work he arrived at a strongly Berkelian idealism (or "mentalism"), arguing that the new physics provides three substantial reasons for seeing reality as "wholly mental": (1) Electromagnetic fields fail to qualify as objective, and hence are effectively "not real at all; they are mere mental constructs of our own" (1942: 200). (2) The reality of the theories of physics is essentially mathematical, and therefore essentially mental. (3) As Haldane suggested, the wave-particle duality implies a view in which "the ingredients of the particle-picture are material, those of the wave-picture mental. ... The final picture consists wholly of waves, and its ingredients are wholly mental constructs." (202) Jeans' philosophical reasoning thus pushed him toward a strong idealism, one that would seem compatible with a form of panpsychism.

In the early 1940s three notable British biologists ventured theories with panpsychist dispositions. Sir Charles Scott Sherrington was known for his research on the physiology of the brain, but in *Man on His Nature* (1941) he delved into mind-brain philosophy. Sherrington argued, much like Bruno, for a dual-aspect theory of reality, one consisting of mind and energy: "[O]ur world resolves itself into energy and mind. These two concepts ... divide, and between them comprise, our world." (348) He was agnostic about interaction between these two realms, stating that we are left with

acceptance of energy and mind as a working biological unity although we cannot describe the how of that unity. ... The evolution of one is of necessity the evolution of the other. There is no causal relation between them; they are both inseparably one. Their correlation is unity. (351–352).

One consequence of this view is that the animate blends seamlessly into the inanimate: "We have difficulty in assigning the lower limit of the mental. It may therefore be that its distribution extends to all organisms, and even further." (354) In other words, "it is as though the elementary mental had never been wanting" (266)—that is, present in all matter throughout the history of evolution.

The second of the three men was Wilfred Agar. A follower of Whitehead's process philosophy, Agar was attracted to Whitehead's concept of the "philosophy of the organism," and he sought a biological theory of the living organism that would correspond to Whitehead's philosophy. Agar's central thesis was that organisms are both percipient subjects and composed of elements—cells—that are themselves percipient; living cells "must also be regarded as feeling, perceiving, subjects" (1943: 8). The logic continues down the chain of being: "A cell, though a subject, must probably also be considered a nexus of living sub-agents." (11)[5]

Agar asserted that "Whitehead's system essentially involves a form of panpsychism" (66), and his analysis demonstrated a deeper philosophical awareness than the other scientists discussed. He accepted most aspects of Whitehead's process philosophy but disagreed on the nature of consciousness. Whitehead saw consciousness as a special and limited case of the more general phenomenon of feeling or experiencing, whereas Agar believed that

the more satisfying hypothesis is that ... all experience is in its degree conscious. ... We must ascribe consciousness to every living agent, such as a plant cell or bacterium, and even (if the continuity of nature is not to be broken) to an electron. (91)

Agar's panpsychism is thus more literal and more far-reaching than Whitehead's, adopting a universalized conception of consciousness.

The third of the biologists was Sir Julian Huxley. Arguing, like the others, that physics and evolution have demonstrated the underlying unity of nature, Huxley embraced a strongly monist perspective that established a deep link between mind and matter. He then adopted a dual-aspect Spinozist ontology: "there exists one world stuff, which reveals material or mental properties according to the point of view" (1942: 140). The material was reality "from the outside"; the mental was "from within." If we accept the continuity of mind and matter that science imposes,

then mind or something of the nature as mind must exist throughout the entire universe. This is, I believe, the truth. We may never be able to prove it, but it is the most economical hypothesis: it fits the facts much more simply ... than one-sided idealism or one-sided materialism.

This is among the clearer and more unambiguous panpsychist statements of the early-twentieth-century scientists.

In fact the arguments of Huxley and the others mentioned above so closely link panpsychism with the scientific worldview that one is inclined

5. The idea that cells might be conscious continues to find adherents. See, for example, Edwards 2005.

to see panpsychism not as a usurper of mechanism but rather as a logical extension of it. All but the most dogmatic critic must allow for at least the possibility that matter itself possesses a mind-like dimension or aspect. On the one hand, such a quality of matter may ultimately be deemed "objective" in some empirical sense, and thus confirmable through the methodologies of science—though perhaps in dramatically revised form. If such is the case, then science may eventually reach a conclusion that undermines its own original mechanistic presumptions.

On the other hand, perhaps something of a Kuhnian paradigm shift will be required before widespread acceptance of panpsychism occurs; this indeed seems to be the more likely alternative. In such a case, the very same physical phenomena will be viewed in a new light—as possessing (perhaps) both mechanical and mental aspects. The mind-like aspects of matter, though, would seem to have no conventional scientific consequences, and hence such a shift would appear to be unlike those which have occurred in the past few centuries of Western thought. One would have to go back to the origins of the mechanistic worldview itself, in the sixteenth and seventeenth centuries, to find a comparable shift in thinking.

In "Gene and Organism" (1953), the zoologist Sewall Wright, then president of the American Society of Naturalists, takes up Whitehead's and Agar's proposal that the concept of the organism should apply to all structures of matter. He defines an organism as any structure in which interrelated parts communicate and cohere in a persistent and self-regulatory manner. He then notes that the concept applies not only to plants and animals, but to human society, and even—anticipating Gaia theory—to the Earth's biosystem as a whole:

[T]he entire array of plants and animals and peripherally the soil and waters of a given region [constitute] an interdependent self-regulatory system, with considerable persistence. ... Since regions [of the earth] are connected, the entire biota and peripherally the surface of the earth form one great organism. (7)

This is one of the few acknowledgments since the time of Fechner that the Earth may be considered as a single organic entity. Furthermore, says Wright, not only the Earth, but the solar system and the universe as a whole each qualify as organisms. At the other end of the scale, atoms and molecules are to be considered organisms; subatomic particles are questionable—not having parts, as he believes—but he feels that their "vibratory character" and persistence put them in the same general category.

As to the question of mind, Wright again invokes an argument by non-emergence, showing that mind must exist both in single-celled organisms and in their constituent parts: "If we are not at some point to postulate the abrupt origin of mind, mind must be traced to the genes, which presumably means to nucleo-protein molecules." (13) This has implications for humans because it entails that "our own apparently unified stream of consciousness is somehow a fusion of the minds of the cells" of our bodies. Wright ultimately concurs with Eddington and Jeans that "the essential nature of all reality is that of mind" (16), though he does acknowledge that his is more of a pluralistic idealism: "reality consists primarily of a multiplicity of minds"—a critical issue from the panpsychist perspective.

Wright continued to elaborate on his panpsychist views over the subsequent 20 years. In an article published in *The Monist* in 1964, for example, he explicitly argues for "dual-aspect or monistic panpsychism." He presents a hierarchy of mind in which each level in the chain of being is enminded, and participates in higher-order mind: "The very fact of interaction, at any level, implies ... that minds are not entirely private. ... They [also] exist as components of a more comprehensive mind." (1964: 284) In a contribution to Cobb and Griffin's 1977 compilation *Mind in Nature*, titled "Panpsychism and Science," he reiterates the same themes and, with admirable clarity, places even more emphasis on the problem of emergence: "Emergence of mind from no mind at all is sheer magic." (1977: 82) Wright asserts that dual-aspect panpsychism is the only logically consistent position.

Several other scientists began speaking out on panpsychism in the 1960s and the 1970s. In *The Nature of Life* (1961), C. H. Waddington discusses approvingly the ideas of Haldane mentioned above. Once again citing evolutionary continuity, Waddington asks:

Are we not forced to conclude that even in the simplest inanimate things there is something which belongs to the same realm of being as self-awareness? ... Something must go on in the simplest inanimate things which can be described in the same language as would be used to describe our self-awareness. (121)

The biologist Bernhard Rensch published about half a dozen pieces arguing for a panpsychic theory of mind. In *Evolution above the Species Level* (1960) he reiterates the evolutionist line that "because of [a] lack of any serious evolutionary gap" one cannot limit mental abilities to the higher organisms. The evolutionary ancestry of living organisms represents a "gapless series of phylogenetic transformations" (334) in which at no point can we logically envision the sudden appearance of psychic abilities; "it is not very probable that in the continuous process of transformation entirely new laws of psychic parallelism [i.e. a mental aspect of things] should have suddenly emerged." On Rensch's view, the defining mental characteristic is sensation; he attributes it not only to all animals but also to plants, owing to the blurring of categories at the micro-organismal level. Even the gap between living and non-living systems is illusory:

Here again it is difficult to assume a sudden origin of first psychic elements somewhere in this gradual ascent from nonliving to living systems. It would not be impossible to ascribe "psychic" components to the realm of inorganic systems ... . (352)

This "hylopsychic" view, Rensch claims, is supported by cognition theory and atomic physics. He concludes that "a hylopsychic concept is well in accord with many findings and facts of the natural sciences, and ... is possibly the most suitable basis for a universal philosophy" (355).

In 1971 Rensch began referring to his system as *panpsychistic identism*. He generalized the conventional identity theory of mind, attributing "protopsychical" qualities to all levels of material organization, and asserting that "all 'matter' is protopsychical in character" (298). Here Rensch begins to treat the subject more systematically. He offers ten nominal facts in support of his thesis: (1) The only reality of which we are aware is that of "experienced phenomena." (2) Dualism is obviously false, and mind and body are an indivisible unity—a fact supported by numerous thinkers throughout history. (3) Phylogenetic development is gapless, and there is no point at which any psychical element could suddenly emerge. (4) The same process occurs in individual development, i.e., from single-celled egg to fetus to person. (5) Sudden emergence of an interactive psychic quality would violate the conservation of energy, or at least introduce an inconsistency in it. (6) Life is rare throughout the universe, and to conjecture the sudden appearance of mind is "more hypothetical" than to presume it present from the beginning. (7) Matter is really just "complexes of energy," and hence amenable to mind-like qualities. (8) Human consciousness arises from chemo-physical brain processes, and thus it is reasonable to believe that the "molecules, atoms, and elementary particles involved are protopsychical in character." (9) Fetal cell tissue is capable of developing into any organ, including the brain, and hence all cells have the ability to yield mind. (10) "It is impossible to point to any fact which would prove that matter is *not* protopsychical in character." (299–301) Such facts, individually, may not be compelling, but for Rensch the overall picture clearly supports a form of panpsychism.

In a 1972 article titled "Spinoza's Identity Theory and Modern Biophilosophy" Rensch compares his views to those of Spinoza, in whom he found the philosophical basis for panpsychistic identism. Then in 1977 Rensch presented five arguments for his system; four of these were reiterations from 1971, and to these he added the fact that since DNA molecules can transmit inherited psychic characteristics from generation to generation, the molecules themselves must naturally have a protopsychic nature.

Rensch's work is notable because he sought detailed empirical, scientific evidence of a panpsychist universe. This, however, is arguably an impossible task, in light of the intrinsic nature of mental experience and the apparent causal closure of the physical world.[6] Perhaps the only such route to panpsychism can be through a detailed understanding of the physiology of human consciousness. If, for example, a basis for our mental experience can be found in certain objective yet universal criteria (such as the quantum collapse theory of Hameroff and Penrose; see below), that could conceivably serve as an objective basis for panpsychism. Apart from such approaches, one is left largely with analogical and metaphysical arguments.

8.3   Bateson

Gregory Bateson researched and wrote on an impressively wide range of subjects, including biology, anthropology, psychology, cybernetic theory, and natural philosophy. A contrarian to the trend of increasing specialization, he was uniquely qualified to comment on the interconnection between nature and mind. His vision of ecological philosophy and the relationship between organic wholes was a predecessor to the more fully developed eco-philosophies of Henryk Skolimowski, Arne Naess, and other environmental philosophers. And his awareness of the importance of concepts such as energy, feedback, and information led to new arguments for

6. Physics describes systems of mass-energy that evolve via specific natural laws that are expressible mathematically. Causality seems to exist entirely within the realm of matter and energy. There is neither room nor evidence for non-physical (i.e., mental or spiritual) causation. Hence the widely held belief that physics is "causally closed."

panpsychism, anticipating later developments in chaos theory and non-linear dynamics.[7]

Bateson's inquiry into mind and nature initially brought him to a qualified version of panpsychism, though he seems to have ultimately abandoned it—for reasons that are not entirely clear. His first investigations in this area occurred in 1968. In an article titled "Conscious Purpose vs. Nature," he expresses—like many other scientist-philosophers of the time—a belief that "the study of evolution might provide an explanation of *mind*" (35). Bateson's first notable point is that the mind is essentially a natural phenomenon, bound up with the complexity of matter. He cites approvingly Lamarck's view that "mental process must always have a physical representation" (36). Furthermore, he asserts that "wherever in the Universe we encounter [a certain degree] of complexity, we are dealing with mental phenomena." In an attempt to elaborate this issue, Bateson observes that complex dynamic systems involve a process of feedback through which they are self-corrective. Examples of natural self-corrective systems include the individual organism, a society of organisms, and the self-sustaining ecosystem. All these levels of organization embody comparable system dynamics, and—by implication—should exhibit qualities of mind. To use his example, a forest ecosystem such as an "oak wood" is fundamentally like an individual organism, reflecting mind from within its bodily, material structure. Bateson refers to this kind of embodiment as "total mind": "This entity [i.e. the individual organism] is similar to the oak wood and its controls are represented in the *total* mind, which is perhaps only a reflection of the total body." (40) But he drops the matter there, only later following up on the implications.

Bateson's 1972 compilation *Steps to an Ecology of Mind* includes the above-mentioned article and a number of other relevant pieces. Preeminent among these is "Form, Substance, and Difference," originally published in 1970. It was in this article that Bateson first presented his famous but vague definition of information as "difference which makes a difference" (1970: 7). He attempts to relate the phenomenon of mind to feedback systems of energy circulation, deciding that it is "pure difference" that matters the most. He is emphatic that it is the circular feedback system itself that is important—that it is in precisely such a system that we observe what can rightly be called mind. On this point he is quite explicit:

7. See, for example, Bateson 1972: 403ff.

The elementary cybernetic system with its messages in circuit is, in fact, the simplest unit of mind ... . More complicated systems are perhaps more worthy to be called mental systems, but essentially this is what we are talking about. The unit which shows the characteristic of trial and error will be legitimately called a mental system. ... We get a picture, then, of mind as synonymous with cybernetic system ... . (1972: 459–460)

Notably, cybernetic feedback systems are ubiquitous in nature. They exist at all levels of organization, from molecular to galactic—anywhere parts interact and persistent structures appear. Therefore, cybernetic mind must be present throughout the universe. That, in fact, is Bateson's conclusion: "we know that within Mind in the widest sense there will be a hierarchy of subsystems, any one of which we can call an individual mind." His elaboration makes clear that such a conception of mind extends not only to small cybernetic systems but also to large-scale ones:

It means, you see, that I now localize something which I am calling "Mind" immanent in the large biological system—the ecosystem. Or, if I draw the system boundaries at a different level, then mind is immanent in the total evolution structure.

The individual mind is immanent but not only in the body. It is immanent also in pathways and messages outside the body; and there is a larger Mind of which the individual mind is only a subsystem. This larger Mind is comparable to God and is perhaps what some people mean by "God," but it is still immanent in the total interconnected social system and planetary ecology.

It is not just a universal Mind, but mind at all levels of existence—true pluralistic panpsychism.[8]

Still, Bateson qualifies his view. The only exceptions for him are the fundamental atomic particles ("atomies"). These particles, being without parts, lack the dynamic feedback interrelationships that he sees as necessary for the process of mind. One of his footnotes is illuminating:

I do not agree with Samuel Butler, Whitehead, or Teilhard de Chardin that it follows from this mental character of the macroscopic world that the single atomies must have mental character or potentiality. I see the mental as a function only of complex *relationship*. (465)

8. This aspect of Bateson's philosophy seems to be rarely acknowledged, even as the concept of "information" is put to use in other panpsychist theories. Bohm (1986) spoke in similar terms, though without citing Bateson. Chalmers (1996: 293–301) developed his own information-theoretic form of panpsychism, but without discussing the related panpsychist views of either Bateson or Bohm.

He repeats the same view in his most philosophical work, *Mind and Nature* (1979: 103): "I do not believe that single subatomic particles are 'minds' in my sense because I do believe that mental process is always a sequence of interactions *between* parts. The *explanation* of mental phenomena must always reside in the organization and interaction of multiple parts." But this is a relatively minor issue, and it doesn't substantially affect Bateson's generally panpsychist outlook.[9]

It is in *Mind and Nature*, however, that Bateson seems to back away from the panpsychist implications of his earlier writings—though, oddly, maintaining the same theory of mind, with presumably the same consequences. Mind still exists in the interrelationship and interaction between dynamic parts. But now this is only a necessary, not a sufficient condition for mind. He lays out six somewhat cryptic criteria for complex systems to possess mind, noting that any system meeting them must be designated as possessing mind.[10] The criteria are very general and would seem to apply to any dynamic system whatsoever. Yet he excludes not only (as before) subatomic particles, but other physical systems too:

There are, of course, many systems which are made of many parts, ranging from galaxies to sand dunes to toy locomotives. Far be it from me to suggest that all of these are minds or contain minds or engage in mental process. The ... galaxy may become part of the mental system which includes the astronomer and his telescope. But the objects do not become thinking subsystems in those larger minds. The [six] criteria are useful only in combination. (1979: 104)

This puzzling statement is potentially inconsistent with Bateson's own standards. If the criteria are valid, they should be valid universally. They appear to occur in combination everywhere. He thus backs away from the logical implications of his own theory—implications he had accepted only

9. The main problem with this view is that mind is no longer truly fundamental, but apparently must radically emerge as soon as a system with "parts" appears—perhaps the first hydrogen atom, or the first proton (with quarks as parts). But this is a philosophical problem that Bateson neither resolves nor even acknowledges.

10. "(1) All mind is an aggregate of interacting parts or components. (2) The interaction between parts of mind is triggered by difference. (3) Mental process requires collateral energy. (4) Mental process requires circular chains of determination. (5) In mental process, the effects of difference are to be regarded as transforms of the events which preceded them. (6) The description and classification of these processes of transformation disclose a hierarchy of logical types immanent in the phenomena." (Bateson 1979: 102)

a few years earlier. Whether he was ultimately able to construct a cohesive and consistent theory of mind remains an open question.

8.4   Other Scientific Interpretations

From the 1970s on, physicists became increasingly involved in the discussion about panpsychism. Evan Walker (1970), for example, argued that quantum processes in brain synapses account for a number of characteristics of consciousness, in particular its existence and non-physicality. He also remarks that, more generally, "consciousness may be associated with all quantum mechanical processes" (175). He closes the 1970 article with this observation:

[S]ince everything that occurs is ultimately the result of one or more quantum mechanical events, the universe is "inhabited" by an almost unlimited number of rather discrete conscious, usually nonthinking entities that are responsible for the detailed working of the universe.

It is a striking view, one that follows from Haldane's related ideas of the 1930s.

Breaking from the evolutionary-continuity approach, Andrew Cochran (1971) argued for a similar perspective. In a rather ingenious argument, he observes that the elements of organic compounds—carbon, hydrogen, nitrogen, and oxygen—have among the lowest atomic heat capacities, which corresponds to a high degree of "wave predominance" (as opposed to "particle predominance"), and hence are the most endowed with the qualities of consciousness. He suggests that "the quantum mechanical wave properties of matter are actually the conscious properties of matter," and therefore "atoms and fundamental particles have a rudimentary degree of consciousness, volition, or self-activity" (236). These ideas would be reflected in the later work of David Bohm, Freeman Dyson, and other physicists.

Beginning in the early 1970s, the biologist Charles Birch wrote a series of essays (1971, 1972, 1974, 1994) and a book (1995) presenting a new interpretation of process philosophy, arguing for a panexperientialist form of panpsychism. His 1974 essay, for example, claims that panpsychism represents a form of evolutionary teleology in which the primordial psychic phenomena of atoms and molecules in the early universe foreshadowed the later appearance of mind and consciousness. And his 1994 speech presents six reasons for adopting the panexperientialist viewpoint: (1) Biology points away from crass mechanism. (2) The process view of true individuals as possessing experience makes intuitive sense. (3) Panexperientialism avoids the emergence category mistake. (4) The "doctrine of internal relations" suggests that true individuals possess unique experiential phenomena. (5) Computers and other mechanisms are not organisms, and thus are inherently limited in their ability to model consciousness. (6) The reality of subjectivity suggests that it has a fundamental place in the universe.

In *Disturbing the Universe* (1979), Freeman Dyson presents his views on a range of subjects, from physics and cosmology to politics and economics. In the penultimate chapter he examines mechanistic philosophy and the concept of the universe as a clockwork machine. He notes that, as one descends the ladder of complexity, things at first appear more mechanical, but then at the level of molecular physics this process reverses itself: "If we divide a DNA molecule into its component atoms, the atoms behave less mechanically than the molecule. If we divide an atom into nucleus and electrons, the electrons are less mechanical than the atom." (248) At the quantum level the observer is intimately bound up with physical events, and thus "the laws [of physics] leave a place for mind in the description of every molecule" (249). The logical continuity of nature then presses us to accept that mind is present and active at all levels of existence:

In other words, mind is already inherent in every electron, and the processes of human consciousness differ only in degree but not in kind from the processes of choice between quantum states which we call "chance" when they are made by electrons.

Dyson readily admitted that such a view is antithetical to conventional science. He cited Jacques Monod as typical of the conventional view, noting that Monod holds out "the deepest scorn" for such an "animist" conception of the world.[11] But Dyson was unfazed. For him the "importance of mind in the scheme of things" is undeniable, whether one considers the role of mind in the electron or in a conception of the world-soul.

Chronologically speaking, Bohm's writings of the 1980s were the next events of significance. I defer this discussion to the next section, which is dedicated to his work.

A brief word is warranted for Michael Lockwood's 1989 book *Mind, Brain, and the Quantum*. Following the approach of Paul Churchland (discussed in

11. See Monod's 1971 book *Chance and Necessity*.

chapter 9), Lockwood employs the methodology of phase-space analysis for his discussion of mind. He concludes that a form of the identity theory is true, one in which mind doesn't reduce to matter but rather "represents the physical world as infused with intrinsic qualities which ... constitute the basis of its causal powers and which include immediately introspectible qualities in their own right" (1989: 159).

Chalmers (1996), Seager (2001), and others have suggested that this view is in itself panpsychist. But Lockwood is very evasive in his terminology. At one point he argues for "a conception of the world as, in some sense, a sum of perspectives" (1989: 177), and later adds "I wish to argue that, in consciousness, that intrinsic nature makes itself manifest" (238). But it is not clear whether such a view qualifies as panpsychism, as he defines it. Other passages seem contradictory. He claims that consciousness comprises only a portion of these intrinsic qualities: "The qualities of which we are immediately aware, in consciousness, precisely *are* some at least of the intrinsic qualities ... specifically, states and processes within our own brains." (159) He then speaks negatively of the panpsychist view in his discussion of unsensed qualities: the "major advantage of holding that phenomenal qualities can exist unsensed" is that "it enables one to halt this slide into panpsychism" (170). And none of his later works suggests anything like an endorsement. If Lockwood's position is a panpsychist one, it is a very tenuous and vague interpretation.

The most recent articulation of a scientific approach to panpsychism, again from quantum theory, was introduced by medical scientist Stuart Hameroff. Working in conjunction with mathematician Roger Penrose, Hameroff developed a theory of human consciousness that was centered on the coordinated collapse of superposed quantum conditions in the brain. Their various presentations of the theory (Hameroff 1994, Penrose 1994a, Hameroff and Penrose 1996, Hameroff 2009) indicate that quantum collapse might be associated with a "moment of experience" in the Whiteheadian sense. This, incidentally, is an interesting reversal of the so-called Copenhagen interpretation of quantum mechanics, in which consciousness causes quantum collapse. On the view of Hameroff and Penrose, precisely the opposite occurs: Collapse causes consciousness.

According to standard theory, atomic and sub-atomic particles appear to evolve into multiple simultaneous superposed states. When an act of measurement is performed, the condition of superposition collapses randomly into one of the states, which then appears as the actual state of the particle. At present there are conflicting views on whether reduction happens in reality or whether it is some kind of artificial or illusory phenomenon. Hameroff and Penrose take it as fact, and further suggest that it happens not merely upon measurement by a subjective observer but independently—as a spontaneous process that they call *objective reduction* (OR). They argue that certain microstructures of neurons—tubular skeletal structures called microtubules—serve as the sites for sustained quantum superposition. Microtubules also allow for a coordination between individual tubulin molecules that results in a large-scale "orchestrated OR" that may produce a unified, large-scale sense of consciousness. Large numbers of tubulin molecules coordinating their effects, and collapsing repeatedly on the order of every 0.5 to 5 milliseconds, are said to account for the apparently continuous stream of consciousness that we normally feel.

On the theory of Hameroff and Penrose, superposed states must be maintained until a quantum gravity threshold is reached; only at that point can OR, and thus conscious experience, take place. A system of fewer elements—fewer neurons, or fewer tubulin molecules—requires a longer, and therefore less likely, time in which to reach the threshold. Complex living organisms are ideal for the OR process, since they possess large numbers of quantum-coherent structures.

Hameroff and Penrose's analysis is primarily focused on the brain and its neurons, but they emphasize that such a process could appear anywhere microtubules are present. Since they are universally present in all living cells, from animals to plants to one-celled life forms, all living beings would presumably experience some degree of consciousness. Fewer tubulin molecules, though, would imply a longer period of time between state collapses, and thus a longer time between moments of experience.[12]

Hameroff independently proceeded to further develop the philosophical implications of the OR theory, linking this process of quantum collapse to a realization of "proto-conscious" events occurring ubiquitously in the quantum realm (1998a, 1998b, 2009) and suggesting that "perhaps panpsychists are in some way correct and components of mental processes are

---

12. The nematode worm *C. elegans* is hypothesized to experience at most two "moments" per second, the simpler paramecium one per minute (Hameroff and Penrose 1996: 51).

fundamental, like mass, spin or charge" (1998a: 121). This would seem to be the logical extension of the Hameroff-Penrose theory, although Penrose seems reluctant to endorse it. He apparently holds that only certain collapse conditions, namely those occurring upon reaching a quantum gravity threshold, count as conscious; and yet it is hard to see what is ontologically unique, with respect to mind, about this particular mode of collapse. And even on this view, a panpsychist interpretation is still possible. Any physical system has at least a statistical likelihood of sustaining a superposed state until the critical threshold is reached. Even a single subatomic particle has a small but finite chance of sustaining superposition until OR occurs: "As OR could, in principle, occur ubiquitously within many types of inanimate media, it may seem to imply a form of panpsychism." (Hameroff and Penrose 1996: 38) Indeed it is, with the qualification that the incidents of *psyche* are, for simple particles, extremely rare: "a single superposed electron would spontaneously reduce its state … only once in a period longer than the present age of the universe." Other theoretical estimates indicate a somewhat more frequent occurrence, such as once every 10 million to 100 million years (Penrose 1994b: 332, 340). Still, a rare psychic event is *psyche* nonetheless.

Hameroff (1998b) adds that his theory "suggests that consciousness may involve a self-organizing quantum state reduction process occurring at the Planck scale [10^{-33} centimeters]," and that "in a panexperiential Platonic view consistent with modern physics, quantum spin networks encode proto-conscious 'funda-mental' experience." With many ongoing developments in quantum theory in general, such a view of mind is likely to undergo continual refinement for the foreseeable future.

The final word in this section goes to John Wheeler. Along with Bateson and Bohm, he was among the first to suggest that information was a potential ultimate ground of reality—see his 1994 essay "It from Bit." Wheeler's acceptance of the quantum as a fundamental principle of the universe suggests that quantum collapses, driven by some kind of observer-process, are universally present. Given the speculative connection between quantum collapse and conscious observation, it is natural to consider the universe as filled with elemental conscious events. Wheeler suggests (1994: 307) that "we may someday have to enlarge the scope of what we mean by a 'who'"—that is, a "who" as any observer or system that induces a quantum collapse. Observing minds could in principle be present even throughout the so-called inanimate realm. A few years before his death, he all but admitted as much: "I find it hard to draw a line between the conscious observer and the inanimate one." (2002)

8.5 Bohm and the Implicate Order

Like many other physicists, David Bohm (1917–1992) had a longstanding interest in developing the philosophical implications of quantum physics. He wrote numerous pieces on the philosophy of physics, and seems to have been especially interested in the process of mind. More than any other scientist-philosopher of the twentieth century, Bohm developed and openly endorsed a form of panpsychism that was grounded in fundamental physical laws—in his case, laws of quantum mechanics.

Bohm's interest in panpsychism began as early as 1957. In his book *Causality and Chance in Modern Physics*, he made just one passing reference to the concept, in the midst of a discussion of his idea of strong emergence—that "new qualities and new laws" can appear because of the "universal process of becoming" (1957: 163) that dominates the universe. Bohm noted that processes of living matter do not fundamentally differ from those of non-living matter: "[W]hen one analyzes processes taking place in inanimate matter over long enough periods of time, one finds a similar behaviour [to living processes]. Only here the process is so much slower ... ." Such a standpoint recalls the arguments of Royce, examined earlier in this volume.

Bohm edged closer to panpsychism in *Wholeness and the Implicate Order* (1980). He states that quantum theory presents a fundamental challenge to mechanism because it exhibits radically discontinuous or quantized behavior, simultaneously wave-like and particle-like properties, and extreme non-locality (a phenomenon in which coupled particles form an instantaneous relationship over any distance whatsoever, leading to a form of communication that exceeds the speed of light). Indeed, he notes that the structure of the universe "is much more reminiscent of how the organs constituting living beings are related, than it is of how parts of a machine interact" (175).

Bohm goes on to argue for a form of neutral monism wherein "both inanimate matter and life [are comprehended] on the basis of a single ground, common to both" (193)—something he designates as the "implicate order."

Repeating his earlier observation, he comments that "even inanimate matter maintains itself in a continual process similar to the growth of plants." In the same way that this common ground unites living and non-living, so too does it unite mind and non-mind: "the implicate order applies both to matter and to consciousness" (196). Bohm sees both sets of dualities as false and fundamentally mistaken. Consequently, he argues, there is a sense in which all matter is both alive and conscious. In his words, "in a wide range of ... important respects, consciousness and matter in general are basically the same order (i.e. the implicate order as a whole)" (208).

Something approaching panpsychism is a natural consequence of such a view. Consider memory, for example. "The recurrence and stability of our own memory ... is thus brought about as part of the very same process that sustains the recurrence and stability in the manifest order of matter in general." The temporally persistent structures of mass-energy that we see around us reflect an ongoing process of recollection by the implicate order, and thus are aspects of mentality.

Bohm explained his theory in less technical terms in a 1982 interview in the journal *ReVision*, where he considered the possibility of a deeper ground underlying both the explicate and the implicate order. When asked if this ground is self-aware, he replied "Yes ... since it contains both matter and mind, it would have in some sense to be aware." (1982: 37) Repeating again his view that "thought and matter have a great similarity of order," he stated that "in a way, nature is alive, as Whitehead would say, all the way to the depths. And intelligent. Thus it is both mental and material, as we are." (39)

In March of 1985, Bohm gave an important speech at a meeting of the American Society for Psychical Research. Published under the title "A New Theory of the Relationship of Mind and Matter,"[13] it combined a direct endorsement of panpsychism with Bohm's first explicit use of the concept of participation as related to a new worldview. Beginning with the panpsychist aspect, there are several passages in which he clearly asserts that mind is found in all systems that contain "information content"—that is, in all dynamically coherent particles or subsystems. This new emphasis on information recalled the work of Bateson, though Bohm did not specifically cite him.

13. The talk was published as Bohm 1986.

Recognizing that the term 'information' implies both a meaning and a consciousness able to perceive that meaning, Bohm notes first of all that, on his interpretation of quantum theory, all physical systems embody information. On his view, "the notion of information [is] something that need not belong only to human consciousness, but that may indeed be present, in some sense, even in inanimate systems of atoms and electrons" (1986: 124–125). Because of the "basic similarity between the quantum behavior of a system ... and the behavior of mind" (130), Bohm argues that mind and matter are intimately connected at all levels of being:

[T]he mental and the material are two sides of one overall process. ... There is one energy that is the basis of all reality. ... There is never any real division between mental and material sides at any stage of the overall process. (129)

The conclusion is a pluralistic panpsychism that reaches up and down the ontological hierarchy:

I would suggest that both [mind and body] are essentially the same. ... That which we experience as mind ... will in a natural way ultimately reach the level of the wavefunction and of the "dance" of the particles. There is no unbridgeable gap or barrier between any of these levels. ... It is implied that, in some sense, a rudimentary consciousness is present even at the level of particle physics. It would also be reasonable to suppose an indefinitely greater kind of consciousness that is universal and that pervades the entire process [of the universe]. (131)

For Bohm, this panpsychism fits together with a world described as fundamentally participatory in nature: "the basic notion is participation rather than interaction" (113). As he sees it, matter is participatory because of the quantum nature of atomic particles. These particles, even if one assumes them (as Bohm did) to be point-like entities, are seen to exist probabilistically: An electron in an atom has a high chance of existing in its so-called proper orbit, but it also has a non-zero chance of existing outside that orbit, across the room, or even across the universe. Each particle exists, in a very real sense, everywhere in the universe at once. Because of this, every particle is in contact with every other particle.[14] All particles thus "dance" together, to a greater or lesser degree. We can clearly see this phenomenon in superconductivity—wherein "electrons are thus *participating* in a common action based on a common pool of information" (122)—or in nonlocal experiments. But even where it is not apparent, this interconnection is

14. Recall Leibniz's view that all monads are in contact with all others. See Leibniz 1714b, section 61.

always present. Echoing a view as old as Anaxagoras, Bohm says "the whole of the universe is in some way enfolded in everything and ... each thing is enfolded in the whole" (114).

On this view of reality, the objectivist stance of an observer dispassionately making observations is fundamentally inadequate. Interaction becomes participation:

[S]uch a complex process of participation evidently goes far beyond what is meant by a merely mechanical interaction. It is therefore not really correct to call what happens a measurement. ... Rather, it is a *mutual transformation* of both systems ... . (124)

Each system changes the other—an idea reaching back to Hartshorne, Schiller, and even Campanella. Bohm concludes, like Wheeler, that

the mechanical notion of an interactive universe is seen to be inadequate. It is in need of replacement by the notion of an objectively participative universe that includes our own participation as a special case. (126)

In 1990 Bohm reissued the 1986 article with substantial changes—confusingly, under the same title. In the new version he clarifies his philosophical terminology without abandoning his central view. He states, for example, that "quantum theory ... implies that the particles of physics have certain primitive mind-like qualities ... (though of course, they do not have consciousness)" (1990: 272). He is clearly refining his ideas, no longer being satisfied to attribute "rudimentary consciousness" to elementary particles.

For Bohm, then, participation occurs both within the material realm, down to the quantum level, and also between the processes of mind that occur at all levels of being. He describes "the essential mode of relationship of all these [levels of mind] as participation" (284), a fact that applies equally to the human scale and to the atomic scale: "For the human being, all of this implies a thoroughgoing wholeness, in which mental and physical sides participate very closely in each other." Such an ontological outlook may be best described as a form of participatory panpsychism.

Bohm's last significant philosophical work, co-written with Basil Hiley, was *Undivided Universe* (1993). Though primarily a technical work in quantum physics, it included a well-developed philosophical analysis that elaborated on earlier themes. The philosophical conclusions at the end of the book were taken largely verbatim from Bohm (1990) and so did not add anything substantially new.

9 Panpsychism from 1950 to the Present

The previous chapter detailed some recent ideas and approaches to panpsychism from within the scientific tradition, broadly conceived. From a philosophical perspective, panpsychism diversified greatly in the middle and late years of the twentieth century, following a number of different routes.

First there was the ongoing development of the Whiteheadian process view, which had been defended and articulated for decades by Hartshorne. His writing was complemented by that of several other process philosophers, most notably Griffin but also including Ford, Birch, De Quincey, and others. The process philosophers have been among the more consistent and vocal advocates of panpsychism over the past several decades, and they deserve credit for keeping the topic alive within philosophical discourse.

Additionally we find a range of other approaches. The panpsychist implications of a part-whole hierarchy, first articulated by Cardano, were adopted and modernized by Koestler. Dual-aspect views, which are at least implicitly panpsychist, were defended by thinkers as diverse as Feigl, Nagel, Globus, Plumwood, and Chalmers. In the work of Abram, Berman, Zohar, Wilber, Harvey, and Orr, populist treatments also emerged. The endorsement of panpsychism by the prominent analytic philosopher Galen Strawson was a major development in the field. So-called Russellian monism has been taken up in earnest by professional philosophers, many of whom spell out the panpsychist implications. And various efforts have been made to build upon the insights of Peirce and to connect recent work in chaos theory and dynamical systems to forms of panpsychism.

9.1 Developments in the 1960s and the 1970s

In the second half of the twentieth century, apart from Hartshorne, a number of philosophical voices argued for variations on the panpsychist theme.

Unsurprisingly, many were from outside the mainstream of traditional academia. Academic philosophy, having become thoroughly immersed in the analytic and linguistic disciplines, seems to have largely abandoned the deeper, more penetrating, more metaphysical questions of mind. Modern philosophy, at least as practiced in the major universities, primarily serves to perpetuate a positivistic, mechanistic worldview. As William James said, philosophy is ultimately about vision. The vision of modern philosophy is predominantly an analytical one, and thus largely sterile and inert: a world of passive matter acted on by blind forces. That such a world can give rise to life and mind becomes an inexplicable fact and an eternal mystery.

Scattered references to panpsychism, many of them confused and ambivalent, continued to appear in the 1950s and the 1960s. Consider the philosopher Herbert Feigl. In 1958 he published a lengthy and influential article, "The 'Mental' and the 'Physical,'" in which he argued for a form of the identity theory that has been interpreted by certain writers as a kind of panpsychism. Identity theories generally equate the physical states of the brain with mental states, typically stating directly that mental states are brain states. On that view, a physical alteration in brain state necessarily implies a changed mental state, in a kind of one-to-one relationship. Such a mind-brain identity presents a number of difficulties, as Feigl points out; one of these is the precise meaning of 'identical'.[1] Under most interpretations, it means that the mental is somehow dependent on or supervenient upon the physical.

If mental states are identical to physical brain or neural states, and if neural states are seen as not fundamentally unlike physical processes in general, then one is strongly inclined toward a panpsychist view. If one accepts an identity theory and yet denies panpsychism, then one necessarily accepts that there is something ontologically unique about the physical processes occurring in the brain, such that they alone give rise to consciousness or mind—a position that smacks of a kind of neo-vitalism and is extraordinarily difficult to defend.

Feigl seems to have recognized this dilemma, and yet he wavers between the two horns. After ruling out many common descriptors of "mental,"

---

1. The other main issues, not exclusive to the identity theory, are the meanings of such notoriously vague terms as 'physical' and 'mental'. Feigl spends considerable time examining these particular matters.

he determines that the two most appropriate terms are "direct experience" (qualia) and "intelligence." Both are required, because if intelligence alone were chosen "as the sole criterion of mentality, then it would be hard to draw a sharp line anywhere within the realm of organic life. Even in the kingdom of plants ... we find processes [characteristic] of purposive behavior." (1958: 411–412) Furthermore, the notion of intelligence "may be attributed not only to the higher animals but also to the 'thinking machines' [computers]" (419).[2] Other putative characteristics of mind are inappropriate: "mnemic, teleological, holistic, and emergent features are not adequate as criteria of mentality, because these features characterize even inorganic processes and structures" (415)—apparently implying that panpsychism cannot be true, by definition.[3]

All this leaves the "raw feels" of direct experience—that is, qualia or sentience—as the critical factor. Sentience can be attributed to things, Feigl argues, only by analogy: "I have no doubt that analogy is the essential criterion for the ascription of sentience." (427) And analogy, of course, is at the heart of many panpsychist arguments. Feigl notes this but then claims that "the panpsychists' hypothesis is inconsistent with the very principles of analogy which they claim to use" (451). This statement is based on "the enormous differences in behavior" between, for example, humans and insects. But this is no real counter-argument. Panpsychism in general accepts large differences in both qualitative states and functional behavior; it merely claims that all structures experience *some* qualia, even if they are unimaginably slight or foreign to us. It is thus not clear exactly how or why the panpsychist hypothesis is inconsistent.

Feigl's wavering on this issue is especially evident later in the essay. On the one hand, "the identity theory regards sentience ... and other [unexperienced] qualities ... as the basic reality" (474). Yet at the same time he seeks to avoid "the unwarranted panpsychistic generalization." However, "one is tempted, with the panpsychists, to assume some unknown-by-acquaintance qualities quite cognate with those actually experienced" (475). A strange sort of ambivalence is obviously present here.

2. Feigl also notes that, under the appropriate definition, "there is no doubt that certain types of robots or computers do think" (423).

3. Though the inclusion of teleology is surprising. Claims of goal-directedness in inanimate systems are generally excluded by conventional science. Natural teleology may be, rather, a complement to a panpsychist metaphysics.

Feigl's position has been interpreted in varying ways, and even at the time it was apparent to many that he was implicitly arguing for panpsychism. He reacted to the criticism shortly thereafter: "Well-intentioned critics have tried to tell me that [my position] is essentially the metaphysics of panpsychism. ... It is not panpsychism at all—either the 'pan' or the 'psyche' has to be deleted in the formulation." (1960: 31) After adding that, in his view, "nothing in the least like a psyche is ascribed to lifeless matter," he concludes that the term 'pan-quality-ism' "come[s] much closer to a correct characterization than 'panpsychism'."

And yet Feigl was never able to shake the panpsychist implications of his view. Popper (1977: 200) made him out to be a virtual panpsychist. Sprigge characterized his position as "to all intents and purposes, panpsychist" (1984: 7). Chalmers (1996: 166) classed him with Russell as a sympathizer of panpsychism. Privately, Feigl seems to have accepted this close association. Grover Maxwell recalled him as having said "If you give me a couple of martinis, a good dinner, and a couple of after-dinner drinks, I would admit that I am strongly tempted toward (a rather watered-down, innocuous) panpsychism."[4] If true, this is indicative of his deep-seated conflictions about the subject.

Another implicit reference to panpsychism came in 1967 with Arthur Koestler's book *The Ghost in the Machine*. Koestler's theory is centered on a triple-aspect hierarchical structuring of reality. On his view, each well-defined structure or object possesses three essential characteristics: Each is composed of parts at lower levels of existence, is a whole in itself, and is a part of larger wholes. In this system—which closely reflects but doesn't acknowledge Cardano's outlook—each thing so conceived is referred to as a holon. Atoms are holons, as are cells, animals, social groups, and the Earth.

Koestler was clear that such an ordering encompasses living and non-living systems, and that it implies a certain common basis for dynamic interaction with the world. The interactive mode of humans relates to our minds, and thus there is the implication that all holons relate to the world in a somewhat mind-like manner:

As we move downward in the hierarchy ... we nowhere strike rock bottom, find nowhere those ultimate constituents which the old mechanistic approach to life led us

4. Globus 1976: 320.

to expect. *The hierarchy is open-ended in the downward, as it is in the upward direction.* (1967: 61–62)

Each holon struggles to maintain its own order of existence ("self-assertive tendency") and yet also seeks to participate in larger-order structures ("participatory or self-integrative tendency"). This much is perhaps clear as it applies to living organisms, but Koestler was compelled by his own theory to acknowledge these tendencies at all levels of being. He saw this immediately and yet recoiled from the panpsychist implications:

It would, of course, be grossly anthropomorphic to speak of 'self-assertive' and 'integrative' tendencies in inanimate nature, or of 'flexible strategies.' It is nevertheless true that in all stable dynamic systems, stability is maintained by the equilibrium of opposite forces, one of which may be centrifugal or separative ... representing the holistic properties of the part, and the other a centripetal or attractive or cohesive force which keeps the part in its place in the larger whole ... . (62–63)

In the appendix Koestler adds that each level of being attains progressively greater consciousness: "Each upward shift is reflected by a more vivid and precise consciousness of the ongoing activity; and ... is accompanied by the subjective experience of freedom of decision." (347) Thus, in spite of his denial of panpsychism, he clearly ascribed mental-like qualities to all levels of existence. Like Feigl, he seems to have been torn by the implications of his own theory.

Koestler appears never to have resolved this conflict. Eleven years later he returned to the issue of mind in nature, explicitly addressing the topic of panpsychism. In *Janus* he observes (incorrectly) that "panpsychism and Cartesian dualism mark opposite ends of the philosophical spectrum" (1978: 229). His "holarchic" system, he claims, "replaces the panpsychist's continuously ascending curve from cabbage to man by a whole series of discrete steps—a staircase instead of a slope." Yet each step represents some level or degree of mentality:

In the downward direction we are faced with a multiplicity of levels of consciousness or sentience which extend far below the human level. ... The hierarchy appears to be open-ended both in the upward and downward direction. (230)

Koestler thus once again accepted the existence of sentience throughout the ontological hierarchy, yet denied that his system was a form of panpsychism. The two views are difficult to reconcile.

The psychiatrist and philosopher Gordon Globus developed a panpsychist reading of the identity theory in the early 1970s. Starting from Feigl's basic conception, Globus emphasized that there is no ontological divide between neural events and general physical events. "The present biological perspective," he wrote, "suggests that physical nonneural events and those physical neural events identical with consciousness per se have similarity qua events" (1972: 299). Thus he was led to ask "Could consciousness per se … be in some way equivalent to the ultimate physical events which comprise reality?" His initial conclusion was that they are, if not identical, at least "congruent."

In 1973 Globus wrote that mind is the process of embodying a physical event. The brain performs this function very well, and in fact "its capability for thus embodying events is identical with its capability of mind" (1134). But the brain is only a special, highly evolved instance of a physical structure. Other systems also embody events; "less evolved organs, organisms, and machines have only a 'protomind' to the extent that they are capable of embodying events." This theory became explicit panpsychism in Globus' 1976 article "Mind, Structure, and Contradiction." Seeking to avoid a naive animism, he articulates a "psychoneural structural identity thesis" that associates mind with all physical structures. Adapting and modifying the Cartesian position into a dual-aspect theory, he argues that mind is "unbounded" whereas brain is "bounded," but that each refers to the same structure of the underlying reality. The structure of the mind and the structure of the brain are *one and the same*, even though the 'stuff' structured is unbounded in the first case and bounded in the second" (282). As an example Globus mentions the sense of sight, in which a pattern of light reflects off some object and reaches the eye:

[T]he electromagnetic waves impinging on the retina … conserves the structure of the "object" from which it has been reflected. … Further, the "stuff" structured varies: from whatever the object "stuff" is, to a light "stuff," and finally to a neural "stuff"—but the structure *per se* is (more or less) maintained. (287)

Structure is thus embodied in many different forms. In humans we recognize mind as one aspect of this. More generally it is an "intrinsic perspective" that varies only according to the particular embodiment. Another of Globus' examples is the following:

[A] brain and a rock are systems differing enormously in "richness" of structure, and the respective "minds" accordingly differ enormously. … Although I appreciate that most will consider it ridiculous to attribute awareness to a rock, for my purposes, I choose to emphasize the awareness intrinsic to rock. (290)

He employs the ancient Continuity argument: "At heart, the issue is just that there is no place to unarbitrarily draw a line (or even a range) in a hierarchy of systems increasing in complexity, above which we can say that mind occurs and below which it does not." The whole notion of mind as emerging only in high-complexity structures is "human chauvinism at its worst." Acknowledging that such a panpsychic worldview is "almost impossible to fathom" from within the scientific mindset, Globus concludes his "defense of panpsychism" with an appeal to intuitive and even mystical insight as necessary for full comprehension. Clearly panpsychism lies fundamentally outside the framework of contemporary mechanistic materialism, and therefore a radical break of some kind is required to deeply grasp and adequately assess such a view.

After these insightful early pieces, Globus moved away from the topic for more than three decades. He returned to it 2009 with an intricate new argument, not for true panpsychism, but for a very widespread presence of qualia in the natural world. Drawing from quantum theory, specifically from quantum thermofield dynamics (QTD), Globus argues that qualia, and hence mind, emerge only where there exists cooperative or correlated dynamics. QTD, he says, "does in fact prescribe a lower boundary below which there can be no cooperative dynamics, and without cooperative dynamics there is nothing mind-like, just the tedious random noise of fully thermalized systems" (2009: 67). This allows us, in some cases, to make precise determinations. Water, for example, can sustain quantum coherence only above a span of about 50 microns—roughly the width of a human hair. "Below the 50 micron threshold, cooperative dynamics cannot be sustained in water" (73), and thus a water-based organism's nervous system must be structured above that threshold to allow for the emergence of consciousness. Globus concludes that, generally speaking, "any structured matter with cooperative dynamics has characteristics of psi [qualia] that arise above the coherence length" (82). Exactly what these systems are remains unclear; presumably they are widespread in the natural world but are certainly not universal. QTD thus "halts the descent into panpsychism," but nonetheless "offers far more than panpsychist scoffers imagine."

9.2 Mind in Nature: Panpsychism and Environmental Philosophy

Any metaphysical system that views all natural objects as endowed with mind-like qualities will have clear implications for one's attitude toward nature and the environment. The growing awareness of environmental problems in the latter part of the twentieth century coincided with the emergence of ecological philosophy and the field of environmental ethics. Thinkers in these areas developed a variety of philosophical systems that attempted to create a deeper and more intimate connection between humanity and nature; these included deep ecology, eco-philosophy, indigenous-culture worldviews, Gaia theory, spiritualism, eco-theology, and various forms of pantheism.

Of particular interest are those philosophical systems that are grounded in animist or panpsychist ontologies. Such systems have their historical roots in a variety of individuals, some of whom I have discussed in previous chapters. One of the earliest was Francis of Assisi, who saw the Spirit of God in all natural things and thus treated everything with the greatest reverence. In the sixteenth century, Bruno's pantheistic and panpsychist metaphysics implied a deeper integration of humanity into the natural order. His system put forth a "call for a healing of the division between nature and divinity decreed by Christianity" (Ingegno 1998: xxi). Calcagno (1998: 208) reflected on Bruno's "effort to reattach the self to its broader natural context—something perhaps which eco-philosophy is attempting to achieve." Leibniz demonstrated evident compassion toward even the smallest of creatures. In a passage titled "Duties to Animals and Spirits" (1784–85), Kant mentions that "Leibniz put the grub he had been observing back on the tree with its leaf, lest he should be guilty of doing any harm to it." The vitalistic materialism of LaMettrie supported his sensitivity and passion for nature; the person who sees all things as animate "will cherish life ... ; he will be full of respect, gratitude, affection, and tenderness for nature ... ; and, finally, happy to know nature and to witness the charming spectacle of the universe" (1747/1994: 75). Schopenhauer was pessimistic about humanity but displayed both admiration and concern for nature; he wrote against cruelty to domestic animals and lamented the damage caused by the advance of industrial society. Goethe's panpsychic worldview was deeply intermingled with his romantic sensitivity to the natural world. And Fechner, of course, grounded his ecstatic love of nature in a thoroughly panpsychic vision of the universe, and he deserves to be held as a founding father of the modern environmental movement; certainly he anticipated much of Gaia theory, more than a hundred years before Lovelock.

In the middle of the nineteenth century, Thoreau's intimate awareness of nature led him to a kind of pantheism in which the Earth was alive and animate, as a single living organism—see "A Winter Walk" or "Succession of Forest Trees" in *Walden*. Perhaps his most explicit writing on the subject is to be found in a journal entry dated December 31, 1851:

[T[here is motion in the earth as well as on the surface; it lives and grows. It is warmed and influenced by the sun—just as my blood by my thoughts. ... The earth I tread on [in winter] is not a dead inert mass. It is a body—has a spirit—is organic—and fluid to the influence of its spirit—and to whatever particle of that spirit is in me. ... Even the solid globe is permeated by the living law. It is the most living of creatures.

Thoreau's sympathies point to a cosmos of universal animation. And if the Earth is seen as animate in itself, what consistent ontology could refrain from accepting something approaching true panpsychism?

A more explicitly panpsychist outlook came from Thoreau's younger contemporary John Muir. Muir developed a profoundly non-anthropocentric philosophy in which all living things possessed the right to self-realization and happiness: "Nature's object in making animals and plants might possibly be first of all the happiness of each one of them, not the creation of all for the happiness of one [i.e. man]." More than this, he considered the possibility that all objects of nature were in some way sensitive and aware:

Plants are credited with but dim and uncertain sensation, and minerals with positively none at all. But why may not even a mineral arrangement of matter be endowed with sensation of a kind that we in our blind exclusive perfection can have no manner of communication with? (in Teale 1976: 317)

Such musings led Muir to a Franciscan outlook on nature in which "every rock-brow and mountain, stream, and lake, and every plant soon come to be regarded as brothers" (321).

Not long afterward, Aldo Leopold, "the father of environmental ethics," also developed strong sympathies toward panpsychism. Leopold was deeply influenced by the panpsychist Russian philosopher Peter Ouspensky, citing him in an early essay titled "Some Fundamentals of Conservation in the Southwest" (ca. 1920/1979). Considering "conservation as a moral issue," Leopold finds the organismic view of the Earth compelling. In the natural processes of the Earth we see "all the visible attributes of a living thing" (139). Furthermore, from this standpoint follows "that invisible attribute—a soul, or consciousness—which not only Ouspensky, but many philosophers of all ages, ascribe to all living things and aggregations thereof, including the 'dead' earth." Leopold is clear that such a view can serve as the foundation for an environmental ethic: "Philosophy, then, suggests one reason why we cannot destroy the earth with moral impunity; namely, that the 'dead' earth is an organism possessing a certain kind and degree of life, which we intuitively respect as such." (140) This declaration constitutes the first invocation of pan-spirituality as a potential remedy for healing the ecological damage brought on by modern industrial society.

Like Thoreau and Muir before him, Leopold was not an academic philosopher. All three men must be excused for relying more on intuitive insight than formal academic argumentation. But there is no doubt that panpsychist beliefs underlay much of their attitudes toward nature.

A deeper union of philosophy, environmentalism, and panpsychism occurred in the work of Albert Schweitzer, who outlined his views on history, culture, nature, and the problem of religious pessimism in *The Philosophy of Civilization* (1949). Schweitzer was heavily influenced by Schopenhauer in two respects. First, he adopted Schopenhauer's ontology of all things as manifestations of pure will—specifically, the "will to live." Second, he inverted Schopenhauer's notorious pessimism, seeing in the will-to-live a profoundly optimistic and altruistic worldview.

Following (like Thoreau and Ouspensky) the ancient Greek conception of life, Schweitzer viewed all things in nature as alive in an extended sense of the word, as manifestations of a dynamic and spiritual cosmos:

The essential nature of the will-to-live is determination to live itself to the full. It carries within it the impulse to realize itself in the highest possible perfection. In the flowering tree, in the strange forms of the medusa, in the blade of grass, in the crystal; everywhere it strives to reach the perfection with which it is endowed. In everything that exists there is at work an imaginative force. (1949: 282)

From such a worldview derives the ethical imperative of *reverence for life*: "Reverence for life means to be in the grasp of the infinite, inexplicable, forward-urging Will in which all Being is grounded." (283) The universal will to live, which is manifest in humans as reverence for life, is realized in the rest of nature as a kind of elemental, life-affirming force: "Nature knows only a blind affirmation of life. The will-to-live which animates natural forces and living beings is concerned to work itself out unhindered." (290)

Nearly two decades passed before there was a reawakening of the connection between panpsychism and environmental attitudes. In 1967, the historian Lynn White Jr. published an influential and controversial article titled "The Historical Roots of our Ecologic Crisis." In assessing the cultural and religious basis for Western attitudes toward nature, White focuses on the inherently alienating aspects of Christianity. In the first place, he argues, it virtually banished spirit from the natural world—excepting, of course, the human soul, and then only as a temporary condition. Second, it put humanity at the head of the corporeal hierarchy. Humans were thus established as radically distinct from, and radically superior to, all other earthly things. With nature despiritualized, humanity was free—even encouraged—to manipulate and exploit nature: "By destroying pagan animism, Christianity made it possible to exploit nature in a mood of indifference to the feelings of natural objects. ... The spirits *in* natural objects, which formerly had protected nature from man, evaporated." (1967: 1205) It was in this sense that White called Christianity "the most anthropocentric religion the world has seen."

Yet White found a potential solution to the environmental crisis even within the Christian tradition—not surprisingly, in the radical views of Saint Francis. Francis' "unique sort of panpsychism" (1207) could serve as a spiritual basis for natural reverence: "The profoundly religious, but heretical, sense of the primitive Franciscans for the spiritual autonomy of all parts of nature may point a direction." This extends Leopold's suggestion that something like a panpsychist outlook could heal our relationship to the natural world.

White's article had an immediate and considerable influence in environmental and theological circles. A minor uproar ensued, and in a little-known 1973 essay he offered a few further reflections on the original 1967 piece. He observed that the ultimate drivers of social behavior are the base value structures of a given society, especially as reflected in that culture's religion. Religion—whether in the overt, classical meaning of the word or in a more subtle, quasi-secular sense—embodies society's fundamental values. White reiterated his view that techno-Christian values have led to environmental destruction as a result of a denial of spirituality to the objects of nature. He reaffirmed his idea that a respiritualization of nature is central to resolving the situation: "The religious problem [now] is to find a viable equivalent to animism." (1973: 62) He noted that recent advances in science, specifically with respect to an understanding of viruses, have "smashed the artificial conceptual frontier between organic and inorganic matter." As before, he observed that such an understanding leads to greater natural reverence. Anticipating debates to follow, he asked "Do people have ethical obligations toward rocks?" (63) But he recognized the inherent difficulties in even posing such a question:

[T]oday to almost all Americans ... the question makes no sense at all. If the time comes when to any considerable group of us such a question is no longer ridiculous, we may be on the verge of a change of value structures that will make possible measures to cope with the growing ecologic crisis. One hopes that there is enough time left.

It seems that, even now, more than four decades later, we have made little progress on this question.

In early 1970, shortly after the publication of White's original article, Gregory Bateson gave a lecture, later published under the title "Form, Substance, and Difference," in which he explicitly located mind in all natural feedback ("cybernetic") systems. He furthermore identified mind as the fundamental unit of evolutionary biology: "This identity between the unit of mind and the unit of evolutionary survival is of very great importance, not only theoretical, but also ethical. It means, you see, that I now localize something which I am calling 'Mind' immanent in the larger biological system—the ecosystem." (1970/1972: 460) The ethical implications of such a panpsychism are, for Bateson, clear. If, he says, you adopt the conventional objectivist materialist view of mind, then "you will logically and naturally see yourself as outside and against the things around you. And as you arrogate all mind to yourself, you will see the world around you as mindless and therefore not entitled to moral or ethical consideration. The environment will seem to be yours to exploit." (462) Continue in this objectivist mode too long and "your likelihood of survival will be that of a snowball in hell." Later in the lecture Bateson reiterates this theme:

[W]hen you separate mind from the structure in which it is immanent, such as human relationship, the human society, or the ecosystem, you thereby embark, I believe, on fundamental error, which in the end will surely hurt you. ... You decide that you want to get rid of the by-products of human life and that Lake Erie will be a good place to put them. You forget that the eco-mental system called Lake Erie is a part of *your* wider eco-mental system—and that if Lake Erie is driven insane, its insanity is incorporated in the larger system of *your* thought and experience. (484–485)

The beginning of a cure for such insanity, then, is a recognition and deep appreciation for the mind immanent in the natural world.

A related idea was independently advocated by the lawyer Christopher Stone in an influential 1972 article "Should Trees Have Standing?" This essay was the first to seriously propose rights for natural objects, and thus to make tangible the concept of intrinsic value. After noting that for more than a hundred years non-human entities such as corporations and nation-states have been granted legal personhood—including the ascription of minds and wills—Stone proceeds to analyze the status of natural beings. Arguing for a change in consciousness or worldview, he says that we must "be able to get away from the view that Nature is a collection useful [but] senseless objects." Even more, "we have to give up some psychic investment in our sense of separateness and specialness in the universe"—such as the notion that we alone are intelligent and enminded. By thinking expansively, we will indeed "recognize more and more the ways in which nature ... is like us" (498). He then quotes a passage in which Dane Rudhyar argues that "consciousness ... exists at animal and vegetable levels, and most likely must be latent, or operating in some form, in the molecule and the atom." Noting that "all the dominant changes we see about us point in [this] direction," Stone makes his basic position clear: Something like panpsychism is true, and it serves as the ultimate basis for seeing intrinsic value in all natural objects. Panpsychism justifies legal rights for nature.

In 1975 Roderick Nash took up Stone's suggestion that human society must find a way to envision the granting of rights to inanimate nature, even to rocks. In the process, he recounts Leopold's hierarchy of expanding rights that culminated in recognizing the rights of "the land" itself. Acknowledging that "the transition from life to the non-living environment is the most difficult part of ethical evolution," Nash is nonetheless confident that "it is possible to conceive of the rights of rocks" (1975/1980: 160). Noting that "there are several intellectual and emotional roads" by which to reach this point, he discusses just two. The first is the Eastern view of a "divine spirit which permeates all things, living and non-living."

The second, implicitly preferable, is the view that "rocks, rightly seen, *are* alive, hence deserving of the full measure of ethical respect accorded to all life." Nash suggests that the current conception of life is too restricted— "perhaps there are ranges of life that also transcend our present state of intelligence."

Nash then touches on the practical matter of how we are to act toward inanimate things that have been granted rights, especially given that we are generally in a poor position to assess their wants or needs:

What, after all, do rocks want? Are their rights violated by quarrying them for a building or crushing them into pavement or shaping one into a statue? ... For the time being, the only way out may be to assume rocks and everything else want to stay as they are. Living things want to live; rocks want to be rocks. (160–161)

He thus argues for a kind of self-realization of all things in nature, of letting them play their natural role in the ecosystem. But to take this approach seems to require, for him, a panpsychist stance; it is something he calls an "essential underpinning" of an environmental ethic.

In 1977 Nash explicitly returned to the subject in an article titled "Do Rocks Have Rights?" Briefly reviewing the history of an expanded moral domain, including the ideas of Leopold, he argues that rocks can fall within the realm of moral regard even without themselves existing as moral beings: "Rocks may not be moral beings, but moral beings can attribute rights to them, claim rights for them, and represent them in the quest for such rights." (1977: 8) He then once again discusses several ways in which we can understand the notion of such rights. One is to assume that rocks have intrinsic interests for themselves. There are a number of ways to envision such interests, ranging from Eastern mystical philosophy to indigenous or native worldviews to a straightforward pragmatic approach in which such interests are taken as a "convenient fiction." Of the latter point, Nash asks "Pragmatically speaking, if it works to produce good results, why not believe it?" (10) This is an interesting approach because it suggests, indirectly, a potential new argument for panpsychism: If a belief in the rights, the interests, and even the psyche of rocks will lead to a better world, then it would be in our interest to adopt it. This anticipates what I will later call the Greater Virtue argument; see chapter 10 for an elaboration.

Beginning in 1979, the journal *Environmental Ethics* published a number of articles addressing such notions as intrinsic value, nonhuman rights, and moral considerability of natural objects. Some of these articles drew from panpsychist theories for their justification. In the first, titled "The Rights of the Subhuman World" (1979), Hartshorne briefly reiterates his view that "every singular active agent [that is, every true individual] ... resembles an animal in having some initiative or freedom in its activity," and hence each such agent possesses "inner aspects of feeling, memory, and expectation" (53). Furthermore, "where there is feeling there is value in a more than instrumental sense." Thus, all individuals possess intrinsic value, and so are worthy of moral consideration. Yet there is the lingering problem of the Whiteheadian view that certain broad classes of natural entities—rocks, plants, mountains, ecosystems—are not seen as true individuals, and hence presumably have less moral standing than fully integrated beings such as atoms, cells, and animals—and perhaps none at all. The implications of this dichotomy for environmental ethics are still open.

In 1982 the environmental philosopher J. Baird Callicott published an article comparing European and Native American attitudes toward nature. The animist worldview of indigenous Americans is well known, and they have traditionally, though not uncritically, been attributed a deep-seated respect for the natural world; it is obvious to connect the two. Most commentators have described this connection in a dispassionate, third-person manner. But not Callicott. After elaborating something of the Indian view—"earth, rocks, water, and wind ... 'are very much alive' ... . Natural entities ... have a share in the same consciousness that we human beings enjoy" (1982: 300–301)—he immediately declares his personal endorsement of it:

The Indian attitude ... was based upon the consideration that since human beings have a physical body *and* an associated consciousness ... , all other bodily things, animals, plants, and, yes, even stones, were also similar in this respect. Indeed, this strikes me as an eminently reasonable assumption. ... The variety of organic forms ... is continuous with the whole of nature. Virtually all things might be supposed, without the least strain upon credence, like ourselves, to be "alive," i.e. conscious, aware, or possessed of spirit. (301–302)

He adds the observation, similar to that of Leopold and Hartshorne, that such a view is conducive to sympathetic approach to nature:

Further, and most importantly for my subsequent remarks, the pervasiveness of spirit in nature, a spirit *in everything* which is a splinter of the Great Spirit, facilitates a perception of the human and natural realms as unified and akin.

Callicott concludes by endorsing a very strong form of panpsychism, approaching that of traditional animism, in which "all features of the environment ... possessed a consciousness, reason, and volition, no less intense and complete than a human being's" (305). Apart from a few comparable remarks by Royce (1898/1915: 230), such a standpoint is unique in Western philosophy.

In 1983 *Environmental Ethics* published an article by Jay McDaniel titled "Physical Matter as Creative and Sentient." Drawing, like Hartshorne, on both Whitehead's process philosophy and ideas in quantum physics, McDaniel argues for a "theology of ecology" based on a view of ordinary matter as "life-like, albeit in an unconscious and primitive way" (1983: 292). Much of the article is a reiteration of standard ideas in process theory and quantum physics, but near the end he begins to draw out some ethical implications: "[The fact that] a rock exhibits unconscious reality-for-itself means that the rock has intrinsic value, for *intrinsic value* is nothing else than the reality a given entity has for itself, independent of its reality for the observer." (315) The ethical implications arising from such a view are reflected in the values of "reverence" and "empathy"—reverence because all things have intrinsic value and thus are worthy of moral consideration, and empathy because all things are, like ourselves, enminded.

Continuing in the same line of argumentation, the philosophers Susan Armstrong-Buck (1986) and James O'Brien (1988) sought to ground the concept of intrinsic value in a panpsychist ontology. Armstrong-Buck pursued McDaniel's theme, further exploring Whitehead's ideas in an environmental context. Although she frequently cited his notions of true individuals as "experiencers" who are creative, self-enjoying, and self-actualizing, she characterized the assertion that Whitehead was a panpsychist as "inaccurate." Her hesitation followed from an assumed definition of panpsychism as meaning that all things are conscious. As she read Whitehead, "intrinsic value resides only in the experiencing of value." Since all things—that is, all true individuals—are said to be experiencers, then all possess intrinsic value. Once again, the moral status of compound or aggregate entities is left undecided.

O'Brien—adopting the perspective of that other great twentieth-century panpsychist metaphysician, Teilhard—spelled out similar conclusions. Embracing Teilhard's panpsychist worldview, O'Brien recounts the thesis that "consciousness exists at all levels in hierarchical degrees" (1988: 332). This is presented as a central reason why all natural objects are "good in themselves" and thus worthy of moral consideration. As in the case of the followers of Whitehead, this is more of an interpretation rather than a direct reading of original works.

In a 1986 lecture that was published in 1991 as "Are There Intrinsic Values in Nature?" Tim Sprigge repeated the view that panpsychism is a basis—in fact, the "only basis"—for intrinsic value in nature. He claims that "there cannot be intrinsic value where there is nothing at all akin to pleasure and pain, joy and suffering" (1991a: 41). Nature, he says, is intimately bound up with mind. This can only be realized either by means of a Berkelian idealism (which he dismisses as too implausible) or more reasonably through a Whiteheadian panpsychic view of nature in which "the inner 'noumenal' essence of all physical processes consists in streams of interacting feeling." Panpsychic-based intrinsic value, combined with a human-centered aesthetic value, constitutes Sprigge's dual-aspect system of ecological ethics.[5]

Also in 1986, something of an ironic twist occurred in a work of analytical philosophy by Martin and Pfeifer, "Intentionality and the Non-Psychological." As will be discussed below, the article was to prove relevant to Val Plumwood's biocentric "intentional panpsychism" of the 1990s. Intentionality, defined as a sense of aboutness or directedness, has been seen by many philosophers, since the work of Brentano in the late nineteenth century, as constituting one of the essential markers of mentality. Will, desire, belief, and knowledge all generally count as intentional qualities. In their essay, Martin and Pfeifer offer up some rather shocking news: Virtually all extant theories of intentionality fail to fundamentally discriminate between humans and natural objects in general, and thus intentionality—and hence mind—would seem to be omnipresent:

We will show that the most typical characterizations of intentionality, including ... Lycan's own suggested characterization and John R. Searle's more extended treatments of the concept all fail to distinguish intentional mental states from non-intentional dispositional physical states. Accepting any of these current accounts will be to take a quick road to panpsychism! (1986: 531).[6]

5. This argument is reiterated in Sprigge 1991b.

6. No doubt both Lycan and Searle were dismayed to hear of this conclusion.

Martin and Pfeifer see panpsychism as a reductio ad absurdum and thus conclude that the standard view of intentionality is defective. Their analysis of current theories, though largely technical, centers on the fact that "recognition" and "awareness of satisfaction" are required as basic aspects of intentionality. They argue that if a thing meets certain "satisfaction conditions" resulting from environmental stimuli, "then clearly that aspect of awareness of satisfaction conditions is something mindless physical objects are equally capable of" (544). Citing the notorious thermostat example, they add that such devices have a "causal disposition" to act in certain ways once various conditions have been satisfied. Plants also exhibit a similar "satisfaction capacity." Consequently, plants and thermostats would, on the conventional reading, have to be conceded intentionality and thus mind.

Recognizing the dreaded conclusion that "someone might interpret it as an argument for panpsychism," and noting sarcastically that "for some, this may be a happy result," Martin and Pfeifer quickly set out to fix intentionality by redefining the essential role that it plays in truly sentient beings. The degree to which they succeed is debatable, and so the theory of intentionality retains some of the larger panpsychic implications.

One environmental philosopher who did take intentionality as a basis for panpsychism was Val Plumwood. In *Feminism and the Mastery of Nature* (1993) she devotes a full chapter to critiquing the conventional mind-nature dualism of mechanistic, Cartesian philosophy. Taking issue with the concept of strong panpsychism—"the thesis that consciousness is fully present everywhere" (1993: 133)—Plumwood opts for a weaker form, later called "intentional panpsychism," in which "*mindlike* qualities" are found throughout nature. She adopts a broad conception of intentionality, treating it as an umbrella term that includes such qualities as "sentience, choice, consciousness, and goal-directedness" (134). So conceived, it applies equally well to objects ranging from humans and other living creatures to natural processes and systems. Employing the Continuity argument, she observes that "intentionality is common to all these things, and does not mark off the human, the mental, or even the animate."

Plumwood's intentional panpsychism is centered on the self-realization of all natural things. She cites notions of growth, function, directionality, goal-directedness of a self-maintaining kind, and flourishing as indicative of the teleology of nature:

Mountains, for example, present themselves as the products of a lengthy unfolding natural process, having a certain sort of history and direction. ... Trees appear as self-directing beings with an overall "good" or interest and a capacity for individual choice in response to their conditions of life. Forest ecosystems can be seen as wholes whose interrelationship of parts can only be understood in terms of stabilizing and organizing principles, which must again be understood teleologically. (135–136)

Such a worldview has a clear bearing on the realm of human ethics:

Human/nature dualism has distorted our view of both human similarity to and human difference from the sphere of nature. ... When this framework of discontinuity is discarded, we can see [support for a worldview] in which nature can be recognized as akin to the human. ... We can recognize in the myriad forms of nature other beings—earth others—whose needs, goals and purposes must, like our own, be acknowledged and respected. (137)

Plumwood's thesis came under criticism from John Andrews in a 1998 article published in the journal *Environmental Values*. Andrews primarily addresses issues tangential to Plumwood's main contention, such as her critique of moral hierarchy, her relatively broad interpretation of intentionality, her discussion of machine intentionality, and her use of the concept of agency. In the end he makes no substantial criticism against either the concept of panpsychism or its use as a basis for environmental ethics. In a footnote, though, he touches on the heart of the matter, the conflict of worldviews:

Where parties to a philosophical dispute disagree over the fundamental intuitive touchstones to which appeal should be made to test the adequacy of a claim, or theory, it becomes difficult to know how to proceed further. ... I can imagine a stone as mindlike ... or I can locate myself within a metanarrative that sees all nature as suffused with mindlike qualities—but [are these] appropriate to the way the world is or [are they] mere anthropocentric projection? What other way of answering this do we have other than to appeal to the very fundamental intuitive touchstones that are at stake? (1998: 395)

The answer, it would appear, is "none." In fact, Andrews' use of the phrase "the way the world is" betrays his own objectivist outlook. To suggest that reality exists in only one way, that there is only one absolute truth to the world, is to adopt a very restricted and almost naive form of realism. The nature of reality has changed countless times in the past, and it will change countless more. Reality is as varied as the sensitivity and subtlety of the mind and the culture that perceives it.

Plumwood (1998) responds ably to Andrews in the same issue of *Environmental Values*, but she does appear to soften her stance on panpsychism. She re-articulates her "thesis that elements of mind (or mindlike qualities) are widespread in nature" (400), but she disavows the view that Andrews attributes to her, namely that "each natural entity has its own distinctive mindlike properties"—her concern being with the terms 'each' and 'own'. In a footnote she adds the following:

I would not be happy to say of such items as mountains that they "have minds" or "have mental states," ... although I am willing to say that mountains express or exhibit elements of mind, or have mind-like qualities. (417)

Most definitively, Plumwood labels as "absurd" the view "that each *individual* natural entity has its own distinctive kind of mind" (400). But it is not at all clear why such a view is absurd. Plumwood gives no arguments, but merely provides an unjustified assertion. Of course, if one were to define mind as something like a fully developed, fully aware, human-like consciousness, few would accept it. But given that there is no consensus on such a definition of mind, there is no *a priori* reason why it would be absurd. Furthermore, Plumwood is suggesting that perhaps not every individual thing has elements of mind, but then which things have them and which do not? And why? Drawing such distinctions presents major ontological problems. Her theory of intentional panpsychism would seem to require further elaboration before it can be fully evaluated as a theory of mind. Yet her view, even loosely articulated, has value as an ethical theory. As she says, the stance of intentional panpsychism is one of "openness to or recognizing the intentionality [or mind-likeness] of the world" (403). Accordingly, we must be "prepared to recognize the other's intentionality as a necessary condition for developing richer experiential, communicative and ethical frameworks and relationships." Such an attitude can clearly be adopted even in the absence of a fully articulated theory of mind.

Plumwood's subsequent book *Environmental Culture* (2002) includes two chapters on the aforementioned subject. One of them—"Towards a Dialogical Interspecies Ethics"—is largely a reprise of her 1998 article. The other—"Towards a Materialist Spirituality of Place"—includes no specific mention of panpsychism but hints at it with talk of nature "participating in mindfulness" (223), of "a fusion of mind and matter" (226), and of "the world as another agent or player" (227).

A more recent articulation of ecological panpsychism occurs in the work of Freya Mathews. In her article "The Real, the One and the Many in Ecological Thought" (1998) and in her book *For Love of Matter* (2003), Mathews develops a sympathetic metaphysical system in which all things participate in the Mind of the cosmos. She justly criticizes conventional materialism as being unable to account for the evident reality of the world: "the *deanimated* conception renders *realism* with respect to the world untenable" (2003: 29). She proceeds to adopt a form of panpsychism and then to articulate a metaphysical worldview that follows from it, emphasizing "encounter" and "eros" as ways of sympathetically interacting with nature. Mathews' work is notable in that it moves beyond mere analysis; she sees both an ecological and axiological imperative in viewing the world from the panpsychist perspective.

The past decade has seen a decline in panpsychist arguments on behalf of nature—a somewhat surprising situation in view of the generally increasing visibility of panpsychism. One of the few such pieces is my article "Ethics, Eco-Philosophy, and Universal Sympathy" (2013), in which I argue that mind in nature is a natural basis for sympathizing with all things. Sentience is typically a justification for ordinary interpersonal (human) sympathy, and the same logic suggests that sentience, awareness, and experientiality in nature should ground an analogous feeling. This in turn lends support to the notion of universal intrinsic value in nature.

9.3   Interdisciplinary and Populist Treatments

Given the inherently unusual nature of the subject, it is not surprising that panpsychism would begin to appear in less formally philosophical and more populist or interdisciplinary settings. I have generally avoided discussion of such works, but a few are worthy of brief mention, if only because the authors have some academic credentials, because the books serve to promote an awareness of panpsychism within society at large, and because such works tend to reach far more people than works of traditional academic philosophy and thus have a greater influence.

Panpsychism, in the guise of animism, first entered a somewhat popular sphere with the release of Morris Berman's book *The Reenchantment of the World* (1981). In a rather simplistic depiction of Western civilization, Berman (a historian) argues that a fundamental shift in consciousness

occurred around the time of Descartes. Our original mode of interaction—
"participating consciousness," defined roughly as an animistic, holistic,
magical way of thinking—gave way to a mechanistic, non-participatory
mindset. This modern form of consciousness, according to Berman, "recognizes no element of mind in the so-called inert objects that surround us."
"One of the goals of this chapter," he announces, "is to demonstrate that
it is this attitude, rather than animism, which is misguided" (69–70). He
then recounts how Newton and Descartes succeeded in overthrowing the
final remnants of animistic and occultist thinking. Berman claims that participating consciousness reemerged only relatively recently, in the ideas of
quantum mechanics: the uncertainty principle, loss of classical determinism, Wheeleresque interactions between observer and observed, and even
panpsychist attribution of mind to quantum particles.

The animistic dimension of participation finds support, Berman argues,
in the work of the psychologists Carl Jung and Wilhelm Reich, who held
that the mind is in the body, not just the brain, and that material objects
possess a kind of indwelling unconsciousness. People comprehend with
their entire physical being; the brain is merely a "thought amplifier" that
accentuates what the body knows. Reich's work, Berman says, is particularly relevant:

Reich supplies that missing link [between animism and participation]. For if the
body and the unconscious are the same thing, the permeation of nature by the latter
explains why participation still exists, why sensual knowledge is a part of all cognition, and why the admission of this situation is not a return to primitive animism.
(180)

Berman concludes with a fairly detailed look at the ideas of Bateson as a
viable path to recovery of the "alchemical world view." There are in fact
some strong elements of panpsychism in Bateson, as was discussed previously in this volume, but Berman alludes to them only indirectly. And he
generally neglects the entire philosophical history of panpsychism.

Two populist books touching on panpsychism appeared in 1990. In *The
Quantum Self*, Danah Zohar's overall approach is to use concepts from quantum mechanics to illuminate issues of selfhood, society, consciousness,
and religion. In a chapter titled "Are Electrons Conscious?" she proposes
a "cautious or limited" form of panpsychism based, apparently, on a dual-
aspect neutral monism. Recalling ideas from earlier in the twentieth century, she emphasizes that the wave-like nature of quantum particles may

be interpreted as mind, and hence "the wave/particle duality of quantum 'stuff' becomes the most primary mind/body relationship in the world" (80). Yet this fact evidently has no bearing on macro-scale inanimate objects, "as there is nothing whatever about modern physics to suggest that mountains have souls or that dust particles possess an inner life" (39). This somewhat gratuitous comment seems intended to deflect the standard criticisms of strong panpsychism, and yet it requires Zohar to answer the question of precisely which objects have dual-aspect minds and why. Not surprisingly, she offers no resolution.

The second work of that year was *The Rebirth of Nature*, by Rupert Sheldrake. A biologist by training, Sheldrake challenges the mechanistic worldview that is at the core of biology by attacking the concept of matter as dead, insentient, and inert. He argues explicitly for a "new animism" that incorporates a strong version of the Gaia hypothesis: "If Gaia is in some sense animate, then she must have something like a soul ... ." (130) He conceives of this soul as the unified field of the planet, aspects of which include the magnetic and gravitational fields that science recognizes. More generally, the planetary soul is a "morphic field"—an entity that organizes, integrates, and coordinates the activities of things in accordance with a preordained teleology.

Morphic fields, Sheldrake writes, are not limited to the Earth; "such fields animate organisms at all levels of complexity, from galaxies to giraffes, and from ants to atoms" (135). They also allow a kind of communication or resonance with other, similar forms of being—whether on the Earth or across the universe. Thus, he sees the cosmos as embracing a teleological synchronicity that unifies and vivifies all things. This is the foundation for his new animism.

As a scientist, Sheldrake seems to recognize that such a view has no direct bearing on scientific inquiry. The effects of this new worldview are to be found exclusively in our relations with the world. He cites three implications:

First of all, it undermines the [anthropocentric] humanist assumptions on which modern civilization is based. Second, it gives us a new sense of our relationship to the natural world, and a new view of human nature. Third, it makes possible a resacralization of nature. (173)

Thus his unique form of panpsychism focuses on the ethical and axiological benefits in a manner reminiscent of Fechner, though without Fechner's extensive analogical argumentation. Not being a philosopher, Sheldrake doesn't develop much of a systematic philosophy; instead he relies on basic assumptions and interpretations, from a biological standpoint, about the nature of reality.

A few years after the publication of the aforementioned books, Koestler's holon theory was taken up and championed by the transpersonal philosopher Ken Wilber. Wilber adopts the basic hierarchical system of Cardano and Koestler and combines it with elements of Teilhard, Plotinus, Spinoza, process philosophy, and various Eastern philosophers, producing a hybrid ontology that is explicitly panpsychist in the sense that all individuals have an "interior" (or "depth" or "Emptiness," as Wilber prefers). His system, laid out in detail in his 1995 book *Sex, Ecology, Spirituality*, envisions reality as a four-part structure in which each holon is at once an individual and a part of a social system and has both an exterior (physical) aspect and an interior ("mental," loosely) aspect.[7]

As explicit as his system is, Wilber has two concerns about the term 'panpsychism'. First, he is worried that most panpsychists ascribe consciousness or some related variant of human experience to all things. His "depth" is "literally *unqualifiable*" (1995: 538), and hence cannot be described in terms relating to our human phenomenology. Sensation, feeling, and even psyche emerge at certain points in the hierarchy of being, and are merely different forms of the more general "depth": "I am a pan-depthist, not a pan-psychist, since the psyche itself emerges only at a particular level of depth." Wilber reiterates this idea in *Integral Psychology* (2000: 276–277).

Second, as is the case with the process philosophers, even Wilber's 'pan' is not so extensive as to include literally all physical things. Aggregates, he explains, have no depth:

I agree entirely with Leibniz/Whitehead/Hartshorne/Griffin that only the entities known as compound individuals (i.e. holons) possess a characteristic interior. Holons are different from mere heaps or aggregates, in that the former possess actual wholeness. ... Heaps [consist of] holons that are accidentally thrown together (e.g. a pile of sand). Holons have agency and interiors, whereas heaps do not. (2000: 279–280)

7. For all of Wilber's impressive citation, *Sex, Ecology, Spirituality* is very light on citing his main predecessors. Cardano appears nowhere, nor does Spinoza, whose dual-aspect panpsychism has much in common. Even Koestler merits only a few brief mentions—surprising, insofar as one of Wilber's central concepts comes from *The Ghost in the Machine*.

He goes on to observe that "the common panpsychist view … is that, for example, rocks have feelings or even souls, which is untenable." Thus—apart from misreading the "common view" of panpsychism—Wilber, like Hartshorne, Griffin, and Leibniz, draws the burden of explaining just how and when an interior appears—or, for that matter, how a *new* interior of a brain is created from the union of independent and preexisting interiors of the neurons. Leibniz's dominant monad, or Whitehead's dominant occasion, was never a satisfactory solution, and unfortunately Wilber offers no better explanation.

The Spell of the Sensuous (1996) is more a poetic essay than a detailed philosophical inquiry but it presents a widely-cited account of something approaching a panpsychist worldview. David Abram argues from a phenomenological basis for a return to an animistic worldview as a remedy for the radical separation of humanity from nature, a separation resulting from Cartesian and mechanistic philosophies. Abram's objectives are to provoke "new thinking" among intellectuals and to suggest a new conceptual approach "to alleviate our current estrangement from the animate earth" (1996: x). He recognizes that panpsychist outlooks in fact have significant potential to alter our philosophical worldview, as they get to the root of the inert-matter view held by mechanists. But he fails to examine its substantial philosophical underpinning. Of all the Western philosophical schools addressing panpsychism, phenomenology—at least, as it is found in the writings of its leading advocates—is among the least relevant.

Related works have continued to appear in recent years. Graham Harvey's *Animism* (2005) and *Handbook of Contemporary Animism* (2015) and Emma Restall Orr's *Wakeful World* (2012), for example, address panpsychist themes from the perspectives of religion, paganism, and Wiccan philosophy. Peter Ells' *Panpsychism: The Philosophy of the Sensuous Cosmos* (2011) is an engaging and popular philosophical examination. Alex Wendt's *Quantum Mind and Social Science* (2015) provides a fascinating application of panpsychism and quantum mechanics to social theory, arguing that something like a group or collective mind is at work in society. For a political scientist, Wendt has an excellent grasp of the relevant philosophical issues, and his impressive bibliography demonstrates his breadth of knowledge on the subject. He deserves credit for examining the larger implications of panpsychism, which are almost completely neglected by academic philosophers.

Most recently we have the work of the medical doctor, theoretical biologist, and complexity theorist Stuart Kauffman, who argues for "a vast participatory panpsychism" based on entangled quantum systems. His book *Humanity in a Creative Universe* (2016a) and his essay "Cosmic Mind?" (2016b) defend a strong panpsychism, in the manner of Penrose, Hameroff, and Wheeler, in which quantum measurement, and the subsequent quantum collapse, indicate the presence of mind.

As I have noted, the authors cited above all bring a degree of academic respectability to the discussion. But in recent years the field has also engaged a number of less credentialed writers who have self-published on related topics, particularly animism. Websites and blog posts are particularly popular, though they often lack the careful research and argumentation of the more professional writers. As always, one must be aware of the source. As a general conclusion, it can certainly be stated that there seems to be a growing awareness of and interest in panpsychism, both within academic philosophy and among the public at large. Whether this portends a fundamental shift in outlook remains to be seen.

9.4   Other Thoughts, Pro and Con

Despite the many sources cited throughout the present work, panpsychism has been, and remains, a decidedly minority view in academia. Philosophical debate on the topic has historically been rare. Its supporters have written defenses, but few have been willing or able to refute them. There was a minor flurry of articles in the early years of the twentieth century, but they had limited effect.[8] The general feeling appears to have been that panpsychism was such a minority view that it could be safely dismissed with a brief comment, or conveniently ignored.

One relatively substantial critique, published in 1922, was Yale philosopher Charles Bennett's review of Perceval Frutiger's book *Volonte et Conscience*. Frutiger advocated a panpsychist metaphysical system that he called "spiritual monism." Bennett (1922: 89) questioned "the general value of a theory of panpsychism" such as Frutiger proposed, and in doing so touched on the pragmatic and utilitarian worth of any such theory:

---

8. See Bakewell 1904a,b; Bawden 1904; Strong 1904a,b; Prince 1904.

Frutiger contends that in a universe so interpreted, morality and religion can breathe more freely; but he has overlooked a most serious objection. The value of … "dead matter" surrounding us is that it gives us a world indefinitely plastic, indefinitely usable. … Put me in a world where all is in some sense (however obscure) spirit, … and you embarrass me strangely. Now I no longer feel free to treat any part of the material world merely as means. The coal for the furnace, the stone that goes into our houses, the steel that goes into our machines—these are now, after some mysterious fashion, my own kith and kin. I must treat them differently now. But how? To that question the panpsychist gives no answer—in which case I have been robbed of a vitally important conception of matter; or else he defines the amount of freedom and spontaneity in the material world so that it is always less than the amount required to make any practical difference … .

Two points stand out here. First, Bennett assumes that panpsychism must have some tangible, practical consequence to be meaningful—something that is arguably untrue. He is looking for mechanistic implications, when it is just such a mechanistic mindset that panpsychism is challenging. He gives no credence to it simply as a metaphysical theory of mind. Second, he inadvertently touches on what we may call the ecological issue: Panpsychism strongly implies a revaluation of the natural world. In that sense, it does in fact have meaningful implications in the sphere of human action, though they are not entailed by it. A new-found sensitivity, respect, and empathy toward natural things have been, for many philosophers, natural corollaries to the panpsychist view. Bennett complains that he may no longer employ the stuff of nature as mere means to human ends—which of course is exactly the point. In the pre-environmentalism era of the 1920s, crude anthropocentrism clearly was the philosophical order of the day.

In the 1950s, Wittgenstein gave short shrift to the view. In the posthumously published *Philosophical Investigations* he asked "Can anyone imagine a stone's having consciousness?" From an analytical perspective, "such image-mongery is of no interest to us" (1953: 119). But apart from such incidental comments, panpsychism went largely undebated in the first half of the twentieth century.[9]

9. One finds a number of scattered references to panpsychism throughout the past 100 years, though most have had little impact. If we survey the field through the 1960s we find such pieces as Salter 1922, Bush 1925, Robinson 1949, Sellars 1960, and Francoeur 1961. In the latter half of the century, we find Bjelland 1982, Kerr-Lawson 1984, and Sharpe 1989. However, not until the advent of consciousness studies, in the 1990s, did panpsychism begin to attract wider attention.

The relative silence of critics was broken in 1967 with the initial publication of the *Encyclopedia of Philosophy*.[10] The general editor, Paul Edwards, had assigned himself to write the putatively objective entry on panpsychism. In one of the more astounding examples of biased writing in modern philosophy, Edwards ridicules the topic at every turn. He portrays panpsychist philosophers as fools, charlatans, or mystics incapable of grasping even the most basic elements of common sense. He calls panpsychism "unintelligible" and a "meaningless doctrine." He makes ludicrous arguments centered on "the 'inner' nature of a tennis ball." Sneering at any supposed consequences of the view—"Is a bricklayer who has been converted to panpsychism going to lay bricks more efficiently?" (1967b/1972: 30)—he likens panpsychism's adherents to religious fanatics. He gratuitously allows that it may be useful "in a pedagogical sense, [to] help school children to understand what a chemist is talking about."

Hartshorne (1990: 393) called Edwards' piece "astonishingly biased" and "only trivially informative." Griffin (1998: 96) declared it "irresponsible" and took Edwards to task for virtually ignoring the process view of Whitehead and Hartshorne. Unfortunately for intellectual integrity, Edwards' article served as the official view on panpsychism for more than 30 years, until the 1998 release of the *Routledge Encyclopedia of Philosophy*.[11] As bad as Edwards' piece was, it did serve, until recently, as a nominally useful starting point for studies of the field (although it mentioned fewer than half of the relevant philosophers, and distorted the views of those it did mention), and it did present one of the first detailed sets of arguments against panpsychism. Perhaps most significantly, it succeeded in establishing the official stance: Panpsychism was to be slandered and abused at every opportunity. Typical was the view of Madden and Hare (1971); in their discussion of James' theory of causality, they referred to panpsychism as "an unmitigated disaster in the eyes of a great many contemporary philosophers" (23). Popper took a similar line shortly thereafter, denouncing the view as "fantastic" and "baseless" (1977: 69, 71).

10. The final and more widely available edition was published in 1972, but with the identical entry on panpsychism from 1967.

11. The new entry, written by the panpsychist Timothy Sprigge, is more sympathetic and more balanced, though unfortunately less thorough.

Even environmental philosophers found reason to be critical. Arne Naess, for one, was unimpressed with a Spinozan form of panpsychism: "The range of predicates such as 'virtuous' or 'in harmony with what is rational' cannot meaningfully be applied to the beings of the mineral kingdom." (1975: 119) Naess found a compatriot in Ernest Partridge, who was quite dismissive of environmentalists tempted by a "primitive belief" in panpsychism. Preferring the derogatory synonym 'animism', he writes:

Believing that nature is alive and sentient, the animist may presume that a cliff "objects" to being reduced to paving stones, or that a tree "objects" to being cut into cordwood. I do not recommend this defense; since few of us believe that rocks or trees have nervous systems or comparable sensory receptors, we are unlikely to be convinced that they are capable of "caring" about their fate. (1984: 105)

Of course, Partridge completely overlooks the fact that nervous systems or sensory receptors are in no way prerequisites for experientiality or subjectivity. He simply presumes this to be true.

In the 1980s and the 1990s, inconsequential and tendentious criticisms continued to appear in the literature. In the midst of a critical analysis of dualism, Geoffrey Madell remarked that

the sense that the mental and the physical are just inexplicably and gratuitously slapped together is hardly allayed by adopting either a panpsychist or a double aspect view of the mind, for neither view has any explanation to offer as to why or how mental properties cohere with physical. (1988: 3)

It is true that most panpsychists take mind as a brute fact of existence. But all metaphysical theories accept certain things as brute; why this counts against panpsychism is unclear.

Gerald Edelman (1992: 212) briefly cites panpsychism as the "most extreme form" of attempts to "make mind and consciousness direct properties of matter." After noting, somewhat patronizingly, that "some very intelligent people have been attracted to panpsychism," he is able to cite only William Butler Yeats, of all people, as an example. This whole approach to mind, for Edelman, is "spooky and mystical." It has no value for a rigorous scientific thinker: "Most good physicists are hardly committed to notions of panpsychism."

The psychologist Nicholas Humphrey occasionally dabbles in philosophy of mind, and he too is quick to dismiss panpsychism. It is "one of those superficially attractive ideas that crumble to nothing as soon as they are asked to do any sort of explanatory work" (1992: 203). Minds are linked to bodies, he says, and bodies need boundaries.[12] Things like force fields, rainbows, snow storms, and swarms of bees are nebulous and diffuse, and thus are intrinsically incapable of mind. Consciousness, furthermore, is tied to self-interest; thus, "we can rule out icebergs or rubber balls or pocket watches or the moon" because they do not care what happens to them. Mind, Humphrey asserts without evidence, is "limited to higher vertebrates such as mammals and birds, although not necessarily all of these" (205). He is aware of the demand that, within a strictly materialist worldview, consciousness must, at some point, have suddenly and dramatically arisen from an utterly unminded material substrate. Panpsychists, as we saw, view this putative event as an inexplicable miracle. But Humphrey, unfazed, says confidently that "consciousness quite suddenly emerged" at some unknown point in evolutionary history. Indeed, he is willing to designate the time before that monumental event as "BC," meaning "before consciousness."

Colin McGinn has repeatedly disparaged panpsychism. He has called it "metaphysically and scientifically outrageous" and then asked "Are we to suppose that rocks actually have thoughts and feelings?" (1997: 34). Elsewhere he has mocked the idea that consciousness is omnipresent by comparing it to the claim that "Elvis is everywhere" (1999: 95) and has asserted that panpsychism entails that "electrons and stars ... literally feel pain, see yellow, think about dinner." It is "very hard to take ... the theory seriously," he has stated, precisely because "it is empty." More recently McGinn has declared the panpsychist view "a complete myth, a comforting piece of utter balderdash" (2006: 93), adding: "Isn't there something vaguely hippyish, i.e. stoned, about the doctrine?" To his credit, he has also articulated some precise counter-arguments; I examine them in chapter 10.

Another critic is Daniel Hutto (2000: 79), who calls Russell's implicit panpsychism "overly liberal." The thought that "pails of water heated by the sun might be having experiences ... is a recognized embarrassment." Panpsychism is "neither attractive nor credible"; rather, it is "awkward" and even "bizarre." William Lycan (2011: 363) suggests that panpsychism

---

12. The question of the boundedness of subjects is indeed an important open issue. For one treatment of the topic, and the potential panpsychist implications, see Skrbina 2009b.

is "ludicrous" because it implies that "a molybdenum atom has either sensory experiences or intentional states." After all, what might it be thinking? "Perhaps it wishes it were a silver atom."

John Searle is another prominent foe. Like many others, he prefers to issue blanket condemnations rather than reasoned critiques. In 1997 he famously called panpsychism "absurd" and "breathtakingly implausible" (48), adding that "there is not the slightest reason to adopt panpsychism" (50). Unrepentant, Searle repeated the same thought some years later, asserting that "consciousness cannot be spread across the universe like a thin veneer of jam" (2013) as if that were the view of current panpsychists. One cannot call the view false, he says; in fact, "it does not even get up to the level of being false. It is strictly speaking meaningless." Clearly Searle has no understanding of the long history of the subject he is criticizing. The level of ignorance displayed by even prominent philosophers can be striking.

Perhaps the most telling statement, though, came from Nicholas Humphrey in 2011. Unhappy with a critical review of his new book by the noted panpsychist Galen Strawson, Humphrey issued this little diatribe in an online forum:

Strawson has not so far responded to my invitation to retract his review of my book. But it's clear from messages I've received from colleagues in philosophy that they see him as an embarrassment to their profession: not only an intellectual ass but unscholarly and lazy too. His ideas about panpsychism have made him a laughing stock. His attacks on attempts to resolve the problem of consciousness as a scientific issue—such as mine—consign him to the nursery.[13]

Well! Clearly we need no longer bother with the topic!

Despite this occasional hostility toward panpsychist theories over the past few decades, a few hardy individuals have continued to offer sympathetic treatments. One of them is Tim Sprigge. In 1983 he published *Vindication of Absolute Idealism*, arguing somewhat obtusely for an idealist form of panpsychism. He has been one of the few recent philosophers to regularly and sympathetically address panpsychism (see his 1984, 1991a, 1991b, 1998a pieces), but overall his theory seems not to have engaged discussion to the degree that, for example, the traditional process view has. On the

13. This public statement, originally issued in early 2011, was reprinted in Strawson 2015c.

negative side, his theory may be seen as perpetuating the mistaken view that panpsychism is necessarily a form of idealism.

Of greater consequence has been the work of the prominent analytic philosopher Thomas Nagel. His 1979 book *Mortal Questions* includes a chapter entitled "Panpsychism" in which he writes that "panpsychism appears to follow from a few simple premises, each of which is more plausible than its denial" (181). The premises he cites are these:

(1) physical reality consists solely of rearrangeable particles of matter
(2) mental states are neither reducible to, nor entailed by, physical states
(3) mental states are real
(4) there are no truly emergent properties.

In effect, this is a more sophisticated version of the Non-Emergence argument. It constitutes perhaps the first formally analytic argument on behalf of panpsychism, and the first in at least a hundred years to arrive at it deductively. Most of the prominent positions of the twentieth century, including those of Whitehead and Teilhard, were based on initial, radical metaphysical conjectures rather than commonly accepted premises.

Following Feigl and Koestler, and despite the force of his own argument, Nagel equivocates. On the one hand he finds the four premises individually compelling. However, after some discussion he concludes "I … believe that panpsychism should be added to the current list of mutually incompatible and hopelessly unacceptable solutions to the mind-body problem." (193) And yet at the end of the chapter he suggests that a form of panpsychism in which the "[material] components out of which a point of view is constructed would not in themselves have to have points of view" (194) might be viable. In other words, atoms may somehow carry with them "proto-mental properties" which, though not mental, combine to create experience and points of view—a kind of atomistic parallelism that recalls Clifford's mind-stuff theory. Nagel thus leaves the door open, but offers no positive theory as to how proto-mental panpsychism might be realized.

Nagel continued to be sympathetic to panpsychism in *The View from Nowhere* (1986), though without significantly developing his ideas. In that book he notes in the introduction that "the general basis of this [mental] aspect of reality is not local, but must be presumed to inhere in the general constituents of the universe and the laws that govern them" (8). In a nod to the philosophical viability of such an "extreme" notion as panpsychism, Nagel remarks that "nothing but radical speculation gives us a hope of coming up with any candidates for the truth" (10) about mind and body. He advocates a neutral monist, dual-aspect theory of mind that is necessarily close to the panpsychist view. In a short section titled "Panpsychism and Mental Unity" he acknowledges this affinity but then adds that the combination problem—the problem of accounting for mental unity—is a major concern. He leaves it at that.

Nagel addresses the topic a third time in *Concealment and Exposure* (2002). That book includes the essay "The Psychophysical Nexus," in which he argues for the irreducibility of consciousness. After rejecting both substance dualism and property dualism, Nagel explores alternative solutions that would account for the "necessary connection" between mind and body. His preferred solution—a kind of non-reductive, dual-aspect neutral monism—again appears amenable to a panpsychist interpretation. He notes similarities to the work of Spinoza and Russell, observing that the latter "holds that physics contains nothing incompatible with the possibility that all physical events, in brains or not, have an intrinsic nature of the same general type" (2002: 209). Near the end of the essay Nagel tackles the sticky issue of how far down, below the level of the brain, one might be able to push this dual mind-matter relation. He notes that the brain must consist of numerous conscious subsystems that somehow combine to form the complex, unified whole, and that, because of this fact, we are logically compelled to consider pushing the mind-matter duality down to the lowest levels of matter:

[T]he active brain is the scene of a system of subpersonal processes that combine to constitute both its total behavioral and its phenomenological character. ... This differs from traditional functionalism ... in that the "realization" here envisioned is not to be merely physiological but in some sense mental all the way down ... . (230)

But he declines to elaborate:

I leave aside the question of how far down these states might go. Perhaps they are emergent, relative to the properties of atoms or molecules. If so, this view would imply that what emerges are states that are in themselves necessarily both physical and mental. ... If, on the other hand, they are not emergent, this view would imply that the fundamental constituents of the world, out of which everything is composed, are neither physical nor mental but something more basic. (231)

This might appear suggestive of panpsychism, but Nagel immediately denies the possibility: "This position is not equivalent to panpsychism. Panpsychism is, in effect, dualism all the way down. This is monism all the way down." Yet it is clear that there are many forms of dual-aspect monism that are panpsychist, and thus simply labeling panpsychism as "dualism" doesn't negate the possibility that Nagel's own system could consistently be conceived as a form of panpsychism. The most that he will allow is that all matter may have "mental potentialities" that are "completely inert in all but very special circumstances" (234). Whether the concept of "universal inert mental potentiality" qualifies as a form of panpsychism is open to debate.

Finally, in *Mind and Cosmos* (2012), Nagel suggests that we should re-conceive our basic metaphysical assumptions. Perhaps experientiality and the corresponding subjectivity do not emerge, but are intrinsic parts of reality. Perhaps all of reality is experiential in some sense. "Perhaps," he writes, "the basis for this identity [of the mental and the physical] pervades the world." (42) Indeed, a complete explanation of reality "may have to be something more than physical all the way down" (53). Again showing no awareness of its lengthy philosophical pedigree, Nagel cautiously sneaks up on panpsychism, tentatively suggesting that it has promise. "So this reduc-tive [monist] account can also be described as a form of panpsychism: all the elements of the physical world are also mental." (57) Unfortunately, he continues to vacillate on the subject:

Without something unimaginably more systematic in the way of a reduction, panpsychism does not provide a new, more basic resting place in the search for intelligibility. ... It offers only the form of an explanation without any content, and therefore doesn't seem to be much of an advance on the emergent alternative. (62)

But he immediately adds that "the proposal is not empty," because it is amenable to naturalistic reductive options that have proved successful in the past. "On the other hand," he states a few lines later, "the idea of reduc-ing the mind to elementary mental events or particles seems unnatural in a way that physical atomism doesn't." One can be excused for not knowing where Nagel comes down on this issue.

A related issue then arises: Are there any outward signs of the inner men-tal life of inanimate structures? Nagel thinks there would have to be. Just as the mental lives of humans correlate with behavioral action, "something analogous must be true at the micro level" (63) if panpsychism is true. Thus, "the protomental will have behavior implications." This presumption is debatable, but we have some recent evidence of such behavioral implications: an attribution of free will to quantum action in the work of Conway and Kochen (2006, 2009). Dyson and Bohm, as was explained above, also offered interpretations that suggest at least some basis for the "behavioral implications" that Nagel calls for. The case for behavioral evidence is stronger than Nagel suspects.

9.5   Dynamical Systems Theory

In the 1890s, Peirce observed that cellular protoplasm was remarkably sensitive to external stimulation, and speculated that this sensitivity was related to mental states, feelings, and perhaps even consciousness[14]: "Feeling may be supposed to exist, wherever a nerve-cell is in an excited condition." (1891/1992: 292) In his five *Monist* essays, Peirce repeatedly examines the dynamical nature of physical systems and the general issue of chance, randomness, and predictability in the universe. He notes that, in a formally mechanistic universe, all future events could be determined by knowing "the positions and velocities of the particles at any one instant" (1892a/1992: 309). But feeling, consciousness, and mind have an innate spontaneity that circumvent any such predictability, and thus "necessitarianism" cannot be true. A corresponding theory—tychism— must hold.

The sensitivity of protoplasm is important because it is "nothing but a chemical compound" (1892c/1992: 347); highly sensitive to stimulation, it thus has a correspondingly large degree of feeling. But all matter is sensitive to a degree, and therefore the most likely inference is that all matter feels in proportion to its degree of sensitivity. In fact, in "Man's Glassy Essence" Peirce anticipates some of the central features of dynamical systems and what would later be called chaos theory:

If, then, we suppose that matter never does obey its ideal laws with absolute precision, but that there are almost insensible fortuitous departures from regularity, these will produce, in general, equally minute effects. But protoplasm is in an excessively unstable condition; and it is the characteristic of unstable equilibrium that near that

14. His earliest such acknowledgment came in his essay "A Guess at the Riddle." See Peirce 1992a: 262–263.

point excessively minute causes may produce startlingly large effects. ... Now, this breaking up of habit and renewed fortuitous spontaneity will, according to the law of mind, be accompanied by an intensification of feeling. The nerve-protoplasm is, without doubt, in the most unstable condition of any kind of matter; and consequently there the resulting feeling is the most manifest. (348)

His conclusion is that "wherever chance-spontaneity is found, there, in the same proportion, feeling exists." And that is everywhere. Peirce thus initiates a new argument for panpsychism, based on the universal sensitivity of matter to external stimulation. Stimulated response, he says, he always accompanied by a degree of feeling. In chapter 6, I called this the Argument from Dynamic Sensitivity.

Theories about dynamical systems were, of course, very primitive in Peirce's time. Henri Poincaré was just conducting his work on the three-body gravitational problem that suggested chaotic dynamics, but Pierce had no knowledge of this. And it would be decades before mathematical theory would develop to the point that chaos theory would become an established discipline. Nonetheless, Peirce's intuition was significant: that mind or consciousness was something intrinsically unpredictable, and that wherever unpredictability was found, there we must also see the presence of mind.

Present-day chaos theory is often described as deterministic, which means that a given system is governed by ordinary non-linear differential equations but yet its evolution over time is inherently unpredictable. This occurs because such a system is highly sensitive to small changes in its environment. Weather is a classic example: Owing to the non-linear dynamics involved with temperature, pressure, humidity, and solar heating, there are fundamental limitations on our ability to precisely predict the weather in the future. Biological systems, from cells up to brains, are also non-linear dynamical systems. Their changes in state over time cannot be predicted in detail. Most generally, all physical systems are subject to non-linear dynamics; this is self-evidently true, given that the fundamental forces of nature—gravity, strong, weak, and electromagnetic—are all non-linear. As such, all physical objects and systems are subject to chaotic dynamics. They are all sensitive, at some level, to small environmental changes.[15]

15. Even a rock is dynamic, both at an atomic scale and, more generally, over long periods of time. Nothing about dynamical systems theory stipulates that the dynamics must happen quickly, or at a macro scale.

Peirce simply speculated that dynamic sensitivity was correlated with mind. But in fact the argument is stronger than he could have known. Chaos theory describes neural system dynamics in a way that offers a satisfying account of many aspects of the mind, including the unity of consciousness, the nature of qualia, and the concept of the personality. This all suggests that chaotic dynamics are a marker for mental processes.

I was one of the first (after Peirce) to make a connection between dynamical systems concepts and the ubiquity of the mind. In a talk given in 1993 (published in 1994 as "Participatory Chaos: An Analytic Model of Consciousness"), I argued that chaotic dynamics were a key to understanding the human mind, and that they implied a natural extension of the mind to all systems in nature. Independently following the approach of Churchland (1986), I proposed that the brain be viewed as a single interconnected feedback system that is describable by a classical mathematical technique known as state-space (or phase-space) analysis. One particular aspect of this analysis has proved particularly useful: The state of any system, at any moment in time, can be depicted as a single point in a multi-dimensional state space. As the physical system changes, the point moves in state space. Thus any dynamical system, no matter how complex, can be depicted in its entirety by the movement of a single point in a multi-dimensional mathematical space. This is an established scientific tool, and it is employed in a number of technical areas.[16]

In the case of the brain, I proposed—as did Churchland (1997)—that the synapse voltage serves as the primary element in defining the state space, and that it captures essential energy dynamics at a level appropriate for grasping something of the mind-brain relationship. The physical brain state is thus defined as the instantaneous, simultaneous value of all synapse voltages. These myriad voltages are represented by a single point in state space, which depicts the dynamically changing states of the brain. As the neural voltages change in real time, the state-space point moves correspondingly through a multi-dimensional space.

I then conjectured that this point be associated with the "unity point" of consciousness. This leads to a number of striking correlations between state-space dynamics—in particular, the nature of the so-called strange attractor—and common-sense notions about the behavior of mind. For

16. Penrose (1989) nicely elaborates on the universality of state-space analysis. See especially pp. 176–184.

example, it helps to explain how the processes of mind can be unpredictable in detail and yet demonstrate long-term stability—as shown in the notion of personality. It suggests a novel reading of the notion of causality between mind and brain.[17] It offers one of the first concrete definitions of qualia: Different regions of state space would correspond to different qualitative experiences. In the end, it provides a reasonable accounting for both "mental unities': that of our instantaneous unified conscious experience and that of our singular, quasi-stable personality. More important for the present study, it naturally leads to a system of panpsychism. Since all physical systems are describable in terms of the motion of a point in state space, and if this point is to be interpreted as the consciousness or mental unity of the system, then clearly all physical systems—i.e., all real objects and collections of objects—possess a mind in an analogical sense. Mind is thus viewed as existing in a parallel, non-physical mental space—described in terms of state space—that is proportional in size and complexity to that of the corresponding physical system. This conception, in turn, suggests a new reading of the dynamics of the mind, one that is compatible with panpsychism.

I am suggesting, in other words, that the state space of physical systems be reinterpreted as a "mind space" in which specific regions correspond to specific qualia or experiential states. As a system or an object changes its physical state, so too does it, in parallel, change its mental state—as indicated by the state-space point. All physical changes have corresponding mental changes. This is not a causal relationship, but simply a parallel evolution through time.

Another facet of the situation is that of the unity of the object in question. Objecthood, or systemhood, is clearly an ambiguous concept. And yet the state-space ("mind") point is always distinct. This suggest that all objects and systems, no matter how diffuse, still possess a unitary point of consciousness. And it implies that myriad levels of mind overlap with one another in a simultaneous but non-interfering manner. This has far-reaching implications for our conception of the mind.

17. On this view, it is incorrect to say either that brain is causal on mind or that mind is causal on brain—both of which views, incidentally, are fraught with philosophical problems. Rather, this theory suggests something approaching a form of parallelism or causal nihilism, in that nothing like the classical notion of causation is advocated.

To take a concrete example, consider a small piece of sandstone consisting of millions of grains of sand held together by a silica-based cement. It appears to us as a single object because the grains are held tightly together in a persistent state, relatively unchanged. We may then make a state-space analysis that corresponds to the force particles (photons) exchanged between the grains of sand.[18] The grains are held continuously in place, and strongly so, and therefore there must be an ongoing and high degree of exchange of photons at the atomic level. The rushing exchange of billions of inter-grain photons maps over to state (mind) space as a single point: the mind of the stone. But owing to the high stability of the relationship between the grains (they scarcely move at all, relative to one another) the state-space point is confined to a very small region. But it does move somewhat, as a result of changes in temperature of the stone, sunlight or rain falling on it, someone touching it, and so on. The stone experiences different qualitative states, different qualia, depending on the environmental conditions it is subject to.

Now take the same number of grains of sand, but form them into a loose pile on a tabletop. As the pile sits there, unmoving, the grains again exchange photons—but this time, far fewer, and far less energetically, given that the grains are just sitting on one another and not tightly fused together with silica. In the corresponding state/mind space, there exists another single point—the mind of the heap. But this mind is much simpler than the stone's: lower in dimension and less energetic, owing to the different photon exchange. We might say that the pile is less "conscious" or less "aware" than the stone, even though both have the same number of particles and roughly the same mass.

Next, gently vibrate the table. The pile will slowly diffuse as the grains spread out. Continue vibrating until no grains are in direct physical contact. We no longer have a pile, but we do still have a "system" of grains. Therefore we still have a mind-space point. But now it is much less intense than even with the pile. The grains exchange few photons—perhaps mostly infrared energy, owing to their temperature—and none that correspond to direct physical pressure. The mind of the system is simpler, less intense, and of lower dimensionality than that of the heap or that of the stone.

18. I presume that the dominant force at the atomic level within the sand is electromagnetic. But there would also be an exchange of gravitons (albeit at a very low level, owing to the low mass of atoms).

Finally, scatter the grains across the room. Now we see no heap, no "system," perhaps not even a single grain. And yet the system still exists; the grains still interact, albeit at an extremely low level—if only via incredibly weak graviton exchange. And if the system exists, so too does its corresponding state-space point. The mind of such a system exists, even if at a very low level, and even if subsumed by myriad other mental systems in the vicinity.

Under such a view—which I call hylonoism—the physical universe has a vast, hierarchical system of minds that exists simultaneously in a parallel mental space. On this view, all systems or objects are enminded, and all participate in countless other systemic minds. The physical universe, which is a vast, interconnected network of energy, has a corresponding *mental* universe, which is a vast, interconnected network of minds or mental states. Although such a "pan-relational" scheme may seem counterintuitive, in fact it aligns with many historical conceptions of mind and panpsychism, and it promises to resolve many open issues of the mind. (For an elaboration, see Skrbina 2009b.)

Another recent connection between dynamical systems and panpsychism was made by Neil Theise and Menas Kafatos. In their articles "Sentience Everywhere" (2013) and "Fundamental Awareness" (2016) they argue that complex systems, in interacting with the world and processing information, experience the world in a mental sense, which Theise and Kafatos call sentience or awareness. Since complexity theory applies uniformly at all levels of material existence, this suggests that a complexity-based awareness exists throughout the universe. In the 2013 article, they state that "a complexity approach shifts autopoetic theory from an emergentist to a panpsychist position, and shows that sentience must be inherent in all structures of existence across all levels of scale" (2013: 378). In the 2016 essay, they change the terminology somewhat, arguing that "a monistic, non-dual field of pure awareness" is at the base of physical reality. They suggest that three guiding principles—complementarity, process, and recusion—operate at all levels of existence, accounting for the hierarchical (or holarchic) structure of the material world. They add that "leading panpsychist approaches" (such as Hameroff's) "may likewise be seen as specifications of processes and mechanisms within the overall framework of Fundamental Awareness."

9.6 Recent Developments in Process Philosophy

An important development occurred in 1988 with the publication of *The Reenchantment of Science*, David Ray Griffin's compilation of articles on "constructive postmodernism" in science. Griffin himself contributed two of the more significant entries: "Introduction: The Reenchantment of Science" and "Of Minds and Molecules." The former presents a series of arguments showing that the modernist ontologies of materialism and dualism are both unintelligible and that they have led to the disenchantment of both science and the natural world. The latter article offers up the concept of panexperientialism as a new postmodern paradigm. Some years later, Griffin published another significant article—"Panexperientialist Physicalism and the Mind-Body Problem" (1997)—and then a major milestone in panpsychist philosophy: the 1998 book *Unsnarling the World-Knot*.

In *Unsnarling the World-Knot*, Griffin gives a full and scholarly exposition of the process view of panexperientialism. Along the way he provides a detailed critique of both materialism and dualism, observing that panpsychist approaches have the potential to resolve a number of otherwise intractable problems. Even though the emphasis throughout is on process philosophy, much of Griffin's analysis applies to panpsychism generally. As the first book-length treatment of panpsychism, *Unsnarling the World-Knot* is a significant event in the history of the subject.

Following Leibniz, Whitehead, and Hartshorne, Griffin offers an updated reading of the process theory of mind and its panpsychist implications, with a focus on the meaning of the compound individual and the nature of freedom. 'Compound individual', a term coined by Hartshorne, refers to an "organism containing organisms" (1936/1972: 54)—that is, a sentient individual composed of lower-order individuals such as cells, molecules, atoms, and at the lowest level, "occasions of experience." This, of course, recalls the issue of aggregates, as elaborated in the previous discussions on Leibniz and Hartshorne. As we saw, the earlier aggregationists had to make unsatisfying metaphysical assertions to account for the restricted appearance of the dominant monad and its unifying power. Griffin attempts to further illuminate the matter, though with arguable success. Ultimately he runs up against the aggregationists' double bind: (1) How do low-order experiences sum up, in certain select objects, to form a single, complex, high-order experience (i.e., the combination problem)? (2) What is ontologically unique about mere aggregates that differentiates them from true individuals?

First take the combination problem: On the process view, occasions begin in a subjective or experiential mode, exist for a short period of time, and then pass away into an objective state. The objective mode is, in turn, the ground or basis for the next moment of subjectivity. Somehow, one (or one series) of these occasions becomes dominant and serves as the integrator of the other sub-experiences. This dominant experience is taken as the consciousness or mind of the person. Specifically, Griffin relates the mind to the experiences of the neurons:

The brain at any moment is composed of billions of neuronic occasions of experience, whereas our conscious experience at any moment belongs to a "dominant" occasion of experience, which is a new higher-level "one" that is created out of the "many" neuronic experiences ... . (1998: 179)

The unification occurs only after the neuronal occasions are completed and exist in their objective state of being. Then the dominant experience comes along and unifies the many objective modes into a single high-level moment of conscious experience. It is, Griffin says, "only in the objective mode that they are a 'many becoming one'" (180). The whole process is repeated endlessly, at very short time intervals: neuronic experiences, becoming objective modes, becoming unified by a dominant experience into a single conscious moment.[19] The string of conscious moments accounts for our colloquial "stream of consciousness."

We don't know much about this dominant experience, other than that it, unlike the Leibnizian monads, is subject to causal influence. It is both caused by the antecedent objective modes of the neurons and causal on them in its power to unify. This two-way causality between the dominant experience (or mind) and the sub-experiences of the brain is the basis for Griffin's interpretation of freedom. And yet we don't have much in the way of theoretical explanation about how or why this happens. The originator of this idea, Whitehead, provided little definitive elaboration.

Then there is the second and more problematic part of the bind: Why don't all collections of occasions have unified experiences? From a theoretical basis there appears to be no clear reason why only certain systems come

---

19. This unification of objective modes seems problematic. How can the unification of multiple *objective* modes result in a collective *subjective* experience? The process philosophers have yet to offer a satisfactory account of this.

to possess a dominant experience. Griffin implies that there is no theoretical basis for determining this *a priori*. Following Hartshorne, he believes that it is strictly an "empirical question" (186). Apparently this distinction between aggregates and true individuals, which Griffin describes as "crucial," is simply a brute fact of existence. And yet nothing of importance seems to turn on that fact. What if all aggregates possessed dominant experiences? What if the nature of this dominant experience was determined by the nature and dynamics of the aggregate—by such factors as the complexity of its hierarchy, the speed at which it interacted, and the quantity of internal sub-experiences? Would we think less of our own minds, or of the theory itself? Again, this whole distinction seems entirely too *ad hoc*; it comes off as a convenient way to deny mind to things that "obviously" do not have it. If there is no theoretical basis for denying this power of unification to all aggregates (and there is nothing in Leibniz or Whitehead that indicates so), then it would seem most reasonable to accept the full implications of the theory.

In the end, Griffin does an outstanding job of elaborating the traditional process theory of mind and the general case for panexperientialism, though he is bound by the inherent limitations of that view. More broadly he succeeds in presenting the case for panpsychism with respect to materialism and Cartesian dualism, capturing many aspects of the contemporary debate.

Following the appearance of Griffin's book were two other notable works: Christian De Quincey's *Radical Nature* (2002) and David Clarke's *Panpsychism and the Religious Attitude* (2003).[20]

De Quincey gives a concise reading of panpsychism throughout history, relating it at many points to the insights of Whitehead and Hartshorne. *Radical Nature* tackles many issues relating to the origins of the panpsychist worldview, and gives the most readable and thorough accounting of it since Paulsen's *History of Philosophy* (1892). It offers an effective overview of the phenomenon of panpsychism in the West.

Clarke, by contrast, presents an abbreviated overview of the concept of panpsychism and seeks to identify it as "the most plausible justification that can be given of religious belief in the eternality of mentality" (2003: 6).

---

20. Clarke's book was accompanied by a small anthology, *Panpsychism: Past and Selected Readings* (2004). This is a moderately helpful collection, though with some questionable inclusions and many notable omissions.

Taking a hard Whiteheadian line, Clarke denies the intelligibility of non-process forms of panpsychism, virtually relegating them to non-existence; he claims, unjustifiably, that "the principal figures in the panpsychist tradition have been careful to exclude such aggregate objects as planets, rocks, and artifacts" (3). In view of his very cursory treatment of all panpsychists before Leibniz and his quick leap to the twentieth-century figures of the process school, Clarke's statement is perhaps to be expected.

9.7 Galen Strawson

Among recent developments in philosophy of mind, and in attitudes toward panpsychism in particular, surely the most significant event has been the public endorsement of the panpsychist view by the prominent analytic philosopher Galen Strawson. The evolution in his thinking, culminating in a landmark 2006 essay, is a remarkable story; it has altered the entire philosophical landscape on the subject at hand.

Strawson took tentative first steps toward panpsychism as early as 1994, when he argued in the book *Mental Reality* that to be a "real" materialist one must accept that "at least some experiential properties [are] fundamental physical properties, like electric charge" (60). This would place mind or experientiality as one of perhaps several fundamental qualities of matter. But precisely where it would be manifest was left unstated, and in any case such a view is far from panpsychism. At the time, Strawson was rather unsympathetic to it, seeing it as a rather desperate move that was potentially justified only because of the inherent difficulties in understanding the nature of conscious experience. He allowed that one version of panpsychism ("experience-realizing"), in which material reality is primary to experiential reality, "seems coherent enough" (76), but evidently not enough so to warrant further discussion.

Strawson further developed his argument in his essay "Real Materialism" (2003a). Real materialism—the view that every real, concrete phenomenon is physical—demands, obviously, that experience, consciousness, and mind also be physical. This, after all, is common sense, unless one is an eliminativist about the mind. Therefore, on the standard view, there exist both *experiential* physical being and *non-experiential* physical being. In fact, physics assumes that nearly all of material reality is non-experiential. But, as Strawson points out, that is purely an assumption; indeed, "we have no good reason to believe [it]" (70). At bottom, we do not know that there is *any* non-experiential being. The only reality that we know—our own minds—is purely and entirely experiential. This we know for certain. Anything beyond it is pure conjecture. Be that as it may, such a philosophical inquiry should be undertaken, Strawson adds, "with a respectful attitude to panpsychism" (75). Once again, highly suggestive but something less than an endorsement. The same sentiment appeared in another essay published in the same year. In a revealing footnote, Strawson writes:

If some form of panpsychism is, as I think, the most plausible, parsimonious, "hard-nosed" option for materialists, the way now lies open for a spectacular *Aufhebung* (makeover, takeover) of Dennett's apparently reductionist, consciousness-denying account of consciousness as "just" "cerebral celebrity" or "fame in the brain" into a fully realist, genuinely consciousness-affirming account of consciousness. This, however, is a story for another time. (2003b: 313)

"Another time" would come in 2006, with the publication of the essay "Realistic Monism: Why Physicalism Entails Panpsychism."[21] In that remarkable essay, Strawson finally elaborates on the panpsychist implications of his real materialism. Now preferring the term 'physicalism' to 'materialism', he reiterates his view that everything concrete is physical, and that experience—at least in the human case—is an intrinsic aspect of physicality. If everything possesses this dual-aspect nature, then a version of panpsychism must obtain:

If everything that concretely exists is intrinsically experience-involving, well, that is what the physical turns out to be; it is what energy (another name for physical stuff) turns out to be. This view does not stand out as particularly strange against the background of present-day science, and is in no way incompatible with it. (2006a: 8)

In other words, "it's already time to admit that in my understanding real physicalism doesn't even rule out panpsychism—which I take to be the view that the existence of every real concrete thing involves experiential being even if it also involves non-experiential being." Strawson immediately clarifies his position in the strongest of terms: "something akin to panpsychism is not merely one possible form of realistic physicalism, real physicalism, but the only possible form, and, hence, the only possible form of physicalism *tout court*" (9).

21. Presented in conferences as early as 2004.

The central argument for such a panpsychist physicalism lies in the inconceivability of the emergence of mind. Strawson reminds us that most physicalists are emergentists who hold that physical matter is wholly and utterly non-experiential. But they also believe that experience is a real, concrete, physical phenomenon. In other words, they hold that the physical phenomenon of mind emerged, in a brute sense, from some non-mental yet still physical stuff. For Strawson that view is sheer nonsense:

I think that it is very, very hard to understand what [this kind of emergence] is supposed to involve. I think that it is incoherent, in fact, and that this general way of talking of emergence has acquired an air of plausibility (or at least possibility) for some simply because it has been appealed to many times in the face of a seeming mystery. (12)

Strawson's anti-emergence argument recalls that of Nagel (1979), but with an emphasis on the supposed dependency of the mental on the physical. If mind emerges from the non-mental physical, it must do so under a condition of "total dependence." This condition of dependency, combined with the assumption of a completely physical universe, entails that mind must be an intrinsic quality of the physical. The physical must be, at least, proto-experiential, in which case it has in fact a mental aspect—and hence, panpsychism is true. Any "radical kind" emergence of mind is impossible because it is inconceivable. "Emergence cannot be brute," because "brutality rules out nothing" (18–19). Reminiscent of the remark by Sewall Wright quoted in chapter 8 above, Strawson observes that any supposed brute emergence is in fact "not emergence at all, it is magic" (21).

Addressing the conventional physicalist philosopher who holds that the universe is almost entirely composed of non-experiential matter, Strawson asks:

Why on earth commit oneself to [a non-experiential reality]? Why insist that physical stuff in itself, in its basic nature, is essentially non-experiential, thereby taking on (a) a commitment to something … for which there is *absolutely no evidence whatever*, along with (b) the wholly unnecessary (and incoherent) burden of brute emergence, otherwise known as magic?

For Strawson, a panpsychist worldview clearly involves a conceptual leap—a leap he is at last prepared to make:

So now I can say that physicalism, i.e. real physicalism, entails panexperientialism or panpsychism. All physical stuff is energy, in one form or another, and all energy, I trow, is an experience-involving phenomenon. This sounded crazy to me for a long time, but I am quite used to it now that I know that there is no alternative short of "substance dualism," a view for which (as Arnauld saw) there has never been any good argument. Real physicalism, realistic physicalism, entails panpsychism, and whatever problems are raised by this fact are problems a real physicalist must face. (25–26)

Among the more serious concerns is the combination problem. "In general, we will have to wonder how macroexperientiality arises from microexperientiality." (26) He defers on an answer, but he clearly suggests that this is neither fatal nor insurmountable.

The same issue of the *Journal of Consciousness Studies* that contains "Realistic Monism" also includes a substantial follow-up essay—more than three times the length of the lead article—in which Strawson adds considerable detail to his argument, responds to critics, and defends a view he calls "equal-status fundamental-duality (ESFD) monism." It is a sort of dual-aspectism in which "all reality is experiential and all reality is nonexperiential" (2006b: 241). Such a view "is the only option short of pure panpsychism [in which 'all being is experiential being'] and radical eliminativism." Later in the piece Strawson sketches out a theory of the subject (or "sesmet")[22] and addresses the question of causality; notably, he argues that under the condition of panpsychism "the causal effect of anything on anything will have an experiential aspect, [and] will indeed be experiential" (260). For those concerned that all such talk "seems like uncontrolled speculation," he adds that "a hard (and genuinely naturalistic) nose for reality obliges one to endorse some sort of panpsychism long before any wild speculation has taken place" (262). Panpsychism is rational, naturalistic, compatible with physics, and fully coherent with our direct experience of the world. All in all, a remarkable pair of essays.

Strawson has continued to comment on panpsychism, though usually as a corollary to other topics. For example, his essay "Nietzsche's Metaphysics" (2015b) touches on Nietzsche's probable endorsement of panpsychism. More significant is a short postscript at the end of "Real Materialism" (2015a) in which Strawson modifies his view of 2006, now preferring the pure panpsychist option: "With Eddington, Whitehead, and others, I think that pure panpsychism / panexperientialism is on balance the most plausible form of materialism, the most scientifically 'hard-nosed,' theoretically

---

22. For an elaboration, see Strawson 2009: 57–65.

elegant, theoretically parsimonious form of materialism." (202) Adopting something of a "Russellian" stance (see below), Strawson notes that physics addresses mass and energy only extrinsically. On his view, energy has an intrinsic nature that is "wholly a matter of experientiality," and is completely independent of the extrinsic reality described by science. There is no clash between panpsychism and physics.

The postscript to "Real Materialism" closes with a strikingly powerful statement: that panpsychism should be the *default view* in metaphysics, and that it is the non-panpsychist theories that bear the burden of proof, should one wish to defend them. "Even if one can't go all the way [to pure panpsychism]," Strawson writes, "one should, I believe, endorse the thesis of the *theoretical primacy of panpsychism*." In other words, "unprejudiced consideration ... obliges us to favor some version of panpsychism ... over all other positive substantive theories" of mind. Most notable is the strong form of this primacy:

[T]he thesis is not just that it would take extraordinarily hard work to justify preferring any substantive metaphysical position that isn't panpsychist. ... It's rather that it can't be done. It can't be done because it requires that one assume the existence of things whose existence one has no reason to assume. ... [T]here is no evidence—there is precisely zero evidence—for the existence of non-experiential reality. Nor can there ever be any. (2015a: 203–204)

The ordinary physicalist stance is that there exists (almost exclusively) non-experiential reality. But this standpoint "confers no theoretical advantages at all, and ... creates some extremely severe—arguably insurmountable—theoretical difficulties." No truly rational thinker would knowingly place himself in such a situation.

The implications of Strawson's words are clear: Not only is panpsychism not "absurd," "crackpot," or "a laughing stock," but it is the most rational, most compelling, and most logical approach to the mind. To hold any other view is to adopt unsupportable assumptions, to believe in sheer magic, or to maintain an anti-rationalist, quasi-religious faith in non-experiential reality. One could hardly make a stronger endorsement.

9.8   Russellian Monism

In the 1920s, Bertrand Russell made an important—though not original—observation about the physical world: that we know it only in an abstract, theoretical, and "external" manner. We can describe forces and motions mathematically, and we have certain scientific devices that give us readings or measurements about physical events. We can, in other words, know the structural content of the material world. But that's all. What matter and energy are in themselves, intrinsically, escapes us. "Physics is mathematical, not because we know so much about the physical world, but because we know so little: it is only its mathematical properties that we can discover. For the rest, our knowledge is negative." (1927b: 125) But extrinsic knowledge is incomplete, because material reality must have a deeper, intrinsic nature to it; it cannot be simply relation, structure, and function.

There are some entities in the physical world, however, that we do know intrinsically: our own minds and their corresponding mental states. These things we know directly and immediately, simply by experiencing them. Correspondingly, there is little or nothing "objective" or measureable about our qualitative mental states. Our minds seem to be utterly nonmathematical, nonstructural. This is a striking and revealing contrast.

Thus stated, we have little more than an updated form of Cartesian dualism: of a *res extensa* and a *res cogitans*. But Russell ultimately went one step further, positing that some form of monism was true. A monistic world presents us with an important metaphysical question: What is the relationship between the physical world, which we know only structurally and extrinsically, and the mental world, which we know only qualitatively and intrinsically? Generally speaking, there seems to be three main possibilities: that the intrinsic are more fundamental and thus ground the extrinsic, that the extrinsic are fundamental and ground the intrinsic, and that something else grounds both the extrinsic and intrinsic. These three positions yield, respectively, idealism, physicalism, and neutral monism.

I won't recount the evolution of Russell's thought here, but he generally defended a neutral monist position in which "sensations" or "percepts" were the underlying stuff of reality. This is problematic, of course, because either term seems to be mental, and thus not really neutral after all. In any case, the net result, as I explained in chapter 7, was arguably a form of panpsychism—or at least a strong sympathy with it.

During the past two decades or so, philosophers have taken to referring the system broadly sketched out above as "Russellian monism." Here I roughly define this as the view that (1) we have only structural, extrinsic knowledge about the physical world at large, (2) our mental states are uniquely known intrinsically, (3) there exists a deeper, monistic basis of both physical and mental reality, and (4) this ultimate basis is either mental or proto-mental in nature. This is not a consensus view, and it seems that every philosopher conceives of Russellian monism in a slightly different way.[23] Stubenberg (2015: 63) refers to the "astonishing flexibility" of the concept, given that it conceivably encompasses monism, dualism, physicalism, idealism, neutral monism, and panpsychism.

Beyond this, there is the notable fact that "Russellian monism" is neither truly Russellian (meaning a position that Russell himself held) nor, strictly speaking, a monism. Russell's own view evolved, and it appears that at no time did he explicitly advocate the fourth point listed above. In fact, "Russellian monism" is *doubly* non-Russellian: If we accept that we generally name things after their originators, we notice that a number of individuals held to something like Russellian monism before Russell himself did. As was noted in chapter 8 above, Eddington (1920: 200) wrote that physics is "knowledge of structural form, and not knowledge of content" and that "all through the physical world runs that unknown content, which must surely be the stuff of our consciousness"—a statement arguably more Russellian than anything Russell himself ever wrote. Nietzsche had similar intuitions. "The triumphant concept of force," he wrote, "needs supplementing: it must be ascribed an inner world which I call 'will to power.'... One must understand all motion, all 'appearances,' all 'laws' as mere symptoms of inner events ... ."[24] Nietzsche also spoke of the "mechanistic senselessness of all that happens" without an inner will or motive force at the center of things.[25]

But the premier anticipator of Russellian monism was surely Arthur Schopenhauer. He was the first to understand that science could only ever grasp the external, spatio-temporal characteristics of matter, and that something "intrinsic"—something non-physical—had to constitute the inner essence of things:

23. For a few competing definitions, see Chalmers 2002: 265; Alter and Nagasawa 2012: 70–71, Rosenberg 2015: 224; Alter and Howell 2015: 277; Kind 2015: 404; Chalmers 2015: 261–262.

24. Nietzsche 2003: 26.

25. Nietzsche 1887/1996: 59.

[Y]ou think you know a dead matter, that is, one that is completely passive and devoid of properties, because you imagine you really understand everything that you are able to reduce to a *mechanical* effect. But physical and chemical effects are admittedly incomprehensible to you so long as you are unable to reduce them to *mechanical*. In precisely the same way, these *mechanical* effects themselves, and thus the manifestations that result from gravity, impenetrability, cohesion, hardness, rigidity, elasticity, fluidity, and so on, are just as mysterious as are those others, in fact as is thinking in the human head. ...

That which is really intelligible in mechanics ... does not go beyond the purely mathematical in every explanation and is, therefore, restricted to determinations of space and time. Now these two, together with their whole conformity to law, are known to us *a priori*; and so they are mere forms of our knowing and belong solely to our representations or mental pictures. Their determinations are, therefore, at bottom subjective and do not concern the purely objective, that which is independent of our knowledge, the thing-in-itself. But as soon as we go, even in mechanics, beyond the purely mathematical; as soon as we come to impenetrability, gravity, rigidity, fluidity, or the gaseous state, we are already face to face with manifestations that to us are just as mysterious as are thinking and willing in man; and thus we are confronted with that which is directly unfathomable; for every force of nature is such.

And so where is that *matter* of yours which you know and understand so intimately that you try to explain everything from it and to refer everything to it? It is always only the mathematical that is clearly comprehensible and wholly explicable because it is that which is rooted in the subject, in our own representation apparatus.

But as soon as something really objective appears, something not determinable *a priori*, then, in the last resort, it too is at once unfathomable. What is perceived generally by our senses and understanding is a wholly superficial phenomenon that leaves untouched the true and inner essence of things. ...

Consequently, with the objective apprehension of the corporeal world, the intellect from its own resources furnishes all the forms of this world, namely time, space, and causality—and with this also the concept of matter, which is thought in the abstract and is devoid of properties and form and, as such, cannot possibly occur in experience. But as soon as the intellect, by means of and in these forms, notices a real intrinsic property (coming always only from the sensation of the senses), that is to say, something which is independent of its own forms of knowledge and manifests itself not in *activity in general* but in a definite mode of acting, then it is this that the intellect supposes to be body, that is to say, to be formed and specifically determined matter—such matter thus appearing as something independent of the forms of the intellect, that is, as something absolutely objective. ...

All the natural sciences labor under the inevitable disadvantage of comprehending nature exclusively from the *objective* side and of being indifferent to the *subjective*. (1851/1974, volume 2: 105–107)

For Schopenhauer, of course, the inner essence is something mental—the will. Thus he can state that "matter is the mere visibility of the will." Were present-day philosophers true to their own history, they would call the view at hand "Schopenhauerian monism"—a bit awkward, but more accurate.

In past decades a number of philosophers—among them Feigl (1958), Foster (1982), Maxwell (1978), and Lockwood (1989)—have emphasized something like Russellian monism. But the explicit connection to panpsychism was first spelled out by David Chalmers. In his 1995 article "Facing Up to the Problem of Consciousness" Chalmers offers an outline of a nonreductive, dual-aspect theory of mind based on a Batesonian reading of the concept of information. Broadly interpreted, he argues that information consists of any change in a physical system, and would thus appear to be omnipresent ("information is everywhere"). "An obvious question," he adds, "is whether *all* information has a phenomenal [i.e. mental] aspect." (217) The answer, he implies, is Yes. Without mentioning panpsychism by name, he cautiously suggests that "experience is much more widespread than we might have believed." The panpsychist conclusion is "counterintuitive at first, but on reflection ... the position gains a certain plausibility and elegance."

Chalmers significantly elaborated his theory in his 1996 book *The Conscious Mind*, though he retains his ambivalence toward panpsychism. He dedicates several pages (293–301) to the question "Is experience ubiquitous?" His approach is focused on the ancient Continuity argument; he observes that "there does not seem to be much reason to suppose that phenomenology should wink out" (294) as one descends the ladder of physical complexity, concluding that it is reasonable to assign experience and even consciousness to a simple feedback system such as a thermostat. He correctly notes that there are no knockdown arguments against this view: "Someone who finds it 'crazy' to suppose that a thermostat might have experiences at least owes us an account of just *why* it is crazy." (295) As to even simpler physical systems, like rocks and electrons, Chalmers allows that "if there is experience associated with thermostats, there is probably experience *everywhere*" (297).

Following in the footsteps of Feigl, Koestler, and Nagel, Chalmers seesaws between endorsing a panpsychist view and hedging his bets. He seems unsure how to label the inner nature of simple physical objects: "I would not quite say that a rock *has experiences*, or that a rock *is conscious*. ... It may be better to say that a rock *contains* systems that are conscious: presumably there are many such subsystems." 'Mind' is not the right word either. He further notes that he "[does] not generally use" the term 'panpsychism', chiefly because that view (he claims) typically implies a system in which simple and fundamental experiences are summed together to form more complex, higher-level experiences.[26] "With these caveats noted," Chalmers writes,

> it is probably fair to say that the view is a variety of panpsychism. I should note, however, that panpsychism is not at the metaphysical foundation of my view. ... Panpsychism is simply one way that [things] might work. ... Panpsychism is just one way of working out the *details*.

Panpsychism is "surprisingly satisfying," but its viability "seems to be very much open." It is a position that Chalmers seems to advocate (340), but he is "unsure whether the view is true or false" (357). Yet on any objective reading of the dual-aspect information theory it seems inevitable. In just what *other* ways, one is tempted to ask, might one reasonably work out the details?[27]

Into the 2000s, discussion on the topic continued unabated. Holman (2008) examines the connection between the Russellian view and panpsychism, though he is not optimistic that the former can be meaningfully cast in terms of the latter. Alter and Nagasawa (2012) offer a detailed look at the subject, comparing and contrasting different variations. Goff (2014) touches on Russellian monism in the course of an assessment of the compatibility of panpsychism with property dualism. And most recently we have the anthology by Alter and Nagasawa, *Consciousness in the Physical World* (2015), which offers a variety of views on the Russellian stance; a number of the pieces, including Stubenberg 2015, Rosenberg 2015, Chalmers 2015, and Kind 2015, examine the panpsychist implications.

Panpsychism is a distinctive metaphysical worldview. As such, it stands in an awkward relationship with conventional positivist, mechanistic thinking. It can seem inconsequential, or even incomprehensible. And yet these are the very hallmarks of new worldviews; anything less would imply

---

26. Without supplying specifics, Chalmers says that "complex experiences are [perhaps] determined more holistically than this" (299).

27. Chalmers' view of mind is closely affiliated with the panpsychism of Spinoza, Bateson, and Bohm; but he doesn't seem to have been aware of these links.

a superficial or minor revision to the prevailing view. Panpsychism offers a fundamental challenge to emergentism and mechanism. And, as many have noted, the problems of mind and consciousness are so difficult, so intractable, that "drastic actions"—perhaps even as drastic as panpsychism—are warranted.

The final step, then, is to consider as a whole the arguments for and against panpsychism, assessing each in light of a deeper sensitivity to the nature of metaphysical worldviews. We may then begin to see, and better appreciate, the broader implications of the panpsychic view.

10 Toward a Panpsychist Worldview

10.1 An Assessment of the Arguments: Opposing Views

Let me reiterate a point I made at the beginning of this book: Panpsychism is a meta-theory of mind, a theory about theories. It is a statement about theories of mind, not a theory of mind in itself. It claims only that all things, however defined, possess some mind-like quality; it says nothing, *per se*, about the nature of that mind, or of the specific relationship between matter and mind. This point lies behind many of the criticisms directed at panpsychist philosophies. The view that panpsychism "crumbles to nothing" (Humphrey) when pressed to do explanatory work is a consequence of the lack of an understanding of what it is. It doesn't claim, and it has no obligation, to provide a positive theory of mind. Therefore it cannot be criticized on that account. Of course, a full and complete conception of the mind would do precisely that, and it should always be our ultimate goal. But arguments for panpsychism stand or fall on their own merits, whether or not accompanied by a detailed thesis of the mind. And I emphasize that any articulation of panpsychism, even if incomplete, has value in itself; any such view carries with it broad metaphysical and axiological implications.

Serious opposing arguments have been, historically, very rare. Perhaps the first philosophical counter-argument came from Thomas Aquinas circa 1260 AD. As I discussed in chapter 2, Aquinas argued against hylozoism by redefining the concept of life. For him life was the power of self-generating motion, something that only plants and animals possessed. Clearly, of course, one can rule out hylozoism or panpsychism by appropriate definition, but to do so is to avoid the issue by failing to address those lifelike or mind-like properties that may be shared by all things.

From Aquinas we must jump some 500 years to Kant's *Critique of Judgment* (1790). The passage cited in chapter 4 demonstrates that Kant ultimately rejected hylozoism. He claimed that "the possibility of living matter cannot even be thought; its concept involves a contradiction, because lifelessness (inertia) constitutes the essential character of matter." Kant too dodged the issue, relying on the etymological definition of inertia as inactivity. He appears to have viewed matter's inability to internally change its "quantity of motion" as indicative of a lack of vital power. As to something more akin to panpsychism, Kant's suggestive comment in the *Critique of Pure Reason* leaves open—but unresolved—the possibility of a panpsychist ontology. One might therefore conclude that his opposition to hylozoism was stronger than his opposition to a form of panpsychism.

Apart from the few remarks cited above, one struggles to find cogent critiques of panpsychism from historical figures. Panpsychism was generally viewed sympathetically, and few saw a need to issue detailed criticisms. When they did, it was typically in the form of a passing condemnation or incidental disparaging comment. Even today, we frequently find trivial or inconsequential critiques that lack all pretense of serious argumentation. However, once we set aside the jokes, superficial remarks, and *ad hominem* attacks,[1] we can distinguish at least seven serious counter-arguments to panpsychism: the combination problem, brute emergence, inconclusive analogy, supervenience, epiphenomenalism, and irrelevance. Below I offer a relatively detailed discussion of the first one—the combination problem—and then cite some representative views for the others.

The Combination Problem   For centuries it has been recognized that there is a potentially serious problem if one considers the possibility that mind exists simultaneously at both higher and lower scales of being. If, for example, the cells that make up an animal are presumed to be sentient or conscious in any fashion, how do the minds of the cells relate to, or perhaps constitute, the mind of the whole organism? If the lesser minds are distinct, why are we not aware of competing subjects within ourselves? If the lesser minds constitute or compose "our" mind, how, exactly, does that work? It seems impossible to imagine, for example, how a billion individually sentient neurons could ever add up to our complex but integrated mentality, or

1. As discussed in chapter 9.

how those same neurons could yield the qualitative sensation of the smell of a rose or the taste of chocolate, or how they could give rise to a singular and unified sense of consciousness at all.

And there are other issues. Our neural cells, for example, are themselves composed of smaller structures, including molecules, atoms, and subatomic particles. Does each level of organization possess its own mind? If so, then any complex being is a nested hierarchy of vast mental complexity. Leibniz's monadology proposed something very close to this view. Nietzsche also believed this to be the case; he held that "our body is but a social structure composed of many souls."[2] And furthermore, does the nesting process continue "upward" to higher orders of being, to a social mind, to a global mind, or to a cosmic mind? Is the universe a vast cosmopolis of enminded beings?

Needless to say, such a situation poses, if not a problem, then at least a very large question for any panpsychist. Perhaps the first to recognize the question, and to criticize panpsychism on the basis of it, was Ralph Cudworth. His magnum opus, *The True Intellectual System of the Universe* (1678), attacked the materialist "hylozoick atheists" of the day, among whom Spinoza was the leading culprit:

[T]his hylozoick atheism was long since, and in the first emersion thereof, solidly confuted by the atomic atheists, after this manner: if matter as such had life, perception, and understanding belonging to it, then of necessity must every atom or smallish particle thereof, be a distinct percipient by itself. From whence it will follow that there could not possibly be any such men and animals as now are, compounded out of them, but every man and animal would be a heap of innumerable percipients, and have innumerable perceptions and intellections. Whereas it is plain that there is but one life and understanding, one soul or mind, one perceiver or thinker in everyone.

And to say that these innumerable particles of matter do all confederate together—that is to make every man and animal, to be a multitude or commonwealth of percipients and persons, as it were, clubbing together—is a thing so absurd and ridiculous, that one would wonder, the Hylozoists should not choose to recant that their fundamental error of the life of matter, than seek shelter and sanctuary for the same, under such a Proteus.

For though voluntary agents and persons, may many of them, resign up their wills to one, and by that means have all but as it were one artificial will, yet can they not possibly resign up their sense and understanding too, so as to have all

2. *Beyond Good and Evil*, section 19.

but one artificial life, sense, and understanding. Much less could this be done by senseless atoms, or particles of matter supposed to be devoid of all consciousness or animality.[3]

Less than a century later, Denis Diderot acknowledged the problem but found it to be no real obstacle to establishing the existence of a collective mind. Referring to a swarm of bees, he wrote that "the cluster is a being, an individual, an animal of sorts." Tight interaction—"continual action and reaction"—is sufficient to establish the unity of the collective mass. "It seems to me that contact, in itself, is enough."[4]

In one of his early writings, Kant made a passing reference to the combination problem. Reflecting on Leibniz's panpsychism, he wrote:

Everybody recognizes [that] even if a power of obscure conception [i.e. perception or intelligence] is conceded to ... matter, it does not follow thence that matter itself possesses power of conception, because many substances of that kind, united into a whole, can yet never form a thinking unit. (1766/1900: 54)

The same thought recurs in his *Critique of Pure Reason* (1781). Anticipating a later and better-known statement by William James, Kant argues that material composites are possible and occur via simple aggregation, but that such aggregation is not possible with mental substances:

Every *composite* substance is an aggregate of several substances, and the action of a composite, or whatever inheres in it as thus composite, is an aggregate of several actions or accidents, distributed among the plurality of the substances ... . But with thoughts, as internal accidents belonging to a thinking being, it is different. For suppose it be the composite that thinks: then every part of it would be a part of the thought, and only all of them taken together would contain the whole thought. But this cannot consistently be maintained. For representations (for instance, the single words of a verse), distributed among different beings, never make up a whole thought (a verse), and it is therefore impossible that a thought should inhere in what is essentially composite. It is therefore possible only in a *single* substance, which, not being an aggregate of many, is absolutely simple. (A352)

Mental combination, it seems, is impossible, on Kant's view.

James is well known for addressing the combination problem, and for his evolving opinion of it. Early in his career, he viewed it as an insurmountable problem, at least for any "mind stuff" theory of consciousness.

---

3. Reprinted on page 290 of Uzgalis 2011. Here the punctuation has been modified slightly for readability.

4. Diderot 1769/1937: 67, 76. See discussion in chapter 4 above.

The very notion of lower-order mental subjects, or mind-atoms, compounding into more complex minds is, he says, "logically unintelligible" because such entities would have to combine upon some non-mental substrate.[5] James' mature thinking, however, reversed that view. In *A Pluralistic Universe* (1909) he dedicates an entire chapter to "the compounding of consciousness." In it he recalls his earlier thinking with disdain: "Twelve thoughts, each of a single word, are not the self-same mental thing as one thought of the whole sentence. The higher thoughts, I insisted [earlier], are psychic units, not compounds ... . The theory of combination, I was forced to conclude is thus untenable ... ." (189) "For many years I held rigorously to this view," he writes. Now, though, he realizes that it "is almost intolerable" and that it "makes the universe discontinuous." (206) If analytic logic drives one to believe in isolated minds, "so much the worse for logic." Hence James' final view: "[T]he self-compounding of mind in its smaller and more accessible portions seems a certain fact ... . Mental facts do function both singly and together, at once." (292) Composition of minds is an evident truth; any so-called combination problem doesn't exist.

But the issue retains force even today. Calling it the "derivation problem," McGinn (2006) argues that, although physical or spatial combination yields many possibilities, "there is no analogous notion of combination for qualia," and "you can't put qualia end-to-end" (96). Thus, he says, "we cannot envisage a small number of experiential primitives yielding a rich variety of phenomenologies; we have to postulate richness all the way down, more or less." And that, McGinn implies, is unacceptable. Lycan makes a similar point: High-level mental properties "must be a function of the mental properties inhering in their subjects' ultimate components." But we cannot even imagine how this might work:

In what way could ... a mental aggregate consist of a host of smaller mentations? Is it that some of my ultimate components are experiencing some of those very same mental states, and when enough of them do, I myself do? Or are the mental state of my components little, primitive states that somehow together add up to macroscopic states such as the ones I am in? Either alternative is hard to imagine ... . (2011: 362)

Perhaps so. But then again, *all* theories of mind and body yield outcomes that are currently "hard to imagine." It is true that the panpsychist needs

5. See James 1890/1950: 149–155.

to explain the emergence of complex mind from simpler mind. But, as I stated earlier, this emergence problem is much more tractable than the miraculous, brute emergence of mind from no-mind. Our current concepts in physics, in fact, give us some models by which to conceive panpsychist emergence—for example, field theory, in which distinct fields combine, overlap, and sum up to larger, more complex fields. Dynamical systems theory, with its notions of deterministic chaos and attractor patterns, may also be useful here. And quantum physics may provide yet other options, including superposition. Any of these is preferable to imagining the unimaginable: mind, consciousness, and experience emerging from that which is utterly mindless.

Brute Emergence   Is brute emergence so inconceivable after all? To this most difficult question, Edwards (1972) has a "simple answer"—essentially, reductive materialism combined with epiphenomenalism. The strong or brute emergentist need simply claim that matter, at some sufficient level of complexity, causes the sudden appearance of mind, but that this same mind has no causal effect on the material substrate from which it arose. "Granting that awareness is not a physical phenomenon, it does not follow that it cannot be produced by conditions that are purely physical." (Edwards 1972: 27) But Edwards doesn't say what these special and unique conditions are. And his theory naturally implies that human minds are epiphenomenal as well—something that few philosophers seem willing to accept.

Popper (1977) also accepts brute emergence. Solidity, he says, radically emerges when a liquid is cooled. Hence radical emergence is no miracle at all. And when a child grows into a adult, its mind correspondingly grows in complexity, but this doesn't imply that the food the child eats, and uses to build its brain, is itself enminded or proto-mental. The unminded food particles, when properly integrated into a nervous system, do in fact yield consciousness. Hence, once again, brute emergence is clearly possible. But of course, all this is just an assertion: It *must* happen, and therefore it does. This is question-begging to the extreme.

As I noted in chapter 9, Humphrey too accepts the thesis of radical emergence. Feedback loops, he says, have an all-or-nothing quality, and the nervous system is a kind of complex feedback loop. "Hence, we may guess that, as the sensory loops grew shorter in the course of evolution and their fidelity increased, there must have been a threshold where consciousness quite suddenly emerged." (1992: 205–206) A "guess," however, is not a rational argument. It would take much more theorizing, backed by considerable indirect empirical evidence, before such a thesis could be accepted.

Inconclusive Analogy   Also known as the "not mental" objection, this is, in essence, a response to both the Continuity argument and the Russellian argument. It was first raised by Edwards; continuity panpsychists, he says, attempt to make a comparison between organic and inorganic things, but "the analogies are altogether inconclusive" (1972: 28). Edwards grants that such things as atomic structure, hierarchical organization, persistence, and laws of physics may be common to all material objects, but he argues that we have no reason to associate them with mental properties.

A similar argument is discussed by Seager (1995) and Lycan (2011), who cast it in terms of intrinsic natures. Lycan briefly cites two related objections. First, "what grounds the assumption that the ultimate constituents of the physical world must have intrinsic properties at all?" (360) Perhaps, Lycan suggests, extrinsic relationships and properties are all there are to such particles. Second, even if we decide that they must have some intrinsic nature, why should we assume that it is mental, or conscious? The reason, panpsychists would say, is that our own firsthand experience of reality suggests that intrinsic natures are experiential. Mind and experience are the most basic facts of human existence, and physicalism still must account for them. At present, it cannot do so. It is plausible that physicalism is inherently unable to account for mind and experience, since it has access only to the exterior of things—their properties and relationships. And yet we know, on the "inside," that mind exists. Our inner nature certainly seems to be mental, and it is likely that the same holds for, at least, the higher animals. And since we cannot justify stopping anywhere along the phylogenetic chain, the logical conclusion is that all intrinsic natures are mental.

Not Testable   Edwards states that there can be no empirical evidence for panpsychism, and that therefore it is unverifiable and non-scientific. "It would probably be pointless," he writes, "to try to 'prove' that panpsychism is a meaningless doctrine." (1972: 28) McGinn (1999: 96–97) concurs, casting it in terms of a "no signs" objection: "regular matter gives no sign of having such mental states: things simply do not behave as if they are in pain or want a drink of water." Furthermore,

physicists have discovered no reason to attribute sensations and thoughts to atoms and stars. They get on perfectly well without supposing matter in general to have mind ticking away inside it. If electrons have mental properties, these properties make no difference to the laws that govern electrons.

Elsewhere (2006: 94) McGinn reiterates the point: "Do the [experiential] properties of elementary particles (or molecules or cells) contribute to their causal properties? If so, how come physics (and chemistry and biology) never have to take account of their contribution?" Churchland (1997: 213) remarks that "modern atomism's experimental and explanatory successes" are vast and well documented, whereas the success of panpsychism "is approximately zero." Modern science can explain a wide range of physical phenomena: chemical elements, the formation of stars, evolution, and the functioning of the nervous system. "At present panpsychism can do none of these things. Not even one. ... No pressing explanatory job exists for it to do." And likewise for Lycan: "panpsychism's most obvious liability is the absence of scientific evidence" (2011: 361).

In principle, this is little different than arguing that neuro-chemical transactions in the brain are sufficient to explain human behavior, and that we therefore have no need to posit the existence of a human mind.[6] At a physical level, brain action can—theoretically—account for everything we do. In humans, it is unreasonable to demand "tests" or "signs" of subjectivity, yet it exists nonetheless. There is no compelling reason why the same could not hold for all objects in the universe.

Supervenience   McGinn asks "Are the [experiential] properties of particles supervenient on their non-[experiential] properties or not?" This is the standard view of reductive materialism—that mind supervenes on the brain. Either way that a panpsychist answers this question, says McGinn, he runs into trouble. If experiential properties are not supervenient, then two particles could be physically identical and yet have radically different

6. This is the well-known "problem of other minds": We cannot even prove the existence of human minds other than our own. As Russell pointed out long ago, the best we can do is make plausible inferences from analogical behavior.

experiential states. But this leads back to the "no signs" problem, and it suggests epiphenomenalism (see below). If particle minds do supervene on their physical properties, "it will be hard to avoid accepting that there is *emergence* there—that combining the [non-experiential] properties in that way gives rise to the [experiential] properties" (2006: 94–95).

But the panpsychist can reply that there is no true "giving rise" to experientiality at all; it is there all along. The emergence that does occur is the soft variety—that of complex mentality arising from simpler mentality. This much is acknowledged, but it is also a much more tractable theoretical problem than the brute emergence alternative. The supervenience relationship is arguably irrelevant for the panpsychist, particularly in its dual-aspect forms.

Epiphenomenalism   "A more worrying difficulty for the panpsychist," according to Lycan (2011: 362), "is the threat of epiphenomenalism." Physics is causally closed, and thus any putative atomic minds have no causal role to play. "They are brought into existence only to do nothing at all." This is an *a priori* "no signs" problem—not only are there no signs of mentality, there can never be any such signs. The panpsychist, of course, can simply respond that epiphenomenalism holds for all minds, human and atom alike. This may be distasteful to some, but there is no logical problem in defending such a view. And it finds support in neurochemistry, which seems to have no need for a causal role for the mind.

Or—and this applies to the "not testable" objection as well—there may in fact be signs that we don't yet recognize or acknowledge. Quantum indeterminacy may be one such sign; chaotic behavior in dynamical systems may be another. Or, as Royce pointed out long ago, the very slow nature of the signs may mislead us into thinking that they do not exist. Mind may have a causal role all throughout nature, and we may simply overlook the form and character of that causality.

Irrelevance   Some ask, What's the point of positing atomic minds if we do not, and cannot, have any conception whatsoever of what they are like? McGinn (2006: 95) raises a related question: "What kinds of [experiential] properties do particles have?" Presuming that atomic minds somehow contribute to or compose our high-level mental states, "they are going to have to be rich and wide-ranging: not just sensory states but also emotional states, conative states, and cognitive states." But such things are inconceivable, he says. We cannot simply postulate their existence. "This is a game without rules and without consequences." Lycan (2011: 363) makes a similar point: "What sorts of mental properties in particular do the smallest things have?" To presume the existence of sensory or intentional states is "ludicrous." "How could [an atom] see, hear, or smell anything? What would be the contents of its beliefs or desires?"

But once again, we need not be able to characterize or relate to these other mental states in order to believe that they exist. This, of course, was Nagel's point long ago (1974): that one need have no conception of what it is like to be a bat, and to echo-locate, in order to accept the very high likelihood that there is *something* it is like to be a bat. What is it like to be a rock, or an atom? Perhaps we can never know. Perhaps we are dealing with fundamental epistemological limitations. But this doesn't preclude arguing that it may be like something, if unimaginably slight, to be such things.

In sum, these counter-arguments generally raise valid and important concerns, but none of them is insurmountable. In large part, they are calls for details. In order for panpsychism to be more widely accepted, philosophers will have to articulate a clear and complete theory of the mind and justify its universal extent. They will have to delineate precisely which objects are enminded, and in what way, and why. If the process philosophers, for example, seek to deny mentality to aggregates and artificially constructed objects, they will have to have a coherent and comprehensible story of how truly integrated beings come to be, and how this existence entails enmindedness. More generally, panpsychist philosophers will have to clearly demonstrate the philosophic payoff—conceptual, metaphysical, ethical—of accepting the validity of such a view.

Not that all this is a guarantee of success. Some critics seem to be terminally dissatisfied. Either they have ruled out panpsychism *a priori*, and therefore no case, no matter how compelling, can win them over, or they make outrageous and impossible demands of the thesis. A good example of the latter is Churchland, who closes his short critique as follows:

Unless panpsychism constructs genuinely explicit theoretical proposals and testable hypotheses, and unless it achieves some systematic successes in experimental predictions and technological control, it will continue to appear to be what it probably is—a theoretical hangover from a less knowledgeable time. (1997: 212)

Is it reasonable to demand of any theory (or meta-theory) of mind that it yield "testable hypotheses," "experimental prediction," and "technological control"? Surely not. Such things apply only to mechanistic conceptions; if these are prerequisites for acceptable solutions, the space of possibilities becomes absurdly small.

When it comes to the mind, we are faced with an array of difficult propositions. Every theory (or meta-theory) has significant, unresolved problems, open issues, or distasteful implications. This alone is striking, given that the mind is the one thing in this universe with which we are most intimately acquainted—precisely because we *are* that thing. Matter is much more poorly understood; we know something of its extrinsic, functional, and structural nature, but really nothing more. We presume that there is nothing mental about matter, but this is a baseless presumption. The alleged causal closure of physics says nothing against experiential matter. Matter can follow all its usual deterministic or quantum laws without infringing on experiential or even intentional qualities. Epiphenomenalism may hold after all. Or, as I have argued elsewhere, the causal closure of the physical may be mirrored by the causal closure of the mental (Skrbina 2014: 240). And there are other possibilities.

10.2   Recapitulating the Central Arguments for Panpsychism

In this chapter and the preceding eight chapters I have attempted to demonstrate something of the breadth and depth of panpsychist thought over the past 2,600 years. In the process, I have identified several distinct arguments in support of panpsychism:

Argument by Indwelling Powers   All objects exhibit certain powers or abilities that can plausibly be linked to noetic qualities.

Argument by Continuity   A common principle or substance exists in all things. In humans, it accounts for our soul or mind, and thus by extrapolation it infers mind in all things. This can also be expressed as a rejection of the problem of "drawing a line" somewhere, non-arbitrarily, between enminded and supposedly mindless objects.

Argument by Design   The ordered, complex, and relatively persistent nature of physical things suggests the presence of an inherent mentality.

Argument from Non-Emergence   It is inconceivable that mind should emerge from a world in which no mind existed; therefore mind always existed, in even the simplest of structures. Also expressed as *ex nihilo nihil fit*, or "nothing in the cause that is not in the effect." Sometimes called the "genetic" argument.

Theological Argument   God is mind and spirit, and God is omnipresent, therefore mind and spirit are present in all things. Or: All things participate in God and thus have a share in spirit.

Argument from Dynamic Sensitivity   The ability of living systems to feel and to experience derives from their dynamic sensitivity to their environment; this holds true for humans and, empirically, down to the simplest one-celled creatures. By extension, we know that all physical systems are dynamic and interactive, if only at the atomic level, and therefore all, to a corresponding degree, may be said to experience and feel.

Intrinsic Nature ("Russellian") Argument   Science describes only the external relations of things, and not how they may be on "the inside," or intrinsically. Firsthand experience of our own bodies suggests that this interior is experiential, and thus mind-like. Continuity among all material objects implies that all have an experiential interior.

The seven arguments listed above constitute the traditional historical cases for panpsychism. In addition, recent philosophical analysis and inquiry has suggested at least five further arguments on its behalf:

Argument from Authority   Not a formal argument *per se*, but a potentially convincing claim nonetheless. Writers as diverse as Bruno, Clifford, Paulsen, and Hartshorne have cited the large number of major intellectuals throughout history who expressed intuitive or rational belief in some form of panpsychism. And in fact the whole of the present work makes this claim.

Naturalized Mind   If the human mind is not to be considered an eternal mystery or a divine miracle, it must be fully, deeply, and rationally integrated into the natural world. No theory does this better than panpsychism.[7]

Last Man Standing   Needless to say, the nature of mind and its relation to the body is generally a very difficult problem, philosophically speaking. Every mind-body theory has major, unresolved problems. But panpsychism is arguably the least problematic, and hence the most plausible (meta-)view.

Theoretical Primacy   Directly attributable to Galen Strawson, who argues that there is, and can be, no evidence of non-mental reality, as assumed by conventional physicalism. Panpsychism, therefore, must serve as the default view of mind, unless and until compelling arguments to the contrary can be derived. This is a kind of "no signs" argument turned against the materialists; the panpsychist places the burden of proof on them to demonstrate that non-experiential matter exists.

Greater Virtue   Panpsychism has a number of beneficial consequences for ethics, the environment, and society generally. It is a positive, generous, and expansive approach to mind. Pragmatically it works to the benefit of all. And unlike (say) religious views, it is eminently rational. Again, not a formal analytic argument but it carries some weight, if only intuitively. Implicitly appealed to by thinkers as diverse as Plato, Campanella, Fechner, Paulsen, and James.

Despite these varied and diverse arguments, conventional materialists can still insist on a "common-sense" standpoint: Humans and certain higher animals are clearly conscious, aware, and enminded, and certain low-level organisms—plants, microbes, and so on—clearly are not (or, at least, these lower creatures act so mechanically that we have no good reason to attribute mind to them). Therefore, materialists say, there must be a dividing line in the organic world, a barrier of sorts, that separates the minded from the mindless. That seems a plausible view until we demand to know precisely where this putative line should be drawn. Clearly it will not suffice to say "somewhere," and leave it at that. If it is to be a credible view, we

7. Attributable to Hartshorne, Griffin, and other process philosophers.

need to know precisely where the line is to be drawn, and we must have a rational argument as to why it is to be drawn just there. This is an exceptionally difficult task. Not surprisingly, few philosophers have taken up this challenge.

But some have. Michael Tye tackles the issue head-on while holding to the standard view that "somewhere down the phylogenetic scale phenomenal consciousness ceases" (2000: 171). The Problem of Simple Minds, as Tye calls it, is the problem of finding the place to draw a line, and he believes that problem to be solvable. In his theory, mind resides only in entities that possess inner states displaying Poised, Abstract, Nonconceptual, Intentional Content (PANIC). Plants fail this test ("there is nothing it is like to be a venus flytrap or a morning glory"), as do paramecia (which give only "automatic responses, with no flexibility in behavior"). Nor do the lower insects qualify: "there is no clear reason to suppose that caterpillars are anything more than stimulus-response devices" (173). Fish, however, are different. They "do not typically react in a purely reflexive manner." They learn by trial and error, and can remember their lessons for substantial periods of time. Fish have "a stored memory representation that has been acquired through the use of sense organs and is available for retrieval" (176), and thus possess inner mental states and are phenomenally conscious. Tye also argues that honey bees—regarded as higher-order insects—have memory-retention capabilities similar to those of fish, and thus are conscious: "honey bees, like fish, *are* phenomenally conscious: there is *something it is like* for them" (180).

As to the further line-drawing question regarding which insects are conscious and which are not, Tye defers: "Where exactly in the insect realm phenomenal consciousness ends I shall not try to say." Whatever the shortcomings of his PANIC theory, Tye is at least willing to acknowledge that, on the standard emergentist view, a line-drawing exercise is demanded, and he makes a brave attempt at it.

When pressed for details, it is clear that the anti-panpsychists have a difficult task at hand. Perhaps the most consistent and parsimonious counterview is the hard-line case: that humans alone have minds and are ontologically unique (perhaps because of their evolutionary status, or their complex neurophysiology, or divine creation) and hence everything else in the cosmos is absolutely mindless. Schopenhauer briefly considered that alternative but declared that it "could be found only in a madhouse"

(1819/1995: 37). René Descartes, John Eccles, and John Searle are among the few who attempt to defend such a claim. Apart from them, who will advocate such a view, and make a convincing claim of it?

10.3   Into the Third Millennium

The mechanistic worldview is deeply imbedded in our collective psyche. For several hundred years, the dominant orthodoxy has implicitly assumed that inanimate things, large or small, are fundamentally devoid of mental qualities. That view has become integrated into our science, our literature, and our arts. It has become incorporated into our deepest social values, and thus it is reflected in our collective actions. We treat nature as an impersonal thing or collection of things without spontaneity, without intrinsic value, and without rights of any kind. Natural resources, including plant and animal species, are generally seen as mindless and insentient objects, and thus as deserving no particular respect or moral consideration. With no deeper meaning or value, they exist solely to benefit us.

The great irony, of course, is that in harming nature we harm ourselves. As we deplete the soil, deforest the land, exterminate species, exhaust the seas, and warm the planet, we are paying a high and growing price. With an ever-growing human population, the situation may well turn catastrophic in the coming decades. All this suggests that our mechanistic worldview is in error: that, by treating nature as mindless, we engage in irrational and destructive behavior. Metaphysics has consequences.

The mechanistic worldview once liberated humanity from religious dogma. Now it appears to have outlived its usefulness. It has become its own dogma, more stifling and destructive than the one it usurped. We may be approaching one of those times in history when fundamental assumptions about the world change. Such changes have happened in the past. The Homeric Greeks came into prominence in a mytho-poetic age full of gods and mysteries, but then the first philosophers appeared, and they imposed an order, a *logos*, on the world, putting reason and rational thinking into a position of preeminence. As they did so, they incorporated many aspects of the older worldview—including the concept of panpsychism, as we have seen. After dominating Western civilization for about 700 years, the Greek *logos* was superseded by the Christian theological worldview. Once again, the older concepts were absorbed and reconceived in a new framework based on faith and revelation. The psyche of the world was now integrated into the notion of God, and God's omnipresence ensured a spiritual dimension in all being.

The theological outlook held for several hundred years, until the Renaissance, when principles of reason and logic reasserted themselves once more—this time in a mechanistic and materialistic guise. Copernicus, Galileo, Hobbes, Descartes, and other thinkers articulated a cosmos of pure mechanical laws, devoid of mind and spirit, even as others—Bacon, Kepler, Newton, Leibniz—saw some reason for retaining a panpsychist universe. This new mechanistic worldview was not atheist; God still presided over the grand system, but he was removed from daily involvement. In like fashion, mind and spirit were drained from nature, leaving a cosmos of insentient particles and forces.

Today the mechanistic outlook has three main pillars. The first is that all non-living things, and most living ones, are utterly devoid of sentience and mind. The second is that reality is intrinsically objective, in the sense that a physical and mathematical description is possible for all that is real. The third pillar relates to the human psyche. In earlier times the soul was a God-given and eternal entity that mysteriously interacted with the body and the physical world. Later the soul was replaced by the mind—a mysterious product of organic processes that magically emerged at some point in evolution and that, as before, mysteriously interacted with the body and the physical world. As a consequence of these three pillars, humanity became radically estranged from nature. Humans alone retained intrinsic value, even as nature became commodified. Humans became cosmological misfits.

A successful worldview is one that transcends its predecessor by discarding certain outmoded aspects and building others into the foundation of a new, more integrated, more harmonious cosmological order. Panpsychism may be poised to fill this role. Its emphasis on mind and "spirit" is, in one sense, a return to the spiritual perspective on nature, in counterpoint to mechanistic materialism. But it is a secular spirituality, one that is compatible with a modern rational outlook. In this sense, panpsychism is fully consistent with modern science. Panpsychism has long been advocated by many scientists and other modern thinkers who, nonetheless, have found conventional science very useful in other areas of inquiry. Yet their larger worldview has rejected the fundamental mechanistic belief that lower animals, plants, and non-living material objects are mindless things. Clearly it has been possible for them to incorporate elements of a mechanistic approach to nature while maintaining a deeper view of all things as enminded or ensouled. And to the extent that they have developed positive new theories of mind, they have been able to create new visions of mind and matter and their interrelationship. This outlook strikes at the heart of mechanistic materialism, and thus holds out the promise of rewriting our view of the universe at large.

Several major thinkers were very explicit that they saw panpsychism as the foundation for a fundamentally new outlook on reality. Epicurus advocated an atomistic ontology and yet saw in the panpsychist atomic swerve the basis for human will, and hence for the very possibility of virtuous action. Francis of Assisi and Campanella advocated a theological form of panpsychism that demonstrated the presence of spirit in the world, and consequently served as a basis for moral action. Leibniz was an early contributor to the mechanistic worldview, but his quanta of the universe, the monads, were fundamentally mind-like entities. Newton was willing to consider the possibility that all matter was alive. LaMettrie was a notorious mechanist, but for him mechanism was no cause for concern; on the contrary, a properly *vitalistic* mechanism was a way of deeply integrating humanity into nature:

Whoever thinks in this way will be wise, just, and tranquil about his fate, and consequently happy. He will await death neither fearing nor desiring it; he will cherish life … ; he will be full of respect, gratitude, affection, and tenderness for nature in proportion to the love and benefits he has received from her; and, finally, happy to know nature and to witness the charming spectacle of the universe, he will certainly never suppress nature in himself or in others. (1747/1994: 75)

Fechner was another who saw panpsychism as the basis for a compassionate understanding of the world. As he said, it "decides many other questions and determines the whole outlook upon nature" (1848/1946: 163). James came to support "a general view of the world almost identical with Fechner's" (1909/1996: 309), and argued that this "pluralistic panpsychic view of the universe … threatens to short-circuit" the cynical worldview of the mechanists, and to replace it with something greater, higher, and more sympathetic.

In the twentieth century, Bateson warned us of the consequences of the standard worldview. If, he said, you adopt the conventional objectivist materialist view of mind, then "you will logically and naturally see yourself as outside and against the things around you. And as you arrogate all mind to yourself, you will see the world around you as mindless and therefore not entitled to moral or ethical consideration. The environment will seem to be yours to exploit." (1972: 462) Bateson lived at a time when the current ecological crisis was just becoming apparent. It was clear to him that this situation was rooted in a defective conception of mind. His outlook was shared by Plumwood, Mathews, and others who saw a subtle form of panpsychism as the foundation of a new, more compassionate, less confrontational environmental ethic.

One of the most poetic expressions of the virtues of the panpsychic worldview was also one of the earliest. Recall Empedocles' beautiful fragment 110, in which panpsychism is seen as the key to revelations about the true nature of the world:

If thou shouldst plant these things in thy firm understanding and contemplate them with good will and unclouded attention, they will stand by thee for ever every one, and thou shalt gain many other things from them; ... for know that all things have wisdom and a portion of thought.

Here Empedocles demonstrates a reverential, almost mystic belief in the power of the panpsychist worldview. It is, he suggests, simply the most enlightening and virtuous standpoint from which to view the cosmos. It is nothing less than the key to ultimate truth.

These beliefs of Empedocles, Fechner, James, Bateson, and others are striking; they suggest that panpsychism is the superior worldview because it leads to a more integrated, compassionate, and sympathetic cosmos. It is life-affirming and life-enhancing. It leads to positive, sustaining values for humanity. It stands in stark contrast to the cynical, isolating, manipulative values of mechanistic materialism. To the extent that these mechanistic values have contributed to our current environmental and social crises, panpsychist values may begin to reverse this process and heal the damage.

To judge the value of something as far-reaching and fundamental as a metaphysical worldview is a difficult prospect. It takes years, even centuries, for the full effects of a new worldview and its corresponding values to be realized. About 350 years passed before the negative effects of the mechanistic outlook became apparent. Thus, today we are likely to be unable to adequately judge the net worth of a panpsychist worldview. And yet the imperative of the present time calls for change. Mechanism is evidently profoundly defective; in any case, it will not last—something will take its place. This new *Weltanschauung* must, for our sake and the sake of the planet, be sustainable, holistic, and compassionate. The evidence is encouraging. Of the dozens of panpsychist thinkers examined in the present work, nearly every one has adopted an optimistic, life-affirming, and sympathetic perspective on the world.

Granting all this, the cynical materialist can still ask "Yes, but is it *true?*" If panpsychism is, in the end, just some happy delusion, we are surely not better off adopting it, or simply pretending it to be true. Agreed. Yet it must be emphasized that truth can be assessed only from within a given worldview. The standard materialist, being fundamentally committed to an anti-panpsychist view, has no unbiased standpoint from which to make a judgment. Thus any ruling of "unintelligible" or "false" is meaningless. Christians have long denounced animism and polytheism as untrue, accusing their adherents of living in a primitive cosmos of omnipresent spirits and ghosts. Likewise, materialists have accused Christians and other theologically minded individuals of buying into a "happy myth" that has no scientific basis. And of course others today blame the materialist mindset as the root cause of many of our present-day social and environmental problems. Objectivity, moral neutrality, and a fundamentally inanimate nature are mechanistic assumptions about the world—presumed but never proven. Mechanistic materialism can thus be seen, like the rest, as a happy myth, one that liberated humanity from stifling theology but which has now reached the end of its useful life.

The evolution of worldviews is one of the great stories of human culture. Worldviews are born, and they are liberating and visionary. They help to define what is true and what is good. They expand to encompass many aspects of society. They undergo gradual evolution and refinement. At some point they grow rigid and inflexible. Ultimately they become self-justifying, self-perpetuating, and finally, self-destructive. Materialism, and the accompanying analytical and logical philosophy, seems to have reached this terminal stage.

Panpsychism—ancient panpsychism—appears able to provide the foundation for a new worldview in a way that deeply addresses the root issues.

It is easy to abuse dead, inanimate matter, or unconscious forms of life. The human who alone has mind, or in whom mind is a contradiction or unfathomable mystery, has no sense of being at home in the cosmos. Consequently he is likely to feel alienated, frightened, distressed, angry, or foolish. It need not be so. Philosophers have envisioned alternative views that have equal claim to validity. We as a civilization need only summon our collective wisdom and courage, learn the lessons of history, and transcend present ways of thinking. Thus has it always been so. Transcendence is in the nature of the cosmos, and only transcendent thinking can carry us forward along our great evolutionary journey.

Bibliography

Abram, D. 1996. *The Spell of the Sensuous*. Vintage.

Agar, W. 1943. *A Contribution to the Theory of the Living Organism*. Melbourne University Press.

Alexander, S. 1914. The basis of realism. In *Realism and the Background of Phenomenology*, ed. R. Chisolm (Free Press, 1960).

Alexander, S. 1920. *Space, Time, and Deity*. Macmillan.

Allison, H. 1987. *Benedict de Spinoza*. Yale University Press.

Alter, T., and Howell, R. 2015. The short slide from a posteriori physicalism to Russellian monism. In *Consciousness in the Physical World*, ed. T. Alter and Y. Nagasawa. Oxford University Press.

Alter, T., and Nagasawa, Y. 2012. What is Russellian monism? *Journal of Consciousness Studies* 19 (9–10): 67–95.

Alter, T., and Nagasawa, Y., eds. 2015. *Consciousness in the Physical World*. Oxford University Press.

Andrews, J. 1998. Weak panpsychism and environmental ethics. *Environmental Values* 7: 381–396.

Aristotle. 1995. *The Complete Works of Aristotle*, ed. J. Barnes. Princeton University Press.

Armstrong, D. 1968. *A Materialist Theory of the Mind*. Routledge.

Armstrong, E. 1973. *Saint Francis: Nature Mystic*. University of California Press.

Armstrong-Buck, S. 1986. Whitehead's metaphysical system as a foundation for environmental ethics. *Environmental Ethics* 8: 241–259.

Augustine. ca. 410. *The City of God*. Reprint: Catholic Way, 2015.

Bacon, F. ca. 1620. *Natural History (Silva silvarum sive historia naturalis)*.

Bahcall, N., Ostriker, J. P., Perlmutter, S., and Steinhardt, P. J. 1999. The cosmic triangle. *Science* 284 (5419): 1481–1489.

Bak, P., and Chen, K. 1991. Self-organized critically. *Scientific American* 264 (1): 46–53.

Bakewell, C. 1904a. Review of *Why the Mind Has a Body*. *Philosophical Review* 13 (2): 220–229.

Bakewell, C. 1904b. A rejoinder. *Philosophical Review* 13 (3): 342–346.

Barnes, J. 1987. *Early Greek Philosophy*. Penguin.

Basile, P. 2007. The compounding of consciousness. In *Consciousness, Reality, and Value*, ed. P. Basile and L. McHenry. Ontos.

Basile, P. 2008. Mind-body problem and panpsychism. In *Handbook of Whiteheadian Process Philosophy*, ed. W. Desmond Jr. and M. Weber. Ontos.

Basile, P. 2010a. It must be true, but how can it? Some remarks on panpsychism and mental composition. In *The Metaphysics of Consciousness*, ed. P. Basile. Cambridge University Press.

Basile, P. 2010b. Materialist versus panexperientialist physicalism. *Process Studies* 39 (2): 264–284.

Basile, P. 2015. Learning from Leibniz: Whitehead (and Russell) on mind, matter, and monads. *British Journal for the History of Philosophy* 23 (6): 1128–1149.

Bateson, G. 1968. Conscious purpose versus nature. In *Dialectics of Liberation*, ed. D. Cooper. Penguin. In *Steps to an Ecology of Mind* (Ballantine, 1972).

Bateson, G. 1970. Form, substance, and difference. *General Semantics Bulletin* 37: 5–13. Reprinted in Bateson, *Steps to an Ecology of Mind* (Ballantine, 1972).

Bateson, G. 1972. *Steps to an Ecology of Mind*. Ballantine.

Bateson, G. 1979. *Mind and Nature*. Ballantine.

Bawden, H. 1904. The meaning of the psychical from the point of view of the functional psychology. *Philosophical Review* 13 (3): 298–319.

Beeson, D. 1992. *Maupertuis: An Intellectual Biography*. Voltaire Foundation, Taylor Institution.

Beever, J., and Cisney, V. 2013. All things in mind: Panpsychist elements in Spinoza, Deleuze, and Peirce. *Biosemiotics* 6 (3): 351–365.

Bennett, C. 1922. Review of *Volonte et Conscience*. *Philosophical Review* 37: 86–90.

Bennett, J. 1984. *A Study of Spinoza's Ethics*. Hackett.

Bergson, H. 1896/1911. *Matter and Memory*. Allen and Unwin.

Bergson, H. 1907/1911. *Creative Evolution*. Holt.

Bergson, H. 1911/1920. *Mind Energy*. Holt.

Bergson, H. 1922. *Duration and Simultaneity*. Reprint: Bobbs-Merrill, 1965.

Berman, M. 1981. *The Reenchantment of the World*. Cornell University Press.

Birch, C. 1971. Purpose in the universe. *Zygon* 6 (1): 4–27.

Birch, C. 1972. Participatory evolution. *Journal of the American Academy of Religion* 40: 147–163.

Birch, C. 1974. Chance, necessity, and purpose. In *Studies in the Philosophy of Biology*, ed. F. Ayala and T. Dobzhansky. Macmillan.

Birch, C. 1994. Why I became a panxperientialist. Presented at conference on Consciousness in Humans, Animals, and Machines, Claremont, California.

Birch, C. 1995. *Feelings*. University of New South Wales Press.

Bjelland, A. 1981. Capek, Bergson, and process proto-mentalism. *Process Studies* 11 (3): 180–189.

Bjelland, A. 1982. Popper's critique of panpsychism and process protomentalism. *Modern Schoolman* 59 (4): 233–254.

Blamauer, M., ed. 2011. *The Mental as Fundamental*. Ontos.

Blamauer, M. 2012. Schelling's "real materialism." *Minerva* 16: 1–24.

Blamauer, M. 2012b. Does the fundamentality of consciousness entail its ubiquity? *Filozofia* 67 (3): 243–253.

Blamauer, M. 2013. The role of subjectivity and the continuity-argument for panpsychism. *Polish Journal of Philosophy* 7 (1): 7–18.

Bohm, D. 1957. *Causality and Chance in Modern Physics*. Routledge.

Bohm, D. 1980. *Wholeness and the Implicate Order*. Routledge.

Bohm, D. 1982. Nature as creativity. *ReVision* 5 (2): 35–40.

Bohm, D. 1986. A new theory of the relationship of mind and matter. *Journal of the American Society for Psychical Research* 80 (2): 113–135.

Bohm, D. 1990. A new theory of the relationship of mind and matter. *Philosophical Psychology* 3 (2): 271–286.

Bohm, D., and Hiley, B. 1993. *Undivided Universe*. Routledge.

Bonansea, B. 1969. *Tommaso Campanella*. Catholic University Press.

Bonifazi, C. 1978. *The Soul of the World*. University Press of America.

Bowie, A. 1998. Schelling. In *Encyclopedia of Philosophy*, ed. E. Craig. Routledge.

Bradley, F. 1893. *Appearance and Reality*. Reprint: Clarendon, 1930.

Brettschneider, B. 1964. *The Philosophy of Samuel Alexander*. Humanities Press.

Brickman, B. 1941. *An Introduction to Francesco Patrizi's Nova de Universis Philosophia.*

Brown, N. 1959. *Life Against Death*. Wesleyan University Press.

Brown, S. 1990. Leibniz and More's cabbalistic circle. In *Henry More: Tercentary Studies*, ed. S. Hutton. Kluwer.

Bruno, G. 1584a. *Cause, Principle, and Unity (De la causa, principio, et uno)*. Reprint: Cambridge University Press, 1998.

Bruno, G. 1584b. *On the Infinite Universe and Worlds (De l'infinito universo et mondi)*. In D. Singer, Giordano Bruno: His Life and Thought, with Annotated Translation of His Work—On the Infinite Universe and Worlds *(Schuman, 1950)*.

Burks, A. 1996. Peirce's evolutionary pragmatic idealism. *Synthese* 106: 323–372.

Burks, A. 1997. Logic, learning, and creativity in evolution. In *Studies in the Logic of Charles Sanders Peirce*, ed. N. Houser et al. Indiana University Press.

Bush, W. 1925. William James and panpsychism. In *Studies in the History of Ideas*, volume 2. Columbia University Press.

Butler, C. 1978. Panpsychism: A restatement of the genetic argument. *Idealistic Studies* 8: 33–39.

Butler, S. 1880. *Unconscious Memory*. Reprint: Longmans, Green, 1910.

Calcagno, A. 1998. *Giordano Bruno and the Logic of Coincidence*. P. Lang.

Callicott, J. B. 1982. Traditional American Indian and Western European attitudes toward nature: An overview. *Environmental Ethics* 4: 293–318.

Campanella, T. 1620. On the Sense and Feeling in All Things and on Magic (De sensu rerum et magia). In *Tommaso Campanella*, ed. B. Bonansea (Catholic University Press, 1969).

Campanella, T. 1638. *Metaphysics (Metafisica)*. In *Tommaso Campanella*, ed. B. Bonansea (Catholic University Press, 1969).

Capek, M. 1961. *The Philosophical Impact of Contemporary Physics*. Van Nostrand.

Capek, M. 1971. *Bergson and Modern Physics*. Reidel.

Cardano, G. 1560. *The De subtilitate of Girolamo Cardano*. Reprint: Arizona Center for Medieval and Renaissance Studies, 2013.

Carus, P. 1892. Panpsychism and panbiotism. *Monist* 3: 234–257.

Cassirer, E. 1927. *The Individual and the Cosmos in Renaissance Philosophy*. Reprint: Barnes and Noble, 1963.

Cassirer, E. 1942. Giovanni Pico della Mirandola. *Journal of the History of Ideas* 3 (2): 123–344.

Cavendish, M. 1655. Philosophical and Physical Opinions. In *Modern Women Philosophers: 1600–1900*, ed. M. Waithe. Reprint: Kluwer, 1991.

Cavendish, M. 1664. Philosophical Letters. In *Women Philosophers of the Early Modern Period*, ed. M. Atherton (Hackett, 1994).

Chaisson, E. 2001. *Cosmic Evolution*. Harvard University Press.

Chalmers, D. 1995. Facing up to the problem of consciousness. *Journal of Consciousness Studies* 2 (3): 200–219.

Chalmers, D. 1996. *The Conscious Mind*. Oxford University Press.

Chalmers, D. 2002. Consciousness and its place in nature. In *Philosophy of Mind*, ed. D. Chalmers. Oxford University Press.

Chalmers, D. 2015. Panpsychism and panprotopsychism. In *Consciousness in the Physical World*, ed. T. Alter and Y. Nagasawa. Oxford University Press.

Churchland, P. M. 1986. Some reductive strategies in cognitive neurobiology. *Mind* 95: 279–309.

Churchland, P. M. 1997. To transform the phenomena. *Philosophy of Science* 64 supplement, S408–S420. In P. M. Churchland and P. S. Churchland, *On the Contrary* (MIT Press, 1998).

Clark, M. 1990. *Nietzsche on Truth and Philosophy*. Cambridge University Press.

Clark, M., and Dudrick, D. 2012. *The Soul of Nietzsche's Beyond Good and Evil*. Cambridge University Press.

Clark, R. 1955. *Herder: His Life and Thought*. University of California Press.

Clarke, D. 2003. *Panpsychism and the Religious Attitude*. SUNY Press.

Clarke, D., ed. 2004. *Panpsychism: Past and Recent Selected Readings*. SUNY Press.

Cleve, F. 1969. *The Giants of Pre-Sophistic Greek Philosophy*. Martinus Nijhoff.

Clifford, W. 1874. Body and mind. In *Lectures and Essays*, volume 2 (Macmillan, 1903)

Clifford, W. 1878. On the nature of things in themselves. Mind, January. In *Lectures and Essays* (Macmillan, 1903).

Cochran, A. 1971. The relationship between quantum physics and biology. *Foundations of Physics* 1 (3): 235–250.

Cobb, J. B., Jr., and Griffin, D. R., eds. 1977. *Mind in Nature*. University Press of America.

Coleman, S. 2012. Mental chemistry: Combination for panpsychists. *Dialectica* 66 (1): 137–166.

Coleman, S. 2014. The real combination problem: Panpsychism, micro-subjects, and emergence. *Erkenntnis* 79 (1): 19–44.

Conway, J., and Kochen, S. 2006. The free will theorem. *Foundations of Physics* 36 (10): 1441–1473.

Conway, J., and Kochen, S. 2009. The strong free will theorem. *Notices of the American Mathematical Society* 56 (2): 226–232.

Cooper, W. 1990. William James's theory of mind. *Journal of the History of Philosophy* 28: 571–593.

Coxon, A. 1986. *The Fragments of Parmenides*. Van Gorcum.

Craig, E., ed. 1998. *Encyclopedia of Philosophy*. Routledge.

Crombie, I. 1962. *An Examination of Plato's Doctrines*, volume 1. Routledge.

Curley, E. 1969. *Spinoza's Metaphysics*. Harvard University Press.

Curley, E. 1988. *Behind the Geometrical Method*. Princeton University Press.

DeGrood, D. 1965. *Haeckel's Theory of the Unity of Nature*. Christopher.

Delahunty, R. 1985. *Spinoza*. Routledge.

De Quincey, C. 1994. Consciousness all the way down? *Journal of Consciousness Studies* 1 (2): 217–229.

De Quincey, C. 1999. Past matter, present mind. *Journal of Consciousness Studies* 6 (1): 91–106.

De Quincey, C. 2002. *Radical Nature*. Invisible Cities.

Dewey, J. 1925. *Experience and Nature*. Open Court.

Dewey, J. 1940. Time and individuality. In *The Later Works*, volume 14, ed. J. Boydston (Southern Illinois University Press, 1988).

Diderot, D. 1754. Thoughts on the Interpretation of Nature. In *Selected Writings*, ed. L. Crocker (Macmillan, 1966).

Diderot, D. 1769. D'Alembert's Dream. In *Diderot: Interpreter of Nature* (Lawrence and Wishart, 1937).

Diderot, D. 1774–1780. *Elements of Physiology*. In *Diderot: Interpreter of Nature* (Lawrence and Wishart, 1937).

Donagan, A. 1989. *Spinoza*. University of Chicago Press.

Dooley, B. 1995. *Italy in the Baroque*. Garland.

Drake, D. 1925. *Mind and Its Place in Nature*. Reprint: Kraus, 1970.

Dulles, A. 1941. *Princeps Concordiae*. Harvard University Press.

Dyson, F. 1979. *Disturbing the Universe*. Harper & Row.

Eddington, A. 1920. *Space, Time, and Gravitation*. Cambridge University Press.

Eddington, A. 1928. *The Nature of the Physical World*. Cambridge University Press.

Eddington, A. 1939. *The Philosophy of Physical Science*. Cambridge University Press.

Edelman, G. 1992. *Bright Air, Brilliant Fire*. Basic Books.

Edwards, J. 2005. Is consciousness only a property of individual cells? *Journal of Consciousness Studies* 12 (4–5): 60–76.

Edwards, P. 1967. Panpsychism. In *Encyclopedia of Philosophy*, ed. P. Edwards. Macmillan.

Edwards, P. 1972. Panpsychism. In *Encyclopedia of Philosophy*, ed. P. Edwards. Macmillan.

Ells, P. 2011. *Panpsychism: The Philosophy of the Sensuous Cosmos*. O-Books.

Endres, M., and Pichler, A. 2013. Ways of reading Nietzsche in the light of KGW IX. *Journal of Nietzsche Studies* 44 (1): 90–109.

Ernst, G. 2010. Tommaso Campanella: The revolution of knowledge from the prison. In *Philosophers of the Renaissance*, ed. R. Blum. Catholic University of America Press.

Fechner, G. 1848. Nanna, or on the Soul-Life of Plants. In *Religion of a Scientist*, ed. R. Lowrie (Pantheon, 1946).

Fechner, G. 1861. On the Soul-Question. In *Religion of a Scientist*, ed. R. Lowrie (Pantheon, 1946).

Feigl, H. 1958. The "mental" and the "physical." In *Concepts, Theories, and the Mind-Body Problem*, ed. H. Feigl et al. University of Minnesota Press.

Feigl, H. 1960. Mind-body, not a pseudo-problem. In *Dimensions of Mind*, ed. S. Hook. New York University Press.

Ferenczi, S. 1926. *Further Contributions to the Theory and Technique of Psycho-Analysis*. Reprint: Hogarth, 1950.

Fierz, M. 1983. *Girolamo Cardano*. Birkhauser.

Ford, L. 1984. *The Emergence of Whitehead's Metaphysics*. SUNY Press.

Ford, L. 1987. From pre-panpsychism to pansubjectivity. In *Faith and Creativity*, ed. G. Nordgulen. CBP.

Ford, L. 1995. Panpsychism and the early history of prehension. *Process Studies* 24: 15–33.

Ford, M. 1981. William James: Panpsychist and metaphysical realist. *Trans Peirce Society* 17: 158–170.

Ford, M. 1982. *William James' Philosophy*. University of Massachusetts Press.

Foster, J. 1982. *The Case for Idealism*. Routledge and Kegan Paul.

Francoeur, R. 1961. *The World of Teilhard*. Helicon.

Freeman, K. 1948. *Ancilla to the Pre-Socratic Philosophers*. Blackwell.

Freudenthal, G. 1995. *Aristotle's Theory of Material Substance*. Clarendon.

Friedman, H. 1986. *Sun and Earth*. Scientific American Library.

Frisina, W. 1997. Minds, bodies, experience, nature: Is panpsychism really dead? In *Pragmatism, Neo-Pragmatism, and Religion*, ed. C. Hardwick. Lang.

Fuller, B. 1945. *A History of Philosophy*. Holt.

Gaskin, J., ed. 1994. *The Elements of Law, Natural and Politic*. Oxford University Press.

Giglioni, G. 1995. Panpsychism versus hylozoism: An interpretation of some seventeenth-century doctrines of universal animation. *Acta Comeniana* 11: 25–44.

Giglioni, G. 2002. Francis Glisson's notion of *confoederatio naturae* in the context of hylozoistic corpuscularism. *Revue d'Histoire des Sciences* 55 (2): 239–262.

Giglioni, G. 2010. The first of the moderns or the last of the ancients? Bernardino Telesio on nature and sentience. *Bruniana e Campanelliana* 16 (1): 69–87.

Gilbert, W. 1600. *On the Magnet (De magnete)*. Reprint: Dover, 1958.

Gill, M., and Lennox, J., eds. 1994. *Self-Motion: From Aristotle to Newton*. Princeton University Press.

Globus, G. 1972. Biological foundations of the psychoneural identify hypothesis. *Philosophy of Science* 39: 291–301.

Globus, G. 1973. Unexpected symmetries in the "world knot." *Science* 108 (4091): 1129–1136.

Globus, G. 1976. Mind, structure, and contradiction. In *Consciousness and the Brain*, ed. G. Globus et al. Plenum.

Globus, G. 2009. Halting the descent into panpsychism: A quantum thermofield theoretical perspective. In *Mind That Abides: Panpsychism in the New Millennium*, ed. D. Skrbina. John Benjamins.

Goff, P. 2009. Why panpsychism doesn't help us explain consciousness. *Dialectica* 63 (3): 289–311.

Goff, P. 2014. Orthodox property dualism + linguistic theory of vagueness = panpsychism. In *Consciousness Inside and Out*, ed. R. Brown. Springer.

Goff, P. 2015. Against constitutive forms of Russellian monism. In *Consciousness in the Physical World*, ed. T. Alter and Y. Nagasawa. Oxford University Press.

Goethe, W. 1828. Commentary on the aphoristic essay "Nature. In *Scientific Studies: Johann Wolfgang von Goethe*, ed. D. Miller (Suhrkamp, 1988).

Greene, R. 1962. Henry More and Robert Boyle on the spirit of nature. *Journal of the History of Ideas* 23: 451–474.

Griffin, D. R. 1977. Whitehead's philosophy and some general notions of physics and biology. In *Mind in Nature*, ed. J. Cobb and D. Griffin. University Press of America.

Griffin, D. R. 1988a. Introduction: The reenchantment of science. In *The Reenchantment of Science*, ed. D. Griffin. SUNY Press.

Griffin, D. R. 1988b. Of minds and molecules. In *The Reenchantment of Science*, ed. D. Griffin. SUNY Press.

Griffin, D. R. 1997. Panexperientialist physicalism and the mind-body problem. *Journal of Consciousness Studies* 4 (3): 248–268.

Griffin, D. R. 1998. *Unsnarling the World Knot*. University of California Press.

Guthrie, W. 1962–1981. *History of Greek Philosophy*, volumes 1–6. Cambridge University Press.

Guthrie, K. 1988. *The Pythagorean Sourcebook and Library*. Phanes.

Haeckel, E. 1868/1876. *The History of Creation*. Routledge.

Haeckel, E. 1892. Our monism. *Monist* 2 (4): 481–486.

Haeckel, E. 1895. *Monism as Connecting Religion and Science*. A. and C. Black.

Haeckel, E. 1899. *The Riddle of the Universe*. Reprint: Watts, 1929.

Haeckel, E. 1904. *The Wonders of Life*. Watts.

Haldane, J. B. S. 1932. *The Inequality of Man*. Chatto & Windus.

Haldane, J. B. S. 1934. Quantum mechanics as a basis for philosophy. *Philosophy of Science* 1: 78–98.

Halton, E. 2005. Peircean animism and the end of civilization. *Contemporary Pragmatism* 2 (1): 136–166.

Hameroff, S. 1994. Quantum coherence in microtubules. *Journal of Consciousness Studies* 1: 91–118.

Hameroff, S. 1998a. Funda-mentality: Is the conscious mind subtly linked to a basic level of the universe? *Trends in Cognitive Sciences* 2 (4): 119–127.

Hameroff, S. 1998b. More neural than thou. In *Toward a Science of Consciousness II*, ed. S. Hameroff et al. MIT Press.

Hameroff, S. 2009. The conscious connection: A psycho-physical bridge between brain and pan-experiential quantum geometry. In *Mind That Abides: Panpsychism in the New Millennium*, ed. D. Skrbina. John Benjamins.

Hameroff, S., and Penrose, R. 1996. Conscious events as orchestrated space-time selections. *Journal of Consciousness Studies* 3 (1): 36–53.

Hamilton, A. 1990. Ernst Mach and the elimination of subjectivity. *Ratio* 3 (2): 117–133.

Hamlyn, D. 1980. *Schopenhauer: The Arguments of the Philosophers*. Routledge.

Hampshire, S. 1951. *Spinoza*. Penguin.

Hampshire, S. 2002. The Spinoza solution. *New York Review of Books*, October 24: 55–56.

Harman, G. 2002. *Tool-Being: Heidegger and the Metaphysics of Objects*. Open Court.

Harris, E. 1973. Body-mind relation in Spinoza's philosophy. In *Spinoza's Metaphysics*, ed. J. Wilbur. Van Gorcum.

von Hartmann, E. 1869. *Philosophy of the Unconscious*. Reprint: Routledge, 1950.

Hartshorne, C. 1936. The compound individual. In *Whitehead's Philosophy: Selected Essays* (University of Nebraska Press, 1972)

Hartshorne, C. 1937. *Beyond Humanism*. Willett, Clark.

Hartshorne, C. 1949. Chance, love, incompatibility. *Philosophical Review* 58 (5): 429–450.

Hartshorne, C. 1950. Panpsychism. In *A History of Philosophical Systems*, ed. V. Ferm. Philosophical Library.

Hartshorne, C. 1977. Physics and psychics. In *Mind in Nature*, ed. J. Cobb Jr. and D. Griffin. University Press of America.

Hartshorne, C. 1979. The rights of the subhuman world. *Environmental Ethics* 1: 49–60.

Hartshorne, C. 1990. *The Darkness and the Light*. SUNY Press.

Harvey, G. 2005. *Animism: Respecting the Living World*. Columbia University Press.

Harvey, G. 2015. *The Handbook of Contemporary Animism*. Routledge.

Heidegger, M. 1927. *Being and Time*. Reprint: SUNY Press, 1996.

Heidelberger, M. 2004. *Nature from Within: Gustav Theodor Fechner and his Psychophysical Worldview*. University of Pittsburgh Press.

Henry, J. 1987. Medicine and pneumatology: Henry More, Richard Baxter, and Francis Glisson's *Treatise on the Energetic Nature of Substance*. *Medical History* 31: 15–40.

Henry, J. 2001. Animism and empiricism: Copernican physics and the origins of William Gilbert's experimental method. *Journal of the History of Ideas* 62 (1): 99–119.

Henry, J. 2011. Omnipotence and thinking matter. In *Materia: XIII Colloquio Internazionale*, ed. D. Giovanozzi and M. Veneziana. Leo S. Olschiki Editore.

Herbert, G. 1989. *Thomas Hobbes: The Unity of Scientific and Moral Wisdom*. University of British Columbia Press.

Herder, J. 1778. On the Cognition and Sensation of the Human Soul. In *Philosophical Writings: Johann Gottfried von Herder*, ed. M. Forster (Cambridge University Press, 2002).

Hill, K. 2007. *Nietzsche: A Guide for the Perplexed*. Continuum.

Hobbes, T. 1655. *On the Body (De corpore)*. In *The English Works of Thomas Hobbes*, ed. W. Molesworth (Bohn, 1839).

Hoeffding, H. 1908. *A History of Modern Philosophy*, volume 1. Macmillan.

Holman, E. 2008. Panpsychism, physicalism, neutral monism, and the Russellian theory of mind. *Journal of Consciousness Studies* 15 (5): 48–67.

Houser, N. 2014. The intelligible universe. *Biosemiotics* 11: 9–32.

Howe, R., et al. 2000. Dynamic variations at the base of the solar convection zone. *Science* 287 (5462): 2456–2460.

Humphrey, N. 1992. *A History of the Mind*. Chatto & Windus.

Hut, P., and Shepard, R. 1996. Turning the "hard problem" upside down and sideways. *Journal of Consciousness Studies* 3 (4): 313–329.

Hutto, D. 2000. *Beyond Physicalism*. Benjamins.

Huxley, J. 1942. The biologist looks at man. *Fortune*, December.

Ingegno, A. 1998. Introduction. In *Cause, Principle, and Unity*, ed. G. Bruno. Cambridge University Press.

Inwood, B., and Gerson, L. 1997. *Hellenistic Philosophy*. Hackett.

James, W. 1890. *Principles of Psychology*. Reprint: Dover, 1950.

James, W. 1902. *Varieties of Religious Experience*. Collier.

James, W. 1909. *A Pluralistic Universe*. Reprint: University of Nebraska Press, 1996.

James, W. 1911a. *Some Problems of Philosophy*. Reprint: Greenwood, 1968.

James, W. 1911b. *Memories and Studies*. Longmans, Green.

James, W. 1912. *Essays in Radical Empiricism*. Reprint: University of Nebraska Press, 1996.

James, W. 1920. *Letters of William James*. Atlantic Monthly Press.

Jammer, M. 1957. *Concepts of Force*. Harvard University Press.

Janaway, C. 2007. *Beyond Selflessness*. Oxford University Press.

Jeans, J. 1932. *The Mysterious Universe*. Macmillan.

Jeans, J. 1942. *Physics and Philosophy*. University of Michigan Press.

Joachim, H. 1901. *A Study of the Ethics of Spinoza*. Reprint: Russell & Russell, 1964.

Jung, C. G., and Pauli, W. 1955. *The Interpretation of Nature and the Psyche*. Routledge.

Kant, I. 1766. *Dreams of a Spirit-Seer*. Reprint: Macmillan, 1900.

Kant, I. 1781. *Critique of Pure Reason*. Reprint: St. Martin's Press, 1965.

Kant, I. 1790. *Critique of Judgment*. Reprint: Hafner, 1951.

Kauffman, S. 2016a. *Humanity in a Creative Universe*. Oxford University Press.

Kauffman, S. 2016b. Cosmic mind? *Theology and Science* 14 (1): 36–47.

Kaufmann, W. 1950. *Nietzsche: Philosopher, Psychologist, Antichrist*. Princeton University Press.

Kaufmann, W. 1967/1972. Nietzsche. In *The Encyclopedia of Philosophy*, ed. P. Edwards. Macmillan.

Kepler, J. 1618. *Harmonies of the World*. Reprint: Prometheus Books, 1995.

Kerr-Lawson, A. 1984. Spirit's primary nature is to be secondary. *Bulletin of the Santayana Society* 2: 9–14.

Kind, A. 2015. Pessimism about Russellian monism. In *Consciousness in the Physical World*, ed. T. Alter and Y. Nagasawa. Oxford University Press.

Kirk, G., et al. 1983. *The Presocratic Philosophers*. Cambridge University Press.

Klausner, N. 1967. Charles A. Strong, realist and panpsychist. *Monist* 51: 267–283.

Klemm, D., and Klink, W. 2008. Consciousness and quantum mechanics. *Zygon* 43 (2): 307–327.

Koch, C. 2012. *Consciousness: Confessions of a Romantic Reductionist*. MIT Press.

Koch, C. 2013. Ubiquitous minds. *Scientific American Mind* 25: 26–29.

Koestler, A. 1967. *The Ghost in the Machine*. Macmillan.

Koestler, A. 1978. *Janus*. Random House.

Kristeller, P. 1964. *Eight Philosophers of the Italian Renaissance*. Stanford University Press.

Kuelpe, O. 1913. *Philosophy of the Present in Germany*. Allen.

Kuklick, B. 1977. *The Rise of American Philosophy*. Yale University Press.

LaMettrie, J. 1745. Natural History of the Soul. In *Machine Man and Other Writings*, ed. A. Thomson. Reprint: Cambridge University Press, 1996.

LaMettrie, J. 1747. *Man, a Machine*. (*L'Homme Machine*). In *Man a Machine: And, Man a Plant*, ed. R. Watson and M. Rybalka (Hackett, 1994).

LaMettrie, J. 1748. *Man, a Plant*. (*L'Homme Plante*). In *Man a Machine: And, Man a Plant*, ed. R. Watson and M. Rybalka (Hackett, 1994).

Lang, K. 1995. *Sun, Earth, and Sky*. Springer.

Leibniz, G. 1686a. Primary Truths. In *Philosophical Essays*, ed. R. Ariew and D. Garber (Hackett, 1989).

Leibniz, G. 1686b. Letter to Arnauld. In *Philosophical Essays*, ed. R. Ariew and D. Garber (Hackett, 1989).

Leibniz, G. 1687. Letter to Arnauld. In *Philosophical Essays*, ed. R. Ariew and D. Garber (Hackett, 1989).

Leibniz, G. 1690. Notes on some comments by Michel Angelo Fardela. In *Philosophical Essays*, ed. R. Ariew and D. Garber (Hackett, 1989).

Leibniz, G. 1695. A New System of Nature. In *Philosophical Essays*, ed. R. Ariew and D. Garber (Hackett, 1989).

Leibniz, G. 1698. On Nature Itself. In *Philosophical Papers and Letters*, ed. L. Loemker (University of Chicago Press, 1956).

Leibniz, G. 1707. Comments on Spinoza's philosophy. In *Philosophical Essays*, ed. R. Ariew and D. Garber (Hackett, 1989).

Leibniz, G. 1714a. Principles of Nature and of Grace. In *Philosophical Essays*, ed. R. Ariew and D. Garber (Hackett, 1989).

Leibniz, G. 1714b. The monadology. In *Philosophical Essays*, ed. R. Ariew and D. Garber (Hackett, 1989).

Leibniz, G. 1716. Letter to Des Bosses. In *Philosophical Essays*, ed. R. Ariew and D. Garber (Hackett, 1989).

Leibniz, G. 1989. *Philosophical Essays*, ed. R. Ariew and D. Garber. Hackett.

Leinkauf, T. 2010. Francesco Patrizi: New philosophies of history, poetry, and the world. In *Philosophers of the Renaissance*, ed. R. Blum. Catholic University of America Press.

Leiter, B. 2013. Nietzsche's naturalism reconsidered. In *The Oxford Handbook of Nietzsche*, ed. K. Gemes and J. Richardson. Oxford University Press.

Leopold, A. 1979. Some fundamentals of conservation in the southwest. *Environmental Ethics* 1 (2): 131–141.

Lewis, D. 1966. An argument for the identity theory. *Journal of Philosophy* 63: 17–25.

Lewtas, P. 2015. Russellian panpsychism: Too good to be true? *American Philosophical Quarterly* 52 (1): 57–71.

Lloyd, A. C. 1959. Parmenides. In *Encyclopædia Britannica*. Encyclopædia Britannica, Inc.

Locke, J. 1689. *An Essay Concerning Human Understanding*. Reprint: Dutton, 1964.

Lockwood, M. 1989. *Mind, Brain, and the Quantum*. Blackwell.

Loeb, P. 2015. Will to power and panpsychism. In *Nietzsche on Mind and Nature*, ed. M. Dries and P. Kail. Oxford University Press.

Long, A. A. 1974. *Hellenistic Philosophy*. Duckworth.

Long, A. A. 1996. Parmenides on thinking being. *Boston Proceedings on Ancient Philosophy* 12: 125–151.

Lossky, N. 1901. Kozlov i Yevo panpsikhism. *Voprosy filosofi i psikhologii* 58: 198–202.

Lossky, N. 1906. The Intuitive Basis of Knowledge. In *A History of Russian Philosophy*, ed. V. Kuvakin (Prometheus Books, 1994).

Lossky, N. 1917/1928. *The World as an Organic Whole*. Oxford University Press.

Lossky, N. 1951. *History of Russian Philosophy*. International Universities Press.

Lotze, R. H. 1971. *Microcosmos*. T. & T. Clark.

Lucretius. 1977. *The Nature of Things (De rerum natura)*. Norton.

Lycan, W. 2011. Recent naturalistic dualisms. In *Light Against Darkness*, ed. A. Lange et al. Vandenhoeck & Ruprecht.

Mach, E. 1883. *The Science of Mechanics*. Reprint: Open Court, 1942.

Madden, E., and Hare, P. 1971. The powers that be. *Dialogue* 10, 12–30.

Madell, G. 1988. *Mind and Materialism*. Edinburgh University Press.

Magee, B. 1983. *The Philosophy of Schopenhauer*. Oxford University Press.

Manjaly, J. 2009. Panpsychic presuppositions of Samkhya metaphysics. In *Mind That Abides: Panpsychism in the New Millennium*, ed. D. Skrbina. John Benjamins.

Martin, C., and Pfeifer, K. 1986. Intentionality and the non-psychological. *Philosophy and Phenomenological Research* 46: 531–556.

Marx, W. 1984. *The Philosophy of F. W. J. Schelling*. Indiana University Press.

Mathews, F. 1998. The real, the one and the many in ecological thought. In *Spirit of the Environment*, ed. J. Palmer and D. Cooper. Routledge.

Mathews, F. 2003. *For Love of Matter*. SUNY Press.

Maxwell, G. 1978. Rigid designators and mind-brain identity. *Minnesota Studies in the Philosophy of Science* 9: 365–403.

McCarthy, J. 1979. Ascribing mental qualities to machines. In *Philosophical Perspectives in Artificial Intelligence*, ed. M. Ringle. Humanities Press.

McDaniel, J. 1983. Physical matter as creative and sentient. *Environmental Ethics* 5: 291–317.

McDougall, W. 1920. *Body and Mind: A History and a Defense of Animism*. Macmillan.

McGinn, C. 1991. *The Problem of Consciousness*. Blackwell.

McGinn, C. 1997. *Character of Mind*. Oxford University Press.

McGinn, C. 1999. *The Mysterious Flame*. Basic Books.

McGinn, C. 2006. Hard questions. In *Consciousness and its Place in Nature*, ed. A. Freeman. Imprint Academic.

McGuire, J. 1968. Force, active principles, and Newton's invisible realm. *Ambix* 15 (3): 154–208.

McGuire, J. 1994. Natural motion and its causes: Newton on the 'Vis Insita' of bodies. In *Self-Motion*, ed. M. Gill and J. Lennox. Princeton University Press.

McHenry, L. 1995. Whitehead's panpsychism as the subjectivity of prehension. *Process Studies* 24: 1–14.

McHenry, L. 2010. Sprigge's ontology of consciousness. In *The Metaphysics of Consciousness*, ed. P. Basile, J. Kiverstein, and P. Phemister. Cambridge University Press.

McRae, R. 1981. Life, vis inertiae, and the mechanical philosophy. In *Pragmatism and Purpose*, ed. L. Sumner et al. University of Toronto Press.

Merchant, C. 1979. *The Death of Nature*. Harper & Row.

Merleau-Ponty, M. 1945. *Phenomenology of Perception*. Reprint: Routledge, 1962

Monod, J. 1971. *Chance and Necessity*. Random House.

Montague, W. 1905. Panpsychism and monism. *Journal of Philosophy* 2 (23): 626–629.

Montague, W. 1912. A realistic theory of truth and error. In *New Realism*, ed. H. Holt. Macmillan.

Montague, W. 1945. Human soul and cosmic mind. *Mind* 54 (213): 50–65.

Moore, G. 2002. *Nietzsche, Biology, and Metaphor*. Cambridge University Press.

Naess, A. 1975. *Freedom, Emotion, and Self-Subsistence*. Universitetsforl.

Nagel, T. 1974. What is it like to be a bat? *Philosophical Review* 83 (4): 435–450.

Nagel, T. 1979. *Mortal Questions*. Cambridge University Press.

Nagel, T. 1986. *The View from Nowhere*. Oxford University Press.

Nagel, T. 2002. *Concealment and Exposure*. Oxford University Press.

Nagel, T. 2012. *Mind and Cosmos*. Oxford University Press.

Nash, R. 1975. The significance of the arrangement of the deck chairs on the *Titanic* (the extension of ethics and humanity). *Not Man Apart* 5, October: 7–9. Reprinted in *Earthworks*, ed. M. Van Deventer (Friends of the Earth, 1980).

Nash, R. 1977. Do rocks have rights? *The Center Magazine* 10 (November/December): 2–12.

Naydler, J. 1996. *Goethe on Science*. Floris Books.

Nehamas, A. 1985. *Nietzsche: Life as Literature*. Harvard University Press.

Newton, I. 1687. *Principia (The Mathematical Principles of Natural Philosophy)*. Reprint: University of California Press, 1934.

Nietzsche, F. 1883. *Thus Spoke Zarathustra*. In *The Portable Nietzsche*, ed. W. Kaufmann (Penguin, 1954).

Nietzsche, F. 1886. *Beyond Good and Evil*. Reprint: Penguin, 1973.

Nietzsche, F. 1887. *On the Genealogy of Morals*. Reprint: Oxford University Press, 1996.

Nietzsche, F. 1906. *The Will to Power*. Reprint: Random House, 1967.

Nietzsche, F. 1954. *Werke*, ed. K. Schlechta. Carl Hanser Verlag.

Nietzsche, F. 1979. *Philosophy and Truth*, ed. D. Breazeale. Humanities Press.

Nietzsche, F. 2003. *Writings from the Late Notebooks*, ed. R. Bittner. Cambridge University Press.

Nisbet, H. 1970. *Herder and the Philosophy and History of Science*. Modern Humanities Research Association.

O'Brien, J. 1958. Gravity and love as unifying principles. *Thomist* 21: 184–193.

O'Brien, J. 1988. Teilhard's view of nature and some implications for environmental ethics. *Environmental Ethics* 10: 329–346.

Orr, E. 2012. *Wakeful World: Animism, Mind, and the Self in Nature*. Moon Books.

Ouspensky, P. 1912. *Tertium Organum*. Reprint: Routledge, 1981.

Pagel, W. 1982. *Paracelsus*. Karger.

Paracelsus, P. 1894. Concerning the nature of things. In *The Hermetic and Alchemical Writings of Aureolus Philippus Theophrastus Bombast*. J. Elliot.

Parkes, G. 1994. *Composing the Soul*. University of Chicago Press.

Parkes, G. 2009. The awareness of rocks: East-Asian understandings and implications. In *Mind That Abides: Panpsychism in the New Millennium*, ed. D. Skrbina. John Benjamins.

Parkinson, G. 1953. *Spinoza's Theory of Knowledge*. Clarendon.

Partridge, E. 1984. Nature as a moral resource. *Environmental Ethics* 6 (2): 101–130.

Paulsen, F. 1892/1895. *Introduction to Philosophy*. Holt.

Peck, A. 1943. Bibliographic footnotes. In *Aristotle, Generation of Animals*. Harvard University Press.

Peirce, C. S. 1891. The architecture of theories. *Monist* 1, no. 1: 161–176. In *The Essential Peirce*, volume 1, ed. N. House and C. Kloesel (Indiana University Press, 1992).

Peirce, C. S. 1892a. The doctrine of necessity examined. *Monist* 2, no. 1: 321–337. In *The Essential Peirce*, volume 1, ed. N. House and C. Kloesel (Indiana University Press, 1992).

Peirce, C. S. 1892b. The law of mind. *Monist* 2, no. 2: 533–559. In *The Essential Peirce*, volume 1, ed. N. House and C. Kloesel (Indiana University Press, 1992).

Peirce, C. S. 1892c. Man's glassy essence. *Monist* 3, no. 1: 1–22. In *The Essential Peirce*, volume 1, ed. N. House and C. Kloesel (Indiana University Press, 1992).

Peirce, C. S. 1934. *Collected Papers of Charles Sanders Peirce*. Cambridge University Press.

Peirce, C. S. 1992a. *The Essential Peirce*, volume 1, ed. N. House and C. Kloesel. Indiana University Press.

Peirce, C. S. 1992b. *The Essential Peirce*, volume 2, ed. N. House and C. Kloesel. Indiana University Press.

Peirce, C. S. 1993. *Reasoning and the Logic of Things*. Harvard University Press.

Penrose, R. 1989. *Emperor's New Mind*. Oxford University Press.

Penrose, R. 1994a. Mechanisms, microtubules, and the mind. *Journal of Consciousness Studies* 1 (2): 241–249.

Penrose, R. 1994b. *Shadows of the Mind*. Oxford University Press.

Perry, H. 1968. *The First Duchess of Newcastle*. Johnson Reprint.

Perry, R. 1935. *Thought and Character of William James*. Little, Brown.

Plato. 1997. *Complete Works*, ed. J. Cooper. Hackett.

Plato. 1953. *Sophist*. Clarendon.

Plumwood, V. 1993. *Feminism and the Mastery of Nature*. Routledge.

Plumwood, V. 1998. Intentional recognition and reductive rationality. *Environmental Values* 7: 397–421.

Plumwood, V. 2002. *Environmental Culture*. Routledge.

Poellner, P. 1995. *Nietzsche and Metaphysics*. Oxford University Press.

Popper, K., and Eccles, J. 1977. *The Self and Its Brain*. Springer.

Porter, J. 2006. Nietzsche's theory of the will to power. In *A Companion to Nietzsche*, ed. K. Pearson. Blackwell.

Priestley, J. 1777. Disquisitions relating to matter and spirit. In *The Theological and Miscellaneous Works of Joseph Priestly*, ed. J. Rutt. Reprint: Kraus, 1972.

Prince, M. 1885. The Nature of Mind and the Human Automatism. In *The Origins of Psychology*, volume 1 (Alan R. Liss, 1975).

Prince, M. 1904. The identification of mind and matter. *Philosophical Review* 13 (4): 444–451.

Reeve, C., and Miller, P., eds. 2006. *Introductory Readings in Ancient Greek and Roman Philosophy*. Hackett.

Reginster, B. 2012. Replies to my critics. *Journal of Nietzsche Studies* 43 (1): 130–140.

Rensch, B. 1960. *Evolution above the Species Level*. Columbia University Press.

Rensch, B. 1971. *Biophilosophy*. Columbia University Press.

Rensch, B. 1972. Spinoza's identify theory and modern biophilosophy. *Philosophical Forum* 3: 193–207.

Rensch, B. 1977. Arguments for panpsychistic identism. In *Mind in Nature*, ed. J. Cobb and D. Griffin. University Press of America.

Richardson, J. 2000. Clark on will to power. *International Studies in Philosophy* 32 (3): 107–117.

Rist, J. 1989. *The Mind of Aristotle. Phoenix series*, volume 25. University of Toronto Press.

Robinson, E. 1949. Animism as a world hypothesis. *Philosophical Review* 58: 53–63.

Rockwell, T. 2013. Mind or mechanism: Which came first? In *Origins of Mind*, ed. L. Swan. Springer.

Rorty, R. 1995. Dewey between Hegel and Darwin. In *Rorty and Pragmatism*, ed. H. Saatkamp. Vanderbilt University Press.

Rosenberg, G. 1996. Rethinking nature. *Journal of Consciousness Studies* 3 (1): 76–88.

Rosenberg, G. 2004. *A Place for Consciousness*. Oxford University Press.

Rosenberg, G. 2015. Causality and the combination problem. In *Consciousness in the Physical World*, ed. T. Alter and Y. Nagasawa. Oxford University Press.

Royce, J. 1892. *Spirit of Modern Philosophy*. Reprint: Houghton Miffin, 1955.

Royce, J. 1898. *Studies of Good and Evil*. Reprint: Appleton, 1915.

Royce, J. 1899–1901. *The World and the Individual*. Macmillan.

Russell, B. 1915. Ultimate constituents of matter. In *Realism and the Background of Phenomenology*, ed. R. Chisolm. Reprint: Free Press, 1960.

Russell, B. 1921. *The Analysis of Mind*. Routledge.

Russell, B. 1927a. *The Analysis of Matter*. Routledge.

Russell, B. 1927b. *An Outline of Philosophy*. Allen and Unwin.

Russell, B. 1940/1949. *An Inquiry into Meaning and Truth*. Norton.

Russell, B. 1956. *Portraits from Memory*. Allen and Unwin.

Salter, W. 1922. Panpsychism and freedom. *Philosophical Review* 31 (3): 285–287.

Sambursky, S. 1959. *The Physics of the Stoics*. Routledge.

Sandbach, F. 1975. *The Stoics*. Chatto & Windus.

Schelling, F. 1797. *Ideas for a Philosophy of Nature*. Reprint: Cambridge University Press, 1988.

Schelling, F. 1800. *System of Transcendental Idealism*. Reprint: University Press of Virginia, 1978.

Schiller, F. 1891. *Riddles of the Sphinx*. S. Sonnenschein.

Schiller, F. 1907. *Studies in Humanism*. Macmillan.

Schiller, F. 1929. *Logic for Use*. G. Bell.

Schilpp, P., ed. 1941. *The Philosophy of Alfred North Whitehead*. Northwestern University Press.

Schleicher, D. 2013. Interview with John Horton Conway. *Notices of the American Mathematical Society* 60 (5): 567–575.

Schnadelbach, H. 1984. *Philosophy in Germany: 1831–1933*. Cambridge University Press.

Schopenhauer, A. 1819. *The World as Will and Idea*. Reprint: J. M. Dent, 1995.

Schopenhauer, A. 1819. *The World as Will and Representation*, volume 1. Reprint: Dover, 1969

Schopenhauer, A. 1836. *On the Will in Nature*, ed. D. Cartwright (Berg, 1993).

Schopenhauer, A. 1851. *Parerga and Paralipomena,* ed. D. Cartwright (Clarendon, 1974).

Schweitzer, A. 1949. *The Philosophy of Civilization*. Macmillan.

Seager, W. 1991. *Metaphysics of Consciousness*. Routledge.

Seager, W. 1995. Consciousness, information, and panpsychism. *Journal of Consciousness Studies* 2 (3): 272–288.

Seager, W. 1999. *Theories of Consciousness*. Routledge.

Seager, W. 2001. Panpsychism. *Stanford Encyclopedia of Philosophy* (online), summer 2001 edition.

Seager, W. 2009. Panpsychism. In *The Oxford Handbook of Philosophy of Mind*, ed. A. Beckermann et al. Oxford University Press.

Seager, W. 2010. Panpsychism, aggregation, and combinatorial infusion. *Mind and Matter* 8 (2): 167–184.

Searle, J. 1997. Consciousness and the philosophers. *New York Review of Books* 44 (4): 43–50.

Searle, J. 2013. Can information theory explain consciousness? *New York Review of Books* 60 (1).

Sellars, R. 1960. Panpsychism or evolutionary materialism. *Philosophy of Science* 27: 329–350.

Shani, I. 2010. Mind stuffed with red herrings: Why William James' critique of the mind-stuff theory does not substantiate a combination problem for panpsychism. *Acta Analytica* 25 (4): 413–434.

Sharpe, R. 1989. Dennett's journey towards panpsychism. *Inquiry* 32 (2): 233–240.

Sheldrake, R. 1990. *The Rebirth of Nature*. Century.

Sherrington, C. 1941. *Man on His Nature*. Macmillan.

Sherrington, C. 1949. *Goethe on Nature and on Science*. Cambridge University Press.

Singer, D. 1950. *Giordano Bruno*. Schuman.

Skolimowski, H. 1990. The world as sanctuary. [summer]. *Quest*.

Skolimowski, H. 1992. *Living Philosophy: Eco-Philosophy as a Tree of Life*. Arkana/ Penguin.

Skolimowski, H. 1993. *A Sacred Place to Dwell*. Element Books.

Skolimowski, H. 1994. *The Participatory Mind*. Arkana/Penguin.

Skrbina, D. 1994. Participatory chaos: An analytic model of consciousness. In *Coherence and Chaos in our Uncommon Futures*, ed. M. Mannermaa et al. Finland Future Research Centre.

Skrbina, D. 2003. Panpsychism as an underlying theme in western philosophy. *Journal of Consciousness Studies* 10 (3): 4–46.

Skrbina, D. 2006. Beyond Descartes: Panpsychism revisited. *Axiomathes* 16: 387–423.

Skrbina, D. 2008. On the problem of the aggregate. In Chromatikon *IV*. Presses Universitaires de Louvain.

Skrbina, D. 2009a. Panpsychism in history: An overview. In *Mind That Abides: Panpsychism in the New Millennium*, ed. D. Skrbina. John Benjamins.

Skrbina, D. 2009b. Minds, objects, and relations: Toward a dual-aspect ontology. In *Mind That Abides: Panpsychism in the New Millennium*, ed. D. Skrbina. John Benjamins.

Skrbina, D. 2009c. Transcending consciousness: Thoughts on a universal conception of mind. *Journal of Consciousness Studies* 16 (5): 79–87.

Skrbina, D. 2010. Whitehead and the ubiquity of mind. In Chromatikon *VI*. Presses Universitaires de Louvain.

Skrbina, D. 2011. Mind space: Toward a solution to the combination problem. In *The Mental as Fundamental*, ed. M. Blamauer. Ontos Verlag.

Skrbina, D. 2013. Ethics, eco-philosophy, and universal sympathy. *Dialogue and Universalism* 23 (4): 59–74.

Skrbina, D. 2014. Dualism, dual-aspectism, and the mind. In *Contemporary Dualism*, ed. A. Lavazza and H. Robinson. Routledge.

Skrbina, D. 2015. *The Metaphysics of Technology*. Routledge.

Smart, J. J. C. 1959. Sensations and brain processes. *Philosophical Review* 68: 141–156.

Smith, T. V. 1934. *From Thales to Plato*. Chicago University Press.

Spencer, H. 1855. *Principles of Psychology*, volume 1. Reprint: Appleton, 1897.

Spencer, H. 1884. Religion: A retrospect and prospect. *Nineteenth Century* 15 (83): 1–12.

Spinoza, B. 1674. Letter to Schuller (#58). In *A Spinoza Reader*, ed. E. Curley (Princeton University Press, 1994).

Spinoza, B. 1677. Ethics. In *A Spinoza Reader*, ed. E. Curley (Princeton University Press, 1994).

Sprigge, T. 1983. *Vindication of Absolute Idealism*. Edinburgh University Press.

Sprigge, T. 1984. Santayana and panpsychism. *Bulletin of the Santayana Society* 2: 1–18.

Sprigge, T. 1991a. Are there intrinsic values in nature? In *Applied Philosophy*, ed. B. Almond and D. Hill. Routledge.

Sprigge, T. 1991b. Some recent positions in environmental ethics examined. *Inquiry* 34: 107–128.

Sprigge, T. 1993. *James and Bradley*. Open Court.

Sprigge, T. 1998a. Panpsychism. In *Encyclopedia of Philosophy*, ed. E. Craig. Routledge.

Sprigge, T. 1998b. Idealism. In *Encyclopedia of Philosophy*, ed. E. Craig. Routledge.

Stack, G. 2005. *Nietzsche's Anthropic Circle*. University of Rochester Press.

Starchenko, N. 1994. Nikolai Lossky. In *A History of Russian Philosophy*, ed. V. Kuvakin. Prometheus Books.

Stone, C. 1972. Should trees have standing? Towards legal rights for natural objects. *Southern California Law Review* 45: 450–501.

Stout, G. 1919a. *Mind & Matter*. Reprint: Cambridge University Press, 1931.

Stout, G. 1919b. *God & Nature*. Reprint: Cambridge University Press, 1952.

Strawson, G. 1994. *Mental Reality*. MIT Press.

Strawson, G. 2003a. Real materialism. In *Chomsky and His Critics*, ed. L. Antony and N. Hornstein. Blackwell.

Strawson, G. 2003b. What is the relation between an experience, the subject of the experience, and the content of the experience? *Philosophical Issues* 13: 279–315.

Strawson, G. 2006a. Realistic monism: Why physicalism entails panpsychism. *Journal of Consciousness Studies* 13, no. 10–11: 3–31. Reprinted with same pagination in *Consciousness and its Place in Nature*, ed. A. Freeman. Imprint Academic.

Strawson, G. 2006b. Panpsychism? Reply to commentators with a celebration of Descartes. *Journal of Consciousness Studies* 13 (10–11): 184–280.

Strawson, G. 2009. Realistic monism: Why physicalism entails panpsychism. (Revision of Strawson 2006). In *Mind That Abides*, ed. D. Skrbina. John Benjamins.

Strawson, G. 2015a. Real materialism (with new postscript). In *Consciousness in the Physical World*, ed. T. Alter and Y. Nagasawa. Oxford University Press.

Strawson, G. 2015b. Nietzsche's metaphysics? In *Nietzsche on Mind and Nature*, ed. M. Dries and P. Kail. Oxford University Press.

Strawson, G. 2015c. Letters to the editor. *Times Literary Supplement* 20 (March).

Strong, C. 1903. *Why the Mind Has a Body*. Macmillan.

Strong, C. 1904a. Dr. Morton Prince and panpsychism. *Psychological Review* 11: 67–69.

Strong, C. 1904b. Reply to Professor Bakewell. *Philosophical Review* 13 (3): 337–342.

Strong, C. 1918. *Origin of Consciousness*. Macmillan.

Strong, C. 1937. *A Creed for Skeptics*. Macmillan.

Stubenberg, L. 2015. Russell, Russellian monism, and panpsychism. In *Consciousness in the Physical World*, ed. T. Alter and Y. Nagasawa. Oxford University Press.

Tallmadge, K. 1944. Nous and naturalism. *New Scholasticism* 18 (2): 185–196.

Teale, E. 1976. *The Wilderness World of John Muir*. Houghton Mifflin.

Teilhard de Chardin, P. 1941. The atomism of spirit. In Teilhard, *Activation of Energy* (Collins, 1970).

Teilhard de Chardin, P. 1947. The place of technology. In Teilhard, *Activation of Energy* (Collins, 1970).

Teilhard de Chardin, P. 1950. *The Heart of Matter*. Reprint: Harcourt Brace Jovanovich, 1979.

Teilhard de Chardin, P. 1952. The reflection of energy. In Teilhard, *Activation of Energy* (Collins, 1970).

Teilhard de Chardin, P. 1959. *The Phenomenon of Man*. Harper and Row.

Teilhard de Chardin, P. 1970. *Activation of Energy*. Collins.

Telesio, B. 1586. *On the Nature of Things* (*De rerum natura*). In *Renaissance Philosophy*, volume 1, ed. A. Fallico and H. Shapiro (Random House, 1967).

Theise, N., and Kafatos, C. 2013. Sentience everywhere: Complexity theory, panpsychism, and the role of sentience in self-organization of the universe. *Journal of Consciousness Exploration and Research* 4 (4): 378–390.

Thiese, N., and Kafatos, C. 2016. Fundamental awareness. *Communicative and Integrative Biology* 9 (3): e1155010.

Thoreau, H. 1851. *Journal*, volume 4. Reprint: Princeton University Press, 1981.

Thoreau, H. 2000. *Wild Fruits*. Norton.

Tononi, G. 2012. Integrated information theory of consciousness: An updated account. *Archives Italiennes de Biologie* 150 (4): 293–329.

Tononi, G. 2012b. *Phi: A Voyage from the Brain to the Soul*. Pantheon.

Tononi, G., and Koch, C. 2015. Consciousness: Here, there, and everywhere? *Philosophical Transactions of the Royal Society B* 370, no. 1668.

Trepanier, S. 2004. *Empedocles: An Interpretation*. Taylor & Francis.

Troland, L. 1918. Paraphysical monism. *Philosophical Review* 27 (1): 39–62.

Troland, L. 1922. Psychophysics as the key to the mysteries of physics and of metaphysics. *Journal of the Washington Academy of Sciences* 12 (6): 141–162.

Tye, M. 2000. *Consciousness, Color, and Content*. MIT Press.

Uzgalis, W. 2011. *The Correspondence of Samuel Clarke and Anthony Collins, 1707–08*. Broadview.

Van Cleve, J. 1990. Mind-dust or magic? Panpsychism versus emergence. *Philosophical Perspectives* 4: 215–226.

Vartanian, A. 1960. Introduction. In *J. LaMettrie, L'Homme Machine*. Princeton University Press.

Velmans, M. 2007. The co-evolution of matter and consciousness. *Synthesis Philosophica* 44 (2): 273–282.

Vietor, K. 1950. *Goethe the Thinker*. Harvard University Press.

Waddington, C. 1961. *The Nature of Life*. Allen and Unwin.

Walker, E. 1970. The nature of consciousness. *Mathematical Biosciences* 7: 131–178.

Weber, M. 2009. Hypnosis: Panpsychism in action. In *Handbook of Whiteheadian Process Thought*, ed. M. Weber and W. Desmond. De Gruyter.

Wendt, A. 2015. *Quantum Mind and Social Science*. Cambridge University Press.

Wheeler, J. 1994. It from bit. In *At Home in the Universe*. American Institute of Physics.

Wheeler, J. 2002. John Wheeler responds. *Discover* 23 (8).

White, L., Jr. 1967. The historical roots of our ecologic crisis. *Science* 155 (3767): 1203–1207.

White, L., Jr. 1973. Continuing the conversation. In *Western Man and Environmental Ethic*, ed. I. Barbour. Addison-Wesley.

Whitehead, A. 1925. *Science and the Modern World*. Reprint: Free Press, 1967.

Whitehead, A. 1926a. *Religion in the Making*. Macmillan.

Whitehead, A. 1926b. Time. In L. Ford, *The Emergence of Whitehead's Metaphysic, 1925–1929* (SUNY Press, 1984).

Whitehead, A. 1929. *Process and Reality*. Reprint: Free Press, 1978.

Whitehead, A. 1933. *Adventures of Ideas*. Reprint: Free Press, 1967.

Whitehead, A. 1938. *Modes of Thought*. Macmillan.

Whitehead, A. 1941. Immortality. In *The Philosophy of Alfred North Whitehead*, ed. P. Schilpp. Northwestern University Press.

Wilber, K. 1995. *Sex, Ecology, Spirituality*. Shambhala.

Wilber, K. 2000. *Integral Psychology*. Shambhala.

Williams, L. 2001. *Nietzsche's Mirror*. Rowman & Littlefield.

Wittgenstein, L. 1953. *Philosophical Investigations*. Macmillan.

Wolfson, H. 1937. Spinoza's mechanism, attributes, and panpsychism. *Philosophical Review* 46 (3): 307–314.

Woodward, W. 1972. Fechner's panpsychism. *Journal of the History of the Behavioral Sciences* 8: 367–386.

Wright, W. 1947. *A History of Modern Philosophy*. Macmillan.

Wright, S. 1953. Gene and organism. *American Naturalist* 87 (5): 5–18.

Wright, S. 1964. Biology and the philosophy of science. *Monist* 48: 265–290.

Wright, S. 1977. Panpsychism and science. In *Mind in Nature*, ed. J. Cobb and D. Griffin. University Press of America.

Wundt, W. 1892/1894. *Lectures on Human and Animal Psychology*. S. Sonnenschein.

Young, J. 2010. *Friedrich Nietzsche: A Philosophical Biography*. Cambridge University Press.

Zohar, D. 1990. *The Quantum Self*. Bloomsbury.

Index